W9-BCZ-916

Daddy

(04- 13027) 4-29-65

MEDIEVAL REPRESENTATION
AND CONSENT

328.42
C

MEDIEVAL REPRESENTATION
AND CONSENT

A STUDY OF EARLY PARLIAMENTS IN ENGLAND AND
IRELAND, WITH SPECIAL REFERENCE TO THE
MODUS TENENDI PARLIAMENTUM

BY

M. V. CLARKE, M.A., F.S.A.

NEW YORK
RUSSELL & RUSSELL · INC
1964

Wingate College Library

FIRST PUBLISHED IN 1936
REISSUED, 1964, BY RUSSELL & RUSSELL, INC.
L. C. CATALOG CARD NO: 64—15027

PRINTED IN THE UNITED STATES OF AMERICA

PREFACE

THIS book, which Miss Clarke began six years ago, was planned
as a short monograph on the *Modus Tenendi Parliamentum*, but
grew gradually into a wide study of fourteenth-century parliamentary institutions. The greater part of it was written during
a two years' struggle with ill-health, and only the author's
spirit and determination made possible its completion a few
months before her death. As her literary executors, we wish
to emphasise the fact that the book as it stands is exclusively
Miss Clarke's work. Our task has been merely the revision
and correction of references, typographical errors and small
points of detail. For inaccuracies of this nature we must be
held responsible, but the typescript which came into our hands
after Miss Clarke's death was, in every respect, complete. In
the work of revising and proof-correcting we have received
invaluable assistance from a number of scholars with whom
Miss Clarke herself had consulted during the preparation of
the book. In particular we wish to thank Professor Hamilton-
Thompson and Mr. J. G. Edwards who read through the whole of
the proofs and pointed out innumerable minor, and some major,
errors which would otherwise have escaped us. For revision of
the chapter on the *Manuscripts of the Modus* we drew freely on
the expert palæography of Mr. V. H. Galbraith, a friend and
colleague to whom Miss Clarke felt herself peculiarly indebted
for help and advice in the examination and collation of manuscripts, and for many stimulating suggestions relating to the
whole subject. Among others who have helped in the revision
of particular sections of the work we wish to thank Miss

27136

J. S. A. Macaulay, Miss D. M. Legge, Mr. C. G. Stone and Miss M. Griffith. The index has been compiled and many references checked and corrected by Miss K. M. E. Murray. Mr. C. M. Morris of Balliol College very kindly made himself responsible for the necessary negotiations with Messrs. Longmans, whose prompt and efficient handling of the proofs has greatly lightened our task. Valuable secretarial assistance was given by Miss M. Crook while the book was being prepared for publication.

Miss Clarke would have wished to thank Somerville College for the generous subsidy which made publication possible. To all those by whose learning she profited during the writing of the book we wish also to express gratitude on her behalf, and we regret the omission of many names which would, no doubt, have appeared in this foreword had Miss Clarke lived to see her book through the press.

L. STUART SUTHERLAND.
MAY McKISACK.

SOMERVILLE COLLEGE,
OXFORD.

TABLE OF CONTENTS

CHAPTER I

INTRODUCTORY

THE Parliament of Great Britain stands on a foundation of representation and consent. Supreme power is vested in the House of Commons, composed of the elected representatives of the nation ; the authority of the executive depends upon the consent of the representatives, organised through political parties aligned in Parliament. The slow unfolding of these powers is the dominant theme of English history, but at every phase the process of growth is complicated and obscure. Parliament has never been the mere stage or setting for great scenes, a passive tool in the hands of its members ; it is itself instinct with the garnered force of tradition and experience, accumulated in six centuries of action. It bears the hall-mark of personality, and, just for that reason, no abstract formula can be found to symbolise its constituent parts. To describe it as the embodiment of the principle of justice in a free society would be to confuse an ideal, seldom recognised, with realities often altogether different. Its history throughout is the history of actual situations and its personality, like its privilege, reveals itself only by employment. To understand its growth we must concentrate upon what is remarkable in its structure. Though functions and principles must also be studied in any full analysis of its constitution, it is from structure alone that the essential quality is derived. For this reason the composition of Parliament is a fundamental problem for the historian. If he seeks for the origin of the institution, as we now know it, he must take as the starting-point of his enquiry the representation of the estates or orders of the realm in a central assembly. It is with Parliament in this sense, the Parliament of estates, that we are here concerned.

The riddle of parliamentary origins cannot easily be read, since the evidence is scattered, fragmentary, and hard to interpret.

Not only are the official records technical and ambiguous, but intelligent contemporary comment is almost altogether lacking. Parliament grew slowly with its roots deep in the soil, hiding its novelty under a protective colour of familiar practice. When first knights and then burgesses and proctors of the clergy were summoned to national assemblies no elaborate justification was deemed necessary ; if chroniclers recorded the facts, they saw no need to discuss them. We have more coherent evidence about the battles of Lewes and Evesham, or the Welsh wars of Edward I, than we can ever hope to have for Montfort's Parliament of 1265 or for any other Parliaments of the thirteenth century. It is true that " a formidable mass of documents " relating to early Parliaments has been preserved, consisting of writs and returns, some drafts of agenda, petitions, statutes, decisions, judgements and executive orders.[1] But the writs and returns are certainly incomplete and the other records are mainly concerned with judicial and administrative business, which would have been transacted in the king's council or high court even if he had never summoned representatives of the Commons. They are, therefore, of disappointingly little value in explaining the presence of representatives and many of them relate to assemblies in which they had no part. Even when a regular series of Parliament rolls begins, these rolls record decisions rather than describe the stages by which those decisions were reached. They tell us little of procedure and nothing explicitly of the ideas underlying it. We are left to guess in the dark at what was in the minds of kings and their subjects as to the nature and functions of Parliaments of estates.

As the difficulties inherent in the evidence have gradually been understood scholars have grown reluctant to commit themselves to any bold solution of the problem of origins. The time-honoured stories, which showed Simon de Montfort as the father of Parliament and Edward I as his wise and generous disciple, have been cast out and nothing as lively or as definite has been allowed to take their place. Like the contemporary chroniclers, historians now seem unwilling to see anything remarkable in the summons of the commons. They will acknow-

[1] See H. G. Richardson and G. O. Sayles, " Early Records of the English Parliaments " (*Bulletin of the Institute of Historical Research*, Vol. V, p. 129, and Vol. VI, p. 129).

ledge no startling innovation, no high motive, no heroic gesture. Everything is keyed down to a sober harmony of normal routine, as if the quiet tones of later medieval glass had replaced the rich colours of earlier craftsmen. This method, admirable in its scientific and critical handling of evidence, cannot be carried beyond a certain point. It displays, so far as the evidence permits, Parliament as it was, but it does not leave room for any process of growth. That which is most remarkable about the sessions of early Parliaments, the coming together, with increasing regularity, of representatives of every grade of free society, is minimised or slurred over, because the records on this side are evasive and obscure. We are told that Edward I summoned—knights and burgesses, not because their consent to taxation was essential, but because it made collection easier and more profitable ; their petitions also informed him about the condition of the realm and their presence helped to break down feudal distinctions between mesne tenants and tenants-in-chief.[1]—They came, in fact, for reasons of administrative convenience, the passive agents of the monarchy. Other scholars state emphatically that " it is from the standpoint of the modern age that the feeble beginnings of popular representation have any importance in parliamentary history . . ." ;[2] even in the reign of Edward II, we are assured, they do not " attach any constitutional importance " to the presence of the commons in Parliament.[3] These and similar conclusions, based on the early records of Parliament, show plainly that we must look elsewhere for knowledge of the beginning of national assemblies, organised on the principles of representation and consent.

There is, however, definite evidence of another kind, which has hitherto been put out of court, owing to its dangerous ambiguity in date and purpose. This is the *Modus Tenendi Parliamentum*, a short, anonymous tract, not later than the end of the fourteenth century, which describes the composition and procedure of Parliament and states the governing principles

---

[1] D. Pasquet, *An Essay on the Origins of the House of Commons*, Cambridge, 1925 (translated by R. G. D. Laffan). The conclusion, stated above, is summarised on pp. 225-6.

[2] H. G. Richardson, " Origins of Parliament " (*Transactions of the Royal Hist. Soc.*, Series IV, Vol. XI, pp. 137 *seq.*).

[3] Richardson and Sayles, " Early Records of the English Parliaments " (*Bulletin of Institute of Hist. Research*, Vol. VI, p. 77).

of its action and authority. Though condemned by Stubbs and other scholars for its "proved worthlessness," [1] we cannot afford to be fastidious about any record of a constructive kind, which is even roughly contemporary. The knowledge gained by piecing together isolated official documents—here a petition and there a writ—is at best, not a picture, but a mosaic, and there is always a risk that the fragments may be put in place upside-down or in the wrong relation to each other. When the total mass of evidence is both disjointed and deficient, we must not lightly discard a document which is a set description of the Parliament of estates, written on a simple and logical plan [2] and with a general meaning that is perfectly clear. [3] It is also significant that the *Modus* is extant in over a score of medieval manuscripts, usually bound up with the coronation order or with the statutes of the realm.

Of greater interest than the description, which is the avowed object of the *Modus*, is its underlying theory of the authority and powers of Parliament. The six *gradus*, orders or degrees, into which the estates of the realm are divided, express a familiar medieval view of the structure of society; upon the ordered movement of the several parts, with each degree in its "authentick place," the "unity and married calm of states" depend. Parliament is at once the visible symbol of this harmony and the active force by which it is secured. The means employed are the gathering together of the estates, either each man for himself

---

[1] *Constitutional History*, III, p. 445. T. F. Tout (*Chapters in Mediaeval Administrative History*, M.U.P. 1928, III, p. 139 n.) considered that it "may well be an idealisation of Parliament any time after 1341." Professor A. F. Pollard (*Evolution of Parliament*, second edition, 1926, p. 433) doubts "if the *Modus* is more scientific than Tacitus' *Germania*, though the author's opportunities for observation must have been far closer. . . ." Elsewhere Pollard has argued in favour of the value of particular passages (*ibid.*, pp. 68 *seq.*).

[2] It has recently been shown that the confused arrangement of chapters in the Latin texts hitherto printed does not appear in the best MSS. See D. E. Hodnett and W. P. White, "Manuscripts of the *Modus Tenendi Parliamentum*" (*Eng. Hist. Review*, Vol. XXXIV, pp. 209 *seq.*). For a discussion of the manuscripts see *infra*, Chapter XV. The new order, as printed in the appendix, will be followed throughout the book. What Miss Hodnett and Miss White counted as Chapter I, however, is here counted as an introduction, and the chapter numbers are changed accordingly.

[3] Since the greater part of this book has been written, Professor Morris has published an article on the *Modus* (*Eng. Hist. Review*, Vol. XLIX, pp. 407-422) in which he brings forward arguments for an early date.

or through elected representatives. The distribution of power is nicely adjusted to give an appearance of equality, but in the last resort authority lies with the representatives of the commons, who control supply. From these statements we are left to infer that Parliament rested ultimately on the principles of representation and consent.

Whatever date or sanction we assign to this doctrine, its general value for the historian of the middle ages cannot be denied. Medieval political theory is only rarely related to actual conditions. The bookish traditions of the schools turned men back to ancient models when they attempted to analyse the principles of government and the overpowering influence of theology concentrated attention on what ought to be, rather than on what was. Even the most daring theorists of the fourteenth century did not venture to make a frontal attack on contemporary political problems. Marsilius of Padua hid his study of the Italian city state under an Aristotelian disguise and Fitzralph set out his theory of dominion in the terms of a feudal society which was already passing away. Lawyers were concerned mainly with the technical problems of their art and were slow to observe or to reflect on the process of constitutional change. For a parallel to the *Modus Tenendi Parliamentum* we must turn to the tracts on tyranny written in Italy in the second half of the fourteenth century.

In the writings of Bartolus of Sassoferrato and of Coluccio Salutati, a jurist and a humanist, the problem of tyranny is discussed, not only in relation to older political forms, but on its merits as a system of government. On the basis of popular sovereignty, they worked out the doctrine of power transferred to the ruler by his subjects, which is the theoretical justification of modern absolutism. In the *Modus* a totally different line of development is implied. Sovereign power, which lies ultimately with the people, is vested, not in their ruler, but in their representatives. Their consent is no mere delegation once and for all, or permanent contract of surrender, but a long series of specific acts ; the sense of responsibility and control is perpetually renewed, both by the election of representatives and by the action of these representatives in Parliament. Thus we find in the *Modus* not only a theory of popular government which is the antithesis of absolutism, but the means whereby that theory could be put into practice. Though it is still far removed from modern doctrines of democracy and the sovereign state, the essential elements of representation and consent are clearly present.

The *Modus* thus contains a description of the composition and procedure of Parliament and unites with it political ideas which must be recognised as the basis of later democratic theory. Its subject matter, therefore, demands respect, and for that reason alone it is impossible to ignore it. It is evident that an examination of its content and of other matters germane to its history must at the same time be an examination into the origin and early history of Parliament. Though the attempt to penetrate a subject so large and so obscure by a single avenue has obvious drawbacks, they are countered, in a measure, by the advantage of stating one particular problem, for which a definite solution will be sought. I propose, therefore, to take the date, the meaning and the validity of the *Modus Tenendi Parliamentum* as the centre of my investigation and to ignore those aspects of parliamentary history which are not directly relevant to it. Within these limits, the method of free enquiry will be followed, however far afield the evidence may lead us. Sometimes it will be necessary to advance with leisure or deviously, as the ground is thick with subsidiary difficulties which must first be cleared away. Because the first official recognition of the *Modus* which is explicitly recorded is its exemplification under the Great Seal of Ireland in 1419, it will be essential to examine the neglected history of the Irish Parliament in the later middle ages. By working from the known to the unknown, from the period to which the oldest manuscripts, both English and Irish, belong (1380-1420) back to the dark period of origin, it is hoped to link together evidence which will at once explain the *Modus* itself and the circumstances in which it was composed. It is feared that the length and range of the enquiry and the need to follow an argument built up by slow degrees will make demands on the patience of readers. The justification of it lies in the hope that an attempt to solve the problem of the *Modus* may contribute towards the greater problem of the origin of Parliament.

CHAPTER II

THE ARGUMENT OF THE *MODUS*

THE *Modus* was written for the glorification of Parliament, the first of a long succession of such works. Though its sober details lack the rhetoric of Burke, we may detect the same spirit of exalted pride and the same feeling for the " particles of venerable rust." The Parliament of the *Modus* is a body already stiff with tradition, sanctified by its sessions under Edward the Confessor and reaching back to a time when there was neither bishop, earl nor baron.[1] The prestige of antiquity is also claimed for the document itself. The author asserts that he is merely recounting how Parliament was held in the reign of Edward the Confessor, that his *Modus* was recited by the more discreet men of the realm before William the Conqueror, and that it was approved and put into practice by him and his successors.[2] In the earlier chapters an attempt is made to maintain this fiction by frequent use of *solebat* and *solebant* and by avoiding, as far as possible, the present and future tenses. In the second and longer part [3] this device is abandoned and we have a frank description of the procedure of Parliament, as it is or as it ought to be ordered.

The end for which Parliament exists is to treat of the king's business and of the common needs of the realm. In the calendar, or standing orders on procedure, its functions are thus defined : " All the business of Parliament ought to be regarded in the following order : first, concerning war, if war there be, and other affairs touching the persons of the king, the queen and their children ; secondly, concerning the common business of the realm, such as legislating, when judgement has been given, against the defects of laws, original, judicial and executorial, which are

---

[1] XXIII.   [2] Cf. *infra*, pp. 330-1.
[3] Part II begins at Chapter VIII, and is clearly marked by a summary of the preceding chapters.

7

especially the common business ; thirdly, private business ought to be regarded and this in the order in which petitions have been filed. . . ." [1] These matters are described as the ordinary routine, but they cover the three functions of government, administration, legislation and justice. The general powers are further defined in the chapters *de casibus et iudiciis difficilibus* and *de auxiliis regis*.[2] Parliament has the duty of arbitrating in all disputes, doubts or difficulties, whether of peace or of war ; in the last resort the proctor of the Parliament [3] shall give judgement which cannot be amended without the consent of the whole body. Finally, Parliament has supreme control over taxation. The king must seek for aids *in pleno Parliamento*, delivering his request in writing to each estate. The consent of all members (*pares*) of Parliament ought to be secured, but here ultimate authority lies with the Commons. In short, Parliament, composed of " the common peers of the realm," is the heart and mind of the body politic.

The king is *caput, principium et finis Parliamenti*,[4] but he is never *solutus legibus*. The obligations imposed upon him far exceed his rights and powers. His functions are primarily ceremonial. He is the president of the assembly, sitting in the seat of honour and he may appoint some one other than the Steward to insure that all men take their places in due order.[5] It is implied that he may choose the place of session and has the right of summons, though it is nowhere explicitly stated. Only one other unrestricted privilege is admitted and that in all probability would not be exercised.[6] The committee of twenty-five, elected to give judgement on difficult cases or disputes, may not reduce itself from three members to one without the king's leave.[7] All other royal acts in Parliament, requiring deliberation or decision, must have the assent of the Council or of the *pares Parliamenti*. It is the king and council who refer difficult cases to Parliament. They may examine and amend the judgement of the committee, but this right can be exercised only *in pleno Parliamento et de consensu Parliamenti*. The few remaining prerogatives are shared with the *pares*. No one may withdraw from the session without the leave of the king and all

---

[1] XVIII.   [2] XVII and XXIII.
[3] The *sola persona* of the committee of twenty-five (XVII).
[4] XXVI.   [5] XIV.
[6] See *infra*, pp. 191-2, 236.   [7] XVII.

his peers.[1]   The judges, who are not members, may be assigned
special powers in Parliament by the king and *pares ;* the chief
clerks are subject to king and Parliament *in communi.*[2]

Against these shorn and parcelled prerogatives stand arrayed
a formidable series of obligations. It is characteristic of the
whole attitude of the *Modus* to the monarchy that the phrase
rex tenetur is used four times.[3] The king is bound to pay the
expenses of those summoned by special writ who have no tenurial
obligation to attend ; he must send writs of summons to the
Cinque Ports ; [4] he must be present in Parliament at mid-prime
and on the sixth day of session ; he cannot absent himself unless
he is ill and his essoin is tested by a parliamentary committee.
It is also his duty to pay the wages of the clerks of Parliament,[5]
to put his requests for aids in writing,[6] and to exhort Parliament to labour for the honour of God and the honour and welfare of the Crown and the realm.[7] He should seek for the advice
and arbitration of each estate in disputes and difficulties.[8] He
ought not and cannot (*nec . . . debet nec potest*) absent himself from
Parliament [9] and he is forsworn (*periurus*) if he dissolves Parliament before all petitions have received an answer.[10] The king
reigns, without him there can be no Parliament,[11] but he is no
more than the servant of the commonwealth. His subjects may
withdraw themselves from Parliament if they maintain, with
particular instances, that he has not ruled them as he ought [12]
and he has no redress against their recalcitrance. The underlying idea is akin to a famous gloss on Bracton : the king in
himself is not sufficient to govern his people ; he has therefore
earls, associates, masters, superiors.[13] Though the *Modus* acknowledged that the king had no peer in his estate,[14] it is throughout
implied that his masters and associates are the *pares Parliamenti*.

This subordination of the Crown to Parliament is quietly
indicated in a matter-of-fact descriptive style, more effective than
a loud fanfare of rebel trumpets. Again and again the manner

[1] XXIV.   [2] XV.   [3] II, IX, XIII, XIX.
[4] Cf. *infra*, pp. 202-3.   [5] XV and XVI.   [6] XXIII.
[7] XII.   [8] XVII.   [9] XIII.
[10] XXIV.   [11] XXVI.   [12] XXIII.
[13] A gloss attributed to John de Longueville, a judge of assize under
Edward II, *Bracton and Azo (Selden Soc.)*, p. 125 ; J. Conway Davies, *Baronial
Opposition to Edward II*, Cambridge, 1918, pp. 16-17.
[14] XXVI.

of treatment reveals the experienced official rather than the doctrinaire politician. Whatever his ultimate purpose may have been, the writer was concerned about ways and means and recognised the value of set forms and traditions. Seven chapters deal with the writs of summons.[1] They must be issued forty days before the date of session ; the persons entitled to special writs are carefully enumerated ; the proctors must have duplicate warrants, one of which shall be handed over to the clerks for enrolment ; the rate of wages is fixed for knights and burgesses. The standing orders on procedure are comprehensive. The business of opening Parliament extends over six days.[2]   On each of the first five days one of the estates must answer a roll call, and heavy fines are levied for default. On the sixth day the king shall attend at mid-prime ; the archbishop in whose province the session is held shall preach or appoint a substitute ; the chancellor or other official shall declare the causes of summons ; the king shall exhort all the estates to labour for God's honour and the common weal. Matters of precedence, seats of honour and rules of debate are also dealt with [3] and the time and manner of dissolution are set out with the same care as for the opening of the session.[4]   The duties of officials, attending or employed by Parliament, are described in five chapters.[5]   Even the doorkeeper and the crier have their sections, and special attention is given to the duties of the clerks. The two principal clerks are immediately subject to the king and Parliament ; they shall enrol all pleas and judgements and deliver the roll to the Treasury before recess, reserving for themselves the transcript or counterroll if they wish to have it. Each of the five junior clerks shall be assigned to an estate to write out questions and answers made in Parliament ; their spare time shall be employed in assisting the principal clerks to enrol. The clerks shall not refuse to anyone a copy of his process and shall charge a fee of tenpence a line for a transcript. As a last refinement of detail, the breadth of the Parliament roll is fixed at ten inches.[6]

It is difficult to go much further in outlining the argument of the *Modus* without coming to a premature decision on the underlying purpose of the whole document. Certain ideas, however, are so clearly expressed that they demand at least a pre-

[1] I-VII.   [2] IX-XII.   [3] XI, XIV, XVIII and XXII.
[4] XXIV.   [5] VIII, XV, XVI, XX and XXI.   [6] XXV.

liminary examination, though the significance attached to them must vary with the date assigned to the composition. These ideas are the unity of Parliament, the peerage or equality of its members and the ultimate ascendancy of the Commons. On each of them the opinion of the writer is stated with directness and force, but he breaks down in an attempt to cover up the fundamental inconsistency of setting equality and ascendancy side by side.

The unity of Parliament is a theme that recurs again and again throughout the *Modus*. At the roll-call the estates must answer in turn and the king must name them all in order in his opening speech.[1] The clerks are subject to king and Parliament *in communi* ; each estate has its own clerk ; speeches must be made so that all may hear, because *omnes pares sunt iudices et iusticiarii*.[2] All must consent to leave of absence for members,[3] to amended judgements in cases of difficulty and to grants of taxation.[4] The procedure when disputes arise is defined with special care.[5] The steward, constable and marshal shall choose twenty-five persons, representing the five estates, who by a process of reduction shall achieve unanimity and ordain for all. Finally, the last chapter, *de gradibus parium Parliamenti*—now given its full significance by its position at the end—enumerates all the estates and reaches a conclusion. Parliament has six estates, and if any one of them, except the king, be absent, Parliament shall still be deemed complete.[6]

The word *par* occurs in two senses in the *Modus*. Neither is equivalent to *peer* in the modern sense of a member of the nobility, since *magnates* is deliberately used for the great nobles as opposed to the Commons.[7] The *pares* of the *Modus* are, in the first place, all who attend Parliament, except officials and servants ; they are members bound to be present either by reason of their dignity and tenures or as duly elected representatives of communities.

---

[1] IX and XII. [2] XI, XV, XVI, and XXII.
[3] XIII and XXIV.   The proctors of the clergy were not represented on the committee to test the king's essoin.
[4] XVII and XXIII. [5] XVII.
[6] Provided that all have been summoned *per rationabiles summonitiones Parliamenti*. XXVI.
[7] XVII and XXIII.   See *infra*, pp. 197-9, for a discussion of the use of the *pares* and *piers* in the fourteenth century.

In its other usage the word bears its normal legal meaning of *equal in degree*, without reference to one degree rather than another. The king *non habet parem in suo gradu ;*[1] no member may sit *nisi inter suos pares ;*[2] disputes or doubts shall be referred by the king to each estate of peers.[3] The last phrase, *cuilibet graduum parium*, seems to bring together the two meanings of the word. Thus, we have unity in diversity. Each man has his place with the peers of his estate, yet all alike are *pares Parliamenti*, members one of another, united by their common tasks and common responsibility. We recognise here the familiar medieval conception that " the Member is but a part of a Whole . . . and, on the other side, that the Whole only lives and comes to light in the Members."[4] The qualities and functions of the members may vary, but on their just coherence the unity of the whole depends.[5] A great fourteenth-century prelate was striving to express this idea concretely when he wrote : " The Crown has the substance of its nature chiefly in the king as head and in the peers of the land as members . . . and this is attached to the Crown in such a way that it cannot be severed without division of the realm. The same law stands for the part as it stands for the whole. . . ."[6]

Since all are equal it should follow that the estates are equal also, forming, not a hierarchy, but a circle like the Round Table of Arthur. In the last chapter we are offered as a conclusion that the five estates under the king (*post regem*) are equal, because if any one of them be absent Parliament shall none the less be deemed complete. The elaborate committee of twenty-five,

---

[1] XXVI.   [2] XIV.   [3] XVII.

[4] Otto Gierke, *Political Theories of the Middle Age* (translated F. W. Maitland), Cambridge, 1900, p. 27.

[5] *Ibid.*, p. 25. Cf. St. Thomas Aquinas, *Summa Theologica*, II, 1, q. 81, a. 1 : " in civilibus omnes homines qui sunt unius communitatis reputantur quasi unum corpus ; et tota communitas quasi unus homo."

[6] The whole passage runs : " A de primes, que la substance de la nature de la Corone est principaument en la persone le Roi come teste, et en les Piers de la Terre come membres, qi tenent de lui par certeyn homage, et nomeement des Prelatz ; quiele chose est si annexe a la dite Corone qele ne poet pas estre sevree sans division du Roiaume : quar une mesme lei est de la parcelle come de lentier, quiele parcelle la meyte de la dite Eveschee." Protest of Grandisson, bishop of Exeter, against attaching the temporalities of his see to the duchy of Cornwall, probably soon after the creation of the duchy, March 17, 1337. Grandisson's Register, ed. F. C. Hingeston-Randolph, Exeter, 1897, Vol. II, p. 840.

reducing itself by election to a single member who cannot disagree with himself, was plainly an attempt to escape from the deadlock of the *liberum veto* without giving up the doctrine of equality.[1] However, the writer refused to be bound by the logic of his own argument, perhaps because it was not an argument at all but a description of the facts. In the same chapter he almost admits, incidentally, the binding force of the majority and he frankly abandons the idea of equal estates in the very circumstances when the predominance of one over the rest would secure a definite advantage. The committee of twenty-five was not composed of five members from each estate, but of two bishops and three proctors for the clergy, two earls and three barons for the secular nobles, five knights, five citizens and five burgesses. Thus a majority of eleven was secured for the Commons. In the chapter *de auxiliis regis* the claim to a predominant voice is explicit.[2] " It is to be understood that two knights who come to Parliament for their shire have a greater voice in Parliament in agreeing or dissenting than the greatest earl in England, and in like manner the proctors of the clergy of a single diocese have a greater voice in Parliament, if they all agree, than the bishop himself ; and this in all things which by Parliament ought to be granted, denied or accomplished. . . . The king can hold a Parliament with the Commons (*communitas*) of his realm without bishops, earls or barons. . . . All things which ought to be affirmed or abrogated, granted or denied, or accomplished by Parliament ought to be granted by the Commons (*communitate*) of Parliament, that is, by the proctors of the clergy, the knights of the shires, by the citizens and burgesses . . . who represent the whole *communitas* of England, and not by the magnates, since each of them is in Parliament for himself alone and for no one else." Thus in the clearest terms the ascendancy of the Commons is maintained in defiance of the general doctrine of equality. The reasons for the inconsistency, whether they arose in the mind of the writer or were indeed part of parliamentary tradition, must form a main branch of our enquiry.

Behind these explicit, though not altogether consistent, ideas, we may discern others upon which the whole structure of Parliament seems to rest. The Commons, clerk and lay, have superiority because they are representatives ; unlike the magnates, they

[1] XVII.　　　　　　　　　[2] XXIII.

Wingate College Library

do not come to Parliament *per se*, but for their communities.[1]
In the chapters on summons, special pains are taken to ensure
that elected members shall carry with them full powers, granted
by their constituents ; they shall come with sealed warrants or
letters of attorney, prepared to act in all things as if those who
chose them were present in person.[2] The purpose for which
these powers are given is that the representatives may answer,
undertake, allege and do their share in all business transacted
in Parliament ; the main business for which their consent is
required, the business which cannot be carried through without
them, is consent to taxation granted to the king.[3] The ultimate
ascendancy of the Commons is obviously bound up with this
control of supply. The author of the *Modus* sets up the consent
of the community to taxation as the key-stone of his arch of
Parliament ; the governing ideas of the whole document are
thus representation and consent.

[1] XXIII.   [2] II, IV.   [3] XXIII.

CHAPTER III

ECCLESIASTICAL CONSENT TO TAXATION UNDER EDWARD III

THE *Modus* does not offer many special clues to the casual enquirer, as it has the detachment and impersonal style of a legal tract. In fact, both its title and its form recall in some ways the short, professional manuals or formularies, popular from the thirteenth century onwards, like *Modus tenendi curias* [1] or *Modus tenendi synodos*.[2] The same volume which contains what is probably the oldest and best text of the *Modus tenendi Parliamentum* also includes, in a collection of statutes and formularies, *Modus amensurandi terram*, *Modus omnium sacramentorum* and *Modus faciendi homagium et fidelitatem*.[3] Our author may have cast his work deliberately into this popular form in order to conceal his identity. Anonymity and the absence of explicit reference to current events certainly help to give authority to the argument of ancient tradition. However, the most ingenious fabricator has a blind spot somewhere and, as experience shows, he always betrays himself by slips, ignorance or unconscious bias in a particular direction. For this reason, our problems of date and meaning may be attacked with some confidence that the clues for solution are there, if only we can find them. We must note, in the first place, that behind the author's baffling manner it is possible to detect that professional bias which is hardly ever permanently hidden. One reference to the judges, though brief, is just severe enough to suggest that the author was not a lawyer,[4] and to deflect

[1] For example, two tracts (*c.* 1307 and *c.* 1342), printed in *The Court Baron*, ed. F. W. Maitland, Selden Society, 1891.
[2] MS. Cotton, *Cleopatra C*, VIII. The MS. belongs to the latter part of the twelfth century, but this title is a later addition.
[3] MS. Cotton, *Vespasian B*, VII, ff. 84, 86-7, 97. See *infra*, Chapter XV, pp. 359-60.
[4] XV, ". . . nec est aliquis iusticiarius Anglie iusticiarius in Parliamento . . ." Cf. *infra*, Chapter X, p. 205.

15

attention towards the only other learned profession. When all the references to the clergy are examined, it becomes clear that the *Modus* has a definite prejudice in favour of the rights and dignity of the Church.

Before embarking on an examination of these references, a point of major interest for our enquiry must be noticed. The ecclesiastical avenue to the history of Parliament is, perhaps, the only one which has not yet been fully opened up. The valuable work of Professor Barker,[1] Professor Powicke,[2] and Dr. Lunt,[3] has been confined either to the general question of early representation, or to particular problems of clerical taxation. The researches of modern scholars into the administrative history of the English Church have been highly specialised,[4] and they have not yet been extended to the frontier lines where lay and ecclesiastical activity meet. Secular historians, as a rule, have either ignored it or have turned towards it only a flickering and uncertain attention. For detailed treatment of the general contribution of the medieval English clergy to political development, we must go back as far as the literature provoked by the Convocation disputes in the reigns of William III and Anne. The Tory Atterbury's *Rights, Powers and Privileges of an English Convocation stated and vindicated* (1700), the Whig Hody's *History of English Councils and Convocations, and of the Clergy's Sitting in Parliament* (1701), and, above all, Wake's great work, *The State of the Church and Clergy of England in their Councils, Synods and Convocations* (1703), to name only a few, attempted to decide the question of the rights of the lower clergy by an appeal to medieval history.[5] These controversialists of the Augustan age were fully alive to the value and abundance of the medieval evidence available. With competitive zeal, they ransacked the archives of episcopal registries and chapter-houses, seeking arguments for or against the independence claimed by the lower house of Convocation, to establish or to destroy the connection with

---

[1] E. Barker, *Dominican Orders and Convocation*, Oxford, 1913.

[2] F. M. Powicke, *Stephen Langton*, Oxford, 1928, Chapter VI.

[3] W. E. Lunt, *Valuation of Norwich*, Oxford, 1926, and a number of special articles, cited *infra*.

[4] For example, Irene Churchill, *Canterbury Administration*, 1933 ; and M. Gibbs and J. Lang, *Bishops and Reform, 1215-1272*, Oxford, 1934.

[5] The massive *Concilia* of David Wilkins (1737) was a by-product of the same movement.

Parliament. Their search for documents, though neither single-minded nor critical, serves to remind us of the wealth of material at command. At a time when the records of shires and boroughs were either concerned only with local affairs or were lacking altogether, the clergy, with their learning, literary traditions and strong sense of the precedent in writing, were eager to gather and keep evidence of each stage of their relations with the secular authority. In their registers and repositories, we find royal writs and returns, letters of summons and proxies, protests and bills of expenses, which illustrate, more fully than anything we have on the secular side, the growth, not only of provincial Convocations, but of Parliament itself. This wealth of evidence is not restricted to the structural side of institutional development. It also contains much that throws light on procedure and on the contemporary attitude to constitutional change. The worth of the chronicler's narrative has always been admitted, but it is not as often realised that his account of sessions in Convocation or of strictly ecclesiastical disputes over taxation has a value for secular history also. Perhaps more illuminating and certainly less well understood are the records of chapters and religious houses ; they show, as it were in miniature, the slow adaptation of means to ends, the shaping of forms and rules, and that friction of minds at work within the same community on common business, which is the essence of politics, when it is translated into the sphere of public law. It is here, for example, that we must look for the most significant early signs of representation and consent and for the slow change from unanimity to the majority decision.

We cannot afford to disregard these sources of knowledge, or to forget that for centuries the authority of the realm was expressed concurrently in Convocation and in Parliament, the one, for its own ends, as representative as the other. From the reign of Edward I, these two together gave a double, yet unequal rhythm to English public life, a rhythm reciprocal enough to render the study of one assembly incomplete if the other be entirely disregarded. Before the lesser partner had finally surrendered all independent motion, the dual authority of Parliament and Convocation was firmly defined by Hooker. " The parliament of England together with the convocation annexed thereunto, is that whereupon the very essence of all government within this kingdom doth depend ; it is even the

body of the whole realm ; it consisteth of the king, and of all
that within the land are subject unto him ; for they all are there
present, either in person or by such as they voluntarily have
derived their very personal right unto." [1]   It is proposed throughout this enquiry to work with Hooker's definition in mind and to
draw freely upon the great store of ecclesiastical evidence, not
only as an aid to the solution of the problem of the *Modus*, but
also in relation to the larger issue of the origin and early history
of Parliament.

Returning to the *Modus*, we find in it a decided bias towards
the ecclesiastical side.   In precedence and in ceremony the Church
has acknowledged superiority.   The estates are named three
times in order of precedence and each time, not only the prelates,
but the lesser dignitaries and the clerical proctors are set above
all the laity except the king : [2]   the archbishops, bishops, abbots,
priors and deans form the second estate, the proctors of the
clergy the third.   The two archbishops have the seats of honour
beside the king, Canterbury on his right and York on his left ; [3]
the sermon at the opening of Parliament is preached by the archbishop in whose province the session is held or by his nominee.[4]
These are formal details, but they take on a significance beyond
mere ceremonial when read in conjunction with other chapters.
The emphatic treatment of the writs of summons to the clergy
and of the ultimate superiority of the proctors over the bishops
in Parliament offer clues to the special intention of the whole
document.[5]

The great prelates ought to be summoned by special writ,
on the same conditions of tenure as the lay magnates.   No lower
clergy ought to be summoned by these writs, though the king
may request their presence, if they be members of his Council
or in other ways useful in Parliament.   The prelates and ecclesiastics who have privileged jurisdictions are required to cause
in each deanery and archdeaconry in England the election of
two proctors from each archdeaconry with full powers to act
for their electors.   The section on the attendance of the lower
clergy differs in several ways from the *premunientes* clause in the
parliamentary writ of summons.[6]   It does not require the attend-

---

[1] *Ecclesiastical Polity* (ed. Oxford, 1890), Vol. II, pp. 546-7.
[2] IX, XII, and XXVI.   [3] XIV.   [4] X.
[5] II and XXIII.   [6] E.g. *Select Charters* (9th ed.), p. 480.

ance of archdeacons, priors of cathedral churches or proctors of their chapters and it greatly increases the representation of the diocesan clergy by demanding two proctors from each archdeaconry instead of two from each diocese.[1] The statement that the choice of proctors shall be for each deanery and archdeaconry is also significant ; it refers to an indirect method of election, in use in certain dioceses, in which a primary or preliminary choice of candidates was made in the rural deaneries.[2] The underlying intention apparently was to enhance the importance of the proctors, an impression strengthened by what follows. Though their attendance is obligatory, the amercement for default—a hundred marks for each archdeaconry [3]—falls not on them, but on the bishops. Again, on the committee of twenty-five the proctors have three representatives and the bishops only two.[4] In short, the bishops have responsibility and the proctors have power. We are thus prepared for the explicit statement in the chapter *de auxiliis regis* : " The proctors of the clergy of a single diocese have a greater voice in Parliament, if they all agree, than the bishop himself ; and this in all things which by Parliament ought to be granted, denied or accomplished." The king can hold a Parliament without bishops, earls and barons, but never without the *communitates cleri et laici*. The three estates of proctors, knights of the shire, and citizens and burgesses represent *totam communitatem Anglie*.[5]

Once attention is directed to the emphasis on the proctorial estate, the doctrines of the *Modus* might appear to point in one direction and it might seem possible to formulate an hypothesis. Though historians have often suggested that the *Modus* is a description of an ideal Parliament, no definite purpose behind the idealisation has hitherto been indicated. Looking at it from the angle of the clergy, we might suppose that its general purpose was to bring to an end the divisions between Parliament and Convocation and between Lords and Commons by insisting upon common sessions of the six estates for common business. The immediate object of the change would be to secure control, especially financial control, for the Commons. Since the Commons are both laymen

---

[1] This is not a slip, as the fine imposed on defaulters was levied *pro quolibet archidiaconatu*. IX.

[2] See *infra*, Chapter XIV, pp. 326-9.

[3] IX.   [4] XVII.   [5] XXIII.

and clergy, the size of the proctorial order seems deliberately increased to insure for them a position of equality. We might, therefore, suppose that the ultimate intention of the writer was to claim for the lower clergy an equal share with the knights and burgesses in all things that were granted, denied and accomplished in Parliament. Orientated in this way, the *Modus* would take on the appearance of an ecclesiastical manifesto, the work of a radical clerk who understood the folly of allowing his order to be extruded from Parliament. What is, in effect, a new constitution, he would be putting forward in the characteristically English guise of a restoration.

If this indeed were the meaning of the *Modus*, it should be possible to discover the date and occasion of its composition. The occasion would presumedly be a time when feeling ran high over the taxation and rights of the lower clergy. It can hardly be later than the rise of the Lollards and the vehement anti-clericalism provoked by them. The clergy were then forced to prefer the protection of the Crown to contention for privilege and to accept without complaint the burdens laid upon them. We may assume that the *Modus* does not belong to any period later than the Peasants' Revolt (1381) and the heresy hunt of 1382. On the other hand, the obscurity that hangs over the history of the proctors in Parliament makes it difficult to fix limiting dates to propaganda to restore them. They are rarely mentioned on the parliament rolls and never after 1332.[1] Indeed, it has never been proved that they were an essential element in Parliament at any stage in its history. Yet in the persistent use of the *premunientes* clause in the writs of summons to the bishops, the proctors had a strong technical justification for a claim to a restoration of rights. Whether present or absent,[2] there can be no doubt that throughout the reign their consent to taxation was seldom given in Parliament[3] and we have no evidence that they had any

[1] *Rot. Parl.* II, p. 64*b*, Parliament held at Westminster, March 16, 1332. " Si alerent mesmes les prelatz et les procuratours de la clergie par eux mesmes," and *ibid.*, p. 65*b*, " avoient les chivalers des countes, citeins et burgeys . . . et auxint la clergie, conge d'aler ver lur pays." The reference for the Parliament at York (December 4, 1332) is not decisive (*ibid.*, p. 67): " lesqueux prelatz od la clergie par eux meismes." The reference in 1333 to " procuratours " (*ibid.*, p. 69*b*) obviously refers only to the proxies of prelates.

[2] See *infra*, pp. 126-7. There is evidence that certain dioceses either sent, or went through the motions of sending, proctors to Parliament throughout Edward III's reign.   [3] See *infra*, Chapter VII, pp. 145-50.

share whatever in parliamentary business after 1333. What we are for the moment supposing to be the argument of the *Modus* would be therefore relevant from the time when we may be reasonably certain that the proctors no longer shared in the work of the Commons in Parliament. We might take 1332 and 1381 as limiting dates and begin by examining the hypothesis of a proctorial paper constitution in relation to this period.

Though the history of the diocesan clergy in the fourteenth century is still obscure, it is possible to test our hypothesis by concentrating on the key problems of finance and representation. From the beginning of Edward III's reign the dual system of granting taxes,—the laity in Parliament and the clergy in Convocation,—was consistently followed. The division was in conformity with the claim of the clergy to privileged isolation and at first it seemed altogether to their advantage. They already understood the value of the conditional grant and were convinced that they could drive the hardest bargains in their own assembly. There was only one obvious weakness. As the ecclesiastical tenth was collected on the assessment of 1291, the Crown asserted the right to tax for the lay subsidy the revenue of all the property acquired after that date.[1] Though the sums thus levied were at first negligible, they formed a perilous precedent, as they interrupted the full application of the doctrine of consent. During the long reign of Edward III the hidden dangers of dyarchy in taxation slowly became manifest. On three sides Convocation was gradually losing its position of equality. A monopoly in legislation was steadily assumed by Parliament, which necessarily weakened the bargaining power of the clergy ;[2] the burden of the foreign wars began to change direct taxation from an emergency measure to the routine of government ; most important of all, the growth of indirect taxation altered the whole balance of the dual system. In 1348 the Commons complained that a tax on wool was, in effect, a

---

[1] This right was asserted by Edward I in 1297, and was acted upon consistently by him and by Edward II. See J. F. Willard, *The English Church and the Lay Taxes of the Fourteenth Century* (University of Colorado Studies, 1907), pp. 219-20.

[2] Sometimes the statute even defeated canon law, e.g. *De Bigamis*, cited T. F. T. Plucknett, *Statutes and their Interpretation in the First Half of the Fourteenth Century*, Cambridge, 1922, p. 37.

tax, not upon the merchants, but on themselves [1] and they demanded that henceforth no impositions, charge or loan should be ordained without the consent of Parliament. The same argument applied to ecclesiastical landlords with equal force, but they were not protected by the remedy, as Convocation had no rights in the matter of indirect taxation.[2] When Parliament acquired a measure of control over the customs it also acquired a general control over taxation which necessarily put the clergy into a position of inferiority.

The danger was recognised by archbishop Stratford in the full tide of his quarrel with Edward III. So much attention has been given to his claims to trial by peers and to a parliamentary enquiry that it has not been observed that he expressed the doctrine of consent to taxation in a manner emphatic enough to recall the *Modus*. His opinions were set out in a letter written to the chancellor on January 28, 1341 ;[3] on the following day he despatched a second draft to the bishops, modified in a way which underlined the constitutional issues involved.[4] The clergy in Convocation, he wrote, had granted the king a tenth on condition that they should pay no other taxes while they were thus burdened. Afterwards Parliament made a grant of the ninth fleece, lamb and sheaf on the express condition that only those prelates who were bound by tenure to come to Parliament should contribute.[5] The prelates were exempt from paying the Convocation tenth and, conversely, the clergy, who " *per baroniam de rege nihil tenent, nec ad parliamentum venire astricti sunt*," [6] were exempt from the parliamentary ninth. In spite of these stipula-

---

[1] *Rot. Parl.* II, 201, " nulle tiele graunte se face par les Marchantz, desicome ce est soulement en grevance et charge de la Commune et noun pas des Marchantz qi achatent de tant les Leines au meyns."

[2] In 1338 Convocation was asked to consent to a parliamentary grant of half the wool of the realm. Canterbury Convocation replied *solutionem vero lanarum expresse negaverunt* (Murimuth, *Rolls Series*, p. 85), making, instead, a grant of a tenth ; York Convocation refused to grant anything (Wilkins, II, 653). Direct grants of wool, which were purveyance by consent, differed altogether from the imposition of customs duties, the true form of indirect taxation.

[3] Walsingham (*Rolls Series*), I, 234-5.

[4] Register of bishop Grandisson of Exeter, A, ff. 235, 236 (in Wilkins, II, 659).

[5] Convocation sat in January 1340 : Wilkins, II, 653 ; Wake, *State of the Church and Clergy*, p. 288. The parliamentary grant was made on April 3, 1340, *Rot. Parl.* II, 112-13.

[6] Walsingham, I, 234.

tions, the king's collectors were compelling prelates and clergy to contribute to both subsidies.[1] This was to the manifest prejudice of prelates, religious and clergy, *cum nec ipsi Parliamento interfuerint predicto, sicut interesse minime tenebantur, nec consensum ad dicte nonae porcionis prestacionem aliqualiter praebuerunt*.[2] If the levy be permitted, the clergy will be constrained by the lay power to contribute to a tax to which they have not given their consent.

The case thus stated by the archbishop is substantially correct and it shows that he was fully aware of the dangers involved in the dual system. A compromise was reached which left the main issue undecided. In the Parliament of May 1341 it was agreed that the ninth should be paid only by prelates *qui tiegnent du roi par baronie et deyvent venir au parlement par somonse*.[3] Heads of religious houses then sought for writs declaring that they had no tenurial obligation to attend Parliament. In these writs a significant clause was inserted : the abbot and his successors are quit, *ita tamen quod ipsi in procuratores, ad hujusmodi parliamenta et consilia mittendos per clerum, consenciant et, ut moris est, pro expensis contribuant eorumdem*.[4] The Crown had accepted the principle of consent, but the claim of the archbishop that the clergy *interesse minime tenebantur* at Parliament was implicitly rejected.

Edward III was thus ready to answer the archbishop's claim that taxes granted in Parliament lacked the assent of the clergy by instancing the summons of the proctors, yet he was by no means prepared to force them to attend. On the contrary, it was just at

---

[1] The collectors had first tried to levy the ninth on all ecclesiastical lands not included in the valuation of 1291, but after a protest in the Parliament of July 1340, they were ordered to desist from the levy on all religious who paid the tenth and were not summoned to Parliament (*Rot. Parl.* II, 119b; *Cal. Cl. Rolls, 1339-41*, p. 613). On January 26, 1341, the king ordered the levy of the ninth on all temporalities whatsoever, and it was against this order that the archbishop's letters were directed (*Cal. Pat. Rolls, 1340-3*, pp. 124-5). See D. Hughes, *Early Years of Edward III*, 1915, Chapter IX, for a valuable account of royal policy.　　　　　　　　　　　　　　　[2] Wilkins, II, 659.

[3] *Rot. Parl.* II, 130. It was ordained at the same time that the ninth should be charged on all ecclesiastical possessions, purchased or appropriated, which was not taxed for the Convocation tenth. See *Chronica Monasterii de Melsa* (*Rolls Series*), III, 24 *seq.*, Chapter VII, for a concrete example of the working of the compromise.

[4] For example, the writ to the abbot of St. Augustine's, Bristol, May 2, 1341, *Report on the Dignity of a Peer*, III, Appendix I, Part II, 528.

this date that the royal and provincial letters from the king and the archbishops, exhorting the full attendance of the clergy, fell out of use.[1] There is, therefore, nothing in the crisis of 1341 to suggest a direct connection with the *Modus*. The compromise reached in Parliament shelved the whole problem of ecclesiastical taxation for a time, and neither side saw any advantage in re-opening it. In 1346 the king even admitted, in reply to a petition of the Commons, that ecclesiastical lands, not valued in 1291, and on which the Convocation tenth was not paid, should be taxed for the tenth, and not for the lay subsidy.[2] At the same time, royal demands for money continued, and the clergy went on bargaining for terms, or bringing forward grievances in their own assemblies and in Parliament.[3]

The next serious clash came in 1356, on the eve of the Poitiers campaign. Canterbury Convocation met at St. Paul's on May 16, and on the following day the king sent an imposing delegation of seven laymen to address the assembly.[4] Shareshull, Chief Justice of the King's Bench, gave warning that nothing must be done to the prejudice of the king or of the law,[5] and then Sir Walter Manny explained the royal needs, and asked for a subsidy of a sexennial tenth to be paid in three years. The clergy debated the request for nearly a week, and on the following Tuesday (May 24), they presented an address to the archbishop and bishops. They complained that the terms of the bargain, made when they granted a triennial tenth in 1352, had not been observed ; that they were bound to pay in the near future a procuration for the cardinals

---

[1] These letters were issued for the last time in 1341. They had always been resented by the clergy as a breach of privilege. See *infra*, Chapter VII, pp. 128 *seq.*

[2] *Rot. Parl.* II, 163 (1346) . . . *des terres dont ils paient nulles dismes soient chargez des dismes come affiert.* This principle does not seem to have been followed in practice, see Willard, *loc. cit.* It was reversed on another petition in 1377, *Rot. Parl.* III, 24b.

[3] For example, the conditions made by the York Convocation in December 1342, and in June 1356 (Wilkins II, 711-12 ; III, 39) ; by the Canterbury Convocation in May 1345, May 1351, May 1356 and February 1360 (*ibid.* II, 727 ; III, 16-17, 38-9, 46-7). Cf. petitions in Parliament 1341, 1344 and 1352 (*Rot. Parl.* II, 129b-30, 151b-2, 244b-5).

[4] The earl of Stafford, Sir Walter de Manny, the judges Shareshull and Henry Green, Sir John de Grey, steward of the household, Thomas de Holand and John de Wynwick, Keeper of the Privy Seal (Wilkins, III, 38-9, where an account of the proceedings is printed from archbishop Islip's Register).

[5] . . . *ne quid per concilium huiusmodi fieret in praeiudicium domini regis iurisve regni sui.*

coming to treat of peace ; and that their benefices had sunk to half their value. The main grievance, however, was definitely constitutional. At the last Parliament the extra duties on wool had been continued for another six years on condition that no fifteenths were levied during that period ; [1] though it should not be so *de jure*, it was, in fact, *ad grave onus cleri, qui a dicto Parliamento non per contumaciam absens erat*. They demanded that they should not be in a worse position (*deterioris conditionis*) than the laity and, in effect, refused to grant any subsidy. The prelates begged for a reconsideration of the refusal, and on the following day it was reported that the clergy, *ad requisitionem prelatorum*, granted a single tenth on condition that their grievances were redressed. A month later the York Convocation made reply to the same effect.[2]

The attitude of the proctors in 1356 thus approached more closely to the plan we are provisionally assigning to the *Modus* than to anything recorded earlier in the reign. It is clear that they recognised the significance of the control of indirect taxation by Parliament, and that they were acting against the bishops as a separate order. Almost the only chronicler who mentions this Convocation emphasises the discord by the statement that while the bishops granted a biennial tenth, the clergy would offer no more than a single subsidy.[3] However, these facts are not in themselves strong enough to support our hypothesis. It is hard to know what meaning should be attached to the plea *absens non per contumaciam*, but it definitely suggests that the proctors were then under no obligation to attend Parliament. There is no sign that blame for their absence was laid either on the king or on the prelates, and no specific claim to representation is asserted. Moreover, the occasion, scarcely noticed by contemporaries, does not seem sufficient to provoke the composition of the *Modus*. The mere fact that the *Modus* appears to be a defence against secular usurpations does not help to fix its date, and it is impossible to isolate the events of 1356 from the mounting tide of ill will between clergy and laity which marks the second half of the reign.

The new anti-clericalism was partly due to suspicion of the

---

[1] Parliament of November 1355, *Rot. Parl.* II, 265b.
[2] June 3, Wilkins, III, 39.
[3] Avesbury (*Rolls Series*), p. 459. Cf. Knighton (*Rolls Series*), II, 86.

French Papacy,[1] and partly to a natural wish to shift the burden of taxation as far as possible on to the shoulders of the clergy. The statutes of Provisors and Premunire (1351 and 1352) were a clear indication of stiffening against papal interference, probably, not altogether unwelcome to English ecclesiastics. More significant of the temper of the Government is the strange case of the bishop of Ely in 1356. He had rashly involved himself in a series of law suits with Blanche Wake, Lancaster's sister, and in a personal quarrel with the king.[2] The situation grew dangerous when his chamberlain slew a servant of the Wake household in a brawl. The bishop himself was brought to trial on the charge of abetting murder and protecting the murderer ; he was refused judgement per pares suos and found guilty by a jury de plebeis ; he was further refused " canonical purgation " by the archbishop, apparently from fear, and his temporalities remained in the king's hand ; finally, when he fled to Avignon and Innocent VI took up his cause, papal bulls excommunicating his judges were excluded from the realm on pain of outlawry.[3] The same bitter anti-clericalism, as Delachenal has shown, wrecked the first treaty of London in 1358.[4] It had been negotiated by two cardinals, and the terms agreed upon were virtually the same as those accepted in 1360. In the Scalachronica it is stated that the Commons in the Parliament of 1358 refused to accept the treaty unless the Pope gave up all claims based on John's surrender and ceased to meddle in the temporal affairs of the realm.[5] In the same spirit

[1] Cf. Knighton, II, 94, Ore est le Pape devenu Franceys e Jesu devenu Engleys. Ore serra veou qe fra plus, ly Pape ou Jesus, which the chronicler said was written in mockery at Vienne and many other places.

[2] He had broken into a hawking-party to reproach Edward III for the false and partial sentences of his judges, saying, " Domine, sic est quod legem in causa mea habere non possum neque justitiam ; potestate, ut credo, regia praepeditus." The king repulsed him in great anger, and there was another stormy scene between them in the Parliament of 1355—wrongly assigned by Wilkins (III, 44-5), who was misled by Parker, to the Convocation of 1360. The full account of the affair, summarised above, is taken from Historiae Eliensis ; Anglia Sacra, I, 655-62. Cf. Knighton, II, 103-4.

[3] Rymer, VI, 65-6, October 10, 1357.

[4] R. Delachenal, Histoire de Charles V, Paris, 1909, Vol. II, Chapter II, iii.

[5] Thom. Gray, Scalachronica, p. 177 : " . . . quelis comunes desagreerent, en playn parlement a Loundres, ou tail du dit tretice, si ensy ne fust qe autre addicioun ne fust ajouste. Ceo fust qe le pape releissast pur ly et sez successours tout le contracte qe le roy Johan avoit fait . . . et qe le seint pier cessast de chos (choses) qen le hour sentremist peniblement. . . ." There follows a summary of papal proceedings on behalf of the bishop of Ely.

of hostility it was proposed in the Parliament of 1365 to withhold Peter's Pence ;[1] the Pope retaliated by reviving his claim to John's tribute, a claim emphatically rejected by the Parliament of 1366.[2] Relations with the Papacy remained unfriendly until the concordat at Bruges in 1375.[3]

The English clergy necessarily suffered from the loss of papal protection, and when the war was renewed in 1369 lay demands for taxation were made in a new spirit of anger and covetousness. Divisions within the Church increased the complexity of the situation. The bishops, either from expediency or from curialist training, generally recognised the wisdom of submission, reserving their energies mainly for combating anti-papal policy. On the other hand, learned clerks like Wycliffe and certain of the friars were coming to look upon the wealth of the Church as a positive evil, and were ready to supply the laity with new arguments for heavy taxation, or even for disendowment. The monks and the diocesan clergy, thus exposed on the right and left flank, were accordingly forced to choose between submission and independent resistance. The situation at this time in some measure corresponds to the political doctrines of the *Modus ;* in order to understand its full significance, it is necessary to examine the sequence of events in the period 1369 to 1375.

The renewal of the French war was discussed in the Parliament of June 1369, and the wool duties were imposed again for three years.[4] The prelates approved the resumption of the style of king of France, but refused to grant an ecclesiastical subsidy until they had consulted their subjects.[5] This consultation evidently took place in diocesan assemblies, as on June 27 archbishop Wittlesey ordered the archdeacon of Canterbury to summon the religious and secular clergy of the diocese to meet at Christ Church, Canterbury, on July 25. Before that date, consultations were to be held in the rural deaneries at fixed times and places ; convents, chapters and the clergy of each deanery were ordered to send proctors to the assembly at Christ Church.[6] We have no record

---

[3] H. B. Workman, *John Wyclif*, Oxford, 1926, Vol. I, 219 *seq.*, summarises
[1] John of Reading, pp. 163-4. Cf. *The Brut* (E.E.T.S.), Vol. II, 316.
[2] *Rot. Parl.* II, 290 ; John of Reading, p. 171.
Anglo-papal relations at this time.
[4] *Rot. Parl.* II, 300b.   [5] *Ibid.*, Wilkins, III, 81.
[6] Wake, Appendix, pp. 70-1. Cf. *infra*, Chapter XIV, pp. 326-9, for a discussion of the use of rural deaneries.

of these diocesan discussions, but apparently nothing was done. On October 11 the king sent a writ to the archbishop ordering him to summon Convocation to grant him help in his urgent necessity. The summons was accordingly issued for January 22, 1370, with a peremptory warning that no excuses for absence would be accepted.[1] When the clergy were assembled at St. Paul's, they were addressed by the chief Baron of the Exchequer, Thomas de Ludlow, supported by the Chief Justices of the King's Bench and Common Pleas.[2] The archbishop also explained the king's necessities, and asked for a triennial tenth. He ordered the religious to withdraw to one part of the cathedral and the proctors of the clergy to another, and there to discuss the amount that they were prepared to grant. They were warned to report their decision in the chapter house on the following day, and threatened with the penalties of contumacy if they were absent. On January 23 the religious and the proctors, except those of Canterbury diocese,[3] offered a biennial tenth on condition that their grievances were redressed. They were ordered to draft petitions for presentation to the king. On the following Tuesday (January 29) the archbishop, supported by nine bishops, explained that *ad relevamen regis et regni* and *ratione potissime iuris naturalis* they must grant a triennial tenth, as the prelates, *iure naturali moti*, had already done. Once more, separate discussions *per gradum* were held, and again the religious and the proctors refused to make a triennial grant. On February 1 the royal commissioners[4] again addressed the whole body, and refused to accept the biennial tenth. The archbishop then begged each bishop to confer with the proctors of his own diocese to bring them to reason. Certain proctors and religious absented themselves from the final decision, and were held contumacious, but those who had the courage to remain repeated their refusal, declaring that they had been ignorant of the larger grant made by the prelates. The archbishop then dissolved Convocation. The obstinacy of the clergy in the end seems to have been wasted, for by April 20 the bishop of London

[1] Wake, Appendix, pp. 71-3.
[2] Wilkins (III, 82 *seq.*) prints a full account of this assembly from the Register of archbishop Wittlesey.
[3] Probably Canterbury claimed exemption on the grounds of ravages by soldiers. Cf. 1360, Wilkins, III, 46-7.
[4] Matthew.Parker, *De Antiquitate Britannicae*, 1572, p. 281, states that this demand was made by Lancaster, Arundel, Warwick and Guy de Brien.

was issuing instructions for the levy of a triennial subsidy, thus overruling the grant for two years only.[1] Similar evidence is extant for other dioceses in both provinces.[2] The chroniclers are agreed that a triennial tenth was granted, Walsingham adding that the clergy put off their answer until after Easter (April 14).[3] It is possible that the clergy were finally forced to consent in diocesan or archidiaconal assemblies,[4] but in any case it is clear that the definite refusal of Convocation was disregarded.

After 1370 the taxation of the clergy does not bear the same constitutional interest, as the savage temper of the laity made serious resistance impossible. In 1371 both Convocations were forced to agree to the tax of £50,000, the same amount that had been granted by Parliament.[5] Evidently there was some resistance from the southern province. Convocation sat from April 24 to May 3, and the Prince of Wales and other magnates made a special appeal at a full session held in Lancaster's palace of the Savoy. In 1373 the southern clergy were ordered to make up a deficit of over £8000, including arrears unpaid by the northern province, on penalty of the seizure of their temporalities.[6] In December 1373 the Convocation of Canterbury granted a single tenth, and York followed suit early in the following year.[7] A late authority records an indignant protest by Courtenay of Hereford, who declared that neither he nor the clergy of his diocese would pay anything until their grievances were redressed.[8] If Courtenay

[1] Sudbury's Register (Cant. and York Soc.), 1918, Vol. I, 75-6.

[2] Issue Roll of Thomas Brantingham, ed. F. Devon, 1835, pp. 137-8 : May 20, orders for the collection of the triennial tenth granted by the clergy, directed to the bishops of St. Asaph, Llandaff, Bangor, St. David's, Coventry and Lichfield, Worcester, Hereford, Salisbury, Bath and Wells ; pp. 138-9, May 21, like orders for dioceses of York, Carlisle, Durham and Lincoln.

[3] Walsingham I, 312 ; Anonimalle Chronicle, ed. V. H. Galbraith, M.U.P., 1927, p. 62, where Convocation is confounded with Parliament. Cf. Murimuth (ed. T. Hog, 1846), p. 207.

[4] This is suggested by Wake (p. 302) on the authority of a writ dated July 26 from the bishop of Winchester to the archdeacon of Surrey with reference to the collection of a grant, recently made by the religious and secular clergy of his archdeaconry when called before the bishop's commissaries.

[5] Wilkins, III, 91. Canterbury Convocation met at St. Paul's on April 24, the northern Convocation at York on July 10.

[6] Ibid. 94, the archbishop's writ, dated August 7, summoning a council of bishops at St. Paul's on October 7. The southern province was assessed at £40,000 ; the northern only at £10,000. The exact sum demanded from Canterbury in 1373 was £8147 11s. 1d.

[7] Ibid. 96-7.   [8] Parker, loc. cit., p. 300.

indeed protested he was probably alone, for the anti-clericalism of the time made argument dangerous. The dismissal of ecclesiastical ministers in 1371 was a sign of the impatience of the war party and a warning of their greed for the wealth of the Church.[1] The chroniclers notice the new temper with dismay and indignation. The *Anonimalle Chronicle* states that the subsidy of 1371 was exacted *pur graunt manauce*, and that the clergy were forced to pay three tenths in a single year.[2] The continuator of the *Eulogium* describes an astonishing scene at the Convocation of June 1373.[3] A special session, attended by the Prince of Wales and the secular magnates, was held at Westminster, to discuss the Pope's demand for a tenth,[4] and the tribute due to him from John's surrender. The debate turned on the temporal lordship of the Papacy and an Austin friar maintained that, though St. Peter held the keys, the sword of power belonged to St. Paul or the lay authority. Though the archbishop protested that there was good counsel in England without the friars, he broke down when the Prince browbeat him by exclaiming *Asine, responde ; tu deberes nos omnes informare.* He weakly admitted that the Pope was not *dominus* in England, and was supported in this denial by the speaker for the monks. The lay magnates then rejected John's submission as *sine consensu regni et baronum, quod legitime facere non potuit.*[5] Even allowing for the narrator's exaggeration, it is clear that the prelates were cowed and overborne by lay authority. Walsingham confirms this impression by his denunciations of Pembroke, who was blamed for the heavy taxation of 1371.[6] He had raved against the rights and liberties of the Church in parliament, and had persuaded the king that the clergy rather than the laity should be taxed in time of war. His arguments were welcomed by the temporal lords, who turned his advice *quasi in consuetudinem* and rejoiced when they were able to lay burdens upon the Church.

[1] Cf. *Brut*, II, 324, the dismissals were done *in hatered of men of holy chirche.*
[2] P. 67.
[3] *Eulogium Historiarum* (*Rolls Series*), III, 337-9. The date is wrongly given as 1374. The circumstances correspond with the summons of the Convocation of Canterbury for May 30, 1373, Wilkins, III, 93, and Wake, p. 303.
[4] The papal demand was issued on February 2, 1373, *Cal. Papal Letters*, IV, 106-7.
[5] The arguments used were, perhaps, those ascribed by Wycliffe to the seven lords in his *Determinacio*, written not later than 1377 (*Opera Minora*, ed. Loserth, pp. 415-30).
[6] Walsingham, I, 314-15. Cf. Higden (*Rolls Series*), VIII, 377-8.

Walsingham's suggestion that the spoliation of the Church had become part of a reasoned and deliberate policy is supported by independent evidence. Wycliffe's famous story of the speech in Parliament about the owl and her feathers probably belongs to 1371. The other birds had given the owl some of their feathers to shield her from the cold. Then the hawk swooped down on them and they asked for the feathers again and, when the owl denied them, each one snatched back his own and escaped from danger. The plucked owl was left more wretched than before. " Thus when war breaks out, we must take from the endowed clergy their temporal possessions, since property belongs to us and to the realm in common. . . ."[1] The same argument was put less picturesquely in eleven articles presented to the Parliament of 1371 by two Austin friars.[2] They maintain that the refusal of prelates and religious to grant taxes, on the grounds that Convocation and all the clergy had not consented, was against the laws of God and Nature. The clergy are bound to give help in time of necessity ; the Decretals and the Fathers agree that ecclesiastical property must be used at a time of common danger. The fact that it is even lawful to kill a priest in self-defence illustrates the way in which necessity overpowers ordinary rules, for no constitution can be upheld against the law of Nature.[3] Therefore, the descendants of the princes and nobles who endowed the Church are entitled to resume at least part of these endowments and the hostile attitude of ecclesiastics to taxation is a great slander to their estate and an evil example to all the people. The implication plainly is that the consent of the clergy to taxation was unnecessary at a time of stress, as the right of Society, as a whole, to help against common danger was based upon the laws of God and Nature. Wycliffe, who had little originality, did not go much beyond this position in the flood of books and pamphlets which he directed against the wealth and temporal power of the Church. He probably became Lancaster's protégé, not because he had new views to put forward, but because he supported the prevailing secularism by the full weight of his learning and skill in dialectics. Until the

[1] Wycliffe, De Civili Dominio (Wyclif Society), II, 7.
[2] Printed from the Cartulary of Bury St. Edmunds by V. H. Galbraith, Eng. Hist. Review, Vol. XXXIV, pp. 579-82.
[3] " . . . en quele necessite nule possession de lour deverroit estre esparni par nule constitucion faite a contraire de deu et de nature." Ibid., p. 581.

concordat with the Papacy was reached at Bruges (1375) and the taint of heresy was definitely attached to Wycliffe's theory of dominion (1377) the laity were able to persuade themselves that the spoliation of the Church was not only expedient but just and godly.

Thus it seems that the circumstances of the period 1369 to 1375 were just of the kind to provoke the expression of the doctrines we have traced in the *Modus*. A hostile court and baronage, supported by the learning of the schools, defended the taxation or even the disendowment of the Church by the dangerous argument of necessity. The prelates, cowed by threats or bought by favour, acquiesced in the repudiation of papal claims and used their authority to wring taxes from their clergy. Of them Wycliffe wrote : " . . . whanne the kyng and lordis axeden of grete prelatis subsidies and dymes for here temperaltes thei graunten hem, so that pore curatis and annueleris may be taxid at here settyng ; and so alle the charge fallith on here pore curatis, and othere and the riche prelatis gon free or hellis wynnen a porcion to hem self of goodis of here pore curatis."[1] The lower clergy, already restless in 1356, obstinately resisted in 1370, debating *per graduum*, opposing their bishops both severally and in full Convocation and refusing to grant the triennial tenth demanded of them. Their refusal was overridden—how it is not clear—and a year later they were forced to consent to the levy of £50,000, collected, one chronicler states, on *minuta* and on benefices never taxed before.[2] The doctrine of consent was set aside and in its place was set the anarchic proposition that no constitution might stand against the laws of God and Nature. In short, dyarchy in taxation had broken down and the obvious remedy was the reunion of Convocation and Parliament.

[1] F. D. Matthew, *The English Works of Wyclif Hitherto Unprinted* (E.E.T.S.) ; *Of Prelates*, Chapter XXXIX, p. 103. Cf. *Of Clerks Possessioners*, Chapter XL, " . . . whanne the kyng hath nede of a taxe, thei wolen not paie for pore men, not withstondynge that thei ben procuratouris of pore men . . . ," *ibid.*, p. 139.

[2] Higden, VIII (*Rolls Series*), 376. Cf. *Cal. Cl. Rolls, 1369-74*, p. 262, October 25, 1371. Order to the sheriff of Cumberland, stating that it was the king's will that all parsons and men of the Church whatsoever should contribute rateably and stipendiary priests of their stipends, all privileges notwithstanding.

CHAPTER IV

THE IRISH CHURCH AND TAXATION IN THE LATER MIDDLE AGES

I

ONCE the view is put forward that the *Modus* might be a proctorial paper constitution, written in the last decade of Edward III's reign to protect the clergy against lay encroachment and episcopal neglect, it might plausibly be argued that certain details of the document conform to this interpretation. The emphatic statement that the proctors of a diocese, if they be agreed, carry greater weight (*maiorem vocem*) than their bishops [1] reads like an echo of the separate diocesan assemblies of 1369 or the private negotiations of the bishops with their clergy in the Convocation of 1370. The instruction to the doorkeeper that he must have knowledge of the persons who ought to enter *ita quod nulli omnino negetur ingressus qui Parliamentum interesse tenetur* [2] recalls the attempt to exclude archbishop Stratford in 1341. The statement that Canterbury must sit on the king's right hand and York on his left [3] exactly conforms to the agreement, reached in 1353, on the long-standing dispute over precedence between the archbishops. *Et cum Eboracensis archiepiscopus ad Parliamentum regis venerit: archiepiscopus Cantuariensis, tanquam praeminentior, ad dexteram partem regis sedebit et Eboracensis in sinistra.*[4] If it be supposed that the *Modus* was written *ad hoc*, as a Utopian project of parliamentary reform, the anachronisms or errors in the description would become much less important, and troublesome details like the absence of dukes, the special meaning of *pares* and the custody of the parliament rolls by the Treasurer might be explained away. The great increase in the number of clerical proctors, usually

---

[1] XXIII.   [2] XX.   [3] XIV.
[4] Stephen Birchington, *Vitae Archiepiscoporum Cantuariensium* in *Anglia Sacra*, I, 43-4.

regarded as an error, would become an integral part of the whole argument. The absence of all reference to the Speaker of the Commons or to the impeachment procedure might also be explained by accepting a date before 1376.

Outside the *Modus* itself a few facts may be gleaned in support of the interpretation we are provisionally considering. Courtenay seems to have posed as the champion of the clergy in 1373 and we find the full text of the *Modus* in the Courtenay chartulary, written early in the fifteenth century.[1] That the document was deemed to have special importance for the Church is suggested by the transcript of the chapter on the summons of the clergy at the end of the Canterbury register of Thomas Arundel.[2] In *De Officio Regis*, written in 1379, Wycliffe twice put forward the idea of joint sessions of Parliament and Convocation. Appeals against the clergy should be heard *coniunctis parliamento et generali cleri sinodo ;* [3] excommunications should be declared and punishments determined by both assemblies sitting together.[4] Wycliffe's purpose was certainly to reduce ecclesiastical privilege, but the means proposed may indicate that the idea of reunion was current at the time. Langland carried it still further when he longed for the day when

> Kynges courte and comune courte, consistorie and chapitele,
> Al shal be bot one courte and one baroun be Justice.[5]

This evidence, it must be admitted, does not amount to much and finds no support either in chronicles or in official records. Throughout the rest of the century the only significant references to proctors of the clergy come from the years 1397-99. In the Revenge Parliament of 1397 Thomas Percy was, at the king's request, appointed proctor for the prelates and clergy, and in the following year, at the Parliament of Shrewsbury, a like duty was assigned to Scrope, earl of Wiltshire.[6] The king's object was to enforce the unanimous consent of Parliament to judgements from which the clergy were excluded by Canon Law, and to proceedings emergent from them,

---

[1] Cf. *infra*, p. 357, for a description of this MS.
[2] Part I, f. 561v., in a different hand from the Register itself.
[3] *De Officio Regis* (Wyclif Society), p. 181.
[4] *Ibid.*, p. 228.
[5] *Piers Plowman*, ed. W. Skeat, *Passus*, III, Text B, ll. 318-19, I, 98.
[6] *Rot. Parl.* III, 348b, 351b, 356b and 359.

and the appointment of a lay proctor to represent them was arbitrary and irregular.[1] In the assembly of estates in 1399 Richard II was deposed by proctors acting for all the orders of the realm ; the bishop of St. Asaph represented the archbishops and bishops and the abbot of Glastonbury the " abbotes and priours and all other men of holy Chirche, seculers and rewelers."[2] Though the committee of deposition, representing the estates, bears a general resemblance to the *Modus* committee of twenty-five,[3] the minor part allotted to the lower clergy does not in any way support our provisional hypothesis. This general lack of corroboration cannot be ignored. Even when full allowance is made for the indifference of the hierarchy and for the panic caused by Lollardy and the Peasants' Revolt, it is difficult to believe that the bold propaganda of the *Modus*, altogether subversive of existing relations between Lords and Commons, Church and secular power, could have been entirely without effect. The evidence of the manuscripts is in itself sufficient to show that from the end of the fourteenth century the *Modus* was well known and frequently copied. Yet it has no certain history until the sixteenth century and even then no trace of our special interpretation can be found.

It might perhaps be argued that the life of Parliament was too vigorous and too much disturbed by party strife to be affected by a paper constitution drafted by a mere proctor of the clergy. If the author of the *Modus* were indeed a sort of Abbé Sieyès, asking *Qu'est ce que le tiers etat ?* he was working against a habit of resistance that was already an English characteristic and there was no hope that his ideal constitution would ever be seriously regarded. In England the political sense of the past has always been kept in strict relevance to problems of the hour, and arguments for a restoration of bygone unity would carry no weight without the backing of partisans in Parliament. At the same time the feeling for continuity and the great tradition of Common Law have always barred the acceptance of any project of reform on its merits alone. English public life, with its conservatism, its energy and its contempt for the merely reasonable, has never had a place either for the paper constitution or for the doctrinaire reformer.

Before, however, we finally abandon the provisional hypothesis

---

[1] In the Merciless Parliament of 1388 the clergy retired without appointing a proctor, which was their proper course.

[2] *Rot. Parl.* III, 422, 423 and 424.   [3] XVII.

which we have put forward concerning the origin of the *Modus*, it must be remembered that we have not only an English, but also an Irish *Modus tenendi Parliamentum*, adapted, it is true, to fit the special conditions of the country, yet also marked by the same emphasis on the rights and duties of the lower clergy.[1] What light does this Irish *Modus* throw upon our problem ? In Ireland English institutions may be observed without the driving force and without the inhibitions of the English genius. The law, the courts and the Parliament, all imported from England, were valued as the institutions of the privileged race, yet everything was on so small a scale and the governing class so individualistic in temper that no corporate stability was achieved. Those English officials who had either rank or ability were mere birds of passage, indifferent to the needs of the colony. The Anglo-Irish were beset by frontier wars, pre-occupied by quarrels and demoralised by the pull of English law against the seeping custom of Celtic society. Parliament, like all Irish institutions, was constantly disintegrating into its component parts and had no strong life of its own in which traditions of law and business could be formed. This lack of integrity or corporate life left it peculiarly open to influence from without. It is true that the influences of English models or of English ideas passed the barriers of English indifference or colonial ignorance only rarely or at haphazard, but this merely served to heighten their effect. Once admitted, they seemed to fossilise into stone, to lose all meaning and to stand as in a magic circle, held fast by the Celtic genius for restless move-ment in the same place.

II

The history of the Irish Parliament is complicated and obscure. First the neglect and then the destruction (1922) of Irish official records have discouraged scholars, though it is improbable that there was ever anything at all comparable to the English series of rolls and bundles of petitions.[2]   Yet enough evidence has survived

---

[1] See *infra*, Chapters V. and VI.

[2] A lawyer at the end of the sixteenth century wrote from Ireland : " And lastly I am to informe your Lordshipp, . . . that there is noe Parliament records here but a fewe and those sithence the time of H. 6, remayning in the Mester of the Rolls office here (and not elsewhere) to be founde, saveing for other records remayning with the chiefe Remembranser, the Auditer and Surveyor, concerning her Majesties revenues and casualties only, and some fewe in the

to show that the Irish Parliament, at least in one respect, approaches closely to the Parliament of the *Modus*. The clerical proctors continued to be an integral part of Parliament down to the Reformation, and at the last they claimed a position of full equality with the other estates. For a few months it even seemed that Henry VIII's ecclesiastical policy, for which Ireland was altogether unprepared, would be blocked by the " proctors of the spirituality." In the spring of 1537 Lord Deputy Grey wrote to Cromwell :—

" The frowardnes and obstynacye of the proctours of the clergy, from the begynnyng of this Parliament, and at this cession, bothe of them the bishops and abbotis, hathe bene soche, that we thinke we can no les do then advertise your Lordship therof. After thassembly of the Parliament, at this cession, some billis were passed the Comon House, and by the Speker delyvered to the Highe House, to be debated there. The spirituall lordes therupon made a generall aunswere, that thei wold not comon, ne debate upon eny bill, till they knewe whether ther Proctours in the Convocation House had a voice or not. . . . I, the Kinges Deputie, called to me all the Kinges lerned Counsaill, to debate withe them aboute ther doubte of ther proctours ; who not oonly shewid unto them thoppinions of the lerned men of Ingland, to gither withe ther awn reasons, that the said proctours had no voice in the Parliament, but also provid unto them by Parliamentes holden there, that it shuld seme by thentries of the rolles, that ther deniall or assent was not materiall, for that it was writtin undre divers actes *procuratores cleri non consenserunt*, and yet were the same actes good and effectuell in lawe. So as, in conclusion, thei condescended, that whan the billes were passed the Comon House, the Speker shuld deliver them to the Convocation House ; but whether thei aggreid or not aggreid, they wold nevertheles procede to [blank].

". . . [It were] well doon that some mean be devised, whereby thei ma[y be] broute to remember ther duties bettir. Excepte the me[ane] may be found that theis proctours may be put from voice [in the] Parliament, ther shall but feue thinges passe for the Kinges prof[ight].

office of chiefe plase, here called the Queenes Bench, concerning matters of Attainder, and a fewe in the common plase concerning some late utlagaries . . ." From *Advice and Directions for summoning a Parliament in Ireland*, *written long since by a learned anonymous lawyer, found amongst Mr. Selden's Papers*, MS. Bodley, Rawl. D. 922, ff. 53ᵛ-54. [The writer suggests that chancellor Gerrard carried many documents to England, but Gerrard's statement, presented to the Privy Council in 1577-78, though it includes many documents, does not contain any citations from rolls otherwise unknown (MS. Rawl. D. 657, printed in *Analecta Hibernica*, Vol. I, Pt. II, pp. 93 *seq.* (Irish Record Commission), Dublin, 1930-34.

For hitherto, synes this Parliament, have they shewid themsilfes in nothing conformable. We thinke that no reasonable man wold judge them to have soche a preemynence in a Parliament, that though the King, the Lordes and Comons assent to an acte, the proctours in the Convocation House, (though thei were but 7 or 8 in number, as sometyme thei bene here no more,) shall stay the same at ther pleasur, be the matter never so good, honeste and reasonable. But it dothe well appere that [it is] a crafty cast, divised betwixt ther masters the bishoppes and them. It is good that we have against the next c[ession], a declaration from thens, undre the Kinges Greate Seale of Ingland, of this question, whether the proctours h[ave a voice] in the Parliament or not ? and that every acte passed [without] ther assentes is nevertheles good and effectuall."[1]

In July 1537 Henry VIII sent instructions for the passing of " an acte to determyne the auctoryte of the proctors of the Convocation, whiche take upon them nowe to dyrect the hoole Parlyament."[2]   The act was passed in the following form :—

" Forasmuch as at every Parliament begun and holden within this land, two proctors of everie diocesse within the same land, have beene used and accustomed to be summoned and warned to be at the same Parliament, which were never by the order of the law, usage, custome or otherwise any member or parcell of the whole bodie of the Parliament, nor have had of right any voyce or suffrage in the same, but only to be there as counsailors and assistants to the same, and upon such things of learning, as should happen in controversie to declare their opinions,—much like as the Convocation within the realm of England is commonly at every Parliament begunne and holden by the Kings highnesse speciall licence,—as his Maiesties judges of his said realme of England, and divers other substantiall and learned men, having groundly enquired and examined the root and first establishment of the same, doe cleerely determine ; and yet by reason of this sufferance and by the continuance of time, and for that most commonly the said proctors have been made privie to such matters as within this land at any time have beene, to be enacted and established, and their advices desired and taken to the same, they now of their ambitious mindes and presumption, inordinately desiring to have authoritie and to intermedle with every cause or matter without any just ground or cause reasonable to the same, doe temerariously presume and

---

[1] *State Papers*, Henry VIII, Vol. II, Part III, 1834, pp. 437-9.   Grey and Brabazon to Cromwell, May 18, 1537.
[2] *Ibid.*, p. 457, the king's instructions to commissioners sent to Ireland, July 31, 1537.

usurpitly take upon themselves to be parcell of the body, in maner clayming that without their assents nothing can be enacted at any Parliament within this land ; which, as it is thought, commeth not without the procurement and maintenance of some of their superiours, to the onely intent that the said proctors, for the more part being now their chapleines and of meane degree, should be the stoppe and lett that the divelish abuses and usurped authoritie and jurisdiction of the Bishoppe of Rome,—(by some men called the Pope)—nor of themselves should not come to light or knowledge, that some good and godly reformation thereof might be had and provided.

"Wherefore, be it enacted, ordeyned and established by authoritie of this present Parliament, that the said proctors ne anie of them so summoned or warned to any Parliament begunne or holden . . . is ne shall be any member ne parcell of the bodie of the same Parliament, ne shall give ne have any voyce, opinion, assent or agreement to anie act, provision or ordinance to bee regarded ne enacted in anie Parliament within this lande ; ne yet their voyces, assents, or agreements or opinions shall not bee necessarie ne requisite to anie such act, etc. . . . the said proctors ne any of them shall be accepted, reputed, demed or taken from the first day of this present Parliament as parcell or any member of the said Parliament or any other Parliament heereafter . . . but onely as counsayllours and assistants to the same, any law, usage, customes, prescription or any other cause or matter, thing or things, whatsoever it or they be, in any wise to the contrary notwithstanding." [1]

A comparison between Grey's letter and the statute itself brings out some points of interest. Grey's account of the forwardness of the Spirituality is certainly disingenuous. He conceals the claim of the proctors to be " parcel " of Parliament, and represents them as wholly obstructive in demanding a right of veto by which they could block all business. It is possible that the prelates had consented to the extrusion of the proctors from the " Common House " on condition that their consent to bills was obtained separately.[2] By his use of the word Convocation Grey suggests that the constitutional position of the Irish proctors was identical with that in England, though, as a matter of fact, this is the first occasion on which the term is applied to general

---

[1] R. Bolton, *Statutes of Ireland*, Dublin, 1621, 28 Henry VIII, c. 12, pp. 113-14.

[2] This consent could easily be interpreted as a right of veto, and may explain the small attendance of the proctors.

assemblies of the Irish clergy.[1] In the statute it is used only for purposes of comparison, but we can hardly doubt that the opinions of the judges and " other substantiall and learned men " were founded upon English precedents. The garrulous preamble virtually admits that these opinions were the sole legal ground for extrusion, and acknowledges that the proctors had, at least, a prescriptive right to be present. The closing words of the enactment—" any law, usage, customes, prescription or any other cause, or matter, thing or things, whatsoever it or they be, in any wise to the contrary notwithstanding "—imply a considerable body of precedent and practice behind conditions in 1537.

There is, indeed, abundant evidence to prove that the presence and the claim of the proctors did not arise merely out of opposition to Henry VIII's policy, but were based on a constitutional practice well established in the fifteenth century. The chief sources of information are the Irish statute rolls and the registers of the archbishops of Armagh. From 1455 onwards the statute rolls [2] refer from time to time to the presence of the proctors and to their share in parliamentary business. In 1455 *lez chivalers et procatours* of the county of Dublin were instructed to appoint collectors for the levy of a subsidy,[3] and in 1459 letters testimonial were tested in Parliament by the lord deputy and by the *lordes spirituels and temporels, procatours and communes*.[4] In 1463 certain privileges of Parliament were established for *chescun ministre du parliament, sibien les seigneuris procatours come communes ;* [5] letters were ordered to be sent to the king from *lez iii estates del dit Parliament, cestassavoir, les seigneurs spirituelx et temporelx, procuratours et communes ;* [6] the dean and chapter of the clergy of Kildare diocese

[1] For the special use of the term in Ireland see *infra*, pp. 56-60.

[2] The statute rolls apparently did not go back beyond 5 Henry VI. They have been published for the reign of Henry VI and for 1-12 Edward IV, *Statute Rolls*, ed. H. F. Berry (Irish Record Office), Dublin, 1910, Vols. II and III. The rolls were destroyed in 1922, but transcripts of eleven, extending from 12-13 Edward IV to 8 Henry VII, are preserved in the Public Record Office, Dublin. The scattered records of earlier enactments have been collected and published in *Statutes, Ordinances and Acts of the Parliament of Ireland, King John to Henry V (Irish Record Office Series of Early Statutes*, Vol. I) ; they contain no references to clerical proctors.

[3] *Statute Rolls*, 34 Henry VI, p. 402.

[4] *Ibid.*, 37 Henry VI, p. 588.   [5] *Ibid.*, 3 Edward IV, p. 144.

[6] *Ibid.*, p. 180. The letters were signed : " By your trewe liege men and moost humble subjectes the lords spirituelx and temporelx prokatours and communes and your counseil of your land of Irland in your ful highe Courte of Parliament ther assembled," p. 187.

were granted leave for three years to appear in Parliament *soulment par une sufficient prokatour*, there to do all things *com les [ditz] dean, Chapitelle et clerge appareount par ii prokatours come ils soloient faire devant cele temps*.[1] In 1465 a complicated financial settlement between the archbishop of Armagh, the Medici bank in London and their agent was revised and established *devant toutz les seigneuries espirituelx et temporelx, procuratours et communes al avantdit Parliament assemblez*.[2] In the same Parliament Michael Tregorre, archbishop of Dublin, brought twelve chaplains as compurgators to clear himself of the charge of assaulting Stephen Fitzwilliam on the king's highway, beating him and robbing him of a halbert worth two shillings. The purgation was heard *coram prefato deputato* [the earl of Desmond] *necnon dominis spiritualibus et temporalibus procuratoribus et communibus terre predicte in dicto pleno Parliamento*.[3]

The Registers of Armagh both supplement the evidence of the statute roll and carry the history of the proctors in Parliament a stage further back.[4] The first reference to them comes from the Register of archbishop Miles Sweteman (1360-80). Writs of summons are entered for the Parliament at Kilkenny, January 7, 1371, and for the Parliament at Ballyduagh, June 8, 1371 ; the archbishop was ordered to attend in person, together with proctors for the dean and chapter of Armagh, and for the clergy of the diocese.[5] Writs of summons to the archbishop alone are entered for five earlier parliaments, and one Great Council [6] and, though the Register is defective, it seems that 1371 was the first year that proctors were summoned. Proctors of the deans and chapters of cathedrals were summoned to a Great Council held at Dublin on February 25, 1372 ;[7] proctors for the chapters and for the diocesan clergy

---

[1] *Statute Rolls*, 3 Edward IV, p. 196.

[2] *Ibid.*, 5 Edward IV, p. 358. Cf. p. 360.   [3] *Ibid.*, p. 348.

[4] These Registers are preserved in the Public Library, Armagh, and there are transcripts in the Library of Trinity College, Dublin.

[5] " Calendar of the Register of Archbishop Sweteman," ed. by H. J. Lawlor, *Proceedings of the Royal Irish Academy*, Vol. XXIX, pp. 233, 248.

[6] *Ibid.* pp. 228, 229, 230, 250. The archbishop was summoned to the Parliament of Kilkenny, February 19, 1366 ; the Parliament of Kilkenny, June 14, 1367 ; the Parliament of Dublin, May 1, 1368 ; the Parliament of Dublin, June 30, 1369 ; the Parliament or Council of Dublin, January 2, 1370 ; the Great Council or Parliament at Dublin, April 22, 1370. See *infra*, pp. 50-51, for these Parliaments held by William of Windsor.

[7] Writ to the archbishop of Dublin, printed by Sir William Betham, *The Origin and History of the Constitution of England and of the Early Parliaments of Ireland*, Dublin, 1834, p. 311.

were summoned to the Parliament of Kilkenny, October 6, 1375.[1] No returns to these writs are entered in the Register, but we have full returns, with names, from fourteen dioceses in reply to the extraordinary summons of two proctors from each diocese to appear before the Council in England in February, 1376.[2] Writs summoning proctors are also extant for the Parliaments of 1378 and 1380.[3]

No register is extant for Sweteman's successor, John Colton (1382-1404). The register of archbishop Nicholas Fleming (1404-15) is defective, and it contains no writs of summons to Parliament.[4] There is, however, ample evidence for the citation and attendance of proctors in the Register of archbishop Swayne (1417-39).[5] Writs of summons for Parliaments and Councils, enjoining the presence of the archbishops and proctors, are entered at least twenty times. The archbishop's return follows a common form. He himself sends two proctors, as he cannot attend in person because of disputes over precedence with the archbishop of Dublin ;[6] the dean and chapter of Armagh cannot obey the mandate as they are *meri Hibernici et inter Hibernicos conversantes, quibus concilium regium non consuevit sicut nec decuit secreta concilii revelari ;* the clergy of the diocese *inter Anglicos* will appear by one proctor whose name is returned. These returns cover the period 1433-51, and they are in themselves proof that the references to proctors on the statute rolls are not merely formal. In Prene's Register, which includes many documents of the archiepiscopates of John Mey (1444-56) and of Swayne, there are returns of proctorial elections for the Parliaments of

---

[1] *Calendar of Sweteman's Register*, p. 285. The archbishops and bishops summoned to the Parliament at Dublin in January 1375 were merely required to come with full powers of consent from their clergy : Lynch, *A View of the Legal Institutions, Honorary Hereditary Offices and Feudal Baronies established in Ireland*, 1830, p. 322.

[2] See *infra*, pp. 52-3.

[3] Lynch, *loc. cit.*, pp. 325-31.

[4] " Calendar of the Register of Archbishop Fleming," ed. by H. J. Lawlor, *Proceedings of the Royal Irish Academy*, Vol. XXX, pp. 94 *seq.* Four out of eleven gatherings are lost.

[5] Register of John Swayne, Public Library, Armagh. I have been able to consult this Register in Belfast, owing to the kindness of Dr. Chart, Deputy Keeper of the Public Records of Northern Ireland, who is preparing it for publication.

[6] On two occasions the archbishop refused to send proctors as his title of Primate had been omitted in the writ of summons.

1441, 1461 and 1465.[1] The Registers of Swayne, Octavian de Palatio (1480-1513), and George Cromer [2] (1522-43) contain a number of references to the taxation of the clergy in which the consent of the proctors in Parliament is definitely stated.[3] Throughout the Registers a few references occur to the payment of the expenses of proctors going to Parliament.[4] The last entry in Cromer's Register describes a session of the *Convocacio cleri* of Armagh at which the clergy elected one proctor to attend the Reformation Parliament in January 1536.[5]

The diocese of Armagh, with a large proportion of churches *inter Hibernicos*, was backward and poor, and it cannot be supposed that the clergy of great dioceses like Dublin and Meath were less willing to obey the writs of summons. Fragmentary survivals of entries on the patent and close rolls indicate the presence in Parliament of proctors from the dioceses *inter Anglicos*. In 1378 the dean, chapter and clergy of Cashel were fined forty shillings because they sent no proctors to Parliament,[6] and in 1380 orders were issued for the collection of a subsidy granted in Parliament by the prelates and clergy.[7] The maintenance of proctorial attendance in the fifteenth century is well illustrated by a list of fines imposed at the Parliament held at Drogheda in 1450 on twenty-seven proctors *pro offensa in dicto Parliamento facta*.[8] The whole history of the parliamentary taxation of the clergy is based upon the consent of the proctors, regularly asked for and given in Parliament.[9] We may therefore conclude, on the evidence of the statute rolls, the Armagh Registers and the official records, that from 1371 onwards proctors of the clergy were summoned to, and attended, the Irish Parliament.

---

[1] Folios 24, 121, 176.

[2] Cromer's Register, which begins in 1518, contains a number of documents of the archiepiscopate of his predecessor, John Kite (1513-22).

[3] See *infra*, pp. 64 *seq.*

[4] Swayne's Register, IV, f. 10 (p. 650 T.), 1447; Prene's Register, f. 24 (1461); f. 165 (1438); Register of Octavian de Palatio, f. 399 (1499). Cf. *infra*, p. 56, and note B.

[5] Part II, f. 93. *Convocacio cleri*, held in Holy Trinity Church, Termonfeckin, December 22, 1535. At this assembly the clergy were informed " quod unus de concilio domini regis monebat supradicto domino primati summum pontificem nomine Pape cum collegio suo non orari publice. . . ."

[6] *Calendar of Patent and Close Rolls, Ireland*, 1828, p. 105, no. 102.

[7] *Ibid.*, p. 109, nos. 100-1.

[8] *Ibid.*, p. 265, no. 13. Some of these persons may have been the personal proxies of prelates.

[9] See *infra*, pp. 59-60.

III

Lord Deputy Grey wrote in 1537 that the denial or assent of the proctors was not material " for that it was written under divers acts *procuratores cleri non consenserunt.*"[1] The phrase has not been traced on the statute rolls and it seems at present impossible to determine what share the proctors had in the work of law-making. The last reference to the proctors in the published statutes (before the act of 1537) belongs to 1494 ; an " act that no great ordnances be in no fortresse, but by licence of the Deputie " was passed " by the advice and assent of his Lords spirituall and temporall, Proctors and Commons in this present Parliament assembled. . . ."[2]

It may be that the consent of proctors to ordinary legislation had become merely formal and was not always necessary. The evidence certainly suggests that their main duty was to discuss, to consent to or to reject proposals of taxation. For that cause they were summoned and for that cause they were willing to attend. Ireland was a poor country, with a weak government and little sense of common responsibility ; to secure consent to taxation was, therefore, a task of great difficulty and importance. Though the reluctance of the English medieval taxpayer is notorious, when it is compared with the Irish attitude it begins to take on an appearance of gracious generosity. In order to understand the contrast and to explain the duties of the proctors it is necessary to summarise the curious history of parliamentary taxation in Ireland.

In Ireland the idea of revenue based on parliamentary taxation lagged far behind the rise of Parliament. The Parliaments of Edward I and Edward II were concerned partly with judicial business and partly with law-making and arbitration between factions.[3] The ordinary revenue was derived from the profits of justice, the Crown lands, escheats, wardship, the farm of shires,

---

[1] Quoted *supra*, p. 37.
[2] Bolton, *Statutes of Ireland*, 10 Henry VII, c. 12, p. 61.
[3] See " The Irish Parliaments of Edward I," H. G. Richardson and G. O. Sayles, *Proceedings of the Royal Irish Academy*, Vol. XXXVIII, p. 128, and my paper on " The Irish Parliaments in the Reign of Edward II," *Transactions of the Royal Historical Society*, Fourth Series, Vol. IX, p. 29. What follows on conditions under Edward III has already appeared in my paper on "William of Windsor in Ireland, 1369-76 " (*Royal Irish Academy*, Vol. XLI, pp. 66-74).

cities and boroughs and the custom duties.[1] The clergy *inter Anglicos* contributed from time to time to the tenths granted to the king by the Pope.[2] Extraordinary aids were raised with the consent of particular persons or communities. In 1300, for example, Edward I demanded a subsidy for the war in Scotland and sent a general writ to his earls, barons, knights and faithful subjects and special writs to the cities and boroughs of Ireland. The justiciar, John Wogan, summoned a Parliament ; before it met he visited twenty-three towns in Leinster and Munster and extracted promises of contribution varying in amount from one to 260 marks. Parliament requested him to raise the rest of the subsidy by further piecemeal negotiation.[3] The counties, liberties, cross-lands (ecclesiastical estates) and boroughs contributed in this way £2361 6s. 8d. ; the magnates served in person in the Scottish campaign of 1301.[4] The plan, which recalls the procedure described in the *Dialogus de Scaccario*,[5] shows an application of the doctrine of consent at its earliest stage. The method was well suited to Irish particularism and was only slowly and with difficulty replaced by consent in a representative assembly.

Edward III's need of money brought new demands for Irish subsidies and, as the papal grants of tenths ceased in 1330, the problem of ecclesiastical taxation began to be seriously considered. A general grant to the king was made in 1335 and at first sight it has the appearance of a parliamentary subsidy. In June 1336 Edward III thanked the prelates, magnates, clergy and communities of cities, boroughs and towns of Ireland for *unum generale subsidium de redditibus, terris et bonis*.[6] The annalist Clyn records that in 1335 the king asked for two shillings

---

[1] On May 15, 1275, the king ordered the Justiciar of Ireland to prevail upon the magnates, commonalty and merchants of Ireland to grant the *Magna Custuma* as it had recently been granted in England, *Cal. Documents Ireland*, Vol. II, no. 1117.

[2] These finally ceased early in Edward III's reign.

[3] *Early Statutes*, pp. 229 seq.

[4] G. H. Orpen, *Ireland under the Normans*, Oxford, 1911-14, Vol. IV, pp. 47-8. In 1292 the "magnates and good men of the land" had granted the king a fifteenth, but there is no indication of how their consent was obtained, *Cal. Documents Ireland*, Vol. III, no. 1090.

[5] *Dialogus*, ed. Hughes, Crump and Johnson, 1902, p. 95 : " Fiunt interdum per comitatus communes assise a iustitiis errantibus . . . que ideo dicuntur communes quia, cognita summa que de comitatu requiritur, communiter ab hiis qui in comitatu fundos habent per hidas distribuitur. . . ."

[6] Rymer, II, Part II, 939.

from each carucate, a tenth from the clergy, and a competent subsidy from the cities and great towns.[1] However, the chronicles [2] and records agree that no Irish Parliament or Great Council was held between 1333 and 1337 [3] and it is also significant that the royal request for aid was sent, not only in a general writ, but separately to the magnates, the prelates and the city of Dublin.[4] From details of the accounts on the Pipe Rolls, it seems probable that, as in 1300, the money was granted locally. In the account of 11 Edward III for Cork city a number of separate payments are recorded as due from individuals or from communities in the county ; [5] in a similar account for Tipperary (11-14 Edward III) it is noted that " the community of county Tipperary, except the market towns, owes £54 7s. 6d. of the subsidy granted to the king for his war in Scotland." [6] The numerous entries dealing with the tax on the clergy relate to grants made by particular dioceses, as, for example, " for the twentieth granted by the bishop and clergy of Meath diocese £32·11s. 9¾d.," [7] or " for arrears of 4s. 7d. owed on the twentieth granted by the diocese of Ossory." [8] A special payment is recorded to the Chancellor of the Exchequer " for his trouble, outlay and expenses in going by order of the king to Meath, and remaining there to stir up the clergy of the diocese of Meath to grant a tenth from their benefices . . . to speed certain arduous affairs of the king." [9] At least for the ecclesiastics, the evidence points definitely to a subsidy raised by local bargains and varying

[1] *Annals of Ireland by Friar John Clyn*, ed. R. Butler, Dublin, 1849, p. 26.
[2] The only Anglo-Irish chronicles of value for the reign of Edward III are Clyne's *Annals of Ireland* (cf. n. 1) and *Annals of Ireland, 1162-1370* (Bodley MS. Laud 526), printed in *Chartularies of St. Mary's Abbey, Dublin (Rolls Series)*, Vol. II.
[3] Parliament at Dublin, June 1333, *Liber Munerum* (ed. R. Lascelles), 1852, I, Part IV, 12 ; and Parliament at Dublin, 1337, *Laud Annals of Ireland*, printed in *Chartularies of St. Mary's Abbey*, II, 380.
[4] Rymer, IV, 641-5. Orders to come in person with horses and arms were sent to the prelates, the earls of Ormonde and Desmond, 54 knights, 109 esquires and 14 Irish chiefs.
[5] *Report 45 of the Deputy Keeper of Public Records, Ireland*, 1913, pp. 41-2. For example, " William son of David de Barry owes £1 ; the community of Carrictothell 6/8 ; of Castle Lyons 6/8 ; of Shandon 5/- ; . . . of Buttevant 10/-." [6] *Ibid.*, R. 47, p. 24.
[7] *Ibid.*, R. 45, p. 50. The tax is usually described as a twentieth, not a tenth, as Clyn states ; Cashel was in arrears on account of the tenth granted to the king by the diocese, *ibid.*, R. 47, p. 27.
[8] *Ibid.*, p. 28, Account for the Cross-lands of Kilkenny, 8-14 Edward III.
[9] *Ibid.*, p. 35, Account for Drogheda on the side of Meath, 12-13 Edward III.

from place to place in the amounts promised. Perhaps the fact that the magnates, as in 1301, were asked for personal service in the field turned attention away from Parliament as a general assembly with the power of consent.

The first true parliamentary subsidy was granted at the Parliament of Kilkenny in October 1346,[1] and it is significant that evidence for it should be derived from records of resistance to its collection. On the Plea Roll of 21 Edward III it is stated that the Parliament of Kilkenny had granted to the king for his Irish wars a subsidy of two shillings on every carucate, a shilling on every half carucate and a shilling from all landless persons possessing goods worth sixty shillings ; and that collectors had been appointed for eleven counties and for the liberty of Trim.[2] Before the end of the year commissioners were appointed to enquire into obstruction to the levy of the tax in the counties of Cork, Kerry, Limerick, Tipperary, and Waterford.[3] Probably as a result of the enquiry, proceedings were taken against the archbishop of Cashel and the bishops of Emly, Limerick and Lismore. On the seventh of January, 1347, they had decreed that any clerk of their province who paid the subsidy should be deprived of his benefice and stripped of his gown and that any layman who contributed should be excommunicated with his children for three generations. On the eighth of February in the same year the bishop of Lismore went *in pontificalibus* to Clonmel and in the middle of the town " excommunicavit et excommunicatos pronunciavit omnes et singulos dictum sub-sidium concedentes, imponentes et procurantes, vel talliagium facientes, necnon scribentes, dictantes, levantes, recipientes vel eisdem considentes [*sic*] auxilium vel favorem prestantes. . . ." [4] We have no clue to the motives behind this vehement opposition, in marked contrast to the grants made freely in 1335. Edward III

---

[1] The prior of Holy Trinity, Dublin, was returning from this Parliament on October 25, 1346, *Account Roll of the Priory of Holy Trinity, 1337-1346*, ed. Mills, 1891, p. 118.

[2] Quoted by Betham, *op. cit.*, p. 292. The counties were Dublin, Meath, Kildare, Carlow, Kilkenny, Wexford, Waterford, Tipperary, Limerick, Cork, and Kerry.

[3] *Cal. Pat. and Cl. Rolls, Ireland*, p. 53, no. 81, December 12, 1346.

[4] Betham, *op. cit.*, pp. 292-3, from the plea roll, 21 Edward III. The bishop of Lismore was cast in damages of £1000. The temporalities of the bishop of Ossory were seized for similar action against the collectors of the subsidy, *ibid.*, p. 294.

hàd then promised that the subsidy would not be drawn into a precedent[1] and perhaps the tax of 1346 was taken as a breach of faith. It is more probable that the novelty of a parliamentary grant instead of a local bargain was resented ; if the proctors were not summoned—and all the evidence suggests this—the clergy were being taxed without their consent.

For over ten years after 1346 no further effort was made to secure a parliamentary grant. Between 1350 and 1355 a subsidy was granted in Munster, probably for local defence, but no details of the levy are recorded.[2] Kildare and Ormonde, the Anglo-Irish justiciars who ruled the country from 1356 to 1361, were more successful in raising money for the Irish wars. Entries on the patent rolls show that Leinster and Munster were taxed in 1358, though not on a uniform plan. The counties of Cork, Limerick and Waterford and the cities of Limerick and Cork granted a tax of two shillings on the carucate.[3] The counties of Dublin, Kildare and Kilkenny granted the wages of a fixed quota of soldiers to serve in the Irish wars.[4] In Kildare these wages were levied at the rate of forty pence on each carucate and on goods to the value of £6 ; a crannock of corn, a crannock of hay and a fat cow were also taken from each carucate.[5] The variations in rate suggest that these taxes were the result of local bargains, and the suggestion is confirmed by the absence of all references to Parliaments or Great Councils between 1351 and 1359.[6] In 1359 an elaborate compromise between local bargains and parliamentary grants was attempted. Following very roughly the provincial divisions of Leinster and Munster, two assemblies were summoned, one to meet at Dublin on the 1st of April and the other at Waterford a week later (8 April).[7]

[1] Rymer, IV, 641-2. Cf. Clyn, p. 26 : " sic ne in consequenciam vel consuetudinem duceretur."
[2] Cal. Pat. and Cl. Rolls, Ireland, p. 67, no. 31 ; the grant was made tempore Thome Rokeby, who was justiciar from December 1349 to August 1355.
[3] Cal. Pat. and Cl. Rolls, Ireland, pp. 71-2, nos. 1-4, 10, 15. The county of Waterford had made the grant spontanea sua.
[4] Ibid., pp. 73-5, nos. 35-6, 55, 64-5, 92. Kilkenny county, for example, granted for a fixed period 12 men-at-arms with horses at 12 pence a day, 60 hobelers at 4 pence, and 200 foot soldiers at a penny halfpenny (no. 64).
[5] Ibid., p. 74, nos. 58-9.
[6] Great Council of Kilkenny, October 31, 1351 (Early Statutes, p. 376) ; and Great Council at Dublin, April 1, 1359 (infra, p.   ).
[7] Cal. Pat. and Cl. Rolls, Ireland, p. 77, nos. 21-5. Cf. Edward I's double Parliaments at Northampton and York, 1283.

The writs show that the commons of the counties, liberties and boroughs were summoned as if for a Parliament,[1] though only the more important lay magnates or bishops are named as specially cited.[2] Immediately after the dates of session orders were issued for the collection of subsidies in both provinces.[3] The subsidy imposed was forty pence on the carucate and sixpence on goods to the value of £1 ; it was apparently the same in Munster as in Leinster. Collectors are named for only two cities [4] and it is possible that the others refused to make a grant. Drogheda was ordered to send eight burgesses to appear before the Council at Dublin because their representatives at the last council had not carried out what they had been ordered to undertake.[5] The share of the clergy in this taxation is obscure. On April 10 the archbishop of Cashel was commanded to levy £10 recently granted by the clergy of his diocese ; like orders were issued to the bishops of Lismore, Limerick and Cloyne.[6] These four prelates had been summoned to the Waterford Council and had probably consented in the name of the clergy of their dioceses. We have no evidence either that the money was paid or that the demand was resisted. The consent of the clergy was anticipated in a similar way at the Great Council of 1369.[7] Then the prelates granted two-tenths to be levied on benefices, on condition that the consent of the clergy was first obtained. The tax was to be collected within a year, but by April 1370 nothing had been done and the archbishop of Armagh was ordered to call

---

[1] There were summoned for Leinster representatives of the city of Dublin, of Drogheda, of the counties of Dublin, Louth, Kildare and Carlow, of the liberties of Meath (Trim), Kilkenny and Wexford, and of the cross-lands of Kilkenny and Wexford. For Munster like summonses were issued to the cities of Cork, Limerick and Waterford, the towns of Kilkenny, Ross, Clonmel, and Wexford, the counties of Kildare, Waterford, Limerick and Cork, the liberty of Kilkenny and the liberty and cross-lands of Tipperary. It is remarkable that the county towns of Kilkenny and Wexford were separated from Leinster and that the county of Kildare and the liberty of Kilkenny were represented in both assemblies.

[2] Only nine persons were specially summoned to Dublin and twelve to Waterford. The sheriff of Kildare and the seneschal of Kilkenny were instructed to return particular persons to the Waterford Assembly.

[3] *Cal. Pat. and Cl. Rolls, Ireland*, p. 77, nos. 32-6, 41 ; p. 79, nos. 110, 111-14, Cl. Roll, 33 Edward III. The letters are dated from April 12 to May 16.

[4] Waterford and Kilkenny.

[5] *Ibid.*, p. 77, no. 42, April 20.   [6] *Ibid.*, nos. 29-30.

[7] Dublin, April 22, 1369. *Cal. of Archbishop Sweteman's Register*, p. 236.

a convocation or council of his clergy to secure their consent.[1] Though we do not know what line of action was taken by the lower clergy in 1359 and 1369, it is clear that the subsidy did not provoke resistance comparable to that in 1347. The experiment of seeking consent in provincial councils, whether deliberately undertaken for the purpose or not, brought the taxpayer a stage nearer to the practice of general consent in Parliament.

After 1359 there was another long interval without direct taxation. Even Lionel, duke of Clarence, seems to have made no attempt to secure a parliamentary grant. A sudden change came when William of Windsor was appointed the king's lieutenant in Ireland in 1369. His first term of office lasted until March 1372 ; though he was then recalled in disgrace, he returned after two years as governor and guardian of Ireland, and held office until early in 1376.[2] The detailed evidence of the enquiry into his administration shows him to have been a vigorous and greedy representative of the Crown.[3] In less than five years he held eight Parliaments and two Great Councils.[4] No legislation is associated with these sessions ; all seem to be an essential part of a new fiscal policy, the purpose of which was to constrain the Irish, not only to bear the cost of their own wars, but also to contribute to the expense of the war with France. The methods and arguments employed and the resistance they provoked altered the form and increased knowledge of the functions of Parliament to an extent which almost entitles William of Windsor to be styled the true founder of the Irish Parliament.

Windsor's first Parliament (Dublin, August 1369) granted new custom duties and imposed on five counties a tax of half a mark on the carucate.[5] In the following spring (April 1370) the Parliament of Dublin appears to have doubled the tax on the

---

[1] Dublin, April 22, 1369.   Cal. of Archbishop Sweteman's Register, p. 236.

[2] He left Ireland on March 21, 1372, was appointed governor and guardian in October 1373, and returned to Ireland on April 18, 1374.

[3] Public Record Office : Council and Parliamentary Proceedings, Edward III, 47-50, Rolls 2 and 3.   Printed as Windsor Documents, Proceedings of the Royal Irish Academy, Vol. XLI, pp. 83 seq.

[4] Parliaments : Dublin, August 6, 1369 ; Dublin, April 22-25, 1370 ; Kilkenny, January 7, 1371 ; Ballyduagh, June 4, 1371 ; Kilkenny, January 14, 1372. Great Councils : Dublin, February 25, 1372, and May 27, 1374. Parliaments : Dublin, January 20, 1375 ; Kilkenny, June 18, 1375 ; Kilkenny, October 6, 1375.

[5] Windsor Documents, pp. 84-5.

carucate, but it is not clear over what area it was collected.[1] The Kilkenny Parliament, held in January 1371, granted a subsidy of £3000, which the Parliament of Ballyduagh (June 8, 1371) increased by £2000.[2] Resistance to the collection of these grants was general and persistent. It was maintained that they were the result of illegal coercion, and no doubt it was to meet the complaints of the clergy that proctors of the clergy began to be summoned to Parliament in 1371. The Anglo-Irish had their connections in England, and, perhaps through Mortimer influence, the intervention of the home Government was secured. In October 1371 Windsor was ordered to stay the levy of the £5000 granted at Kilkenny and Ballyduagh,[3] and in May 1372 the king ordered the collection of the new custom duties to be suspended.[4] The Parliament held at Kilkenny in January 1372 and the Great Council in Dublin a month later were probably summoned by Windsor in a desperate attempt to secure confirmation of the earlier grants.[5] He was recalled in March, and an enquiry into his administration dragged on until the autumn of 1373. He was then reappointed as governor and guardian of Ireland, and orders were issued for the collection of the disputed subsidy.[6] He held three Parliaments in 1375. At the first (Dublin, January 17) he secured grants from individuals for the maintenance of his retinue ;[7] and at the second (Kilkenny, June 18) the clergy and commons of Munster, Kilkenny and Wexford made a grant of 400 marks.[8] At the autumn Parliament (Kilkenny, October 6) Nicholas Dagworth, specially commissioned by Edward III, explained the king's heavy expenses, and asked for a special subsidy.[9] The request was emphatically refused on the plea of poverty. An attempt to force consent by summoning two proctors from each diocese and two commoners from each county, city and borough to meet the king's Council in England provoked a storm of resistance, and in February

---

[1] *Windsor Documents*, Article 14, p. 86.
[2] *Ibid.*, Article 18, p. 87.
[3] *Cal. Cl. Rolls, 1369-74*, October 20, 1371, pp. 256-7. Cf. pp. 259, 262.
[4] *Ibid.*, May 28, 1372, p. 380.
[5] The magnates and commons were forced to seal a letter to the king declaring that the tallage and subsidy had been granted freely and without coercion (Inquisition Meath, II, cap. 7), in *Windsor Documents*, p. 115.
[6] *Cal. Cl. Rolls, 1369-74*, December 20, 1373, p. 529.
[7] *Cal. Pat. and Cl. Rolls, Ireland*, p. 95, no. 200.
[8] *Ibid.*, p. 98, no. 264.
[9] *Windsor Documents*, p. 123.

1376 Windsor was recalled to meet new charges against his administration.[1]

The articles of impeachment, drafted in Ireland, charge William of Windsor and other high officials with tyrannical misconduct and embezzlement in every department of government, but the main emphasis throughout lies on unlawful taxation without the free consent of subjects. It was maintained that the custom duties were imposed by the Parliament of 1369 *sine assensu et contra voluntatem communium et mercatorum eiusdem terre ;* [2] the tax of half a mark on the carucate was also imposed against the assent and will of the commons of Meath.[3] At the Parliament of Kilkenny in 1370 the knights of the shire for Meath, pledged when they were elected to refuse a subsidy, were coerced into assenting to a tax of a mark on the carucate ; [4] they were terrorised by the imprisonment of the members for Louth who had refused consent.[5] The grants made in the Parliaments of 1371 were also contrary to the pledges of elected representatives. The members for Meath at the Parliament of Kilkenny resisted for two or three days the demand for a subsidy of £3000.[6] At Ballyduagh consent to an additional £2000 was forced by the inconvenience of the place of session ; it was three leagues from the city of Cashel, in a waste land, without houses or provisions.[7] Finally, the summons of clerical and lay representatives to appear before the English Council in February 1376 drew forth a series of returns which were almost certainly part of a concerted plan of action.

We have evidence that the governor and Dagworth made every effort to influence the elections. In Dublin county, perhaps regarded as a test case, the county court was assembled on no less than five separate occasions in the hope of securing

---

[1] The earl of Kildare was appointed justiciar of Ireland on February 16, 1376, as Windsor and other officials were summoned to England, *Cal. Pat. Rolls*, p. 244.

[2] *Windsor Documents*, Inquisition, Meath, III, cap. 2, p. 116.

[3] *Ibid.*, cap. 1, p. 113.

[4] *Ibid.* I, cap. 3 ; II, cap. 3, pp. 114-15.

[5] *Ibid.*, p. 115. Cf. the coercion of the two members for Drogheda in Louth for refusing consent, *ibid.* IV, cap. 2, p. 117.

[6] *Ibid.* I, cap. 4, p. 114.

[7] *Ibid.* II, cap. 6 ; III, cap. 7 ; IV, cap. 5 ; VI, cap. 7, pp. 115, 116, 118, 121-2. The townland of Ballyduagh lies four miles S.E. of Cashel, in the parish of Railstown.

favourable returns.[1] Feeling evidently ran high as the elections were keenly contested, three separate parties putting forward candidates at one time and two at another. The differences were probably local or personal,[2] as all parties were agreed in resistance to taxation. In spite of the addresses of special messengers and threats of heavy amercements, each assembly refused to concede to their chosen representatives the power of consent to taxation. The general result of the elections throughout the country is equally significant. The counties of Dublin, Louth, Kildare, Meath and Kilkenny protested that the summons was contrary to their rights and liberties ; they agreed to elect representatives out of reverence for the king, but they refused to give them the power of consent to taxation. Like refusals were made by the city of Dublin, the town of Drogheda, and the clergy of Armagh, Kildare, Lismore and Waterford. The counties of Waterford and Tipperary made elections, saving their liberties ; a like reservation was made by the city of Kilkenny. Elections without reservations were made by the poor or remote counties of Wexford, Limerick, Cork and Kerry ; [3] by the cities or towns of Limerick, Cork, Ross, Wexford and Youghal ; and by the seven dioceses of Dublin, Ossory, Ferns, Limerick, Emly, Cloyne and Kerry.[4] The returns made it clear that no subsidy would be granted by the prosperous areas of Leinster and, probably for that reason, the whole project was abandoned, at least as far as taxation was concerned. The episode is important as the first struggle between the home government and the Anglo-Irish which can properly be called both political and constitutional. The main issue, it is clear, was the right of consent to taxation.

In maintaining for their defence the doctrine of consent, the

---

[1] The county court met on the following dates :

> November 13, 1375. No agreement.
> November 17, 1375. No agreement.
> November 18-19, 1375. Two persons elected ; protest by petition.
> December 22, 1375. Three separate elections by three distinct parties.
> February 14, 1376. Two separate elections by two parties.

The new elections of December and February were made by special order of the government, *Windsor Documents*, pp. 127-30.

[2] The local objection to the candidates first returned was that they were " cousins germane and of one assent," *ibid.*, p. 127.

[3] The county of Carlow refused to make an election, pleading poverty.

[4] The dioceses of Cashel and Meath elected only one proctor, Leighlin refused to elect on plea of poverty, and Tuam made no return.

Anglo-Irish were tacitly forced to admit the power of their own Parliament to impose taxation. By the addition of clerical proctors William of Windsor had made it fully representative, and from this time onward the parliamentary right of taxation does not seem to be disputed. None the less, the idea of local consent died hard. The peculiar conditions of the country, with its incessant and half isolated border wars, kept alive for a time the custom of local taxation for frontier defence, authorised by local representative assemblies. In August 1381, at a Great Council at Clonmel, the magnates and commons of seven southern counties agreed to provide the earl of March with 15 men-at-arms and 150 archers for six months, and the clergy of the ten dioceses of the same area granted £78 6s. In 1388 the clergy and commons of county Dublin made a grant for the maintenance of 80 men-at-arms,[1] and we have evidence of a long series of similar local grants in the reign of Henry IV.[2] There is no record of the practice under Henry V, but it seems to have revived again in 1423, when the commons and clergy of Meath and Louth, in county or diocesan assemblies at Trim and Ardee, granted money for defence against Irish enemies.[3] From that time onwards no clear reference to the practice has been traced. In the second half of the century parliamentary consent to taxation was recognised as obligatory, and neglect to secure it was apparently deemed to be treason.[4] The evidence, therefore, suggests that the custom of local taxation through local assemblies gave way to taxation by Parliament in the first quarter of the fifteenth century, though we may suppose that local levies caused the revival of local bargains from time to time.

At the same time local control over the collection of taxes continued to be closely associated with parliamentary consent. The few references to taxation on the statute rolls imply that when taxes were granted in Parliament a fixed quota was assigned to each civil or ecclesiastical area, and that local collectors were then

---

[1] *Cal. Pat. and Cl. Rolls, Ireland*, p. 141, no. 190.

[2] *Ibid.*, p. 158, nos. 114-15, 119; p. 161, nos. 61-2; p. 166, nos. 242-3, 253, 14; p. 178, no. 77*c*; p. 201, no. 113.   Cf. *infra*, p. 108, n. 3.

[3] *Ibid.*, p. 230, nos. 112-15, 121-2.   The commons of Meath granted 360 marks, the commons of Louth £40, the clergy of Meath 120 marks, and the clergy of Armagh 9 marks.

[4] This was secured by that statute of assent and disassent, the date and meaning of which are discussed *infra*, pp. 106-7.

made responsible for the levy.[1] In 1467-68 it was ordained that for one year only the Lord Lieutenant and Council should reach an agreement about the subsidy by treating with six gentlemen from each county ; two of the six were required to be *spirituelx hommes*, who should also be responsible for the collection of the tax, *sicome il est use en le subsidie le roy*.[2] In 1471-72 the assessment for the county of Meath was committed for two years to six persons, two of the spirituality—the bishop of Meath and the abbot of Navan—and four of the temporality.[3] These arrangements correspond with the instruction to the knights and proctors of the county of Dublin to appoint collectors for the subsidy in 1455.[4] The evidence not only suggests that subsidies were normally granted by clergy and laity together, but that each estate exercised a measure of control over the levy through the appointment of collectors. The special privilege of the clergy lay, not in the place where their consent was given, but in a more direct control over the collectors. The difference between lay and ecclesiastical arrangements is clearly indicated in a statute of 1485, which granted a tax of a mark on the carucate.[5] The knights of the counties and the proctors were ordered to name to the Clerk of the Rolls or to the Clerk of Parliament sufficient collectors for the levy. Forfeiture of one-twentieth was imposed as a penalty on all failing to make such nomination by the Sunday following, with the explicit reservation that the clergy of Armagh, Dublin, Meath and Kildare should have two weeks after that date to elect their collectors.[6]

---

[1] Cf. the English allotment of Danegeld by counties. In 1485, for example, Parliament granted £100 from the four counties of the Pale to be levied at the rate of 70 marks from Meath, 40 from Dublin, and 20 each from Kildare and Louth (2 Ric. III, c. 14, transcripts of unpublished statutes, Public Record Office, Dublin).

[2] *Statute Rolls*, 7 and 8 Edward IV, p. 469. The enactment begins with the phrase : " Que come il est ordeine par estatute que assent et disassent est treisoun, ceo nient obstaunt. . . ." The statute referred to is discussed in the following chapter.

[3] *Ibid.*, 11 and 12 Edward IV, pp. 766-8.   [4] *Ibid.*, 34 Henry VI, p. 402.

[5] 2 Ric. III, § 17, transcripts, *loc. cit.* The grant was made : " que par la dit auctorite si bien chivalers pur countees et proctours pur clergees, deanes et chapitrees et chescun de eaux, eint plein power, cest assavoir, lez chivalers pur countees pur lez charues de terre come lez proctours pour lour spiritualx possessiouns."

[6] " . . . purvieu toutz foitz que lez clergees de Ardmagh, Divelin, Mith et Kildare eient ii semayns apres le dit dimenche del space de eslier lour collectours." The four dioceses represent the four counties of the Pale, the county of Louth being equivalent to Armagh *inter Anglicos*.

The evidence from the statute rolls is confirmed and carried further by three of the Registers of Armagh, which contain the records of the diocesan assemblies in which the clerical tax collectors and assessors were appointed. The Register of archbishop Swayne has a series of royal writs and returns, covering the period 1438-51, which show plainly the working of the machinery by which the clergy were taxed.[1] After Parliament had granted a subsidy, a writ was issued to the archbishop, informing him of the amount due from his diocese and enjoining him to convoke his clergy. The archbishop then cited the clergy *inter Anglicos* to appear before him or his commissary at a fixed time and place, in order that they might assess themselves and appoint collectors for the several rural deaneries. This assembly was known as a Convocation.[2] It is an institution of which we know nothing in detail before 1438 and nothing at all before 1370. We may suppose that it had its origin in diocesan assemblies summoned by prelates to discuss the demands for local or general subsidies made by the lieutenants of Edward III. The earliest reference to it is an order from William of Windsor to archbishop Sweteman to call a convocation or council of his clergy to give their consent to certain taxes granted by the prelates at a Great Council in Dublin.[3] The collectors of the tax were perhaps appointed from the first by this assembly, as a schedule of their names is appended to the entry of the writ. When in 1371 proctors of the clergy began to be summoned to Parliament the duty of electing them fell naturally to the same body ; the scanty evidence for proctors' wages suggests that Convocation both authorised the payment and appointed collectors for the levy.[4]   Between 1370 and 1438, when the records

---

[1] The earliest of these entries describes a Convocation held at Drogheda on February 10, 1438, at which the clergy of Armagh *inter Anglicos* elected assessors for a subsidy granted by them, through their proctor, Henry Nangle, in the Parliament held at Dublin on November 13, 1437 (Swayne's Register, IV, f. 10).

[2] The first Convocation in the English sense of the term was summoned for May 18, 1613.

[3] *Cal. Sweteman's Register*, p. 236. The writ was issued on April 6, 1370. Cf. *supra*, p. 41.

[4] Cf. *supra*, p. 43 and note. In 1438, for example, the archbishop ordered that the wages of two proctors should be collected by assessors elected " per dictum clerum et ad hoc specialiter deputatos " at the rate of four pence in the mark and four pence on the carucate, Prene's Register, f. 165. The Convocation held on May 14, 1499, agreed that the Prior of Ardee should have his expenses for attending Parliament as proctor, Register of Octavian de Palatio, f. 329, cf. *nfra*, p. 61.

begin, these irregularly summoned meetings of the diocesan clergy gradually hardened into a permanent institution, shaped and maintained to take the strain of increasing financial pressure from the government. The rise of Parliament and the disappearance of local bargains forced the original purpose of consent to give way to the new purposes of representation and diocesan control. Our knowledge of this remarkable bridge between the opposed systems of parliamentary and provincial taxation is tantalisingly scanty and almost altogether limited to the single diocese of Armagh. We have, however, enough evidence to show that the sessions of Convocation were not purely formal and that its function of serving as a check on Parliament continued to be understood. In the later Registers of Armagh there are no entries of the writs ordering the archbishop to summon the diocesan clergy. Much more interesting, however, are the summaries of business transacted in Convocation, preserved in the Registers of Octavian de Palatio (1480-1513) and George Cromer (1522-43).[1] They show that the main function of Convocation continued to be the election of collectors of the subsidy, though other diocesan business was discussed and decrees of the archbishop were promulgated. In the Convocation held at Drogheda in May 1496 the clergy were ordered to ring church bells during thunderstorms under penalty of fines.[2] A year later the archbishop asked Convocation to grant him a subsidy ; the clergy withdrew apart to discuss his request and finally agreed to give him five shillings in the mark.[3] There seems no doubt that Convocation was a body primarily concerned with finance and that the task of safeguarding diocesan interests helped to foster traditions of independence and initiative. In 1496, for example, the clergy rejected the rate at which the Government proposed to levy the subsidy granted by Poynings' Parliament (December 3, 1494). Parliament had agreed to a subsidy at double the usual rate, as it had formerly been raised when William, bishop of Meath, was deputy.[4] The clergy and

---

[1] Examples of these minutes are printed at the end of the chapter, Note A.

[2] The minutes of this Convocation are printed infra, p. 60, Note A.

[3] Infra, p. 61. In 1523 archbishop Cromer was granted 18 pence in the mark by Convocation, but he seems to have had difficulty in collecting it (Cromer's Register, ff. 13, 14, 33).

[4] The double subsidy for the bishop of Meath was granted by the Parliament held at Drogheda, December 6, 1476, 16 and 17 Edward IV, cap. 4, Transcripts, loc. cit.

others present in Convocation declared that the king had been *sinistre et non recte informatum* in thinking the former double subsidy paid by the diocese to be £44, when in fact it was only 29 marks 7 shillings, that is, twice the usual amount, 14 marks 10 shillings. The facts put forward by the clergy are confirmed by numerous entries in the Registers and they maintained their point by appointing collectors for the lower rate.[1] The value of Convocation as a taxpayers' association was thus fully demonstrated.

The records in Cromer's Register, which includes the second half of the primacy of Kite, contain evidence, not only of regular sessions of Convocation, but also of a clear distinction between it and the diocesan synod. Between 1518 and 1535 we have minutes for no less than thirteen Convocations and sixteen synods, each meeting annually in normal years.[2] In the synod, which usually sat in June or July, general ecclesiastical business was transacted. Convocation, held in November or December, appointed collectors of the parliamentary subsidy and, incidentally, dealt with other business brought before it. In 1520 the clergy of the deanery of Ardee disagreed over the choice of a collector; four on one side elected the abbot of Knock and four on the other side the vicar of Kildemock; finally, with the consent of both parties, the vicar-general, who was acting for the archbishop, appointed the abbot of Knock.[3] The contested election lays bare the constituencies within Convocation itself, which secured the maximum of local control by subdividing the electors in their several rural deaneries. It also clearly implies that Convocation still valued the privilege of appointing collectors, and the implication is borne out by evidence of resistance to the archbishop's claim to nominate the collector for the deanery of Drogheda.[4] At the last Con-

---

[1] Printed *infra*, pp. 60 *seq.*

[2] A list with dates of these Convocations and synods is printed in Note B at the end of the chapter, together with examples of the minutes of both types of assembly in note A, pp. 64 *seq.*

[3] Cromer's Register, Part II, f. 4 : "... clerus decanatus de Athirde 4 ex una quaque parte elegerunt abbatem de Knoke et vicarium de Kildymoke 4 ex alia parte ; unde ex consensu partium vicarius generalis elegit in collectorem eiusdem decanatus fratrem Johannem Kerule, abbatem de Knoke." Knock was an abbey in N.W. Louth ; Kildemock is a parish in co. Louth.

[4] The claim was made at the Convocation of 1520 and apparently admitted : " Predictus vicarius generalis protestabatur quod dominus Primas consuevit

vocation before the Reformation, held at Termonfeckin (Louth) on December 22, 1535, royal letters were read ordering the clergy to appoint collectors and to elect a proctor to attend Parliament in the following month. Collectors were appointed in the usual way and master William Hamling, vicar of St. Peter's, Drogheda, was chosen as proctor, *nemine tunc de presentibus reclamante preter eundem vicarium et dominum Ricardum Grey, procuratorem proprietariorum predicte ecclesie Sancti Petri*.[1] The double functions of Convocation were thus in full working order down to the end and by this means the doctrine of consent was maintained.

Thus, by the fifteenth century the constitutional position of the Irish clergy was altogether different from that in England. They had no national or provincial convocation and they had, therefore, no system in any way resembling English dyarchy in taxation. Prelates and proctors were full members of Parliament, with equal rights of assenting to or rejecting requests for supply. It is true that the Parliament to which they belonged was held static by the pull between a greedy, half-alien executive and subjects obsessed by personal ambitions and wrongs ; under the continual strain the idea of parliamentary unity could never be realised. Yet the persistence of individualistic interests, constantly and violently upheld, was by no means a dead loss to Anglo-Irish society. It is probable that the bond between the national tax granter and the local tax payer has never been stronger, at least as far as the clergy are concerned. The vestiges of the old system of local bargains survived in the diocesan Convocations, by means of which the clergy retained control over taxes granted in Parliament. These diocesan arrangements made it almost impossible for the consent of the proctors to become a mere form, as they were bound to face their constituents shortly after they had agreed to taxation. The democratic principle of consent by the parties concerned was thus consistently applied and it is clear that the proctors of the clergy of a single diocese had " a greater voice in Parliament, if they all

eligere collectorem in decanatu de Drogheda . . . [after an account of the other elections] Item, in decanatu de Drogheda rector de Bewly in collectorem eligitur, ut vicarius generalis retulit." In 1533 the archbishop himself, and in 1531 and 1535 (Sep.) the vicar-general (Alex. Plunket and Cormac Roth), were elected collectors for Drogheda, Cromer's Register, Part II, ff. 4, 59, 74, 91. On all other occasions the clergy elected in the usual way, e.g. *infra*, pp. 64-8.

[1] Cromer's Register, Part II, f. 93. Printed *infra*, p. 68.

agree, than the bishop himself." In fact, the clergy of the Irish Parliament are the clergy of the *Modus*, alike in status, rights and duties. It remains to enquire whether any direct connection can be traced between the two.

NOTE A

CONVOCATIONS OF THE CLERGY OF ARMAGH, 1496-99

I. CONVOCATION AT DROGHEDA, May 19, 1496

Registrum Octaviani de Palatio, f. 327*a*.

Convocacio cleri diocesis Armachane inter Anglicos celebrata in ecclesia parochiali sancti Petri de Drogheda Armachane diocesis, coram reverendissimo in Christo patre et domino, domino Octaviano Dei et apostolice sedis gracia Archiepiscopo Armachano, tocius Hibernie Primate, xix die mensis Maii, anno Domini millesimo CCCCLXXXXVI. Lecta litera patenti domini Regis de subsidio regio vel dimidia parte eiusdem in festo Pasche iam ultimo preterito debita, dominus Primas statuit quod quandocunque fulgur et tonitruum evenerit rectores vicarii et clerici parochiales intendant et procurent in omni ecclesia campanas pulsari quamdiu obscuritas vel signum huiusmodi fulguris et tonitrui in aere apparuerint, sub pena cuiuslibet rectoris iii s, cuiuslibet vicarii ii s. et cuiuslibet clerici parochialis xii d. Et clerus dominum Thomam Waren rectorem de Clonmore in decanatu de Drogheda ac Patricium Cullyne, firmarium de Stabanane in decanatu de Atrio Dei [1] et Ricardum Whyte firmarium ecclesie de Tempylton [2] in decanatu de Dundalk elegit eiusdem subsidii collectores. Ac iniungitur toti clero quod deinceps literas domini Primatis contra quoscunque effectualiter exequantur et dissolvitur convocacio. Citatur quoque dominus Ricardus Gefrey, rector de Beveley ad Termonfeghyn in crastino certis articulis etc. sibi proponendis responsurus cui comparenti iniungitur expellere a cura et curia sua illam scandalosam (?) personam cumque diffamatus est et post festum Sancti Michaelis Archangeli iam proxime futurum ne sit sibi propinqua spacio trium miliarium, sub pena iuris et dictus dominus Ricardus rector concordavit cum dicto domino Primati pro omnibus pronuncicionibus sibi incumbentibus eidem domino Primati debitis a retro existentibus non solutis, pro quibus idem dominus Ricardus rector sponte et voluntarie promisit solvere xii salmones citra vel modicum post festum Nativitatis Sancti Johannis Baptisti, tunc proxime sequentis.

[1] Ardee.
[2] An alternative name for Kilmore, in the townland of Templeton, now in the parish of Carlingford.

II. CONVOCATION AT ARDEE, January 10, 1497

Registrum Octaviani de Palatio, f. 329a.

Convocacio cleri diocesis Armachane inter Anglicos celebrata in ecclesia parochiali beatissime virginis Marie de Atrio Dei,[1] Armachane diocesis, coram reverendissimo in Christo patre et domino, domino Octaviano Archiepiscopo Armachano tocius Hibernie Primate, x die mensis Januarii anno Domini millesimo CCCCLXXXXVI[to] vocatis omnibus de clero et preconizatis, dictus dominus Primas decrevit absentes contumaces et in penas contumaciarum suarum huiusmodi procedendum fore ad acta huiusmodi convocacionis, perlectis postmodum per eundem dominum Primatem nominibus quorundam ecclesiasticorum virorum diocesis predicte diversas ecclesias insimul retinencium in quadam papiri scedula contentis assignatur terminus eisdem nominatis et perlectis et eorum cuilibet xxii dies eiusdem mensis Januarii apud Termonfeghyn ad ostendendum pro se qua auctoritate dictas ecclesias detinent, curam animarum exercent et sacramenta ecclesiastica ministrant. Quo facto exposito per eundem dominum Primatem clero predicto, de necessitatibus et egestatibus suis atque dampnis rogavit clerum eundem de competenti subsidio subvenire. Qui quidem clerus se a latere declinans et insimul de subsidio huiusmodi communicans demum eis placuit eidem domino Primati subsidium v s. de qualibet marca ecclesiarum dicte diocesis Armachane inter Anglicos iuxta taxam unacum summis super quemlibet presbiterum curatum et non curatum per eandem diocesim inter Anglicos constitutum per certos cessores seu distributores, videlicet, vicarium de Termonfeghyn et dominum Thomam Waren capellanum beate Marie virginis in ecclesia parochiali sancti Petri de Drogheda una cum rectore de Carryk,[2] ita quod ipse nullum verbum cum eis loquatur in decanatu de Drogheda, priorem de Atrio Dei[1] et dominum Thomam Rowe capellanum, cui iniunctum est huiusmodi subsidium super capellanos assidere, sub pena excommunicacionis in decanatu de Atrio Dei.[1] Ac priorem et vicarium de Dundalk in decanatu de Dundalk per dictum dominum et clerum electos, videlicet viii d. super quamlibet marcam stipendiorum et proventuum suorum annuatim assidendos. Ita quod dicti cessores nomina huiusmodi capellanorum una cum summis super eos assidendis dicto domino Primati in scriptis presentant citra diem eiusdem mensis Januarii, et desolvitur huiusmodi convocacio.

---

[1] Ardee.
[2] Carrick or Carrickbaggot.

III. CONVOCATION AT DROGHEDA, May 14, 1499

Registrum Octaviani de Palatio, f. 329*b*.

Convocacio cleri diocesis Armachane inter Anglicos celebrata in ecclesia parochiali sancti Petri de Drogheda Armachane diocesis, coram reverendissimo in Christo patre et domino, domino Octaviano Dei et apostolice sedis gracia Archiepiscopo Armachano tocius Hibernie Primate, xiiii die mensis Maii, anno Domini millesimo CCCCLXXXXIX ad eligendum collectores subsidii regii termini Pasche tunc proxime precedentis. Lecta litera patenti domini regis de dicto subsidio colligendo, predictus clerus, transiens a latere elegit pro toto anno sequente in decanatu de Atrio Dei [1] magistrum Jacobum Mcmahown rectorem de Dervere [2] et dominum Symonem Gefrey vicarium de Termonfeghyn in decanatu de Drogheda ac Robertum Ivers priorem de Kilmaynane [3] rectorem de Kylmor [4] in decanatu de Dundalk et dictus dominus Primas notificavit eidem clero omnia beneficia et ecclesias ad hospitalem et domum de Kylmaynane [3] infra diocesim Armachanam pertinencia seu appropriata eo quod frater Robertus Ivers prior de Kylmaynane [3] ad exhibendum titulos beneficiorum et ecclesiarum huiusmodi canonice citatus non comparuit nec aliquem titulum alicuius ecclesie predicte nobis exhibere curavit vacare et quisque idoneus ea prosequeretur ad ipsum dominum Primatem veniret et collacionem inde obtineret et iniunxit omnibus de clero predicto quod satisfaciant Priori de Atrio Dei [1] expensas suas in Parliamentis regiis existentibus procuratores cleri a retro existentes sub pena in literis dicti domini Primatis inde directis contenta et dissolvit convocacionem huiusmodi primitus inhibicione per dictum dominum Primatem facta quod nullus emat decimas ecclesiarum a quacunque ecclesiastica persona contra formam constitutionum provincialium in ea parte editarum et precipue decimas ad hospitale Sancti Johannis Jer⟨us⟩olimitani in Hibernia in diocesi Armachana existentes sub pena in eadem constitucione contenta.

IV. REDUCTION OF TAXATION BY CONVOCATION, June 11, 1496

Ibid., ff. 330*a*-330*b*.

Certificatorium cleri quod non tenentur ad summam petitam in literis regiis datis desuper.

Excellentissimo in Christo principi et domino suo serenissimo

---

[1] Ardee.   [2] Darver.
[3] Kilmainham, co. Dublin, the chief house of the order of Hospitallers in Ireland.
[4] Kilmore in the townland of Templeton, now in the parish of Carlingford (cf. p. 60, n. 1).

domino Henrico, Dei gracia regi Anglie et Francie et Domino Hibernie inclitissimo humilis vestre regie celsitudinis orator continuus Octavianus eadem gracia archiepiscopus Armachanus, tocius Hibernie primas, salutem et regnorum prosperitatem in eo per quem reges regnant et principes dominantur. Cum regia vestra magestas literas vestras patentes nobis duxerit dirigendas per quas nos rogastis quatinus cum clerus diocesis nostre Armachane, per Johannem Casshell priorem domus Sancti Johannis Baptiste de Athirde [1] procuratorem electum ad comparendum pro eodem clero in vestro regio Parliamento apud Drogheda die veneris proxime post festum sancti Andree apostoli anno regni serenitatis vestre decimo coram potenti viro Edwardo Poyninge milite deputato vestro terre vestre Hibernie tento, auctoritate eiusdem Parliamenti propter certas consideraciones dederunt et concesserint magestati vestre pro termino quinque annorum a festo Pasche tunc sequente de clero predicto et croceo eiusdem tale duplicatum subsidium quale tempore Willelmi nuper episcopi Midensis deputati locumtenentis predicte terre vestre Hibernie fuerat usitatum et levatum prout in actu inde edito plenius continetur dimidietatem predicti duplicati subsidii vobis pro termino Pasche iam ultimo preterito racione eiusdem actus debitam de assensu cleri nostri predicti et aliorum quorum interest super clerum et croceum predictos assideri ac idem subsidium cum assessum fuerit de clero et croceo predictis levari et colligi ac denarios inde provenientes ad receptum scaccarii vestri Hibernie vel certis receptoribus per vos assignatis per indenturas inde debite conficiendas liberari faceremus ceteraque fieri procuraremus prout in predictis literis vestris patentibus plenius continetur. [virtute] quarum literarum patentium cleri predicti et aliorum in ea parte interesse habendum certis die et loco fieri mandavi convocacionem Qui quidem clerus et alii ut prefertur interesse habentes in dicta convocacione comparentes audita per eas lectura et forma vestrarum predictarum literarum patencium dixerunt vestram regiam excellenciam sinistre et non recte fuisse informatum ubi vestra regia celsitudo in eisdem literis patentibus asseruit predictum duplicatum subsidium tempore predicti Willelmi nuper Midensis episcopi deputati locum tenentis Hibernie ad summam quadraginta et quatuor librarum se extendisse cum sicut ipse clerus et interesse habentes ut affirmant satis certi et experti dicunt pro certo supradictum duplicatum subsidium tempore predicti Willelmi nuper Midensis episcopi deputati locum tenentis vestri terre vestre Hibernie usitatum et levatum de clero et croceo predicto summam viginti et novem marcarum ac septem solidorum prout eis auctentice et evidenter constare dicunt non excessisse cuius dimidietatem ultra summam quatuordecim marcarum decem solidorum et duorum denariorum dicunt extendere non debere. Igitur

[1] Ardee.

predictus clerus cum aliis supradictis interesse habentibus in dicta convocacione eorum comparentes predictam dimidietatem supradicti subsidii duplicati vestre predicte magestati pro termino Pasche iam ultimo preterite racione predicti actus debitam secundum formam et exigenciam eiusdem actus Parliamenti ad quatuordecem marcas decem solidos et duos denarios assiderunt ac dominum Thomam Waren rectorem ecclesie de Clon'more in decanatu de Drogheda Patricium Cullyne de Stabanane firmarium ecclesie de Stabanane in decanatu de Athirdie ac Ricardum Whyte firmarium ecclesie de Tempilton in decanatu de Dundalk huiusmodi dimidietatis subsidii duplicati in collectores elegerunt ceteraque paratus sum adimplere prout predicte litere vestre patentes exigunt et requirunt. Et sic vestram predictam regalis excellencie magestatem certifico presencium per tenorem datum in meo manerio de Termonfeghyn sub meo sigillo quo utor ad maiora xi die mensis Junii anno regni eiusdem magestatis vestre undecimo.

f. 330b.

EXAMPLES OF RECORDS OF SYNODS AND CONVOCATIONS, 1518-35

Registrum Georgii Cromer.   Part I.

f. 6,
T.[1] p. 24.
[July 6,
1518].

Sinodus cleri Armachani inter Anglicos celebrata sexto die mensis Julii anno domini millesimo CCCCCXVIII in ecclesia Sancti Petri de Drogheda, Armachane diocesis, coram magistro Alexandro Plunket utriusque iuris bachalario reverendissimi in Christo patris et domini Johannis [Kite] archiepiscopi Armachani totius Hibernie primatis ipso in remotis agente vicario generali, assistente sibi magistro Jacobo White, archidiacono Armachano, Missa de spiritu sancto celebrata processioneque solenni in solita et consueta forma unacum sermoniis peracta cum cantatione hymni *Veni Creator Spiritus*, supradictus vicarius generalis sinodum huiusmodi usque post nonas illius diei ad eundem locum ad pulsationem magne campane continuavit. Qua hora adveniente preconizato clero ac communicatione inter vicarium generalem et clerum huiusmodi communiter pro utilitate ecclesia habita.

f. 6,
T. p. 25.

In predicta sinodo ordinatum fuit quod nullus ad curam animarum infra diocesim predictam inter Anglicos admittatur nisi per approbationem et institutionem ordinarii admittatur.

Item, ordinatum fuit in eadem sinodo quod quilibet curatus diocesis antedicte insinuat et faciat testamenta et verum inventarium omnium bonorum infra parochiam propriam decedentium ordinario

---

[1] T. = Transcript by Henry Upton (eighteenth century), preserved in the Public Library, Armagh.

infra mensem immediate post mortem testatoris sub pena refusionis debiti valoris portionis archiepiscopi de bonis ipsius curati hoc negligentis ordinario applicande.

Item, ordinatum fuit quod quilibet curatus testamenta decedentium veraciter et formaliter concipiat annum diem mensem et locum conditi nomina testium executorum et legatariorum ac debita que debentur testatoris et que debet ac legata in se continentia.

Item, ordinatum fuit quod omnes et singuli curati quaslibet senten- f. 6, tias censure ecclesiastice et alia mandata que ordinatius ad ipsos T. p. 26. direxerit debite exequantur et per literas suas signatas vel sigillatas aut subscriptas quid super eis directis mandatis fecerint sub pena solutionis refusionis contentorum pro quibus litere emanarunt certificabunt. Quibus publicatis in vulgari predictus vicarius generalis dissolvit sinodum quo ad presentes et solventes sinodalia et quo ad absentantes decrevit contumaces et in penam contumacie fore excommunicandos vel ecclesias fore suspendenda.

Registrum Georgii Cromer. Part II.

Convocatio cleri Armachani inter Anglicos celebrata coram f. 3, magistro Alexandro Plunket, vicario generali Johannis [Kite] archi- T. p. 414. episcopi Armachani, totius Hibernie primatis, ipso in remotis agente, in ecclesia parochiali sancti Feghini de Termonfeghin quinto die mensis [Nov. 5, Novembris, anno domini millesimo CCCCCXVIII. 1518].

Vocatis vocandis de clero predicto presentatis et perlectis literis patentibus domini regis pro subsidio regio per dictum clerum concesso ad summam XIXli. XIIIs. IIIId. levando et collectoribus inde constituendis commisso quoque per ipsum vicarium generalem et exposito clero predicto quod collectores desuper nominent et eligant. Declarato in dicta convocatione per ipsum vicarium de remedio providendo contra fratres vagabundos petentes elemosinas et curam animarum ac contra admissionem ordinarii exercentes nulla privelegia auctoritatemve desuper exhibentes.

In eadem convocatione ordinatum fuit quod nullus frater ad Part II, curam animarum absque admissione ordinarii infra diocesim predictam f. 3, admittatur nisi saltem privilegium desuper ostenderit neque aliquis T. p. 415. questor vel mendicans ad querendum aut mendicandum in aliqua ecclesia sine literis commendatoriis loci ordinarii aut exhibitione privilegii ipsorum admittatur.

Item, in decanatu de Drogheda pro anno instanti dominus Johannes Geragh, curatus ecclesie de Kilclogher[1] in collectorem subsidii predicti eligitur.

Item, in decanatu de Athirde[2] frater Laurentius Thonder, prior

---

[1] Kilclogher or Clogher.   [2] Ardee.

domus seu prioratus sancti Johannis Baptiste de Athirde,[1] in collectorem subsidii predicti in eodem decanatu est electus.

Item, in decanatu de Dundalke frater Georgius Werdon, prior domus seu prioratus sancti Leonardi de Dundalke predicta, in collectorem ut supra est electus.

Part II, f. 3, T. p. 416. Insuper dominis Thoma Duffy vicario de Kildimok,[2] servienti ecclesia de Morston [3] et Jacobo Mcdueny, servienti ecclesia de Shearliston,[4] examinatis super conventione illorum super servitio ecclesie de Morston [3] ex sinistra conventione ipsorum vendentes et ementes servitium predicte ecclesie hincinde precio 11 nobilium. Idem vicarius generalis ipsos dominos Thomam et Jacobum suis demeritis ex confessione ipsorum id exigentibus ab ingressu ecclesie suspendebat et similiter ecclesiam de Shearliston propter ruinam suam a divinis suspendebat.

Primo die mensis Decembris articulato vicario predicto quod intromisit se divinis post suspensionem predictam, unde vicarius generalis assignavit eidem XVI diem eiusdem mensis allegaturo causam si quam habet rationabilem quare deberet dictus vicarius decerni tanquam irregularis. Quibus die et loco comparente personaliter dicto domino Thoma, idem diem lune proximo tunc sequentem in eodem loco Part II, f. 3, T. p. 417. infra quem quidem diem lune, videlicet, XVII die predicti mensis, memoratus vicarius generalis in hac parte deliberatus ad requestum ipsius vicarii de Kildimoke suspensionem predictam eidem vicario tunc iurato stare mandatis ecclesie relaxavit ipsumque attollendo in premissis absolvit et secum in quanto potuit dispensavit.

Registrum Georgii Cromer. Part II.

f. 4, T. pp. 418-9.

[March 30, 1520] Convocatio cleri Armachani [5] [inter Anglicos celebrata in ecclesia parochiali] sancti Feghini de Termonfeghin coram magistro Alexandro Plunket vicario generali Johannis [Kite] archiepiscopi Armachani totius Hibernie primatis, ipso in remotis agente, penultimo die mensis Martii anno domini millesimo CCCCCXX.

Vocatis vocandis de clero predicto perlectis literis patentibus domini regis pro subsidio regio [5] [de clero predicto levando et collectoribus desuper eligendis] [5] lato quod contumaciarum absentium decreto et in penam contumaciarum suarum fore procedendum ad actum convocationis et absentes fore [5] [   ] predictus vicarius generalis protestabatur quod dominus primas consuevit eligere collectorem in decanatu de Drogheda. Clerus decanatus de Athirde iiii ex unaquaque parte elegerunt abbatem de Knoke et vicarium de

---

[1] Ardee.　[2] Kildemock.　[3] Mosstown.　[4] Shanless or Shenlish ?
[5] The MS. is damaged ; words in brackets have been supplied.

Kildymoke iiii ex alia parte ; unde ex consensu partium vicarius generalis elegit in collectorem eiusdem decanatus fratrem Johannem Kerule, abbatem de Knoke.

Item, de decanatu de Dundalke electus est Walterus Bedlu de Part II, Roth, miles firmarius ecclesiarum de Ballibalryke,[1] Kylkerly,[2] Kene,[3] f. 4, T. pp. 419- Deken,[4] Philipston [5] et Castelton [6] in collectorem eiusdem decanatus. 20.

Item in decanatu de Drogheda rector de Bewly [7] in collectorem eligitur ut vicarius generalis retulit.

Registrum Georgii Cromer. Part I.

Nomina citatorum ad ultimum convocationem et non comparentium. f. 84, In primis etc. T. p. 284. [1521].

Vicarius de Drummyn.[8]
Vicarius de Drumcarr.[9]
Vicarius de Monfeliston,[10] excusatus.
Vicarius de Clonkene.[11]
Curatus de Taloniston.[12]

Decernuntur contumaces pena reservata recitentur ad sanctum Petrum de Drogheda XIX die Decembri etc. Quibus die et loco decernuntur contumaces pena reservata ad huc.

Convocatio cleri Armachani inter Anglicos celebrata coram magistris Part II, Cormaco Roth ac Petro Snake in decretis bacallariis presidentibus f. 16, huiusmodi convocationi auctoritate Georgii archiepiscopi Armachani T. pp. 460-1. totius Hibernie primatis, in ecclesia sancti Petri de Drogheda XIX die mensis Januarii anno domini millesimo CCCCCXXIV vocatis tunc [Jan. 19, de clero vocandis factaque fide de citatione eiusdem cleri exhibitisque 1524]. et perlectis literis patentibus domini regis de subsidio regio termini Michaelis ultimi preteriti ad summam XIXli. XIIIs. IIIId. dictum clerum concernentem levando et scaccario domini regis solvendo. Predicti presidentes decreverunt omnes absentes contumaces et in penam contumaciarum suarum ad actum convocationis procedendum fore ulteriori pena reservata domino primati, vero procedentibus ad electionem collectorum elegerunt ut sequitur—

In primis, in decanatu de Drogheda dominum Octavianum Rounsell, rectorem de Clonmore in collectorem subsidii huiusmodi.

Item, in decanatu de Atrio Dei [13] elegit clerus dominum Thomam Duffy, vicarium de Kildymoke.

[1] Ballybarrack.
[2] Killincoole ?
[3] Kene, Cain or Iniskin ?
[4] Kane ?
[5] Philipstown.
[6] Castletown.
[7] Beaulieu.
[8] Dromin.
[9] Drumcar.
[10] Manfieldstown or Mandevillestown.
[11] Clonkeen.
[12] Tallanstown.
[13] Ardee.

Item, in decanatu de Dundalke elegit clerus [1] dominum Simonem
Betagh in collectorem eiusdem decanatus.

Cum his iniunctum erat clero predicto quod bis in hebdomada
habeant processiones circa cemiterium, videlicet, qualibet feria quarta
et sexta cum cantatione responsorii recordare, cum his dissolvitur
convocatio.

Registrum Georgii Cromer.   Part II.

f. 93,
T. pp. 789-
90.
[Dec. 22,
1535].

Part II,
f. 93,
T. p. 790.

Anno domini MDXXXV mensis Decembris die XXII in ecclesia
sancte trinitatis de Termonfeghin.

Convocatio cleri Armachani inter Anglicos celebrari assignata
per reverendissimum in Christo patrem et dominum Georgium
[Cromer] permissione divina archiepiscopum Armachanum totius
Hibernie primatem, domino Willelmo Mann, rectore ecclesie de Monfeliston [2] presidente eidem convocationi perlectisque literis domini
regis de subsidio suo summe XIIIs. IIIId. legalis monete Hibernie de
et super qualibet carrucata terre nunc occupata ad quodlibet festum
sancti Michelis archangeli levando : perlectoque eidem clero brevi
regio de procuratoribus prius eligendis ad comparendum pro clero
predicto in Parliamento regio apud Dubliniam XX die Januarii proximo
futuro, cum continuatione et prorogatione dierum et locorum tunc
sequentium factaque monitione eidem clero quod unus de concilio
domini regis monebat supradicto domino primati summum pontificem
nomine Pape cum collegio suo non orari publice pro eo vocatis tunc
primitus de clero vocandis et illis exceptis decano et capitulo com-
parentibus dictoque clero desuper communicante et deliberante elegerunt in procuratorem Parliamenti magistrum Willelmum Hamling,
vicarium ecclesie sancti Petri de Drogheda, nemine tunc de presentibus
reclamante preter eundem vicarium et dominum Ricardum Gray,
procuratorem proprietariorum predicte ecclesie Sancti Petri.

Item, in decanatu de Dundalk dominus Alexander del Palatio
in collectorem subsidii regii ibidem protermino predicto eligitur.

Item, in decanatu de Drogheda dominus Octavianus Rounsell.

Item, in decanatu de Atrio Dei Adam Syr de Stabanan, firmarius
rectorie ibidem.

---

[1] Cf. Ardee, f. 74, T. p. 717. Convocation, December 4, 1533. " . . . in
decanatu de Drogheda si quis eligeret dominus primas antedictus. Item in
decanatu de Atrio Dei prior domus seu prioratus sancti Johannis Baptiste de
Atrio Dei. Item in decanatu de Dundalk vicarius de Korlingford (Carlingford)."

[2] Manfieldstown or Mandevillestown.

NOTE B

CONVOCATIONS AND SYNODS OF THE CLERGY OF ARMAGH DIOCESE, 1518-35

(Compiled from the Register of Archbishop George Cromer)

6 July, 1518	Synod, St. Peter's, Drogheda.	
5 Nov., 1518	Convocation, Termonfeckin.	Collectors elected.
3 July, 1520	Synod, Drogheda.	
19 Dec., 1520	Convocation, Drogheda.	
30 Mar., 1521	Convocation, Termonfeckin.	Collectors elected.
2 July, 1521	Synod, Drogheda.	
21 Nov., 1521	Convocation, Drogheda.	Collectors elected.
1 July, 1522	Synod, Drogheda.	
24 Nov., 1522	Convocation.	Collectors elected.
31 July, 1523	Synod, Drogheda.	
20 Nov., 1523	Convocation, Drogheda.	Collectors elected.
13 June, 1524	Convocation, Termonfeckin.	Subsidy discussed.
5 July, 1524	Synod, Drogheda.	
19 Jan., 1525	Convocation, Drogheda	Collectors elected.
4 July, 1525	Synod, Drogheda.	
[1] (Jan.-March), 1526	Convocation, Drogheda.	Collectors elected.
3 June, 1526	Synod, Drogheda.	
2 June, 1527	Synod, Drogheda.	
6 April, 1528	Convocation, Termonfeckin.	Subsidy granted to the archbishop.
30 June, 1528	Synod, Drogheda.	
[1] (July-Aug.), 1529	Synod, Drogheda.	
[1] (June-July, 1530)	Synod, Drogheda.	
4 July, 1531	Synod, Drogheda.	
1 July, 1533	Synod, Drogheda.	
4 Dec., 1533	Convocation, Drogheda.	Collectors elected.
30 June, 1534	Synod, Drogheda.	
6 July, 1535	Synod, Drogheda.	
17 Sept., 1535	Convocation, Termonfeckin.	Collectors elected.
22 Dec., 1535	Convocation, Termonfeckin.	Collectors elected.

[1] The dates in parentheses are inferred from the position of the documents in the Register. Unless otherwise stated, all the place-names referred to in these documents are parishes in co. Louth, that part of the diocese of Armagh which lay *inter Anglicos*.

CHAPTER V

THE MANUSCRIPTS OF THE IRISH *MODUS TENENDI* *PARLIAMENTUM*

THE manuscripts of the Irish *Modus Tenendi Parliamentum*, unlike those of the English version, are few and hitherto they have not been above suspicion. There are seven extant. Six are transcripts made in the seventeenth century, and upon certain of these the best published text of the document has been based. The seventh manuscript was briefly and inaccurately described in the eleventh report of the Historical Manuscripts Commission.[1] It was then part of the Bridgewater or Ellesmere collection, which was acquired in 1917[2] by the Huntington Library, California ; by means of photographs and through the courtesy of its custodians, it has now been examined. It is thus possible, for the first time, to bring under review the evidence about all the extant manuscripts and to put forward certain conclusions as to their classification, authenticity, and origin.

Two versions of the Irish *Modus Tenendi Parliamentum* have been edited for publication, one (1692) by Anthony Dopping, bishop of Meath, and the other (1910) by Dr. Robert Steele. Dopping's edition[3] is admittedly based on a manuscript which has disappeared without leaving a trace, but it is, in the main, identical with two seventeenth-century transcripts, E. 3. 18, 1-10, in Trinity College, Dublin, and Additional MS. 33505, a roll

[1] *Report XI*, Appendix, Part VII, 129. "*Modus tenendi Parliamenta* in Ireland, exemplification by Sir John Talbot ' de Halomshire,' Lieutenant of Ireland, at Trym, 12 Jan. an. Hen. [VI] 6 [1428] of articles written on a parchment roll taken with Sir Christopher Preston at the time of his arrest at Clane ; together with articles written on a paper schedule and taken at the same time, as to the form of election of the king and doing homage ; fragment of Great Seal."

[2] *Bulletin of the Huntington Library*, no. 1, May 1931, p. 48.

[3] First edition, Dublin, 1692 ; new edition, Dublin, 1772.

acquired by the British Museum in 1889. It will be convenient to call Dopping's text and the manuscripts in agreement with it the Irish transcripts. The other version was edited by Dr. Steele [1] from a transcript made by William Hakewill, a well-known lawyer and antiquary of the first part of the seventeenth century.[2] Hakewill's transcript was the source of Selden's copy, now in the Library of Cambridge University.[3] A third copy, E. 318, ff. 10-15, is in Trinity College, Dublin ; though virtually identical with the Hakewill transcripts, it bears a note stating that it was written for Daniel Molyneux, Ulster King-of-Arms (1597-1632), from an original " remayning in the hands of " Sir Robert Cotton.[4] An incomplete transcript, preserved among the Rawlinson manuscripts in the Bodleian Library, was the work of the Irish historian Ware († 1666) ; it occurs among series of extracts from manuscripts in the Cotton collection.[5] These four manuscripts form a second group which may be styled the English transcripts.

The classification is based upon definite textual variations between the two groups. Though many of Dopping's readings may be accounted for as failures to read or to understand an abbreviated script, there are larger differences which cannot be explained away by any theory of a corrupt text or a careless copyist. The Irish transcripts insert a longer and substantially different section

---

[1] *Bibliotheca Lindesiana*, Vol. V ; a *Bibliography of Royal Proclamations of the Tudor and Stuart Sovereigns and of others published under authority, 1485-1714*, Robert Steele : Vol. I, England and Wales, Oxford, 1910, pp. clxxxviii-cxcii.

[2] The transcript is signed " concordat cum originali : W.H." It is now in the possession of the executors of Mr. Voynitch, New York, and a rotograph of it is in the British Museum, Department of Manuscripts (MS. Facs. Suppl. I (1)). My thanks are due to Dr. Steele for information as to the ownership and also for drawing my attention to Additional MS. 33505.

[3] MS. Mm. VI, 62, ff. 45-9, and British Museum, Department of Manuscripts, MS. Facs. Suppl. I (i) (rotograph). The Cambridge MS. contains Selden's *Baronage of England* and a collection of notes and documents relating to Parliament.

[4] F. 15, " This is a true copy of the exemplificacioun under the greate seale of Ireland, remayning in the hands of Sir Ro. Cotton, Knight, Daniel Molyneux, Ulster King-of-Arms." The Dublin MSS. have been described with extracts by Miss O. Armstrong, *Proceedings of the Royal Irish Academy*, Vol. XXXVI, p. 256. Cf. *Dublin University Magazine*, Vol. XVIII, pp. 305 *seq.*, for an account of the Molyneux family in the seventeenth century.

[5] Rawlinson MS. B. 484, f. 51ᵛ. It contains only the *inspeximus* clause, the proem and the first three chapters.

under the heading *Sessiones in Parliamento ;* they contain only the opening words of the chapter describing the procedure to be followed at an election of a chief governor ; they omit altogether the succeeding chapter on the oath of the governor. The main difference, however, lies in the absence of the exemplification clauses ; these occur only in the English transcripts. They begin with the statement that the document is an *inspeximus* of divers articles contained in a certain parchment roll, found when Sir Christopher Preston was arrested at Clane and exemplified by John Talbot of Hallamshire, King's lieutenant in Ireland, and his council at Trim on January 9, 1419. As a postscript to the *Modus,* thus exemplified, there is appended another *inspeximus,* also omitted in the Irish transcripts ; the coronation oath in its third and final recension as a catechism put to the king by the archbishop. This exemplification is dated at Trim on January 12, 1419, and the names of the clerks who made it are entered at the end. The differences between the two groups are thus considerable and important enough to require serious consideration.

There is, however, no evidence to warrant the subdivision of the English group into Hakewill and Cotton transcripts. The slight variations may readily be accounted for as the slips of copyists ; the exemplification clauses and the coronation postscript occur in the three complete manuscripts. It seems evident that both Hakewill and Cotton had the same original in their hands. Certain facts make it possible to fix the date in a preliminary way.[1] Selden did not use Hakewill's transcript in the first edition of *Titles of Honour* (1611), though he refers to it definitely in the edition of 1631 ;[2] Cotton's library was sequestrated by royal order in 1629 ; Molyneux, who acquired his copy through Cotton, died in 1632. It is, therefore, safe to put the limiting dates for the transcripts as 1611 and 1632.

The original manuscript, which does not appear in any of the Cotton catalogues, seems to have disappeared soon after the transcripts were made. The last to write as if he had seen it was Coke ; in the *Fourth Institute,* written between 1628 and 1633, he described it as " a parchment roll," but made no statement about its custody.[3] Prynne, writing in 1647, specifically denied

---

[1] See *infra,* pp. 81-6 *seq.,* for a full discussion of this date.
[2] *Titles of Honour,* ed. 1631, pp. 743-4.
[3] 4 *Institute,* Cap. I (ed. 1648, p. 12).

that any exemplification was extant,[1] and we may conclude that by that date the original manuscript had disappeared. As we shall see, it was already lost and forgotten among the archives of the Egerton family.

The original from which the Irish transcripts were derived has never been traced, though the evidence for its transmission extends over nearly a century. In his preface Dopping describes how he came to possess the manuscript and gives an account of its provenance.

" It came to my Hands among other Manuscripts and Papers of my ever honoured Uncle Sir William Domvile, late Attorney General in this Kingdom, which he was pleased to bequeath as a Legacy to me, and he told me in his Life-time, upon an occasional Discourse concerning it, that it was bestowed on him by Sir James Cuffe, late Deputy Vice-Treasurer of Ireland, that Sir James found it among the Papers of Sir Francis Aungier, Master of the Rolls in this Kingdom, and Sir Francis his Grandson, the Right Honourable the Earl of Longford has lately told me, that Sir Francis had it out of the Treasury of Waterford." [2]

Dopping has left no description of the manuscript, though he maintained : " That the Character, Ink and Parchment, are all so many Arguments for the Antiquity of it, and may convince any Person that is unprejudiced in the Controversy, that it could not be so late as the Time of King Henry the 6th. . . ." William Molyneux, with the document before him, wrote six years later : " I must confess it has a Venerable Antient Appearance." [3] These words

---

[1] " These exemplifications (for ought I can learn) being neither of them extant, nor yet so much as once mentioned by master Richard Bolton (a great Antiquary) in his Collection of the Statutes of Ireland . . ." (*The Levellers Levelled*, 1647, p. 18).

[2] Dopping, introduction, pp. 3-4. Bolton, a contemporary of Aungier's, states that he had seen certain Irish statutes preserved " in the Treasory of the citie of Waterford " (*Statutes of Ireland*, 1621, p. 67, n.). Cf. *Report on the Public Records*, 1812, p. 302, where it is stated that no statutes had been found in Waterford, but that enquirers had been told " that when the old Exchange at Waterford was pulled down, about Forty years since, the Mayor ordered several Cart Loads of very old Manuscripts to be thrown in a Heap in the Street, and burned as useless Lumber . . ."

[3] *The Case of Ireland's being bound by Acts of Parliament in England, stated*, Dublin, 1698, p. 36 : " Whilst I write this, I have this very Record now before me, from the Hands of the said Bishop of Meath's Son, my Nephew, Samuel Dopping ; and I must confess it has a Venerable, Antient Appearance, but whether it be the True Original Record, I leave on the Arguments produced for its Credit by the said Bishop." William was the grandson of Daniel Molyneux, for whom the Cotton transcript was made.

could not then have applied to the seventeenth-century transcript in Trinity College, which was probably a copy made before publication for Dopping or for one of his friends. Aungier, through whom the manuscript is traced to the treasury of Waterford, was master of the rolls between 1609 and 1621, and thus had access to the records. The pedigree is confirmed, at one point at least, by a note at the end of the transcript in the British Museum : " Originale hujus transcripti penes Willelmum Domvile, militem, Attornatum hujus regni Generalem, remanet, MDCLXXVI."¹

The printed editions of the *Modus* thus depend altogether on seventeenth-century transcripts, falling into two groups and each derived at first- or second-hand from a lost original. It is remarkable that each original should have disappeared almost as soon as it was copied and used by lawyers and publicists. The coincidence is a sharp reminder that in England and in Ireland the *Modus* was held to have a direct bearing on contemporary political controversy ; in England it was the bulwark of the parliamentarians, and in Ireland it served as the main historical argument for the independence and antiquity of the Irish parliament. It is, therefore, impossible to accept the transcripts as genuine without close examination, as there was a direct motive for forgery on both sides of the channel.

In England the political value of the Irish *Modus* was limited to the proem, stating that Henry II had imposed it on his Irish subjects, and to the exemplification clauses ; these passages were cited as proof of the antiquity and official character of the English version. Coke, with characteristic inaccuracy and confidence, accepted the whole document, with all its implications.² Selden rejected the proem altogether and was careful to qualify the statement that the *inspeximus* was under the Great Seal by the phrase " as I have heard," thus showing that he had never seen the original.³ Prynne, who maintained that the English *Modus* was a " modern consarsination " written about the end of Henry VI's reign " by some unskillfull Botcher," ⁴ wholly rejected the Irish

---

¹ Additional MS. 33505, presented by William Boyd in 1889. Possibly this is " the copy of the Irish Modus in the German MSS." to which Duffus Hardy mysteriously refers in his edition of the English text (p. xxiv).
² Coke, 4 *Institute*, Cap. I (ed. 1648, p. 12).
³ *Titles of Honour*, pp. 743-4.
⁴ *Brief Register of Parliamentary Writs*, 1664, Part IV, 554.

version as " a meer Forgery "[1] and " a spurious late Imposture."[2]
He heaped abuse on Coke for his " supertranscendent credulity to
believe and affirm,"[3] and concluded that the Irish *Modus* was " so
palpable an Imposture, as Mr. Selden [*Titles of Honour*], Archbishop Usher [in his Letter to Mr. William Hackwel] and others
have discovered it to be."[4] Prynne's anxiety to discredit the
Modus as " a most Notorious new-fangled Anti-parliamentary
Fiction "[5] led him to stretch Selden's cautious words beyond their
meaning, and we may reasonably suspect that he has done as much
for Usher's letter, which is no longer extant. Elsewhere he states
that Usher wrote to Hakewill saying that he must be mistaken in
his exemplification,[6] but no details of the arguments are recorded.
Prynne, in short, puts forward no specific evidence to support his
contention, except the disappearance of the original manuscript ;
his judgement is important mainly as the vigorous expression of
hostile contemporary opinion.

As there were two distinct original versions, it will be convenient to examine separately the claims of each series of transcripts.
With regard to the Irish group, it is obvious that Dopping's
knowledge was limited to his own manuscript. For example,
the last chapter of his text breaks off in the middle of a sentence ;[7]
in the preface he writes " after the Word *censeatur*, there should be
added *constituatur Justitiarius per Consilium* " ;[8] in the English
transcripts the sentence ends altogether differently, with a long
description of the mode of summons proper for a special council to
elect a justiciar at a time of casual vacancy. Dopping had clearly
never seen this section in the English form, nor did he know that
his text lacked both an additional chapter on the custody of the
document and the postscript on the coronation oath. He knew
that other transcripts contained the exemplification clauses, but

---

[1] *Brief Register of Parliamentary Writs*, 1664, Part IV, p. 560, margin.
[2] *Brief Animadversions . . . to the Fourth Part of Coke's Institute*, 1669,
p. 249.
[3] *Brief Register*, Part IV, 603.
[4] *Ibid.*, Part I (1659), p. 405. The words in brackets are taken from
Prynne's marginal notes.
[5] *Ibid.*, Part IV, 604.
[6] *Brief Animadversions*, p. 7. Cf. *infra*, p. 83, for Usher and the Irish
Parliament.
[7] " Et etiam Rex vult ut absente Rege a dicta terra sine procuratore ejusdem
terrae quocunque alio nomine senceatur——," p. 22.
[8] P. 9.

his knowledge was drawn from Coke and Selden and not from any examination of manuscripts.[1] He recognised the value of these clauses as evidence of antiquity and quoted in full the whole passage from *Titles of Honour*.[2] If he had not been acting in good faith, he could easily have incorporated it in his text instead of printing it in the preface. It is, in fact, almost inconceivable that any copyist or forger, working from the English transcripts, should omit the clauses which seemed invaluable as corroborative evidence.

This first impression of the independence of the Irish transcripts is confirmed by a detailed scrutiny of the text. The textual differences between the two groups are both numerous and significant. In the first place, Dopping's text contains so many verbal errors that the meaning is sometimes altogether lost. Either he was using a corrupt text or else he was too ignorant to understand and to transcribe what was before him ; the absence of any attempt at emendation suggests the latter view. Such mistakes as *dentus gradus* for *quintus gradus* in the section *De Gradibus* and the consistent rendering of *nisi* as *ni* are errors of the kind easily made by a scribe unfamiliar both with the subject-matter and with the signs and contractions of medieval handwriting.[3] However careless he was, these errors would hardly have been made by the copyist of a seventeenth-century transcript. Apart entirely from obvious errors and slips of the scribe, the Irish transcripts have a number of variant readings and changes in word order, hardly possible if one text were derived directly from the other.[4]

The only substantial additions to the text in the Irish transcripts are the titles of the chapters and a longer version of the section *Sessiones in Parliamento*. The titles are not mere translations from those of the English *Modus* nor do they read as if they were composed in the seventeenth century. Two titles occur which are not in any other version : *Amerciamenta Absentium* and *Perjurus Rex*. The second of these is inserted before the chapter called *De Departitione Parliamenti* in the English version and it is taken from the last two words of the first sentence. It was no

---

[1] Preface, pp. 4-6.   [2] *Ibid.*, p. 6.
[3] Cf. also *viguit* for *viginti*, § 3 ; *meorum* for *in eorum*, § 7 ; and *Di* for *Si*, § 16.
[4] For example, *alocandum* for *locandum*, § 2 ; *Omnes senatores et quilibet comes* for *omnis et quilibet comes*, § 3 ; *justitiarius nullus sit* for *nullus justiciarius est*, § 6.

doubt added for purposes of emphasis. The title *De fine Parliamenti* is obviously out of place, as it breaks into the middle of the next sentence.[1] This suggests that the chapter headings and some additional comments were originally in the margin and were used as titles by some one who imperfectly understood them. These differences show that Dopping's text was independent of the English transcripts and was probably based upon a contracted medieval manuscript. It is also significant that no insertions can be detected which are relevant to Irish political controversies in the early seventeenth century. According to Dopping's pedigree the manuscript was at that time never in the hands of the opposition. Taken from the treasury at Waterford, it passed from Aungier, master of the rolls (1609-21), to Cuffe, deputy vice-treasurer at a rather later date, and from Cuffe to Domvile, who was attorney-general after the Restoration. It is, therefore, hard to believe that it was concocted by the party opposed to the Government in the parliaments of 1613 and 1634. It seems much more probable that the revival of political opposition under James I, acting on the new learning of officials like Davies and Molyneux and of scholars like Usher and Ware, provoked a search for documents and precedents which might serve as weapons in contemporary controversy.

The probability is strengthened by a comparison between Dopping's text and the transcript [2] taken from Domvile's original, a comparison which suggests that each was copied independently from the same manuscript. In Domvile's transcript the scribe frequently left a space for a word that he could not read ; later, in a different ink and, possibly, a different hand, the omitted words were inserted, but in writing so much smaller that the spaces left were not completely filled in. These additions very often correspond to obvious mistakes in Dopping's text and point to a common difficulty in reading the original. It is also easy to see that Dopping had not Domvile's transcript to help him. In Chapter III,

---

[1] § 18 " . . . nullus solus potest nec debet decedere a Parliamento sine licencia Regis et omnium parium Parliamenti ; et hoc in pleno Parliamento.
De fine Parliamenti.
Ita quod inde fiat mencio in rotulis Parliamenti. . . ."
[2] Additional MS. 33505. It is worth remembering that the date of Dopping's text is 1692, and that of Domvile's transcript 1676. Domvile was Dopping's " ever honoured uncle " (*supra*, p. 73).

for example, he misread *sectatores* as *senatores*, and gave the non-sensical *viguit libras* as the value of a fief where Domvile had *XX libras*. On the other hand, both agree in omitting about eighteen words in Chapter XVI, probably a line of the original, and both break off at the same point in the middle of the first sentence of Chapter XX. We may, therefore, conclude that the transcripts were derived from a common original, which the scribes had difficulty in reading and which was probably at least as old as the sixteenth century.

Before the discovery of the Huntington manuscript, the authenticity of the English transcripts was less easy and more important to establish. The story told in the exemplification clauses is extraordinary enough to strain credulity to its limit. The Irish *Modus*, written on a parchment roll, was found on Sir Christopher Preston when he was arrested at Clane ; it was solemnly exemplified by the lord-lieutenant and his council at Trim on January 9, 1419 ; at the same time the coronation oath of the king was also exemplified and on January 12 letters patent were issued to give a public ratification to the whole business. The Irish *Modus* with its codicil was, in effect, the Magna Carta of Ireland, a declaration of the supremacy of parliament and the law. Talbot, the lieutenant, was a strong fighting man and the champion of the English interest. How could it come to pass that he should give official sanction to a document subversive of royal rights and found upon the person of a prisoner ?

To answer this question fully a detailed examination of Anglo-Irish politics at the beginning of the fifteenth century would be necessary. Here it is sufficient to point out that the *Modus* was a convenient weapon for the Irish Butlers to use against the English Talbots in the feud that lasted almost as long as the Lancastrian dynasty. A contemporary chronicler, Henry of Marlborough, states that on June 26, 1418, the earl of Kildare, Sir Christopher Preston, and Sir John Bedlow were arrested at Clane and committed to ward in the castle of Trim.[1] Marlborough was then

---

[1] " Anno 1418 . . . apud Clane in die sanctorum Johannis et Pauli arrestati sunt comes Kildarie, dominus Christopherus Preston et dominus Johannes Bedlow, et positi in castro de Trym, quia voluerunt loqui cum Priore de Kilmaynam [Thomas Butler]," Cotton MS. *Vitellius E.* V, 259ᵛ. This manuscript belongs to the second half of the sixteenth century ; for a later copy see Bodleian, Laud Misc. MS. 614, ff. 81-100ᵛ, the fourth volume of Carew's collection. Mr. R. A. B. Mynors has drawn my attention to a third manuscript,

vicar of Balscadden, co. Dublin, and, as part of Preston's manor of Gormanstown lay in his parish, he was certainly in a position to know the facts.[1] Further, on November 1, 1418, the Regent, Bedford, wrote to Talbot ordering him to send Kildare, Preston, and Bedlow, lately arrested and now in prison at Trim, to appear before the king's council at Westminster on February 3, 1419.[2] There is also corroborative evidence of an entirely different kind. At the end of the document occurs a note : *ex per Johannem Parsant et Wm. Sutton, Clericos.* These names appear frequently on the Irish patent and close rolls between the reigns of Richard II and Henry VI,[3] and it is difficult to imagine a forger equipped with the exact knowledge necessary for their insertion. Talbot's motive in consenting to the exemplification remains obscure, though no doubt the provoking cause was the summons of his prisoners to England. He evidently feared the outcome [4] and hastened to compound with his enemies. Perhaps his consent was given in return for a promise of silence : a tacit indemnity bartered for a Charter of Liberties.

Thus by strong, though circumstantial, evidence, the authenticity of the English transcripts can be established, in spite of the

apparently of the fifteenth century. It is preserved in the library at Troyes (MS. 1316) and, according to the catalogue, the title is identical with that in the Cotton manuscript (*Catalogue général des Manuscrits des Bibliothèques publiques des départements*, Vol. II, 541-2). Holinshed drew upon Marlborough for his *Historie of Ireland*, 1577, and it was partially printed in Camden's *Britannia*, 1607, I, 832-6). English translations were published in *Historie of Ireland* by Hanmer, Campion, and Spenser, ed. James Ware, 1633, pp. 207-23, and Richard Gough's *Britannia*, 1789, III, Part II, 690-3.

[1] The full title of the chronicle runs : " Chronica excerpta de medulla diversorum cronicorum, precipue Ranulphi monachi Cestrensis, scripta per Henricum de Marleburge, vicarium de Ballischadan, una cum quibusdam capitulis de cronicis Hibernie, incepta anno domini 1406 regis Henrici quarti post conquestum septimo," f. 197. Marlborough's continuation covered the years 1406-28. Cf. *Cal. of Pat. and Cl. Rolls, Ireland*, p. 152, nos. 38-9, for a reference to Marlborough in 18 Richard II.

[2] Rot. Cl., 6 Hen. V, m. 16 ; transcribed in Bodleian, Rawlinson MS. B. 491, f. 80.

[3] *Cal. of Pat. and Cl. Rolls, Ireland, passim.* Passavant and Sutton were clerks almost continuously in the employment of the Crown, the one from 1386 to 1435 and the other from 1381/2 to 1441. There are twenty-seven references to Parsant or Passavant and thirty-four to Sutton. The identification of the clerks was made by Dr. Steele in his edition of the Irish *Modus, loc. cit.*, p.cxcii, n.

[4] It was not to Henry V's interests to oppose the Butlers in 1419, as Thomas Butler, prior of Kilmainham, was bringing an Irish contingent to the siege of Rouen, *Archaeologia*, XXI, 54, 57. Cf. *Cal. Pat. Rolls, 1416-22*, p. 202.

disappearance of the original noted as suspicious by Prynne. Should any doubt still linger, it is altogether cleared away by the discovery of the Huntington manuscript, which must be identified as the document exemplified in 1419.[1] The document measures 15½ by 19 inches.   The lower half of the right-hand edge has been gnawed by rats, injuring the text in certain places.   The writing, though very small, is legible, and it appears to be a typical hand of the early fifteenth century, without any peculiarities suggesting Irish provenance.[2]   At the foot of the document, appended in the usual way, is a fragment of the Great Seal.[3]

Collation with Hakewill's manuscript (printed by Dr. Steele) shows at once that we have the document described by Selden and Coke.   The text is substantially the same throughout and the few gaps in the seventeenth-century transcript correspond to the damaged places on the Huntington manuscript. Hakewill's variants are, for the most part, corrections of the faulty grammar of the original, which bears marks of careless haste. Though the list of variant readings is long, most of them have no more than verbal importance.   Twice the contracted form of a word in the original makes it possible to substitute an expansion in the plural number for one in the singular, thus doing away with a difficult reading.   In the chapter *de absentia regis* the reading *comitibus terre* is better than *comite terre*, as in Ireland no one earl had precedence over the rest.   Again, in the chapter describing the election of a justiciar at a time of casual vacancy *cum iustic'* may be expanded *cum iusticiis* instead of *cum iusticiario*, which in the context is nonsense.

---

[1] MS. E. L. 1699.   Dr. Hubert Hall who saw the manuscript in 1931 put me in touch with Mr. R. B. Haselden, curator of manuscripts, who very kindly sent me photographs of the document and seal.   The text is reproduced here by the courtesy of the Director of Research, Huntington Library, Dr. Max Farrand.

[2] For this opinion my thanks are due to the late Mr. T. Gambier-Parry.

[3] The seal, which is of yellow wax, has been badly damaged.   The obverse shows a king, crowned and holding the sceptre and orb ; he is enthroned on a carved seat with canopy.   On the reverse are the royal arms.   No other examples of the medieval Irish Great Seal appear to be recorded ; the oldest in the British Museum is that of Elizabeth (W. de G. Birch, *Catalogue of Seals*, 1887-1900, IV, 696).   Through the kindness of Professor E. Curtis, who is calendaring the Ormonde MSS., and of Mr. Charles McNeill, I have knowledge of a number of medieval exemplars, preserved among the Ormonde deeds and the municipal archives of Dublin.

The legal part of the Bridgewater or Ellesmere collection, to which the manuscript belonged, was assembled by Thomas Egerton, first Lord Ellesmere and chancellor of England (1603-17). His ownership fits in well with the little that we know of the manuscript in the seventeenth century. Selden knew of it at a date later than 1611 and before 1631 ; Molyneux no doubt had his transcript before the sequestration of the Cotton Library in 1629. Both refer to the original as " in the hands of " either Hakewill or Cotton, apparently careful not to style them owners. Hakewill heads his own transcript : " A Copie of an Exemplificacion under the Greate [seal of Ireland] 6 H. 4,[1] of which I have seene the original under seale . . ." [2] The owner is nowhere mentioned and it almost looks as if his name were deliberately withheld, possibly because his right of possession was official rather than personal. Now both Hakewill and Cotton must have known Ellesmere while he was chancellor and, if we suppose that he lent the *Modus* first to one and then to the other, the date of the transcripts must lie between 1611 and his death in 1617. If the *Modus* had come to Ellesmere by reason of his office, it is conceivable that he would not wish his ownership to be known ; a like scruple would hardly be felt after his death either by his son or by his widow. The collection included other documents of Irish provenance, notably an act of the Irish parliament, with the Great Seal attached, suspending Poynings' Law in 1537.[3] It is impossible to prove definitely how they came into Ellesmere's hands, though circumstantial evidence points not only to a date in the summer of 1613, but also to a possible provenance in Ireland.

In 1613 the Irish parliament met for the first time since 1586, and its summons brought a group of the Anglo-Irish again into political opposition.[4] The deputy, Chichester, had secured a protestant majority by creating thirty-nine boroughs and allotting two members to Dublin University. Before parliament was opened ten recusant lords, led by Gormanston, protested against

---

[1] This mistake in the date was repeated by Coke, and has since mislead many scholars.
[2] Dr. Steele's edition, *loc. cit.*, p. clxxxviii.
[3] *Hist. MSS. Comm.*, *loc. cit.*, p. 129.
[4] See Richard Bagwell, *Ireland under the Stuarts*, 1909, Vol. I, Chapter VII, for an account of this parliament.

Chichester's methods and refused to attend the upper house.[1] The recusants in the Commons demanded a purge of the house before the Speaker was elected. When this was denied, they declined to accept Sir John Davies, the Crown nominee, chose one of themselves, Sir John Everard, and refused to name tellers for a division. Everard seated himself in the Speaker's chair, whereupon, in the words of the recusant petition, " Sir Olyver St. John, with others with like violence and force, thrust the said Sir John Davyes into the Speakers chair upon the saide Sir John Everard, and the treasurer, Sir Richard Winckfelde, Sir Olyver St. John and the rest, taking hold of Sir John Everard pulled him downe to the grounde, toare his gowne, hurte his arme and his legge . . . "[2] The recusants, thus routed, seceded from both houses and sent a deputation, headed by Lord Gormanston, to lay their grievances before the king. James, after long enquiry, gave decision against them.[3] Three leading commoners were imprisoned ; resistance collapsed ; in the later sessions of Parliament the deputy had no difficulty in carrying his legislative and fiscal proposals. Yet the organisation of resistance was the first sign of political life in Ireland for nearly half a century, and it inevitably brought with it a revival of interest in the history and the authority of the Irish Parliament.

As chancellor, Ellesmere was involved in the enquiry that followed the protest of the recusant party ; he was also connected with Davies by ties of friendship and family.[4] As soon as news

[1] *Cal. of State Papers, Ireland*, May 17, 1613, p. 342.

[2] Bodleian, Laud Misc. MS. 612, f. 261*b* : " A true declaration of the pro- cedinge in the Lower House in the parlyament holden at the Castle of Dublyn, the xviiith of May, 1613 " (f. 259*b*). Cf. another version of the same episode in " slow motion " : " Mr. Treasurer and Mr. Marshal [Wingfield], gentlemen of the best quality, took Sir John Davies by the arms and lifted him from the ground and placed him in the chair upon Sir John Everard's lap, requiring him still to come forth of the chair ; which he obstinately refusing, Mr. Treasurer, the Master of the Ordnance, and others whose places were next the chair, laid their hands gently upon him and removed him out and placed Sir John Davies quietly therein " (*Cal. of Carew MSS., 1603-1624*, p. 273, from " A true Declaration of the Protestants of what passed the day before the beginning of the Parliament the first day and the Friday following, in the Lower House or Chamber in Dublin ").

[3] April 20, 1614. James was not conciliatory : " What is it to you if I made many or few boroughs ? What if I had made 40 noblemen and 400 boroughs ? The more the merrier, the fewer the better cheer " (*ibid.*, p. 290).

[4] In 1601, through Ellesmere, Davies was reinstated as a member of the Middle Temple, from which he had been expelled ten years earlier. In 1599

of the uproar over the Speaker's election was known in England he wrote to Davies asking for information in order that " the cavils and objections of the adverse party " might be answered.[1] No doubt he was soon supplied with full information and the relevant documents and it is possible that among them was the exemplified *Modus*. Yet Davies, though certainly a student of Irish history, never betrays any knowledge of our document.[2] In fact, in a speech delivered when he was accepted as Speaker, he declared that " this high extraordinary court was not established in Ireland . . . till towards the declining of the reign of Edward 2 " ; the invasion of Edward Bruce, " by the testimony of the best antiquaries, was the first occasion of instituting this High Court of Parliament." [3] If he had read even the proem of the *Modus*, with its reference to Henry II as the founder of Parliament, he would hardly have spoken with so much emphasis. As a like ignorance is shown by the learned Usher,[4] another staunch supporter of the Crown, it seems that the Irish *Modus* was at this time unknown to members and friends of the Government. Unless we suppose that both Davies and Usher

he wrote a sonnet of condolence on the death of Ellesmere's second wife (*Poems*, ed. A. B. Grosart, II, 1876, 112-13) ; he also dedicated to him at some length his Reports on Irish Law Cases, published in 1615 (*Works*, ed. A. B. Grosart, Blackburn, 1869, II, 249-87). The edition of *Orchestra* preserved in the Ellesmere collection is said to contain a poetical dedication to Ellesmere which does not appear to be in print. The family connection may be illustrated by a letter to Davies in Ireland from William Ravenscroft, in which he writes : " I am commanded by Sir John Egerton [Ellesmere's son] . . . to put you in mind of his Irish harp " (*Cal. of State Papers, Ireland, 1606-8*, pp. 127-8). Ellesmere's first wife was Elizabeth Ravenscroft. Later, this John Egerton (first earl of Bridgewater) married Frances Stanley, his step-sister and the aunt of Ferdinando, earl of Huntingdon, who married Lucy, daughter and heiress of Davies. Through Lucy the Davies manuscripts passed to the Huntingdon family and became ultimately part of the Carte collection, now in the Bodleian Library.

[1] *Cal. of State Papers, Ireland, 1611-14*, p. 356, May 31, 1631, from Bodleian, Carte Papers, Vol. 61, f. 565-6. Ellesmere went on : " it will not stand onely in discourse of reason, but must also be supported by warrant of lawe and the customs and usages of Parlement in England."

[2] He published in 1612 *A Discoverie of the True Causes why Ireland was never entirely subdued, nor brought under Obedience of the Crowne of England*. Much of this essay deals with the history of Ireland in the middle ages.

[3] Speech delivered on May 21, 1613, printed by J. Lodge in *Desiderata Curiosa Hibernica*, Dublin, 1772, I, 175-95.

[4] " Of the first establishment of English Laws and Parliaments in the Kingdom of Ireland," written by James Usher and dated October 11, 1611 (J. Gutch, *Collectanea Curiosa*, Oxford, 1781, I, 23 *seqq.*).

deliberately concealed what they knew, we must assume that the document did not reach England through official channels.

The line taken by the recusant opposition can be traced in the series of petitions presented to the deputy or to James I between 1612 and 1614.[1] These petitions deal mainly with the particular abuses of the time : the new enforcement of the oath of supremacy,[2] the creation of boroughs, the partisanship of returning officers, and the suspension of the law of residence which allowed the deputy to pack the Commons with officials. Two points of constitutional law were raised.[3] Before Parliament met the recusant lords complained that they had not been consulted about the heads of bills to be proposed, though they were members of the Irish council within the meaning of Poynings' Act. They also protested against the " omitting of many of the ancient nobility [of Ireland] and the summoning of others [of England and Scotland] to have voice and place in Parliament, who are already parliant [4] [sic] in other kingdoms."

The recusants came to London with their petition in the early summer of 1613.[5] No doubt they brought documents to support their complaints, and it must be admitted that the Act suspending Poynings' Law and the *Modus*, both in the Ellesmere collection, would have been matter in every way cogent to the issue. When their case came up for hearing before the king and council (July 8-17, 1613 [6]) decision was postponed pending an enquiry in Ireland, and it is reasonable to suppose that the relevant legal documents were handed over to the chancellor for investigation.[7]

[1] Twenty-one petitions were presented during this period (*Desiderata Curiosa Hibernica*, Vol. I, and *Cal. of State Papers, Ireland, 1611-14*).

[2] Ellesmere and Bacon gave a judicial opinion (undated) on the enforcement of the oath (*Cal. of State Papers, Ireland, 1606-8*, pp. civ-v, from Carte Papers, Vol. 61, p. 83).

[3] *Ibid. 1611-14*, pp. 342-3. Both points are made in the same petition.

[4] The word *parliant* is not in the *New English Dictionary ;* it probably means no more than " speaking in other parliaments."

[5] *Desiderata Curiosa Hibernica*, I, 206-7. Those who went to England were Lord Gormanston and Lord Dunboyne, Sir Christopher Plunket, Sir James Gough, William Talbot, and Edward Fitz-Harris. Six others were summoned at a later date.

[6] Gardiner, *History of England*, II, 293-4, on the authority of Brit. Mus. Lansdowne MS. 156, ff. 241-2.

[7] An alternative possibility is that certain documents came to Ellesmere through his friend Francis Bacon, who was the king's main adviser in the business.

The leader of the recusants is nowhere specifically named, but the evidence all points to the leading Roman Catholic peer and premier viscount of Ireland, Jenico Preston, Lord Gormanston. He was one of the chief landlords of the Pale and he had already suffered from the new severity shown to loyalists of his faith. In the panic which followed the Gunpowder Plot he was the first petitioner in an address to the deputy, signed by 218 of the nobility and gentry of the Pale, in which they asked for " the private use of our religion and conscience." [1] When he pressed for an answer " importunately and peremptorily," he was imprisoned in Dublin Castle for a short time.[2] Gormanston was then only twenty years of age, yet he already stood out as one of the most forward of the recusant party. His later relations with the Government were not improved by the facts that his sister was the wife of Sir Cahir O'Dogherty, who rose in rebellion in 1608, and that his brother was a captain in O'Neill's Irish regiment, then stationed at Brussels in the service of Spain. His position as leader in 1613 is shown by the fact that his name heads almost all the petitions.[3] In a contemporary " note of the lords and recusants in the Houses of Parliament that were the principal disturbers of the same," Gormanston's name is given first and he is described as " forwardest in delivering petitions." [4] The commission of enquiry sent to Dublin by James I reported that he alone came to Parliament attended by followers : " only Lord Gormanston came to the city with 100 horse (as is confessed), whereof there were not 20 of his own retinue ; the rest were his friends and kinsmen that went out of Dublin to meet him, the rather because his lady came in his company." [5] The public

---

[1] *Cal. of State Papers, Ireland, 1603-6*, pp. 362-5.

[2] *Ibid.*, p. 371, Davies to Salisbury. Cf. *ibid.*, pp. 367 *et seq.*, for Chichester's letter to Salisbury describing the petition and the measures taken against the chief promoters.

[3] This cannot be accounted for solely by his rank, as several times Barry of Buttevant and Roche of Fermoy, who claimed precedence above him, signed below him, e.g. signatures to the petition to Chichester, May 17, 1613 (*Ibid.*, p. 342). It must, however, be admitted that disputes over precedence between the three were frequent (*Complete Peerage*, Vol. I, Appendix A ; *Desiderata Curiosa Hibernica*, I, 204 *seq.*).

[4] *Ibid.* I, 391 *seq.* The full note on Gormanston runs : " Forwardest in delivering petitions, contesting when he should attend the deputy to church, his misbehaviour to the deputy at the time of the powder treason, his contention [over precedence] with the lord Barrye, in presence of the lord deputy."

[5] *Cal. of State Papers, Ireland, 1611-14*, pp. 445-6.

procession, whatever the pretext, is a traditional political gesture in Ireland, and it serves to mark out Gormanston as the leader of the recusant party.

The significance of Gormanston's leadership to the present issue turns on his family and his inheritance. He was the direct descendant of that Christopher Preston who owned the parchment roll of the *Modus* which Talbot and his council exemplified in 1419. Nowhere was this particular copy of the *Modus* so likely to have been preserved as at Gormanstown. No man is more likely to have brought it to England in 1613 than the leader of the recusant lords, himself the inheritor of a family tradition of aristocratic resistance, and the descendant of almost the first champion of the Anglo-Irish Parliament. On this evidence it is thus possible to put forward certain hypotheses : that in the summer of 1613 Gormanston brought forth from the archives of his house the *Modus* which his ancestor had forced an English lieutenant to exemplify two centuries earlier ; that it was impounded by the English council and thus passed into the possession of the English chancellor, Ellesmere ; and that Ellesmere permitted Hakewill and Cotton to have it in their hands as an historical curiosity, before it was lost to sight again in another muniment room for over three hundred years.

Though it is impossible to consider here the general relation of the Irish to the English version of the *Modus*, the result of a close textual comparison of the two cannot be ignored, since it leads directly to the identification of the manuscript which served as the bridge between them. The changes and additions which adapted the English *Modus* to Irish conditions were cleverly drafted in general terms ; they offer little direct help in fixing a date, though they seem to belong to a period not earlier than the end of the fourteenth century.[1] For the purpose of tracing the origin of the text we must depend mainly on minor textual variations which occur throughout the whole document. These variations are distinct, numerous, and of the type which cannot be explained away as the errors of a scribe. For example, the English proctors *peritos et idoneos* elected *ad illud subeundum, allegandum et faciendum* become *sapientes et competentes* elected

---

[1] For example, the chapter on the election of a justiciar corresponds with the procedure followed when the earl of March died in 1382 (*Cal. of Pat. and Close Rolls, Ireland*, p. 111, no. 39).

ad respondendum et supportandum, locandum et faciendum.[1]   Variations of this kind, where the difference lies in verbal expression and not in meaning, occur throughout the whole text.   They at once suggest that the Latin of the Irish *Modus* has been reached through the medium of translation.

This conjecture passes into certainty when the French translation, extant in two fifteenth-century manuscripts [2] (the Courtenay cartulary and the Finch-Hatton roll), is compared with the Latin versions.   In words, word order, and special peculiarities it is the bridge between the English and the Irish *Modus*.[3]   The proctors are *sagez [et] covenables*, elected *a respoundre, supportere, alowere et faire ;* in the same way *autre justice covenable, honest et de beal parlaunce* is the link between *alius idoneus honestus et facundus justiciarius* and *alius sapiens et eloquens ac honestus.*[4] In the chapter *De Loquela Regis post Pronunciationem* the French word order, as well as a change in wording, is repeated in the Irish version ; " Prout maius et principalius hoc ad Dei voluntatem primo, et postea ad eius et eorum honores, et commoda fore intelligerint et sentierint " (English version) becomes " sicut principaliter intendunt hoc esse, primo ad voluntatem Dei et postea ad honorem et proficuum regis et ipsorum presencium " ;   the transition stage in the French is " si come ceo pluis principalment estre endenderount [*sic*] et senterount, primerment a la volunte Dieu, et depuis al a [*sic*] honour et profit du Roy et lour mesmez." [5]   Perhaps the simplest example of a change in the Latin reached through translation occurs in the chapter *De Gradibus Parium :* " rex est caput, principium et finis Parliamenti " becomes, through the French " Le roi est chief de Parlement, commenciounri [*sic*] et fyne de mesme le Parlement,"

---

[1] II.   Compare variations of exactly the same kind in the chapter on the knights of the shire.

[2] The Courtenay cartulary, now in possession of Sir A. P. Vivian, and a parchment roll (F.H. 2995) among the manuscripts of the earl of Winchilsea, the Finch-Hatton collection, now deposited with the Northamptonshire Record Society, County Hall, Northampton.   My thanks are due to Miss Joan Wake for her help in tracing the latter manuscript.   The Courtenay *Modus* was transcribed by D'Ewes in the manuscript now Harley 305, ff. 284 *seqq. ;* I have not seen the original, and my thanks are due to Miss M. Coate, who has examined it, for the information that the *Modus* text is still in the cartulary. The Finch-Hatton MS. was edited by T. D. Hardy, *Archæological Journal*, Vol. XIX, 1862, pp. 266 *seq.*

[3] A detailed textual comparison is printed as a note at the end of this chapter.

[4] XI and 14.   [5] XII and 14.

" quia est caput comensor et finis Parliamenti."[1] Finally, the absurd statement in the Irish *Modus* that the Parliament roll should be ten inches long (*decem polices in longitudine*) is explained by the vagueness of the French phrase *en largesse X poutz*.[2]

A casual omission makes it possible to narrow down still further the origin of the Irish text. In the chapter *De auxiliis Regis* one of the three normal aids, *filios suos milites faciendo*, is left out both in the Irish version and in the French translation in the Finch-Hatton manuscript. It is correctly given in the Courtenay manuscript,[3] a fact that suggests that the omission is a slip peculiar to one manuscript. The probability that the Finch-Hatton manuscript supplies, not only the text, but the actual exemplar from which the Irish *Modus* was derived is increased by an Irish entry on the dorse of the roll. This is a petition from the archbishop of Cashel " a trespuissaunt seignur Thomas de Lancastre, fitz le roy, Seneschal Dengliterre et lieutenaunt Dirlande," asking for leave to parley with Irish enemies and English rebels and to supply them with food, notwithstanding statutes and ordinances to the contrary.[4] Thomas of Lancaster (duke of Clarence from 1412) was lieutenant between 1401 and 1413, but he resided in Ireland only for two short periods, 1401-3 and 1408-9. The form of the entries on the unique Irish Council Roll of 16 Richard II suggests that petitions were not addressed to the lieutenant when he was out of Ireland, but to his deputy, the justiciar.[5] We may, therefore, assign, though not with certainty, the archbishop's petition either to the years 1401-3 or to 1408-9 ; at least, it undoubtedly belongs to the reign of Henry IV. We can, however, do no more than guess why it was endorsed on the *Modus* roll. Hardy puts forward a suggestion made by Graves (the editor of the

[1] XXVI and 8.

[2] The English version reads *in latitudine decem pollices*, XXV and 17.

[3] From the Harley transcript, f. 291ᵛ. It is possible that the Courtenay MS. had also an Irish connection, as Philip de Courtenay was lieutenant in Ireland, 1383 to 1386.

[4] Printed by Hardy, *Archæological Journal, loc. cit.*, p. 274. Similar petitions from the bishop of Waterford and Lismore and the archdeacon of Glendalough are entered on the Irish Council Roll of 16 Richard II (*Rolls Series*), nos. 105 and 107, pp. 114-16, 117-18.

[5] In 1392-94 the earl of Ormonde was justiciar, but there was no lieutenant during his term. It is, however, unlikely that a petition of this type, the answer to which would depend on personal knowledge of the applicant, would be addressed to any one outside the country.

Irish Council Roll), that " the roll was brought over in the time of Thomas of Lancaster's Lieutenancy ; and, when the petition came before the Council, it was temporarily endorsed upon it, until it could be regularly enrolled on the Council Roll." [1] This explanation is not convincing. The council received the petition itself and there was no reason why it should be copied before it was entered, with endorsement, on the Council Roll in the ordinary way. It seems much more probable that the Finch-Hatton document then belonged to the archbishop of Cashel, and that his petition was copied on to it, perhaps in order to preserve a form of request likely to be repeated from time to time.[2]

Now the Irish *Modus* contains two specific references to the archbishop of Cashel which bear out the suggestion that the connection between him and the French roll was not fortuitous, but personal. In the chapter *Sessiones in Parliamento* the precedence of Cashel is carefully secured ; if parliament should meet outside the province of Dublin the archbishops of Armagh and Cashel shall sit on the right of the throne, Dublin and Tuam on the left.[3] The significance of the arrangement lies in the fact that Parliament almost always met in the provinces of Dublin or Cashel, and that the archbishops of Armagh and Tuam were almost invariably absent. In his own province, therefore, Cashel would take precedence of Dublin. More remarkable is the statement in the concluding chapter that the *Modus* shall be preserved for the people of Ireland by the archbishop of Cashel, *tanquam in medio terre*. The reason given for the archbishop's custody seems absurdly thin. No doubt the underlying motive was to keep the *Modus* out of official hands, but the choice of the archbishop as custodian points definitely to a personal connection between Cashel and the document.

The person for whom this function was designed was almost certainly Richard O'Hedigan, archbishop of Cashel between 1406 and 1440. The Butler estates lay partly in his diocese and at

[1] *Archæological Journal, loc. cit.*, p. 274 n.

[2] The only other note on the dorse of the roll is a prophecy of St. Hildegarde, directed against the Mendicants. This is very unlikely to be the work of a council clerk.

[3] A dispute over precedence may have arisen at the parliament of Ballyduagh near Cashel, held in June 1371.

least one member of the family was grateful to him for education.[1] That he stood at the extreme left of the anti-English faction is shown in a series of accusations brought against him in the parliament of 1421 : " that he made very much of the Irish and loved none of the English nation ; that he had bestowed no benefice upon any Englishman and that he counselled other bishops not to give the least benefice to any of them ; that he counterfeited the king's seal and letters patent and that he set himself up to be king of Munster." [2] It was in this parliament that nineteen articles of complaint against the policy of the Crown were drafted for presentation to Henry V by the archbishop of Armagh and Sir Christopher Preston ; [3] the charges brought against O'Hedigan may represent the counter-attack of the English party. How O'Hedigan came to be connected with the French manuscript from which the Irish *Modus* was derived remains uncertain, though his alliance with the Butlers must have had something to do with it. At least it is clear that the English *Modus* had travelled nearly as long a way round before it reached the form in which it was exemplified at Trim in 1419, as the Irish version was to travel without further change in the next five centuries.

[1] The Psalter of Cashel (Bodleian, Laud MS. 610) was written in Irish (1453) for Edmund, son of Richard Butler, who was brother of the fourth earl of Ormonde. It contains a marginal note : " May blessings attend the soul of the Archbishop of Cashel, Richard O'Hedigan, for it was under his tuition that the possessor of this book, Edmond, the son of Richard, son of James Butler, was educated " (f. 116). The translation is taken from C. O'Connor's *Bibliotheca MSS. Stowensis*, Bucks, 1818, I, 201.

[2] Chronicle of Marlborough, *sub anno* 1421, f. 260ᵛ. The full entry runs : " Eodem tempore accusatur Richardus Ohedian, Cassellensis a Johanne Gese, episcopo Lismorensis et Waterfordensis, de 30 articulis. 1. Quod favit Hibernicis et nullum Anglicum dilexit. 2. Quod nulli Anglie dedit beneficium, et sic iubebat aliis episcopis quod non darent Anglicis minimum beneficium. 3. Quod fecit sigillum regis Anglie et literas patentes regias. 4. Quod ordinavit se regem Momonie. 5. Accepit annulum de imagine beati Patricii, quem obtulit comes Desmonie, et dedit meretrici sue. Et multa alia enormia dedit in scriptis, et vexati sunt domini et communes per eos."

[3] *Early Statutes*, pp. 562 seq.

NOTE A

COLLATION OF TEXTS

Latin Text, English Version.	French Text, English Version.	Irish Text.
II.	**ii.**	**2.**
per ipsos decanatus	par eaux mesmes deanes	et [de] se ipsis decanis
eligi facerent duos peritos et idoneos	ferroient eslier deux sagez convenables	faciant eligere duos sapientes et compe- tentes
ad respondendum,sub- eundum, allegandum et faciendum idem quod facerent omnes et singule . . . archi- adiaconatuum	a respoundre suppor- tere alowere et faire mesme ceo qe toutz et checunz . . . et arche- deaknyez ferroient	ad respondendum et supportandum locan- dum et faciendum quod quilibet et omnes . . . et archidiacon- atibus facerent
una liberabitur	lune serra delivre	unum deliberetur
III.	**iii.**	**3.**
ad valentiam comitatus integri	a value dune Countee entiere	ad valenciam unius comitatus integre
viginti feoda unius militis	vint feez de chivaliere	viginti feoda militum
libratas	livers	libras
IV.	**iv.**	**4.**
ad respondendum, subeundum, allegan- dum et faciendum	a respoundre supporter alowere et faire	ad respondendum sup- portandum allocandum et faciendum
tunc solebant habere breve de magno sigillo custodi Quinque Por- tuum quod ipse ration-	avoir brief de la graunt seale direct a Gardeyne de lez Cynk portz qils ferroit tielx	habeant breve direc- tum senescallo . . . quod faciat dictos milites suos habere de

Latin Text, English Version.	French Text, English Version.	Irish Text.
abiles sumptus et expensas suas huiusmodi baronibus habere faceret de communitate . . .	Barouns aver reisonablez costagez et lour despensez de communalte . . .	communitate sua racionabiles custus et expensas suas . . .
redierint	reviendrount	revenire
V. eligi facerent	v. ferroient eslier	4. faciant eligere
per ipsum comitatum	omitted	omitted
idoneos, honestos et peritos	convenablez honestez et sagez	competentes honestos et sapientes
VI. de Civibus	omitted	omitted
VI and VII. mandari	vi. envoies	5. mittendum
X. magnus clericus discretus et facundus	xiv un graunt clerc sage et de bele parlance	14. aliquo solempni clerico
XI. alius idoneus, honestus et facundus justiciarius vel clericus	xv. ou autre Justice convenable honest et de beal parlaunce	14. vel alius sapiens et eloquens ac honestus
pronunciare causas Parliamenti	monstrer lez causez de parlement	monstrabit causas Parliamenti
specie	especial	specialiter

Latin Text, *English Version.*	*French Text,* *English Version.*	*Irish Text.*
XII.	xvi.	14.
rogare debet	doit prier	debet predicare
prout maius et principalius hoc ad Dei voluntatem primo, et postea ad eius et eorum honores et commoda fore intelligerint et sentierint	come ceo pluis principalment estre enderount [*sic*] et senterount primerment a la volounte Dieu, et depuis al a [*sic*] honour et profit du Roy et lour mesmez	sicut principaliter intendunt hoc esse, primo ad voluntatem Dei, et postea ad honorem et proficuum regis et ipsorum presencium
XIV.	xviii.	10.
camerarii	chaumberlayns	camerarii (*Dopping*)
qui sunt	si . . . soieint	si sint (*Dopping*)
XV.	vii.	6.
irrotulabunt omnia placita	enrollerount communes plees	irrotulandum communia placita
nisi quatenus assignata vel data fuerit eis nova potestas in Parliamento per regem et pares Parliamenti	(si) noun novelle poiara eaux soit assigne et done en parlement par le Roy et lez piers du parlement	nisi nova potestas ei assignetur per regem et pares Parliamenti in Parliamento
immediate subiecti regi	saunz meisnez subigiz al Roy	subiectus erit sine medio regi
XVII.	ix.	16.
casus difficilis	dure case	si dubius casus vel durus . . .
emergat	aveigne	advenerit
adeat per se	aleit par soi	eat quilibet gradus
qualiter melius	en quele meillour	in quo meliori modo
representant	sount presentz	presentes sunt

Latin Text, English Version.	French Text, English Version.	Irish Text.
inter regem et aliquos magnates, vel forte inter ipsos magnates	parentre le Roy et lez autres graundees ou parentre les graundeez	inter regem et alios magnates vel inter magnates
negotium illud	tiele bosoigne	talis causa
tribulentur	troublez	turbe⟨n⟩tur
casus difficilis . . . emergat	dure cas aveigne	durus casus . . . advenerit
et huiusmodi	ou a⟨u⟩tre cas semblable	vel aliquis alius similis casus
valeant	purrount	possint
XVIII. ut de	x. sicome	13. sicut
XIX. non in privato nec in occulto loco	xi. en lieu appert	12. in aperto loco
XXIII. instanti	xxii. esteaunt	15. existente
vel filios suos milites faciendo	omitted	omitted
huiusmodi	tielx	talibus
hoc patet	ceo appiert	quod apparet
absque	saunz	sine
licet communitates, cleri et laici, summonite essent ad Parliamentum	si lez communaltez de clergie et layez estoient somouns a le parlement	si (communes) clericorum et laicorum sint sumoniti . . . ad Parliamentum
in quibusdam articulis quod ipse eos disrexerat, tunc Parliamentum nullum esset omnino	en queux articles eux ne governeroit . . . a donques le parlement serroit pur nul	causas in quibus rex eos non recte gubernaverit tunc Parliamentum tenebitur pro nullo

Latin Text, English Version.	French Text, English Version.	Irish Text.
oportet quod omnia que affirmari vel infirmari concedi vel negari vel fieri debent per Parliamentum per communitatem Parliamenti concedi debent	il est busoigne et toutz chosez queux devount estre grauntez faitz affirmez ou donez par le parlement qils soient graunteez par communalte de le parlement	necessarium est quod in omnibus concedendis faciendis affirmandis et donandis per Parliamentum quod sunt concessi per communes Parliamenti
XXIV.	xxiii.	18.
contrarium permittat	fait le contrarie	contrarium fecerit
recedere	departier	decedere
non valeat	ne purre	non possit
Departitio Parliamenti ita usitari debet	A le departier de le parlement	Ad departicionem Parliamenti
et publice proclamari	et crie en apert	et proclamari debet in aperto
quod cuilibet medetur	qa a [sic] chescun est fait medicine	cuilibet peticioni medicina racionabilis facta est
XXV.	xxiv.	17.
in latitudine decem pollices	en largesse x poutz	decem polices in longitudine
XXVI.	xxv.	8.
Rex est caput, principium et finis Parliamenti . . . rege solo est primus gradus	Le Roi est chief de parlement commenciounri [sic] et fyne de mesme le parlement . . . le Roy soul est le primer degre	de rege solo est primus gradus Parliamenti quia est caput comensor et finis Parliamenti
censetur esse plenum	est juggez estre playn	iudicatum est esse plenum.[1]

[1] My thanks are due to Miss K. M. E. Murray for tabulating these parallels.

CHAPTER VI

THE IRISH *MODUS* : ITS HISTORY

I

IN examining the history of the Irish *Modus* we began by looking on truth " askance and strangely." The appearance of the manuscripts in the seventeenth century, based on two independent originals, each lost within a few years of transcription, was ambiguous enough to awaken suspicion. For forgery, however, we could find only the motive without the means. The transcripts could not be explained without assuming medieval documents as their origin and in the search for these documents the main derivation of the text was laid bare. It was discovered that all matter common to the English and Irish versions was, in the Irish form, drawn from a French translation of the English *Modus*. The priority of the English *Modus* was thus definitely established. Further, the particular French manuscript, which was used as the source of the Irish Latin text, was identified as a parchment roll associated with an archbishop of Cashel in the reign of Henry IV. Following hard on this date came the strange story told in the exemplification clauses ; this was confirmed by independent contemporary evidence—the names of the attesting clerks, a letter close and an entry in the Annals of Marlborough. We must, therefore, not only recognise the Irish *Modus* as a genuine medieval document, but also accept it as an Anglo-Irish charter of liberties imposed on the English lieutenant in January 1419.

So much, at least, we may take as established. We are thus free to go on to the consideration of three dependent problems ; what happened to the *Modus* in Ireland after 1419, how and why did it originally come from England, and what is the significance of its Irish history for the value and origin of the parent version ? Once answers have been found to these questions it will be possible to turn again to the main problem of the date and meaning of the English *Modus*.

II

The years immediately following the exemplification of the *Modus* are among the most obscure in Irish medieval history. The Annals of Marlborough, except for one brief entry, come to an end in 1421 and the statute rolls do not begin until 1426-27. The evidence extant mainly consists of articles of complaint sent to England, the registers of Armagh and the meagre calendar of patent and close rolls. In none of these has any reference to the *Modus* been traced. If the story of the feud between the Butlers and the Talbots were known in detail, it would, perhaps, show that the powers and procedure of Parliament continued to be a matter of contention, though, on the whole, the evidence suggests that the issues of conflict were personal rather than constitutional. It may be that the death of Sir Christopher Preston in 1422 removed the only man who understood the policy underlying the exemplification at Trim. Whatever the cause, the reign of Henry VI seems to be a time of uneasy and aimless movement, filled with the confused noise of faction and frontier warfare. The limits of English rule shrank gradually to little more than the confines of the four counties of the Pale ; within that narrow orbit the weakness and disorder of the colony was so great that in 1453 the archbishop of Dublin himself was kidnapped by pirates in Dublin Bay and carried off for ransom to Ardglass in county Down. Hostility to the English Talbots turned by a natural transition into hostility to the Lancastrian dynasty, and the Anglo-Irish, partly through a traditional loyalty to the house of Mortimer, warmly supported the Yorkist cause.

A significant change came over the Irish system of government in the middle of the fifteenth century, about the time when Richard of York became king's lieutenant. Hitherto Parliament had met infrequently and its proceedings were limited almost altogether to public business. As writs of summons are often missing, we can judge the number and importance of Parliaments only by the survival of legislative enactments. In Henry IV's reign we have records of the acts of two Parliaments, of one under Henry V and of four in the first twenty-four years of Henry VI.[1] Between 1447 and the deposition of Henry VI, ten Parliaments were held for which statute rolls are extant ; that of 1460, the last of the reign, passed sixty-three statutes in four separate sessions.[2] Under Edward IV and Richard III the change was stereotyped in constitutional practice. Rolls were preserved for twenty Parliaments and, as they were sometimes prorogued as often as five or six times, the number of sessions must be counted as nearly double.[3] The statutes passed were also numerous ; 109 in 1463-64, 91 in 1471-72, 92 in 1475-76 and 60 in 1479-80. Many of these acts were either of merely local interest or else settlements of private disputes ; they resemble closely the kind of business that appears on the Council Roll of 1391-93. In fact, Parliament seems to have taken over much of the judicial and administrative business that once had belonged to the council, that is, the reverse of Fortescue's plan for the governance of England was put into practice in Ireland.

The change is unmistakable, but it is, at least at present, impossible to say whether it was begun by Richard of York. It coincides fairly closely in point of time with his coming to Ireland in 1449 and it was certainly followed out by both his sons. There is, however, little in Yorkist policy as a whole to suggest that any system of parliamentary government would take its origin from the dynasty. It seems more probable that the weakness of the English in Ireland revived again the idea of parliamentary supremacy expressed in the *Modus* and that Richard of York and his successors found it convenient to give a free hand to its supporters. The last statutes passed by the Irish Parliament before the deposition of Henry VI indicate definitely the bargain wrung from Richard of York when he took refuge in Ireland after his flight from Ludlow. Though the Anglo-Irish had

[1] There are references in the official records and in Marlborough to other Parliaments for which no statutes are extant. The earliest statute roll belongs to 5 Hen. VI.

[2] List of Irish statute rolls, *Supplement to Report VIII on the Public Records of Ireland*, 1819, p. 354.

[3] E.g. 7-8 Ed. IV, 6 sessions ; 11-12 Ed. IV, 5 sessions ; 15-16 Ed. IV, 3 sessions ; 16-17 Ed. IV, 3 sessions ; 19-20 Ed. IV, 4 sessions ; 2 Ric. III, 3 sessions ; *ibid.*, pp. 355-6.

received him as if " another Messiah had descended to them," [1] they were quick to make their own terms. The letters patent by which the king had appointed York lieutenant for ten years were confirmed by Parliament and it was enacted that any " imagining, compassing, excitement or provocation, confederacy, assent or rebellion " against him be deemed treason.[2] On the other hand, the liberties of Ireland were confirmed and it was expressedly declared that the land of Ireland is and at all times has been corporate of itself and free of the burden of any special law of England.[3] The immediate purpose of the declaration was to render illegal appeals under the seal of England or prosecutions before the English Constable and Marshal : " it has not been seen or heard that any person . . . resident in any other Christian land so corporate of itself ought to obey any mandate, within the said land given or made, under any other seal than the proper seal of the same, by which any person should be had or compelled to go . . . out of the said land." [4] Thus the Anglo-Irish seized the opportunity of a common fear of Lancastrian reprisals to assert that their country was *corporate de luy mesme* and bound only by the laws of the Irish Parliament.

Too little is known of these forty odd years of parliamentary rule for any final conclusion to be reached,[5] but the evidence clearly indicates that the Irish Parliament of that time was the Parliament of the *Modus*. It was a Parliament supreme over the council in its judicial functions and in its right to make, not ordinances, but statutes ; a Parliament in which peers gave

---

[1] Whethamstede, *Reg. S. Albani* (*Rolls Series*), I, p. 367.

[2] Statute Rolls, 38 Henry VI, cap. V, p. 643. This Parliament, which was presided over by Richard of York in person, was held at Drogheda on February 8, 1460, and was later prorogued to Dublin. York did not return to England until September.

[3] *Ibid.*, pp. 638, 644-6, cap. I-III, VI. The preamble to cap. VI runs : " Item, al requisicioune dez communes, Que come la terre dirland est et a toutz foitz ad este corporate de luy mesme de lez auncientz leies et custumes usez en le mesme franchisie de le charge dascune especiale ley del Reaume dengleterre, saue taunt soulment tielx leies sicome par les seigneures espirituelx et temporelx et lez communes du dit terre avoient eu en graund Counseile ou parliament illeosques tenuz admisez, acceptez, affermez et proclamez, acordaunt as plousors a[unci]entz estatutes dent faitz. . . ."

[4] *Ibid.*, p. 645.

[5] The statute rolls for the period 1472-85, and the Registers of Armagh have not yet been printed ; these are the main sources of evidence for the period.

judgement upon petitions brought before them and whose members were amerced for absence from sessions. In it all powers of taxation were vested and further administrative control was maintained by the naming of lay collectors in Parliament. It was, in short, a Parliament of six orders, grouped in a strange hieratic equality as King, Lords Spiritual, Lords Temporal, Proctors, Knights, Burgesses ; the Lieutenant, who represented the king as the first order, was bound by his oath of installation [1] to guard the law, liberties and rightful customs of the land of Ireland, which was *corporate de luy mesme.*

It can hardly be accidental that the only official and specific reference to the *Modus* as a repository of constitutional law should belong to this Yorkist period of Irish parliamentary history. The reference occurs at the end of a complicated quarrel over the election of the justiciar at a time of casual vacancy. The right of election was guaranteed by the *Modus,* but, as it carried with it the control of the Government, it was naturally suspect by the new dynasty. The Yorkists could not rule Ireland without the help of the Anglo-Irish (especially the great house of Geraldine, under the leadership of Desmond and Kildare), yet they naturally feared that their supporters would turn again to king-making. The situation was complicated by the fact that Clarence was lieutenant of Ireland from 1462. Once Edward IV was aware of a disloyal alliance between his brother and Warwick it became essential that the lieutenant's deputy should be a faithful servant of the Crown. For this reason Tiptoft, earl of Worcester,[2] was sent to replace Desmond as deputy in the autumn of 1467 and we can hardly doubt that he was instructed to act promptly against the supporters of Clarence. At a Parliament held in February, 1468, he procured the attainder of Desmond, Kildare and one of the Plunkets on the vague charge of " diversez causes, horribles treisouns et felonies, perpensez et faitz . . . sibien en alieaunce, fosterage et alterage ove les irrois, enemies le roy." [3]   A few days later Desmond was arrested

---

[1] It is significant that the only extant record of the oath in full—apart from the *Modus* itself—belongs to the year 1461 (*Cal. Pat. and Cl. Rolls, Ireland,* 1828, Vol. I, Part I, p. 269, nos. 61-2).

[2] " . . . trux carnifex et hominum decollator horridus," *Warkworth's Chronicle (Camden Soc.),* p. 63.

[3] *Statute Rolls,* 7 and 8 Edward IV, cap. 17, p. 464.

and summarily executed.[1] Kildare escaped and made his own peace with the king; his restoration to favour, on condition that he brought the Irish of Leinster to peace according to his power,[2] was no doubt partly due to the army of Irish rebels and English enemies with which Garret of Desmond was invading the counties of Kildare and Meath.[3] Clarence was also reconciled and reappointed lieutenant in the autumn of the same year, and Kildare was once more his deputy. However, in March 1470 the quarrel between the brothers broke out again. Clarence was "utterly discharged" from the Government of Ireland and Tiptoft was appointed in his place. When Tiptoft was captured and executed[4] in the brief hour of Lancastrian triumph, the Anglo-Irish straightway seized the opportunity of the vacancy to elect Kildare as justiciar. It was the choice of Kildare that provoked the disputes as to the right of election set out in the *Modus*.

In the Parliament of November 1471, when Clarence was again lieutenant, the question was at once raised. It is clear that the title of Kildare to the office of justiciar, which he still held,[5] had been challenged and that he was determined to justify his election. At the request of the Commons, it was enacted :

[1] It is much less probable that the reason for Desmond's execution lay in his "Irish methods" and treasonable relations with Celtic chiefs (G. H. Orpen, *Eng. Hist. Review*, Vol. XXX, p. 343) than that his connection with Clarence had alarmed the king. An Anglo-Irish story (*Book of Howth*, ed. J. S. Brewer and W. Bullen, Calendar of Carew MSS. 1871, pp. 186-7) puts the blame on the queen, Elizabeth Woodville, whom the earl is said to have offended by open speaking against her marriage. This may represent a garbled tradition of an alliance between Desmond, Clarence and Warwick, dating from the Woodville marriage. In September 1484 Richard III instructed the bishop of Annaghdown to inform the earl of Desmond that "albe it the fadre of the said erle, the king than being of yong age, was extorciously slayn and murdred by colour of the lawes within Irland by certain persones than havyng the governaunce and rule there, ayenst all manhode, reason and good conscience, . . . the kinges grace alweys contynueth and hathe inward compassion of the deth of his said fadre, and is content that his said cousyn, now erle, by alle ordinate meanes and due course of the lawes, when it shall lust him, at any tyme herafter to sue or attempt for the punyshement therof." MS. Harley 433, f. 265[b], *Letters of Richard III and Henry VII (Rolls Series)*, Vol. I, 68.

[2] *Statute Rolls*, 7 and 8 Ed. IV, cap. 57, p. 586.

[3] *Ibid.*, 7 and 8 Ed. IV, cap. 69, p. 617. Cf. *Annals of Ireland by Four Masters*, ed. J. O'Donovan, 1856, *sub anno* 1468.

[4] October 18, 1470, C. L. Scofield, *Life and Reign of Edward the Fourth*, 1923, Vol. I, 547.

[5] " Statuta ordinaciones et acta in quodam Parliamento domini regis apud Dublin . . . [November 29, 1471] coram Thoma fitz Morice comite Kildarie, Justicia ipsius domini regis terre sue Hiberni tento . . ." *Statute Rolls*, 11 and 12 Edward IV, p. 713.

" Whereas Thomas Fitz Morice, earl of Kildare, the King's Justice of Ireland (this land being without a governor, by the avoidance of the earl of Worcester, calling himself lieutenant of the said land, and his deputy), was elected Justice of the said land by the King's Council and the gentry of the same land. This notwithstanding, certain persons object that the election of the said earl to be Justice would not be effectual in law. Whereupon, the premises considered : It is published, declared and ordained, by the authority of the said Parliament, that the said election be good and effectual in law, and that by the same authority the said election be ratified, approved and confirmed, and all grants, acts, ordinances and statutes, made by the said Justice, shall be good, legal and effectual in law in all points, as they have been by Justices in this land before this time. . . ." [1]

The final doom of Clarence in 1478 raised again the same issue. Thomas of Kildare had died in 1477 while acting as deputy, and his son, Gerald, the eighth earl, was first elected as Justiciar and then served as deputy. Clarence was attainted in February 1478, and, as it had happened when Tiptoft was executed, Kildare was again elected to fill the casual vacancy. Though Edward IV in March appointed Suffolk as lieutenant and in July replaced him by his third son, George of Windsor, Kildare continued to hold office, summoning a Parliament at Naas in May and July of the same year.[2] When Grey of Codnor came to Ireland as Deputy, a Parliament held summoned by him at Trim (November 1478) not only declared void all Acts of the Parliament at Naas, but also passed an act which defined in a significant way the conditions of an election of a justiciar.[3] This Act, passed at the request of the Commons, confirmed the general procedure laid down in the *Modus*, adding new geographical limitations which the decline of the colony had made necessary. The text runs as follows :

[1] *Statute Rolls*, 11 and 12 Ed. IV, cap. 4, p. 715.
[2] Transcripts of Irish Statutes in the Public Record Office, Dublin. Parliament met at Naas on May 29, 1478, and passed twenty-four Acts ; it was prorogued to July, when further Acts were passed. The record is imperfect.
[3] *Ibid.* Parliament at Trim on November 6, 1478 ; it was adjourned first to Drogheda (November 19), and thence to Dublin (May 31, 1479). A document in which the king gives judgement as to the validity of these rival Parliaments is published in J. T. Gilbert's *History of the Viceroys of Ireland*, Dublin, 1865, Appendix, pp. 592 *seq.*

"Before this time there has been great ambiguity and doubt among the judges of Ireland as to the manner and form of the election of a Justiciar for the land. Some hold the opinion that election should be made only by seven persons of the King's Council and others maintain that election belongs to the lords spiritual and temporal and other more honourable persons of the four adjacent counties, acting with the whole Council.

"Wherefore, by authority of Parliament, it is ordained that the said Justiciar shall be elected by the whole Council and the archbishop of Dublin, the Primate of Armagh, the bishops of Meath and Kildare, the mayors of Dublin and Drogheda for the time being and the lords spiritual and temporal of Parliament of the four counties of Dublin, Meath, Louth and Kildare. They shall be duly summoned by writ to come within fifteen days to Dublin or to Drogheda and the majority of those who come shall make an election which shall be deemed and judged good and effectual in law. By the same authority it is ordained that any other manner or form of election of a Justiciar shall be judged and held to be null and void in law, notwithstanding any statute, use or custom held before this time to the contrary." [1]

Though the reference is not specific the procedure described is, in fact, no more than an amplification of Chapter 20 of the *Irish Modus*. The changes are matters of detail : the time of summons is limited to fifteen days ; certain prelates are specially named ; the mayors of Dublin and Drogheda and *aultres pluis honourables de les IIII countees parochiens adiunauntz* are substituted for the form *ad minus comitatus proxime*. The preamble seems to indicate that seven of the council, no doubt the permanent officials, had been trying to override the general right of election, defined in the *Modus* and, as we have already seen,[2] exercised at least as early as 1382 and 1403. The occasion of the statute suggests that Kildare, and possibly his father before him, had been elected by the council alone.

If this were all, we should still be in doubt as to whether the drafters of the statute had the formula of the *Modus* in their minds or were merely legislating in accordance with a practice of long standing. The doubt is resolved by another enactment, passed less than a decade later by the second Irish Parliament of Richard III. Here we find, not only an identification of the seven

---

[1] 18 Ed. IV, Roll 3, cap. 10 (Transcripts, Public Record Office, Dublin).
[2] *Supra*, pp. 86, n. 1.

councillors who claimed a monopoly right of election, but also a reference to the *Modus* itself of a kind which shows plainly how it was regarded :—

" At the request of the commons, it is ordained by the authority of this Parliament that the statute of Henry Fitzempress, for the election of a governor for this land when there happens to be a voidance of a loyal governor, shall be confirmed, ratified and adjudged good and effectual in law. And when it shall happen to come to pass at any future time that this land of Ireland in any manner whatsoever shall be void of any such manner of governor, then so often as this may happen, by authority of this Parliament, Thomas Fitzgerald, Chancellor of Ireland, Lord Rowland FitzEustace, Treasurer of Ireland, Philipp Bermingham, chief justice of the King's Bench,[1] Thomas Plunket, chief justice of the Common Bench, Oliver Eustace, Chief Baron of the Exchequer or his deputy for the time being, Thomas Dowdall, clerk and keeper of the rolls and records of the king in his chancery in Ireland, and John Estrete, sergeant-at-law of the king in Ireland and each of them severally, by the authority of this Parliament, shall be adjudged fully and severally to have and to hold each of their said offices for the term of their lives, notwithstanding any manner, matter, cause or thing had or to be had to the contrary. And by the same authority it is fully lawful to them or to the greater part of them, as to all other manner of persons or to the greater part of them who shall severally have and hold any of the said offices by reason of the death of any officer holding any of them, by gift under the witness of Gerald, earl of Kildare, in any manner, as governor of the said land, according to the tenor, usage and execution of the said statute of Henry Fitzempress, wherein it is specified that, with the assent of the nobles of this land, on each such voidance there shall be elected a noble lord to be governor and to have the governance as Justice of Ireland, to have and to enjoy the office in accordance with ancient usage, used and executed at this time.

" And by the same authority it is fully lawful for each such governor so elected to hold Parliaments and Great Councils and so to act that the law of the land shall be duly administered and executed for the public good, in every manner in which it has been administered and executed by any manner of governor and that the same shall be adjudged as good and as effectual in law as anything done by any manner of governor at any time in the past, provided

---

[1] *chiefe justice de chiefe place le roy en Irland.*

that the said election shall be made each time by the lords spiritual and temporal and the nobles of the said land.

" It is also provided that no Parliament shall begin except once a year." [1]

This clumsily worded statute represents a compromise. We may suppose that the permanent officials regarded the act of 1478 as an instrument which might be used to destroy them. The new Governor or justiciar, like a monarch at his accession, might dismiss them and appoint his own creatures in their stead. The danger of a voidance by violent death was increased by the fact that the deputy, Kildare, was at that very time " attendaunt lez guerres le roy en lez marches dicest terres, subduant sez Irrois ennemiez pour le encresce de bone publique dez subgittes le roy." [2] A life-interest in their offices was, therefore, fully secured to the seven chief officials whose names and titles are fully set out in the statute. No other reference is made to the council and we may conclude that at this time its membership was limited to the Chancellor, the Treasurer, the Chief Justice of the King's Bench, the Chief Justice of Common Pleas, the Chief Baron of the Exchequer, the Clerk and Keeper of the rolls and records of Chancery and one sergeant-at-law.

The constitutional interest of this implicit definition of the council is, for our purposes, overshadowed by the reference to the statute of Henry FitzEmpress, *le statute de Henry fitz Emprice.* It is an unmistakable citation of the *Modus* under a title drawn from the proem, *Henricus, Rex Anglie, conquestor et dominus Hibernie.* The election of a justiciar, it is enacted, shall follow the form prescribed in that statute, thereby cancelling the new provisions added by the Act of 1478. By leaving out all mention of the four counties of the Pale and the mayors of Dublin and Drogheda, the unofficial element taking part in the election is both reduced in size and made more aristocratic. *Lez seigneurs espirituelx et temporalx et lez noblez del dit terre*, to whom the right of election is assigned, represent a group of persons less popular and more indefinite than *lez seigneurs . . . et aultres*

[1] Stat. 2 and 3 Ric. III, cap. 8 (Transcripts, Public Record Office, Dublin). The text of the statute has been printed by Walter Harris, *Hibernica*, Pt. II, pp. 216-18 (ed. 1770), and by R. Steele, *Tudor and Stuart Proclamations*, Vol. I, p. cxix, n. 8.

[2] Stat. 2 and 3 Ric. III, cap. 4 (Transcripts, Public Record Office, Dublin).

pluis honnourables de les IIII countees parocheins adiunauntz of 1478 or *aliisque proceribus et discretis viris ad minus comitatus proxime* of the *Modus* itself.

It seems then that the *Modus* was specifically cited in the Parliament of 1485 in order to modify the statute of 1478 in the interests of the officials and the magnates. Even the clumsy phrasing of the statute may be due to a wish to stretch the sanction of the *Modus* to cover the life-appointments of the seven councillors.[1] We cannot say whether the original form of the document was deliberately revived as a whole, or if it were no more than the programme of constitutional government by which the Yorkists were, professedly, guided. It is, perhaps, significant that the deputy, Gerald FitzThomas, earl of Kildare, was the grandson of the earl who had been taken prisoner with Preston at Clane in 1418 and that his kinsman, Thomas, was Chancellor of Ireland at the time. A Geraldine tradition of a half-forgotten political conspiracy may have led to a search in Chancery for the document exemplified before Talbot and his council in 1419. It must, however, be admitted that an hypothesis of a statute, claiming the sanction of a rebel programme over half a century old, is not in itself convincing. It fails to take into account either the undoubted revival of Parliament along lines laid down in the *Modus* or the fact that the act of 1478 was primarily directed against Kildare himself. It also disregards other evidence, strong though circumstantial, indicating that the Statute of Henry FitzEmpress was not the first transmutation undergone by the *Modus*. It is this evidence which we must now consider.

The fact that the *Modus* was cited as a statute in 1485 throws light upon a mysterious allusion to a statute of assent and denial which occurs three times on the statute rolls, without reference to the date or circumstances of its enactment. In the Parliament of 1467-69 it was enacted that the lieutenant and the majority of his council should have power to consult with the six most honourable gentlemen of a county and to agree with them as to the amount by which their county should be taxed, notwithstanding " que come il est ordeine par estatute que assent et disassent

---

[1] For the same reason, the last sentence of the statute, forbidding the holding of Parliament more than once a year, may have been inserted. It is clear that the frequent sessions of Parliament were becoming a burden.

est treisoun."[1] Some words, it is clear, are missing from the *non obstante* clause ; perhaps it should run : *que come il est ordeine par lestatute que assent et disassent [hors de Parlement] est treisoun.*[2] Two further references, almost within the same decade, leave us in no doubt as to the title of the statute and also give indications of its content. In the Parliament of 1476-77 a statute was passed granting a subsidy at a double rate to the deputy. To it was attached a rider by which the lords and commons of Meath were fully pardoned for all that they had done against any statute, act or ordinance in lately assenting to and paying twenty shillings on the carucate within the county, " lestatute del assent et disassent ou ascun autre estatute, acte, ordinaunce ou provisoun nient obstaunt."[3] The lords and commons of Meath had evidently made a local grant to the deputy—he was the bishop of Meath—for which they were indemnified by Parliament, the statute of assent and denial notwithstanding. In the following Parliament (1479-80) it was ordained at the request of the Commons that Kildare and certain other persons in the counties of Kildare, Meath and Louth should have power to levy subsidies lawfully at their discretion and to name assessors and collectors of taxes, " lestatute del assente et disassente ou ascun aultre estatute, acte, ordenaunce ou provisioun en contrarie fait nient obstaunt." This power was to hold good until the meeting of the next Parliament.[4]

The resemblances between the three passages are very close. Each time the reference to the statute occurs in a *non obstante*

---

[1] 7 and 8 Ed. IV, cap. 20, *Statute Rolls*, p. 468.

[2] Perhaps the missing words were merely *etc.* It is surprisingly early to find reference to treason by statute.

[3] Stat. 16 and 17 Ed. IV, cap. 4, Parliament at Drogheda, December 6, 1476, adjourned to Dublin, January 14, 1477 (Transcripts, Public Record Office, Dublin). The clause runs : " Et que par lauctorite avantdit toutz seigneurs et communes de lavantdit counte de Mith et chescun de eaux soient pardonez, relessez, clerez, quitez et autrement dischargez de toute ceo qils firent encontre la forme et tenour dascun estatute, act ou ordinaunce en assente, graunte, leve et paiement fesaunt ore tarde de XX s. del charue de terre deins le dit counte de Mithe, lestatute del assent et disassent ou ascun autre estatute, acte, ordinaunce ou provisoun nient obstaunt ; et que par la dit auctorite commissions soient faitz et directes as collectours de tielx baronies queux ne ount pas paiez le dit subsidie deins le dit counte de Mithe, oue si ample power come il est accustume devant cest temps. . . ."

[4] Stat. 19 and 20 Ed. IV, cap. 34, Parliament at Dublin December 10, 1479, prorogued to Naas, May 8, 1480, and to Dublin, May 15 and July 10, 1480 (Transcripts, Public Record Office, Dublin).

clause and in each context Parliament is granting power for or regularising the levy of local subsidies. It seems obvious that the statute contained a strict prohibition of extra-parliamentary taxation. Both context and title suggest an Act with a formula expressing the idea that all proposals for the levy of taxes must be brought before Parliament for assent or denial. No such Act is extant either on the Irish statute rolls or among the collections of statutes earlier than 1426. Moreover, the form of reference, by title instead of the regnal year, is unusual ; the only other medieval Irish statutes generally known by special names are the Great Statute of Kilkenny and Poynings' Law. To these we must add the so-called Statute of Henry FitzEmpress, which, as we have seen, was the name given to the *Modus* in 1485. Now in the chapter *de adiutoriis postulandis* [1] (§ 15) the doctrine of parliamentary consent to taxation is stated with an emphasis on the special function of the Commons even greater than in the English *Modus*. " It is necessary that in all things conceded, done, affirmed and granted by Parliament the Commons of Parliament shall consent, which Commons consist of the proctors of the clergy, the knights of liberties and counties and the citizens and burgesses. Each of the peers of Parliament is in Parliament for himself and all the peers are judges and justices . . . but the Commons are petitioners and to them it also belongs to grant or to deny subsidies." *Communes vero . . . auxilii concessores vel negatores*, it must be admitted, comes very near to *le statute del assent et disassente*.

In a previous chapter we have already traced the slow process by which a system of parliamentary taxation was established in Ireland.[2] It was not until the prolonged struggle with William of Windsor (1369-75), that the Anglo-Irish were forced to admit the power of Parliament to impose taxes ; even after that date the system of local bargains persisted for nearly forty years. The last series of local grants of subsidies belongs to the reign of Henry IV,[3] that is, to the reign to which we have traced the French manuscript from which the Irish *Modus* was translated.

[1] The English title is *de auxiliis regis*.   [2] *Supra*, pp. 44-60.
[3] Louth and Meath, 1400 ; Dublin, Meath, Louth, Kildare and Carlow, 1401 ; Kildare and the clergy of Armagh and Meath, 1402 ; Dublin, 1404 ; Wexford, Kilkenny and the towns of Wexford and New Ross, 1412 (*Cal. Pat. and Cl. Rolls, Ireland*, pp. 158, no. 114-16, 4-5 ; 161-2, nos. 61-5 ; 166, nos. 242, 250, 253 ; 178, no. 77c).

Local bargains for taxation seem to have ceased altogether under Henry V and few later examples [1] have been traced, if we exclude those of the reign of Edward IV for which the statute of assent and denial was suspended by Parliament.

The evidence thus points to a definite change in practice following on the repeated demands for local grants made throughout the reign of Henry IV. The change apparently came about in the succeeding reign and three references in the statute rolls indicate that by the time of Edward IV it was supposed to have taken the form of the statute of assent and denial. In 1419, as we have seen, after a prolonged struggle, the Anglo-Irish, led by Preston and Kildare, had forced the deputy and council to exemplify the *Modus.* No doubt their main purpose was to assert the general principle that even the representative of the king himself was below Parliament and the law of the land,[2] but the fiscal exactions levied locally under Henry IV must also have given a special value to the chapter *de adiutoriis postulandis*.[3] The time and occasion of the *Modus* are thus in agreement with the time and purpose of the statute of assent and denial, and we can hardly hesitate to identify them. We may conclude, therefore, either that the statute was § 15 of the *Modus* itself or else, much less probably, that a lost statute was based upon it, which enacted that taxation without parliamentary consent was treason. If this conclusion be accepted, then the whole argument that the Yorkist policy of governing Ireland through Parliament had a direct connection with the *Modus* is strengthened almost into certainty.

After the short reign of Richard III we hear no more of the *Modus* until the eve of the Reformation. The favour shown by the Anglo-Irish to Yorkist pretenders helped to bring about a reversal of English policy. The independence of the Irish Parliament was destroyed by the statute known as Poynings' Law (1494), which made the consent of the English council a necessary preliminary to legislative proposals. Even with this safeguard, the Tudors feared the Irish Parliament. It was

---

[1] E.g. taxation of Meath and Louth, 1423 ; *Cal. Pat. and Cl. Rolls, Ireland,* p. 230, nos. 112-15, 121-2.

[2] This is clearly brought out by the codicil exemplifying the Coronation oath.

[3] It is, perhaps, significant that the full phrase " communes vero querentes et auxilii concessores vel negatores " occurs only in the exemplified version of the *Modus,* § 15.

summoned only eleven times between 1485 and 1603.[1] Much
of its work was taken over by the council and its functions as a
high court fell into abeyance. The Government depended for
revenue either on custom duties and forfeitures, or on uncon-
stitutional exactions for payment of troops, known as *cess* and,
in fact, no more than the coyne, livery and harbourage prohibited by medieval statutes. At first the Anglo-Irish hardly
understood that the atrophy of Parliament carried with it loss of
independence. The Commons probably regarded Parliament
mainly as a tax-granting body and, therefore, were unlikely to
clamour for frequent sessions. The magnates were either
preoccupied by rebel schemes in support of Simnel or Warbeck,
or else they were drawn into the great quarrel between Geraldines and Butlers, which, as Campion says, caused " much ruffle
and unquietness in the realme " throughout the first half of the
sixteenth century.[2] The aim of each faction was to secure the
office of deputy-lieutenant for its leader and in the effort to
gain or to hold it all other issues were forgotten. Even an English
governor was often welcomed as a partisan by one party or the
other in the hope that enemies might be branded as traitors.
The struggle for power gradually became a struggle for survival
and so passed into the long series of rebellions which led in the
end to the re-conquest of Ireland under Elizabeth. It is, in
short, hardly too much to say that the policy of the *Modus*, which
took shape in the first heat of the feud between Talbots and
Butlers, perished a century later in the feud between Butlers
and Geraldines.

Though the secular magnates, partly through Tudor policy
and partly in their passionate concentration on factious ends,
let slip their hold on Parliament, the *Modus* itself was not
altogether forgotten. This is proved by a long extract from it
preserved in the *Liber Niger* or Register of John Allen, archbishop of Dublin, 1528-34.[3] The date of the transcript, as shown
by a marginal note made by the archbishop himself, was 1533
and probably the occasion was the summons of Parliament in

[1] Parliament met in 8, 10 and 24 Hen. VII ; 7, 25, 28 and 33 Hen. VIII ;
3-4 Philip and Mary ; and 2, 11 and 27-8 Eliz.
[2] *A Historie of Ireland*, ed. James Ware, p. 106.
[3] Printed in *Eng. Hist. Review*, Vol. XLVIII, pp. 599-600. The following
four paragraphs are substantially the same as my note, *ibid.*, pp. 598-9.

that year. The chapters wholly or in part transcribed are, in the order of the Register, *Sessiones in Parliamento* (10), *Amerciamenta Absentium* (11), *Summonitio* (1), *Summonitio Clericorum et Laicorum* (2 and 3), *Gradus Parliamenti* (8), and *De adiutoriis postulandis* (15). The chapter *Sessiones in Parliamento* is the fuller version, as printed by Dopping ; the phrase *ad pedem dextrum regis sedebit cancellarius* has a marginal note—which fixes the date of transcription—*tempore meo* 1533 *orta est controversia inter me et Armachanum etiam tunc cancellarium regis hic.*[1] The immediate purpose of the transcript was probably to provide evidence to maintain Allen's claim, as archbishop of Dublin, to sit on the right hand of the throne. The chapter on amercements is worded differently from any other version and it is combined with the chapter requiring forty days' notice of summons. The chapters dealing with the summons of clergy and laity are run together ; much is omitted, but there are also unique additions. The brief extracts from § 8 and § 15 are combined with phraseology which appears to be taken from the English *Modus*. The whole transcript ends with a sentence that does not stand in any other version, Irish or English.

Thus Allen's notes from the *Modus* do not correspond exactly to either of the two groups of manuscripts, of which we have already traced the history. On two points he follows Dopping's text [2] and there is no indication that he had used the exemplified version. In one place he adds a detail which occurs only in the English *Modus*.[3] Minor additions which do not occur elsewhere are the wording of the amercement clause and the statement that prelates come to Parliament at their own expense. More interesting is the addition of the adjective *rurali* before *decanatu*, as it serves to emphasise the survival of the Irish rural deanery as the unit of taxation and representation. The main interest, however, lies in the concluding passage, which is partly a conflation of § 2, § 4, § 5, § 8, and § 15, and also contains a phrase based on Chapter XXII of the English version :

" Ecce tres gradus Parliamenti, scilicet : de procuratoribus cleri in una domo, qui erunt duo sapientes [a quolibet decanatu

---

[1] Allen was murdered in 1534.

[2] The chapter *Sessiones Parliamenti* and the phrase *ante primum diem Parliamenti* instead of *ante Parliamentum* (§ 1).

[3] XIV.

rurali vel archidiaconatu cum warentis] cum mandato duplicato superiorum sigillis sigillatis, quorum unum deliberetur clerico Parliamenti irrotulandum, alter remaneat apud se ipsos. In secunda autem tam milites comitatuum quam cives civitatum et burgenses oppidorum. In tertia vero pares curie sedentes, nisi loquatur aliquis eorum, quia tunc surgat citra regem, ut audiatur ab omnibus.

"Nunc Parliamentum non adjournetur, nisi de consensu majoris partis omnium doctorum trium graduum sive domorum."[1]

Whatever its origin, the description of the Irish Parliament as divided into three orders or houses is of great interest. It is in agreement with Grey's account of separate sessions of proctors in 1537[2] and we cannot doubt that Parliament was divided in this way in 1533. At first sight it looks as if Allen had begun by copying notes from the Irish *Modus*, using the text later known as Dopping's ; then he turned to the English version and borrowed from it the reason why peers must stand when they speak ; lastly, he added certain observations of his own. This theory, however, breaks down under close examination. The re-wording of the amercement clause seems pointless, as it is no shorter and less well expressed than the original ; for the same reason, it is difficult to explain why, if Allen were borrowing from the English *Modus*, he did not take the exact wording before him. Further, the statement that Parliament shall not be adjourned without the consent of the three orders or houses neither appears in the *Modus* nor does it express sixteenth-century practice. It is not by any means the kind of constitutional doctrine that an Englishman and an archbishop was likely to formulate in 1533. It has, however, an Irish parallel of significant date. In 1410, in the Parliament held by Thomas Bacagh, a petition was put forward —" That Parliments shall not be adiorned or dissolved without resonable cause shewed in the Parliment, and by the advyse of the Lordes and Commens."[3] The reply that " the Governenor is pleased that the forme of adiornment of Parliments shall be

---

[1] *Eng. Hist. Review*, Vol. XLVIII, p. 600. Cf. English *Modus*, XXII : " Omnes pares . . . sedebunt, et nullus stabit nisi quando loquitur et loquitur ita quod quilibet de Parliamento eum audire valeat . . . stabunt omnes loquentes ; causa est ut audiantur a paribus, quia omnes pares sunt iudices et iusticiarii."

[2] *State Papers*, Henry VIII, Vol. II, Part III, pp. 438-9.

[3] *Early Statutes*, p. 520. Only a translation of the original roll is now extant. The first recorded adjournments of the Irish Parliament were in 1406 and 1416, *Annals of Henry of Marlborough*, Dublin, 1633, *sub anno*.

keept after the maner of England " may have served to provoke an enquiry into the English manner of keeping Parliament and thus have helped the vogue of the *Modus*. The parallel sentence in Allen's transcript, stating the necessity of the consent of Parliament to adjournment, suggests that a recension of the *Modus* was drafted soon after 1410.[1]

If this were so, the recension must have been modified considerably at a much later date. The division into three houses does not correspond with the divisions in the other versions of the *Modus*, where the dividing line is drawn either between spiritual and temporal members, or between *pares* and *communes*. It seem probable that the separation of the proctors into a separate house did not take place until the sixteenth century, perhaps not before 1533. In that year Parliament met for the first time since 1521 ; it may be that in the interval the tradition of joint sessions had been broken. We cannot assign Allen's notes to an earlier date with any reasonable probability and we may conclude that they were taken from a lost recension of the *Modus* and modified in the sixteenth century by the insertion of the reference to three houses.

No one in Ireland at the time was more likely to undertake the work than Allen himself. He was, Campion writes, a man " of deepe judgement (and) in the Cannon law, the onely match of Stephen Gardener." [2] He would naturally incline to regard the Irish order of proctors as equivalent, in part at least, to the English Convocation, and be anxious to bring Irish practice more into line with English procedure. He would not, however, be prepared, on that account to betray the rights of the clergy. The selections of chapters from the *Modus* and the new matter added to them have a certain unity of their own ; they all bear, one way or another, on the dignity and privileges of the Church. The year 1533 was a time when the Church in Ireland was looking to her defences ; that " two-handed engine," the Lords and Commons of the English Parliament, stood " ready to strike once and strike no more." In England the northern Pilgrims in 1537 cited Magna Carta with its *ecclesia libera sit* as their warrant for rebellion ; the *Modus*, perhaps, was intended to serve the same

---

[1] Allen's *Nunc* certainly suggests contemporary practice, but there is no evidence to support it.

[2] *Op. cit.*, p. 120.

purpose in Ireland. If this were indeed the intention, it was at once cut short by that Irish goddess of mischief, whose lust to kill was slaked more often by innocent than by guilty blood. Archbishop Allen was murdered by Silken Thomas [1] in the summer of 1534 and he was succeeded by George Browne, a recreant monk and the willing tool of Cromwell. In the Parliament of 1537/8 there was no one to use the defence lying to hand in the *Liber Niger*. The proctors were expelled from Parliament, as no longer " parcel or any member " of it, and by this means that three-fold unity of Proctors, Lords and Commons which had been the heart and mind of Irish public life, was broken in fragments. Thus the archaism of the Irish medieval Parliament and its fidelity to the plan of the *Modus* involved it in the downfall of the medieval Church.

III

The entry in the *Liber Niger* recalls attention to the history of the manuscripts and to the problem of their origin. It has been seen that we have evidence of three distinct but closely allied versions known in Ireland between the years 1418 and 1533—the Dopping text, the exemplified *Modus* and the document used by archbishop Allen. All three bear signs of a common origin as translations from the French roll associated with the archbishop of Cashel in the reign of Henry IV.[2] The exemplified version is longer and more complete than the Dopping text. We know that it was found with Sir Christopher Preston when he was arrested in June 1418 and we may conclude that it represents the final or definitive draft. Dopping's text was, perhaps, a little earlier in date, composed before the quarrel with Talbot led the conspirators to add the installation oath of the justiciar

---

[1] Lord Thomas Fitzgerald, grandson of the earl of Kildare, who was deputy in 1485. He rose in rebellion because he heard a false rumour of his father's execution in England. Campion (*op. cit.*, p. 118) says he heard the news through a letter which a man picked up at random " in the morning for some paper to drawe on his straite hosen, and, as the devill would, he hit upon the letter, bare it away in the heele of his hose . . . at night againe he found the paper unfretted and musing thereof began to pore on the writing, which notified the Earle's death. . . ."

[2] The evidence is hardly sufficient to establish a clear connection between the French MS. and Allen's notes. However, the use of the Irish form *sapientes* when the English *Modus* would have read *idonei* indicates that the original English version was not consulted.

and the king's coronation oath and to name Cashel as the place where the document should be preserved. Its discovery in the Treasury at Waterford suggests that it was regarded as official ; perhaps it was deposited there by the earl of Ormonde. Allen's notes, in spite of an obvious addition of the sixteenth century, were probably taken from another draft, which the reference to adjournment helps to connect with the year 1410. This recension may have belonged to Cranley,[1] one of the leaders of the con-stitutional party opposed to Talbot, and through him it may have passed into the registry of the archbishops of Dublin. Though it is impossible to assign a precise date to the composi-tion, the first drafts may date from the reign of Henry IV and the final or exemplified version cannot be later than the summer of 1418.

The composition of the Irish *Modus* was provoked by the financial exactions and high-handed rule of English lieutenants. No doubt all grievances of English origin were less tolerable after the Lancastrian revolution had lowered the prestige of the monarchy and had drawn attention back to the doctrine that the king must rule under the law. Sir Christopher Preston has already been suggested as the man who may have undertaken or directed the work of composition.[2] He and Cranley were the leaders of the constitutional party ; the final draft was found in his possession and it was exemplified before he was sent to answer to the English council. He himself, as the Gormanstown Register shows, set a high value on precedents and legal forms ; two chronicles are connected with his family, at least one of which was probably composed under his patronage.[3] Finally, his father, Sir Robert Preston, played a prominent part in affairs just at the time when the English *Modus* first seems to have reached Ireland.

It is to the fourteenth-century history of the English *Modus* in Ireland that we must now turn, and here it must be admitted that the evidence is altogether circumstantial. During or im-mediately after the rule of William of Windsor (1369-75), we find that the Irish Parliament changed fundamentally both in form and in function. The doctrine of taxation by the consent

---

[1] Cranley was archbishop of Dublin, 1397-1417, Justiciar of Ireland, 1414, and deputy from 1416 to 1418.
[2] *Supra*, p. 86.   [3] *Supra*, pp. 78-9.

of elected representatives given in Parliament was accepted ; two proctors from each diocese were added to the Commons ; the obligation imposed on lay magnates to attend Parliament became exclusively tenurial and the issue of writs of summons was restricted to earls and barons. It can hardly be a coincidence that each of these changes brought the Irish Parliament nearer to the Parliament of the *Modus*.

We have already traced out the history of the proctors in the Irish Parliament [1] and it is not necessary to go over the ground again. It will be remembered that they were first summoned to Parliament in 1371, in accordance with the new fiscal policy of William of Windsor, and that they remained an integral part of Parliament until 1537. Through the Registers of Armagh, we have seen how closely proctorial representation was bound up with taxation and how a system of consent and supervision was worked out in diocesan convocations and rural deaneries along lines indicated in the *Modus*. In contrast to this enlargement of ecclesiastical representation was the limitation of the attendance of lay magnates, brought about by the adoption of the doctrine of barony by tenure.

The early writs of special summons to the Irish Parliament, as far back as they can be traced, were issued to all persons of importance whose presence was desired, irrespective of conditions of tenure. They were not even restricted to tenants-in-chief ; in 1310, for example, eighty-eight secular persons were summoned to Parliament by special writ and at least twenty-five of them were small landowners, vassals of absentee lords like Roger Mortimer and the earl of Ulster.[2] This practice continued until the end of Edward III's reign, though the number of persons who received special writs declined. Then in 1372, the year after the first summons of proctors to Parliament, William of Windsor issued writs for a Great Council on a new principle.[3] The only lay peers who received a special summons were the earls of Kildare and Ormonde. In writs to the sheriffs or

---

[1] *Supra*, pp. 36-43.
[2] *Early Statutes*, pp. 258 *seq.* I have discussed these writs in *Irish Parliaments in the Reign of Edward II*, Trans. Royal Hist. Soc. 4, ix, pp. 35-7, 58-9.
[3] The writs, taken from " Chancery Roll. Dub. 46 E. 3," are printed by W. Lynch (*A View of the Legal Institutions, Honorary Hereditary Offices and Feudal Baronies established in Ireland*, 1830, pp. 318 *seq.*). Cf. *Cal. Pat. and Cl. Rolls, Ireland*, p. 83, nos. 110-18.

seneschals of Dublin, Meath, Louth and Kildare, in addition to the usual formula for the election of two knights, a *premunire* clause was inserted, commanding the attendance of certain named persons under penalty of a fine of 100 marks.[1] The names of fifteen magnates usually summoned by special writ [2] appear in this way, together with the names of seventy-two other persons,[3] landed gentry of lesser degree. Lynch, who mistook this assembly for a Parliament, thought that Windsor's object was to secure a majority of lay magnates over the prelates.[4] In support of this explanation he cites Spenser's account of a tradition current in Ireland at the end of the sixteenth century.

" Edward the thirde . . . beinge greatelye bearded and crossed by the lords of the Clargie, they beinge then by reason of the Lord Abbotes, and others, too manye and to stronge for them, so he could not for theire frowardnes, order and reforme thinges as he desyred, was advised to dyrecte forth his writtes to certaine gentlemen of best abyllitie and trust, intytlinge them therein Barrons to serue and sytte as Barrons in the next parlament, by which meanes he had so manye barrons in his parlament, as were able to weighe downe the Clargie and theire freindes the which Barrons they saye were not afterwardes Lordes, but onelye Barronytes, as soundrie of them doe yett retaine the name. . . ." [5]

Spenser's statement has interest as a sign that the extraordinary summons of 1372 [6] made a deep impression. There is, however, nothing in contemporary records to show that laymen were more favourable to Windsor's fiscal policy than the clergy. This Great Council, like the Parliament held at Kilkenny in the

---

[1] For example, in the writ to the sheriff of Dublin (Lynch, *loc. cit.*, p. 320) : " . . . et ulterius premunire facias Thomam Talbot, militem [and fifteen others named] et quemlibet eorum in fide et ligeancia quibus nobis tenentur quacunque excusacione cessante et sub pena C marcarum nobis solvendum ibidem ad diem illum [February 25] personaliter intersint. . . ."

[2] E.g. in the writs of summons to the Parliament at Dublin, January 1375 (*ibid.*, p. 323). Twenty-five others then received special writs whose names were not on the writs of 1372.

[3] Six named burgesses from Drogheda and the twenty-four jurats of the city of Dublin were also summoned. The only elected members were the representatives of the four counties and two citizens of Dublin.

[4] *Op. cit.*, p. 124.

[5] *A View of the State of Ireland, 1596*, ed. W. L. Renwick, 1934, p. 184.

[6] Possibly the tradition relates to the special summons of a large number of laymen to the Parliament of January, 1375, *infra*, pp. 120-1.

previous month, was probably summoned in a last desperate effort to secure ratification of the grants exacted from previous assemblies.[1] The writs of summons to the Council were issued only ten days before the date of meeting (Feb. 15 for Feb. 25), and the short notice no doubt explains why Windsor did not call a Parliament. Perhaps for a like reason he summoned the magnates through the sheriffs, though it may be that he had observed the purely traditional system of issuing writs and hoped to turn it to advantage. Perhaps by the new method he hoped both to increase the revenue from fines [2] and to reduce the pride of the magnates by reminding them that their titles to the rank of baron were defective. Moreover, the omission from the sheriffs' writs of the earl of Desmond and twenty-two other persons summoned by special writ in 1375 [3] indicates clearly enough a policy of deliberate selection or packing.

William of Windsor returned to England in March 1372, and an enquiry into the abuses of his administration was begun. No writs are extant for the Parliament summoned in his absence (Jan. 1374), but we know that a message of complaint was sent from it to England. For the first Parliament held after his return writs of special summons were issued to forty lay magnates in the usual way.[4] Two other Parliaments were summoned in the same year (June and October, 1375) and, as they obstinately refused to grant supply, Windsor then tried the extraordinary expedient of summoning the Commons only to meet the king and council at Westminster in February 1376. This summons

---

[1] *Supra*, pp. 50-54, for a more detailed summary, with references, to the actions of William of Windsor.

[2] There is ample evidence that fines for absence were exacted from the time of Edward II. Cf. Lynch, pp. 53, 56, 57 and 58, and *Cal. Pat. and Cl. Rolls, passim*. The calendars of the Irish Pipe Rolls (Reports of the Deputy Keeper of Public Records, Ireland) contain a number of examples of fines for absence from Parliament, many of which belong to the Dublin Parliament of January, 1331. They suggest that there was no fixed scale of penalties and no approximation to the fines laid down in the English *Modus* (cf. *infra*, pp. 219-20). For example, the earl of Kildare was fined £100 (Report 43, p. 35), the bishop of Killaloe £40 (Report 54, p. 49) ; Richard de Tuit £20 (Report 44, p. 23) ; the abbot of Wetheney (Owney, co. Limerick) £18 (Report 43, p. 49) ; the sovereign and provosts of Youghal £20 (Report 43, p. 51) ; the sovereign and baillifs of New Ross £10 (Report 53, p. 28) ; and the sheriff of Waterford £10 (Report 44, p. 25). Cf. *Annals of St Mary's Abbey, Dublin (Rolls Series)*, II, 375 (1331) and the Irish *Modus*, § 10.

[3] Lynch, pp. 321-5.

[4] *Ibid.*, Parliament met on January 17, 1375.

is in itself evidence that less resistance was expected from the Commons than from the magnates. The list of lay magnates, who received special summons to the first Parliament of Richard II contains twenty-five names, excluding five members of the council ; unfortunately it is defective and we cannot tell how many names are missing.[1] In 1380 only twenty-one persons were summoned in this way [2] and henceforth the number of lay peers remains fairly constant at or about this figure. In other words, not much more than half the lay magnates specially summoned to the first Parliament of 1375 remained permanently peers of Parliament.

The explanation of this marked decline in numbers seems to be found in the case of Walter Lenfaunt, who in 1377 petitioned the Crown for remission of a fine imposed upon him for absence from the Parliament of 1375.[3] Lenfaunt pleaded that he had been summoned *tanquam tenentem per baroniam*, although he had never held by that tenure. His petition was tried before the Treasurer and barons of the Exchequer ; it was found that he did not hold by barony and the fine was remitted. At the same time a general principle was expressly stated : " It does not belong to the law and custom hitherto used in this land, that any persons not holding by barony should be summoned to our Parliaments nor for their absence should the same be amerced." [4] The same principle was applied in the case of Thomas Verneille, heard in the same year.[5] Verneille had petitioned for a remission of his fine for absence on the grounds that he could not attend Parliament without the destruction of his lands by Irish enemies and also that none of his ancestors were ever summoned before this time to Parliament except among the Commons. The second plea was rejected altogether and, though the fine was remitted by reason of the Irish wars, it was found that Verneille's estates in Meath were sufficient to justify his summons as a baron.[6] A number of other persons

---

[1] Lynch, pp. 325-8. [2] *Ibid.*, pp. 328-31.
[3] *Cal. Pat. and Cl. Rolls of Ireland*, p. 103, no. 89. The case is fully discussed by Lynch, pp. 62-3, 124-6.
[4] " Non est iuris seu consuetudinis in dicta terra nostra hactenus usitatae, quod aliqui, qui per baroniam non tenuerunt ad parliamenta nostra summoneri seu occasione absenciae suae ab eisdem amerciari deberent."
[5] Lynch, pp. 126-7.
[6] Verneille was summoned to the Parliaments of Richard II.

were fined for absence in 1376 and 1377 [1] and it seems that these decisions were taken as test cases. Names like Power of Donhill, Calf of Norraghmore, Hussey of Galtrim, and Nangle of Navan disappear from the lists of lay tenants specially summoned to Parliament, though they retained the title of baron in legal proceedings and in all official documents.[2]

It is, as Lynch writes, " evident . . . that the feudal parliamentary dignities of Ireland were governed solely by the principle of Tenure." [3]   The English doctrine of barony by writ was not accepted, even though it was in conformity with the practice followed until the end of Edward III's reign. The doctrine of tenure by barony was adopted as the sole qualification for parliamentary peerage and this is identical with the doctrine of the *Modus*. " Every earl and baron and their peers, that is, such as have lands and rents to the value of one whole earldom, or twenty knights' fees . . . or to the value of a whole barony, that is thirteen knights' fees and a third, which make four hundred marks, ought to be summoned and to come to Parliament ; and no others of the laity or clergy [4] of lesser possessions ought, at their own costs, to appear on account of their tenures, unless the king should summon his counsellors or other wise men for some necessary cause. . . ." [5]   It is certainly significant that this doctrine was suddenly applied and acted upon in Ireland in 1377.

The third sign of the influence of the *Modus* during the closing years of Edward III's reign was that the doctrine of parliamentary consent to taxation was definitely accepted by the Anglo-Irish. We have already seen [6] how they were driven into this new position by the pressure to grant taxes put on them by William of Windsor, pressure culminating in the summons of representatives of the commons to Westminster. It has not hitherto been remarked that the extraordinary summons of the Commons in 1375 was a particular application of a plan implicit

---

[1] Lynch, pp. 62-3.   [2] *Ibid.*, pp. 132, 163-4.
[3] *Ibid.*, p. 131.   [4] The English version omits *vel clerici*.
[5] § 3. In the English version the phrase about counsellors appears in a slightly different form in the previous chapter. It is worth noting that writs of special summons to members of the Irish council were issued for the Parliament of January 1375, and from that time an issue of this kind became a usual practice—*Ibid.*, p. 324.
[6] *Supra*, pp. 50-54.

in the *Modus* itself. The writs of summons were directed to the bishops, sheriffs or seneschals and mayors or sovereigns ; they were commanded to send two proctors, two knights, and two citizens or burgesses from each diocese, county and city or borough.[1] No writs of special summons were issued, as the presence of spiritual and temporal lords was not desired. Though the summons roused vigorous opposition, no protest against the exclusion of the magnates is recorded. Emphasis throughout was laid either on the unprecedented citation to England, or on the right of consent. Four dioceses, five counties and the electors of Dublin and Drogheda clearly recognised the underlying purpose of the summons and refused to grant to their representatives any power to consent to taxation. It was, however, never asserted that the Commons without the Lords would be incompetent to grant a subsidy. Now this exactly conforms with the principle laid down in the *Modus*. " All things which ought to be affirmed or abrogated, granted, or denied or accomplished by Parliament ought to be granted by the Commons, that is, by the proctors of the clergy, the knights of the shires, by the citizens and burgesses, who represent the whole community of England, and not by the magnates, since each of them is in Parliament for himself alone and for no one else." [2] The same principle is reiterated in the Irish version, with the significant addition *communes . . . auxilii concessores vel negatores*. Thus the constitutional crisis of 1375 suggests that both parties, the English executive and the Anglo-Irish opposition, accepted the doctrine of the *Modus* that ultimate responsibility for taxation lies with the Commons.

We have found that attendance of proctors, barony by tenure and the consent of the Commons to taxation were all established as part of Irish constitutional practice at the end of Edward III's reign. Each can be traced directly to the *Modus* and the conclusion can hardly be avoided that each took its origin from the document itself. How it came to be known in Ireland at this time can only be conjectured. William of Windsor may have introduced it as part of his policy of forcing Parliament to undertake full financial responsibility. He was certainly acting in accordance with it when he caused proctors to be summoned

[1] *Supra*, p. 51.   [2] XXIII.

and when he tried to compel the Commons to grant taxes in 1375. At an early stage in the conflict between him and the Anglo-Irish, knowledge of the document must have passed to the opposition. Perhaps Sir Robert Preston, Chief Justice of Common Pleas, was the man who first understood its constitutional importance.[1] He was one of the commissioners who in 1373 enquired into the abuses of Windsor's rule and he was summoned by special writ as a councillor to the Parliaments of 1375 (January), 1378 and 1380.[2] We may suppose then either that Windsor brought the *Modus* to Ireland in order to instruct the colonists and found them only too willing to use it as a defence,[3] or that Preston or some other Anglo-Irish official brought it forward and forced the executive to admit its authority.

IV

Whether the *Modus* was first sponsored in Ireland by Windsor or by Preston must remain uncertain, but there can be no doubt that, once it was known, it carried the sanction of authority. In the middle of the fourteenth century the Irish Parliament lay open to the pressure of society because it was not an instrument of power either for the magnates or for the Crown. By the greedy energy of Windsor its starved and stunted frame was suddenly driven into movement; at the same time the motive for independent action was supplied by the doctrines of the *Modus*. Movement and motive together brought rapid growth. Rooted in the two-fold authority of king and subjects, Parliament within a decade increased its stature and rounded out its contours. The principles of barony by tenure, attendance of clerical proctors and parliamentary taxation through representatives were either recognised or established and with them Parliament at last grew to a position of mastery. Whether that position was to lie in the control of the Crown or of subjects became the dominant issue. The Anglo-Irish were quick to see both their danger and their opportunity and to appropriate the *Modus* to themselves

---

[1] *Supra*, p. 115. [2] Lynch, *loc. cit.*, pp. 324, 327, 330.
[3] Another, less certain, example of the influence of the *Modus* may be seen in the protest made by the prelates, lords and commons in June 1382 against the holding of Parliament in the absence of the lieutenant, Roger Mortimer (cited in full by Steele, *Proclamations*, I, pp. cxxvi-vii, n. 46, from *Report of Searches*, 1806, no. 17).

for the definition and the defence of their constitutional rights. From this appropriation the draft of a special Irish version, its exemplification at Trim with the coronation oath as a codicil, and its later disguises as the statutes of Henry FitzEmpress and of assent and denial followed in logical sequence. Through Windsor and the *Modus* something new and difficult had been put into the currency ; from that time forward Parliament, either in fact or in theory, remained at the centre of Irish political life.

However, for the main purpose of our enquiry, the interest lies less in the *Modus* as an Irish Magna Carta than in the circumstances of its first appearance in the country. It is clear from the outset that it was acknowledged to bear the stamp of authority. In admitting so much we are forced to abandon the hypothesis already put forward to explain its origin. If the English *Modus* were indeed the work of a discontented proctor, drafted to maintain the rights of the lower clergy and to protest against the taxation of 1370, it is incredible that the king's representative in Ireland should have used it forthwith to instruct the Anglo-Irish in the powers and privileges of Parliament. Alternatively, it is even more absurd to suppose that Preston or some other leader of the opposition was able to pass off a document thus concocted as an authoritative statement of constitutional law. Whatever its origin, the *Modus* in the " seventies " carried the weight of official sanction. To maintain that it was then newly-minted, and, in fact, no more than a wild-cat paper constitution contrived by an unknown radical member of Convocation, would involve balancing the whole Irish parliamentary system on the point of a needle.

We are then driven to the alternative conclusion, that in the closing years of Edward III's reign the English *Modus* had a definite official standing. When it became known in Ireland, it at once served to shape and to develop the Irish Parliament in a way that would have been impossible without a background of authority. The Irish history of the *Modus*, therefore, proves that in the period 1369 to 1377 the English version had a recognised constitutional standing. As the theory of an origin in Convocation about the year 1370 can no longer be sustained, we must look further back for its beginning. The facts suggest that in England, where Parliament had grown with great rapidity in the reign of Edward III, it was already old-fashioned, while the Irish, with their half-formed and half-understood system of government, still required the direction of an authoritative summary of the functions and powers of Parliament. This is the more probable because the English, with their formal conservatism based upon law, have always been slow to admit the difference between the legal and the actual, especially where the rights of others are concerned. The English who applied the *Modus* to Ireland no more understood that it represented a by-gone stage of their own political experience than their descendants understood in 1782 that legislative independence without Cabinet responsibility was a form of government which England had already outgrown.

CHAPTER VII

PROCTORS IN PARLIAMENT AND IN CONVOCATION

On the Irish evidence we have reached the conclusion that in England, at the end of Edward III's reign, the *Modus* was invested with prestige and authority and that it cannot be taken as the work of a free-lance or Utopian dreamer, writing at that time. We must, therefore, seek for its origin at an earlier date. Its Irish origin has also thrown into bolder relief both an ecclesiastical bias and a special emphasis on the ultimate superiority of the Commons. It has become clear that these characteristics are of first importance in fixing the time and motive of composition, though we are not yet committed to any theory of origin. The *Modus* is certainly not in agreement with much that we know of Parliament in the second half of the century, but this may not also be true of an earlier period. It may have been the outcome of an older movement of ecclesiastical discontent, or it may belong to a time when the clergy had a larger share in the work of Parliament. The stress laid upon the superiority of the Commons may have its counterpart in actual conditions, or it may express the hope of some forgotten political reformer. To examine these or similar possibilities it will be necessary to turn back to the first half of the century and to compare the content of the *Modus* with parliamentary conditions, so far as they are known to us.

In the search for the latest date in which the Parliament of the *Modus* seems to be in harmony with the Parliament of the day, we may take as a starting-point the separation of the estates, as it is on this subject that the divergence between the two is, by the end of the century, most clearly marked. The beginning of the joint session of knights and burgesses, which was to grow into the House of Commons, belongs to the first decade of Edward III's reign. Though the first specific reference to the union of the two orders occurs in 1341,[1] the date should probably be put as early as 1332. From that time the knights and burgesses nearly always voted subsidies jointly, no doubt because the commutation of the tenth and fifteenth for a lump sum did away with the need for a separate bargain with each estate.[2] For our particular purpose not much stress can be laid on the consolidation of the lay Commons. The rolls and chronicles show that their sessions were regarded as extra-parliamentary and that they continued to come to Parliament to make requests and to report decisions. The *Modus* certainly assumes that each estate will debate apart before common decisions are reached, but the extra-parliamentary union of two of them does not necessarily conflict with this assumption. We cannot argue that the consolidation of the lay Commons was later in date than the description in the *Modus*. The secession of the clerical proctors is altogether different. Their withdrawal ran directly counter to the whole theory of the ultimate responsibility of the Commons, clerk and lay, which is set out in the *Modus*.

We have already seen that the last decisive reference to the presence of proctors in Parliament, as an estate, occurs on the roll of 1332.[3] About the same time the practice was established by which clerical grants were made in Convocation only, thus destroying the only compelling motive for proctorial attendance in Parliament.[4] In 1341 archbishop Stratford definitely stated that the clergy were in no way bound to attend Parliament (*interesse minime tenebantur*[5]). Though Edward III made a formal denial of this claim,[6] he did not attempt to press his point ; in fact, it was in the same year that the royal and provincial letters enjoining attendance ceased to be issued.[7] There was certainly no dramatic secession of proctors. For at least

---

[1] " . . . les chivalers des counteez, citeyns et burgeys de par eux," *Rot. Parl.* II, 127.

[2] The tenth and the fifteenth were commuted for £38,000 in 1332.

[3] *Rot. Parl.* II, 64b. Cf. *supra*, Chap. III, p. 20.

[4] See *infra*, pp. 146-7.

[5] " . . . cum nec ipsi Parliamento interfuerint predicto sicut interesse minime tenebantur . . . ," *Register of Grandisson*, ed. F. C. Hingeston-Randolph, Exeter, 1897, II, 938.

[6] " . . . ita tamen quod ipsi in procuratores, ad huiusmodi parliamenta et concilia mittendos per clerum, consentiant . . . ," *Report on the Dignity of a Peer*, IV, 528.

[7] *Infra*, pp. 128 *seq.*

another hundred years, a few seem to have attended from time to time, enough to justify an occasional reference to *la clergie de la roialme* or to proctors and prelates in Parliament.[1] The position was clearly defined in 1380, when the lay Commons proposed that a tax of 50,000 marks should be imposed on the Church. The clergy replied that their grant was never made, nor ought to be made, in Parliament and that they should be as free from lay constraint as the laity were free from that of the Church.[2]

It was natural that the lower clergy should prefer the direct profits of separate discussion and separate bargains to the shadowy advantage of co-operation with the laity. They had no wish to attend Parliament, once they had ceased to grant supply there, and the king had nothing tangible to gain by insisting upon their presence. Their failure to come into a general system of taxation was no doubt due to a long tradition of separatism, but for our purposes that tradition has less significance than the means by which it was defended. From the time of John's submission to Innocent III and the new *entente* between the Papacy and the Crown, the clergy had realised that both independence and fiscal immunity were slipping from their grasp. The inclusion of their proctors in the Parliaments of Edward I and Edward II was the visible sign of secular victory. Once the king had established the right to tax spiritualities,[3] the clergy were bound in self-defence to attend the assemblies at which taxation was imposed. A levy sanctioned by Parliament was at least better than arbitrary extortion, but it did not follow that the general principle of parliamentary taxation was accepted by the Church. It is, therefore, necessary to examine the evidence for their attitude to representation in Parliament.

The folly of open resistance, even with full papal support, was fully demonstrated by Edward I's dramatic outlawry of the

---

[1] Cf. *Rot. Parl.* II, 151 (1344); *Cal. Cl. Rolls*, 1371, pp. 286-7; royal letters to the archbishops refer to " procuratoribus vestris ac prelatis in ultimo parliamento nostro," quoted by Wake, *op. cit.*, p. 303. It is possible that here personal proctors are meant.

[2] " . . . lour grant ne feust unques fait en Parlement, ne ne doit estre, ne les laies gentz devroient ne ne purroient constreindre le clergie, ne ne poet ne doit en celle partie constreindre les layes gentz ; mais leur semble, que si aucun deust estre frank ce serroit pluis tost la clergie que les lays gentz," *Rot. Parl.* III, 90.

[3] See *infra*, pp. 263-4.

clergy in 1297. The price that the king paid for his victory was the loss of the good will of the Church for his new Parliament of estates. Clerical proctors were summoned for the first time to the same assembly as the lay commons in the Model Parliament of November 1295. Boniface VIII issued the bull *Clericis Laicos* in February 1296 and its terms left no way to compromise open. When Edward I forced the clergy to choose between the immunity claimed in the bull and their right to protection at common law, they had no alternative but surrender to the Crown. Coercion of this kind was not a propitious beginning for a great constitutional experiment. The clergy remained in a state of uneasy wakefulness and throughout the next forty years they adopted an attitude of ingenious obstruction to the new parliamentary system. If they could not directly defy the authority of royal writs, at least they were able to safeguard the rights of their order by an insistence upon technical detail, which often brought parliamentary business, so far as it concerned them, to a standstill. Soon the most useful methods of obstruction were found to be objections to the form of summons and revival of the ancient dispute between the provinces of Canterbury and York. It is necessary to consider briefly how each of these methods was applied, in order to understand the ultimate withdrawal of the lower clergy from Parliament.

Edward III asserted in 1341 that the proctors of the clergy were bound to attend at Parliaments and councils,[1] but the insincerity of the statement is proved by the fact that in the same year the special royal letter enjoining attendance ceased to be issued. This letter is important for our purposes, as its issue and the resistance it provoked throw light on the whole problem of the clergy in Parliament.[2] It first appeared in 1282, as a royal writ to the archbishops, commanding them to cause their prelates and the proctors of chapters to come before the king or his commissioners in provincial assemblies at Northampton and at York.[3] At Northampton the southern clergy refused to answer the royal commissioners, chiefly because many were absent, owing to

---

[1] *Supra*, p. 126, n. 6.

[2] Its history has been traced by J. Armitage Robinson in " The Convocation of Canterbury : its Early History " (*Church Quarterly Review*, Vol. LXXXI, pp. 81 *seq.*

[3] *Select Charters*, p. 459 : " mandamus . . . venire faciatis coram nobis."

the improper method of summons (*modo debito non vocati*). It was, therefore, necessary for archbishop Peckham to summon a second assembly to meet in London.[1] Edward I learnt his lesson and did not again use the objectionable form *mandamus . . . venire faciatis*. In 1294 he summoned for the first time all the clergy of the realm to one assembly; writs were issued to the archbishops and bishops with a clause *vocantes prius*, enjoining the attendance of archdeacons and proctors of chapters and dioceses.[2] The form of citation was evidently deemed unsatisfactory and in 1295 the *premunientes* clause was devised and attached to parliamentary writs sent to the prelates. It was used again by Edward I in 1296, 1300, 1305 and (January) 1307, and in the writs for Edward II's Parliaments of 1307, 1309 and 1311.[3]

We have no record of protests either against the summons of the lower clergy to Parliament or against the *premunientes* formula. The attitude of the bishops may, perhaps, be inferred from a note preserved in the register of bishop Giffard of Worcester.[4] It is undated, but from internal evidence it obviously relates to a discussion of the still novel *premunientes* clause, with reference to the writs issued for the Parliament of March 1300.[5] It runs as follows :

[1] Peckham, *Epistolae* (*Rolls Series*), II, 508 *seq*.

[2] *Select Charters*, p. 476. The ecclesiastical assembly was summoned for September 21 ; the lay commons were summoned to Parliament on November 12 in the same year.

[3] *Parl. Writs*, II, ii, pp. 1, 24, Appendix, p. 37. Cf. *Rot. Parl.* I, 189-91, for a long list of proctors attending the Parliament of Carlisle (1307) ; the names of the proctors for the diocese of Carlisle are recorded for the Parliament of April 1309 (Halton's Register, ed. W. N. Thompson and T. F. Tout (*Cant. and York Soc.*), 1913, I, 314).

[4] Giffard's Register, on a slip attached to f. 442. On f. 441ᵛ there is a copy of agenda for the council, headed : " Tractatus habendus coram domino episcopo et suis cons' apud Hertl' (Hartlebury, Worc.) anno xxxiii (1300-01).' My thanks are due to the late Professor A. E. Levett for calling my attention to this passage, which is not reproduced in the published calendar of the register. She suggested that it may be a rough minute of a discussion held in the bishop's council.

[5] Bishop Giffard died in 1302 ; the only Parliaments summoned with the *premunientes* clause before that date were those of 1295, 1296 and 1300. The minute is obviously associated with the agenda for the council at Hartlebury, held in the bishop's thirty-third year of office, that is, in 1300-01, as he had been granted the temporalities of the see in June 1268.

" As to the seventh article, concerning proctors to be sent to the Parliament of the king, let the lord (bishop), by reason of his barony, send there his essoiner and proxy, if it be necessary, and . . . let the official cause the royal writ to be explained to the prior and chapter, the archdeacons and the clergy, but let him not persuade anyone to go to London." [1]

The intention of this laconic order is clear enough. The bishop and his council were prepared to obey the letter of the royal command, but, beyond an official premonishment, they would take no steps to see that it was carried out.

The troubles of Edward II's reign soon had an effect on the whole position and brought about a revival of the provincial letter and *mandamus* of 1282. A conflict between Crown and clergy was inevitable. On the one hand, the king's need for money led him to press hard for ecclesiastical subsidies ; on the other, the clergy had the strongest motive for using tactics of obstruction, which the struggle over Gaveston and the Ordinances gave them time to develop. The first irregularity and the first protest occurred in connection with the prorogued Parliament of 1311. Parliament, summoned in the usual way, had sat in London from August 8 to October 9, when it was prorogued to November 5.[2] Writs without the *premunientes* clause were issued to the bishops, ordering them to reassemble on the appointed day.[3] On October 8 archbishop Winchelsey was required (*mandamus . . . quod premuniatis*) to summon the clerical proctors to come on November 18, with power of consent only, instead of the normal powers *ad faciendum et consentiendum*.[4] There is no evidence to show that Winchelsey acted on this order and he seems to have made an effective protest at once. Little more than a fortnight later (October 27) the king sent him an apology for the wording of the writ, promising that any prejudice contained therein should be corrected in Parliament ;

---

[1] " Item, ad septimum articulum de procuratoribus mittendis ad Parliamentum regis, quod dominus (episcopus), racione baronie sue mittat excusatorem ibidem et procuratorem, si necesse fuerit, et quod . . . officialis breve regium priori et capitulo archidiaconis et clero faciat exponi, sed neminem ad eundum London. inducat."

[2] *Parl. Writs*, II, ii, 44-57 ; Appendix, pp. 37-9, 41.

[3] *Durham Register (Rolls Series)*, I, 108-10. The lay commons were ordered to meet on November 12.

[4] *Parl. Writs*, II, ii, 57 *seq.*

he also allowed him to alter the date of summons to December 2.[1]

It is not easy to be sure what lay behind the revival of the older formula. The Ordinances and the exile of Gaveston were the chief business of the Parliament of 1311. The Ordainers had been given power up to September 29 and Parliament had been summoned to hear and to consent to what they had ordained —" quod enim omnes tangit ab omnibus debet approbari." [2] Edward II had been reluctant to face Parliament, going on pilgrimage to Canterbury to avoid it, but he was forced to agree to the publication of the Ordinances before the end of September.[3] His need of money probably explains why Parliament was not dissolved, but merely prorogued. By the Ordinances he had lost the *Nova Custuma* and he had been granted no parliamentary subsidy since 1309. In the early summer of 1311 the clergy had been asked to give a shilling in the mark, to be levied on their spiritualities, for the expenses of the Scottish war.[4] York Convocation refused ; [5] the Canterbury clergy seem to have granted a penny in the mark,[6] though no trace of receipts has been found.[7] We may suppose that the king resolved to exact in Parliament at least the shilling in the mark, which had been demanded in May and that the clergy, already burdened by papal tenths, were prepared to resist. A note on proctorial letters for the Parliament of 1311, issued by the prior and chapter of Worcester, runs as follows : " . . . That these proxies were not delivered, because the clergy is not bound to obey the

[1] R. Brady, *Continuation of the Complete History of England*, II, 111. The archbishop's amended letter is printed by Wake, *op. cit.*, Appendix, p. 34. Cf. Reynolds' Register (Worcester), ed. R. A. Wilson (*Worc. Hist. Soc.*), 1927, p. 28 ; and Register of Simon de Gandavo (Salisbury), ed. C. T. Flower and M. C. B. Dawes (*Cant. and York Soc.*), 1934, Vol. I, 410.

[2] *Vita Edwardi II* in *Chronicles of Edward I and Edward II*, Vol. II (*Rolls Series*), p. 170.

[3] They were published at St. Paul's on September 27 and again on October 5; on October 11 the great seal was affixed to them, and they were despatched to all the counties of England. *De Antiquis Legibus Liber*, Appendix, p. 251 (*Camden Soc.*) ; *Annales Paulini* in *Chronicles of Edward I and Edward II*, Vol. I, p. 270 (*Rolls Series*).

[4] *Cal. Pat. Rolls, 1307-13*, 1311, p. 341.

[5] Greenfield's Register (York), ed. A. Hamilton-Thomson (*Surtees Soc.*), I, 137-8 ; *Historical Letters and Papers from Northern Registers (Rolls Series*), pp. 210-11 ; Durham Register, I, 6-7.

[6] Register of Simon de Gandavo, Vol. I, 429 *seq.*

[7] W. E. Lunt, *Clerical Tenths Levied in England* (*Haskins Anniversary Essays*), Boston and New York, 1929, p. 179, n. 169.

king's call, without the command of the archbishop."[1] This
is the first clear sign of a policy of obstruction and, perhaps, it
is significant that it should come from Worcester. Walter
Reynolds, bishop of Worcester, was virtually Chancellor at the
time ;[2] it may have been his suggestion that the *mandamus*
form should be revived, in order that the clergy should attend
in force to grant a subsidy. No doubt the design, whether his
or another's, was understood in his own diocese. At all events,
the danger of allowing a precedent for indirect royal coercion to
be established was understood by the clergy as well as by their
archbishop.

Winchelsey was strong enough to secure both a modification
of the original mandate and a promise that the words of prejudice
should be corrected in Parliament. Though the situation changed
altogether when he was succeeded in 1313 by the time-server
Reynolds, his protest set an example which was followed by the
clergy throughout the whole middle period of the reign. During
this time disputes over the form of parliamentary summons were
almost continuous and it will be useful to discuss them in some
detail. It may be noted at the outset that the clergy were not
united in a common policy of resistance ; three parties may
be distinguished among them, parties which overlap and correspond roughly to the groupings of the magnates. In the first
place, Reynolds' party consisted of Caesarian prelates and clerks ;
following the lead of men in power at the court, they were indifferent to constitutional forms and ready to acquiesce in a policy
of heavy taxation. Opposed to them were the great mass of the
lower clergy, determined to defend their order against spoliation.
They seem to have hoped for greater financial independence,
if their assemblies were cut loose from Parliament ; though they
held firmly to the doctrine of consent, they took only the nar-
rowest view of the consenting body and failed to recognise
that the smaller the assembly, the easier it was to coerce it.
Nothing is known of their leaders, but we may guess that direction came from the university men, doctors and masters, whose
names and degrees appear frequently on proctorial returns.

---

[1] Cited by Wake, *op. cit.*, p. 260, from the margin of the Great Register of
the prior and chapter of Worcester, f. 50.
[2] Tout, *Place of Edward II in English History*, M.U.P., 1914, p. 324 ;
Conway Davies, *Baronial Opposition under Edward II*, pp. 118-19.

Between these extremes stood a middle party, which seems to have been led by Stapeldon of Exeter, with a certain backing from Cobham of Worcester and Simon of Ghent, bishop of Salisbury. They understood the value of constitutional forms and, though they protested against irregularities either in letters of summons, or in the composition of Parliament and Convocation, they were not merely obstructive, and freely admitted the paramount importance of Parliament.

The provincial letter, that is, the *mandamus* embodied in a covering order from the archbishops, was nothing more than a whip, issued to secure full attendance of the clergy for purposes of taxation. It appeared again in 1314, when a Parliament, summoned for April 21, was prorogued because of the war with Scotland.[1] Royal writs were sent to the archbishops, requiring them to summon the clergy to assemblies at Westminster and at York ; the bishops also received letters with the *premunientes* clause.[2] The writs explained that the presence of the clergy was required in order that they should treat with royal commissioners about a competent aid. These meetings were certainly not Parliaments, as they were both provincial and entirely ecclesiastical, but they were also not true Convocations, since abbots and priors were not summoned in the ordinary way. We have knowledge only of what happened in the southern province. The Canterbury clergy met and issued eight *rationes* against the form of summons.[3] They protested against the action taken by the Crown and reminded the archbishop that in Winchelsey's time (1311) it had been agreed in Convocation that a summons of this kind was an unprecedented injury to the Church. The words *venire faciatis* were regarded as particularly offensive. It was also urged that the metropolitan had only a limited jurisdiction and that, if this order were obeyed, both bishops and clergy would suffer ; that the clergy were not wont to be summoned to an exempt place (Westminster) ; and that the omission of abbots and priors was a threat to the unity of the Church, the more serious because those abbots who had been summoned did not bear with them the consent of their convents and, therefore, were unable to bind them. For all these reasons the clergy prayed for the revocation of the writ. That the protest

[1] *Parl. Writs*, II, ii, 121. [2] *Ibid.* I, ii, 122-3 ; Wilkins, II, 442.
[3] Wilkins, II, 442-3 (May 20, 1314).

was effective is proved by the issue of a summons in the normal form for a Convocation at St. Paul's in the following July.[1] The stand made by the clergy in 1314 shows that Winchelsey's protest of 1311 had general support.

However, neither the king nor the archbishop was prepared to make a permanent surrender and the clergy were summoned to York (September 9, 1314) under the double form, *premunientes* and *venire faciatis*.[2] There is no record of any protest. It was the period of Lancastrian ascendancy and for a time Lancaster and archbishop Reynolds seem to have presided over the council.[3] They may have been responsible for another (the fourth) irregular summons of the clergy to the Parliament held in January 1315.[4] As in the previous autumn, the clergy were cited both through their bishops, under the *premunientes* clause, and through the archbishops, under *venire faciatis*. That the procedure was deeply resented is made plain by entries in the registers of Exeter and Salisbury and by a formal protest put forward by the clergy in Parliament. The bishop of Salisbury, Simon of Ghent, wrote to Reynolds that the larger and wiser part of his clergy dreaded the mandate, as prejudicial to himself and to them ; from fear, he made a return, saving all ecclesiastical liberties.[5] In the Exeter register it is recorded that the bishop of that diocese alone refused to make a return.[6] Neither register mentions any specific reason for objecting to the writ. As Simon of Salisbury, pleading illness, was absent from Parliament,[7] Stapeldon of Exeter probably acted as the leader of resistance. The protest offered to the archbishop by the clergy is entered in his register.[8] It concentrated upon two points raised in the *rationes* of 1314. The clergy had been summoned to a secular court (Parliament), which *tam racione fori quam eciam loci* was against the canons ; no

[1] Wilkins, II, 444-5, for July 1314.   [2] Greenfield's Register, I, 154.
[3] Conway Davies, *op. cit.*, p. 397.
[4] *Parl. Writs*, II, ii, 136-8 ; Greenfield's Register, I, 154.
[5] Register of Sim. de Gandavo, Vol. I, p. 550-1 ; Stapeldon's Register (Exeter), ed. F. C. Hingeston-Randolph, Exeter, 1892, p. 122.
[6] " Memorandum quod nullum missum fuit certificatorium per episcopum Exoniensem." Then follows the Salisbury return, after which is written : " Omnes, vero, alii episcopi certificarunt quod executi sunt mandatum," *ibid.*, p. 121.
[7] Register of Sim de Gandavo, pp. 551-2.
[8] Stapeldon's Register, p. 122. The protest was made " per clerum coram domino archiepiscopo et suffraganeis suis," at the house of the Carmelites on March 3, 1315.

abbots nor priors (except from cathedrals) had been summoned, which was a danger to the unity of the Church. The clergy stated expressly that they would not be able to obey mandates of this kind in future, without injury to ecclesiastical liberties and peril to their estate.[1] The protest was apparently directed against the archbishop ; by summoning a part of the clergy to Parliament, as if to a provincial council, he was extending his powers unlawfully. As supply was not refused, the grievance was probably deemed to be primarily ecclesiastical ; though conditions for the grant were laid down, they contained no reference to the form of summons.[2] It may be that Stapeldon, supported on the bench only by the absentee bishop of Salisbury, was able to direct the protest of the clergy, but was not strong enough to insist upon a new summons. The fact that a tenth was granted is proof that irregularities of summons or of composition were not thought sufficient to invalidate the whole procedure. The protest was plainly a failure, as not even a promise of amendment had been secured.

In the following year the clergy were summoned to the Parliament of Lincoln (January 1316), by double writs from the archbishops and bishops ; the archbishop did not quote the royal mandate in his letter, perhaps seeking to mollify his critics, perhaps exalting his own authority.[3] Owing to illness, he was not at Lincoln, and in his absence the constitutional party seems to have prevailed. In an angry letter, sent out on March 3, he summoned the clergy to St. Paul's on April 28, explaining how proceedings in Parliament had been vitiated by the number of absentees and by the failure of the bishop of London to make proper returns. Those present at Lincoln had agreed to a subsidy, on condition that the absent should be summoned by the archbishops *ad tractandum et consentiendum* . . . *in loco debito*.[4] We know from other sources that parlia-

---

[1] Stapeldon's Register, *loc. cit. ; Parl. Writs*, II, ii, 139. The protest is also entered in Mortival's Register (Salisbury MS.), liber II, f. 121ᵛ, under the year 1321.
[2] Swinfield's Register (Hereford), ed. W. W. Capes (*Cant. and York Soc.*), pp. 497-8 ; Wilkins, II, p. 451.
[3] *Parl. Writs*, II, ii, 152, 154 ; Wake, *op. cit.*, Appendix, p. 41.
[4] Wilkins, II, 456 ; Wake, *op. cit.*, Appendix, pp. 42-3. In the writ issued by the bishop of London the failure at Lincoln is glossed over, and it is merely stated that, owing to the archbishop's illness, the summons to Lincoln had been changed to St. Paul's (Mortival's Register, liber II, ff. 17ᵛ-18ᵛ).

mentary business had at first been delayed by the absence of Lancaster and others ; on February 4 it was decided to proceed with petitions without them.[1] The bishops of Salisbury and Exeter were both appointed auditors and on the following day the clergy were promised that their petitions should receive consideration.[2] On February 7 the bishops of Salisbury, Exeter, Norwich and Chichester were sworn of the king's Council. Lancaster arrived a few days later (February 12). On February 16 royal writs were issued to the archbishops, ordering the summons of provincial Convocations to ratify the grant made in Parliament.[3] They were issued on a date between certain conferences held to discuss supply and the Scottish war (February 13-14), and the grant of an aid by the laity (February 20) made after Lancaster's ascendancy in the council had been secured (February 17). The decision to summon the Convocations was probably taken during the conferences and it seems to indicate the influence of some one independent alike of the king's party and of Lancaster. The evidence points to Stapeldon. Though sworn of the council on February 8, his name is absent from the list of councillors appointed after the bargain with Lancaster, though the other bishops retained their places. Stapeldon's exclusion was probably due to some policy adopted during the session, and it may well have been support of the clergy in their stiffness over supply and insistence on special Convocations. The grudge against him must have grown when it was found that two sessions of Canterbury Convocation and four of York were necessary before grants were finally made in October and November, 1316.[4]

In 1318 and 1319 the clergy were summoned to the Parlia-

[1] *Rot. Parl.*, I, 350*b seq.* Cf. Conway Davies, *op. cit.*, pp. 408 *seq.*, for the outline of events.

[2] These petitions were the basis of the *Articuli Cleri*, published November 24, 1316. Cf. Mortival's Register, *op. cit.*, liber II, ff. 73ᵛ-7, where the articles are headed : " Carta regis super responsionibus suis factis ad gravamina ecclesie Anglicane illata porrecta in Parliamento Linc' per prelatos."

[3] Wilkins, II, 456 ; Wake, *op. cit.*, Appendix, p. 42.

[4] Canterbury Convocation met on April 28 and on October 11, 1316 (Wilkins, II, 456-7, 458). A half or a third was asked for, but the *communitas cleri* refused to grant more than a tenth (*Vita Edwardi II*, pp. 225-6). York Convocation was summoned for April 16, June 11, October 25, and November 23, 1316 ; on the last day a tenth was granted (Wilkins, II, 462 ; *Records of Northern Convocations*, pp. 66-8).

ments of York by the *premunientes* clause only,[1] showing that the protest of 1316 was for a time effective. Yet in 1318 supply was refused both by the northern and by the southern provinces. The Canterbury clergy pleaded the absence of their archbishop and the fact that they could act only in the common assembly of their province.[2] The clergy of York declared that no grant could be made *absque convocatione prelatorum et cleri*.[3] It was necessary to hold another series of Convocations. Canterbury refused to grant a tenth until the Pope gave leave [4] and in the north nothing was done in two Convocations, though a tenth was finally granted in the second Parliament of York.[5] In these years the issue was plainly not the form of summons, but taxation itself. At the same time the obstructive shifting of the venue from Parliament to Convocation and, in the north, from Convocation back again to Parliament, raised the whole question of the place where the clergy ought to grant supply. In the writs summoning bishops to the two Parliaments of 1320 the *premunientes* clause was omitted for the first time since 1309.[6] The obvious reason for omission was that no requests were made for supply, but perhaps we may also catch a reflection of official disgust with the exasperating tactics of delay adopted by the proctors. Whether they wished to attend or not, to ignore them was a definite indication that their place in Parliament was not yet firmly established and, at least for the bishops, the whole question was thus pushed firmly into the foreground.

The Parliament of 1321 was summoned when the Marchers were already in arms. In the writs to the bishops the *premunientes* clause reappeared ; they were accompanied by the provincial letter in which the archbishop paraphrased the royal mandate, as he had done in 1316.[7] Mortival of Salisbury drafted his return in the exact form used by his predecessor in 1315 ; it is entered in his register with a note, dated July 12, 1321, that it

---

[1] *Parl. Writs*, II, ii, 182, 197.
[2] *Ibid.*, p. 196. Cf. a royal letter to St. Augustine's, Canterbury, Wilkins, II, 485.
[3] *Ibid. ; Records of Northern Convocations*, pp. 68-9.
[4] 1319, Gravesend's Register (London), ed. R. C. Fowler (*Cant. and York Soc.*), pp. 203-4, 207-9. Cf. *Annales Paulini*, p. 286, for an account of the debate.
[5] *Records of Northern Convocations*, p. 70 ; Wilkins, II, 485-6.
[6] *Parl. Writs*, II, ii, 215, 219. For 1309 see *ibid.*, p. 40.
[7] Wilkins, II, 507-8. I have not found a similar provincial letter from York.

was not delivered to the archbishop, because the mandate seemed prejudicial and because other bishops did not wish to make returns.[1] Three days later Parliament met and we may suppose that the attendance of proctors was scanty. It may have been partly on this account that the Despensers later pleaded that they were condemned *absque clero*.[2] It is also possible that the absence of the clergy and the discontent of certain prelates gave rise to Edward II's curious plan of playing off the Convocation of Canterbury against Parliament in December 1321,[3] in order to revoke the judgement against the Despensers. Though he seems to have secured the formal declaration that he sought, there is ample evidence to show that both the clergy and some of the prelates explicitly referred the decision back to Parliament.

This attempt to use Canterbury Convocation for an entirely secular purpose demonstrated the chaos into which the whole conception of the political function of the clergy had fallen. In the same year the irregular provincial assemblies summoned by Lancaster in the North showed open contempt for the idea of a royal Parliament of estates.[4] It is impossible to imagine that the danger as well as the inconvenience of the situation escaped the notice of the king's officials and councillors. The issue was greater than that raised by the disputes with the clergy, since it involved, not only the technical questions of the form of writs and the place where ecclesiastical taxes should be granted, but also the composition and powers of Parliament itself. When Parliament met at York (May 1322), after the royalist victory at Boroughbridge, a solution was sought for in the legislation known as the statute of York. It affirmed that " matters which are to be established for the estate of our lord the king and of

---

[1] " Datum London. ii Idus Julii, anno predicto (1321). Hoc certificatorum non fuit . . . archepiscopo liberatum, eo quod mandatum predictum preiudiciale ut premittitur videbatur, et alii episcopi ad mandatum predictum certificare noluerunt," Mortival's Register, liber II, f. 121ᵛ. Armitage Robinson wrote : " we hear of no protest on the part of the clergy," *op. cit.*, p. 123.
[2] *Chron. Bridlington* in *Chronicles of Edward I and Edward II*, Vol. II (*Rolls Series*), p. 70. Later Stapeldon (Register, p. 443) stated that he was not present when judgement was given ; he may have withdrawn for reasons of policy.
[3] *Infra*, pp. 168-70, where this assembly is fully discussed.
[4] *Infra*, p. 163.

his heirs, and for the estate of the realm and of the people, shall be treated, accorded and established in Parliaments, by our lord the king and by the assent of the prelates, earls and barons and the commonalty of the realm." [1] The statute of York was thus designed to integrate the estates of the realm in Parliament. Its ambiguous phrasing was probably deliberate. Not only were the special grievances of the clergy ignored, but it was not even clear whether grants of supply were among the " matters to be established," or if the clerical proctors were an integral part of the " commonalty of the realm."

If this interpretation of the statute of York be adopted, it becomes possible to understand why the clamour of clerical complaint died away soon after 1322, though the objectionable provincial letter contined to be used until 1341.[2] The last recorded protest was made, not in Parliament, but in the Convocation of Lincoln, summoned to grant supply in January 1323.[3] Archbishop Reynolds convoked the assembly at the royal command and Edward himself had ordered about fifty abbots to appear in person at Lincoln.[4] A Peterborough chartulary records the royal summons with the comment " mirabile in oculis audiencium et videncium." [5] It was, perhaps, the abbots who engineered the petitions of the lower clergy, in which they repeated the protest of 1314 and declared that they were not wont to be convoked by royal authority. The purpose of the session was to secure a grant of supply, already discussed both at the Parliament of York [6] and at a council of prelates.[7] The clergy now flatly refused to make a grant, resisted the justices and magnates sent to bully or to entreat them and included in their protest a long statement of ecclesiastical grievances.[8] Once again, not the constitutional, but the financial

---

[1] *Statutes of the Realm*, I, p. 189. The whole problem of the interpretation of the statute will be discussed in Chapter VIII.

[2] It was used in 1322 for the Parliament of York, Wilkins, II, 516.

[3] *Ibid.* II, 517-19. [4] *Parl. Writs*, II, ii, 281-2.

[5] Cotton MS., Vespasian E, 21, f. 50, quoted by Armitage Robinson, *op. cit.*, p. 124.

[6] Wilkins, II, 515-16. Apparently the prelates and clergy at York promised a grant.

[7] Mortival's Register, liber II, f. 135ᵛ. The *congregacio prelatorum* was summoned for June 9.

[8] Lincoln, January 13, 1323 (*Hist. Roffensis* ; *Anglia Sacra*, I, 362-3).

side of their grudge against authority seems uppermost. There is no longer any record of episcopal support ; on the question of writs and returns the registers of Salisbury and Exeter are suddenly silent. In short, the long quarrel over the form of summons, which had come to a head in 1321 and 1322, died away in an ambiguous compromise.

Thus the practice was established that the clergy should be summoned to Parliament by the *premunientes* clause [1] and by the provincial letter. The king and the archbishop gained little by their victory. They failed either to compel attendance or to vest an exclusive right of consent to ecclesiastical taxation in the clergy in Parliament. The historical interest of the *venire faciatis* writ and the provincial letter lies, not so much in their effect, as in the period during which they were employed. They serve to define the time when the king sincerely wished the clergy to attend Parliament, that is, experimentally in 1283 and later, when the *premunientes* clause was found insufficient, almost continuously from 1311 to 1341. By the same means we may also define the period of lively controversy over the right of summons and the form in which it should be expressed, a period which can hardly be extended beyond the years 1311 and 1322. If it be supposed that the *Modus* has any bearing on the dispute, we must look for its origin between these dates.

Before reaching even a tentative conclusion as to the relation between the *Modus* and the form of ecclesiastical summons, we must turn to the resistance of the clergy to extra-provincial citations, the other method of obstruction, which grew up about the same time and lasted for over ten years longer. The perennial dispute between the two archbishops over the primacy made it easy to evolve obstruction of this kind. In the north Lanfranc's settlement of 1072 had never been accepted as final and quarrels invariably broke out when one archbishop attempted to erect his cross in the province of the other.[2] As long as the clergy

---

[1] It was omitted in the summons of bishops to Ripon for November 14, 1322 (*Parl. Writs*, II, ii, 261), but the return of Halton of Carlisle (Register, II, p. 232) shows that this assembly was not a Parliament, but a great council.

[2] For examples of the stiff attitude of archbishops Peckham and Winchelsey, see Peckham, *Epistolae*, III, 869-70, 893-4, 906-7, 908, 945-6 ; and *Lit. Cant.*, I, 26-7, 30-1, 32-3, for the years 1299, 1306 and 1307 or 1309.

met in separate assemblies, there was no reason why the dispute should affect them, but once prelates, dignitaries and proctors were summoned to Parliaments, provincial ill-feeling was bound to be aroused. The Scottish war led naturally to sessions of Parliament at York and thus arose a new source of annoyance to the richer and more influential clergy of the south. Yet the sense of injury cannot have been altogether spontaneous, as it grew up slowly to support or even to replace the earlier protests against irregular summons. The sequence of events suggests that the dispute between the archbishops offered to the clergy an opportunity to manufacture a case against the parliamentary attendance, which they already disliked.

No open objection was raised to the summons to the Parliament of York in September 1314, though it followed hard on the *rationes* presented by the Canterbury clergy in the previous May.[1] There is ample evidence of friction between the archbishops, in spite of the king's attempt to prevent it.[2] Apparently an agreement was reached, *cum cleri consensu*, but it was purely temporary, arranged to cover the attendance of archbishop Reynolds, as Chancellor.[3] In the following year archbishop Greenfield visited Gloucester and all who showed reverence to him on his progress with cross erect were excommunicated by the bishop of Worcester, at Reynolds' command.[4] The quarrel was given notoriety and a certain political tinge by the countenance given to Greenfield by his cousin, John Giffard of Brimpsfield, and other Lancastrian magnates in the neighbourhood.[5] That the repercussion of these quarrels on Parliament was well understood is shown by a letter from Edward II to Reynolds, sent before the session of the second Parliament at York (Michaelmas 1318).[6] The king urged Reynolds to attend in

---

[1] *Supra*, pp. 133-4.
[2] Greenfield's Register, I, 98-100, August 31, 1314. The archbishop warned the dean and chapter of York that they must forbid any reverence to the archbishop of Canterbury, while on procession, threatening both excommunication and interdict. Cf. *Cal. Cl. Rolls*, 1313-18, p. 194 ; Wilkins, II, 448.
[3] Trokelowe, *Annales (Rolls Series)*, p. 88.
[4] Greenfield's Register, I, 273 *seq.* Further disputes broke out when archbishop Melton returned from Avignon through London in 1317, *Annales Paulini*, p. 281 ; Rymer, II, Part I, 339.
[5] Greenfield's Register, I, 278.
[6] *Lit. Cant.* I, 38-40. The chapter of Canterbury should be warned to send some one to Torksey to act on their behalf.

person and to arrange for a halt at Torksey on his way north, in order that he might reach an agreement, concerning cross-bearing in procession, with the archbishop and chapter of York. Reynolds had intended to go to York—he said so in a letter to Prior Eastry, dated September 16 [1]—but he must have changed his mind, as his absence was afterwards explicitly commented on in royal writs.[2] It may be that the Torksey conference broke down and that Reynolds took fright, fearing to injure his dignity by entering the northern province. We have no record of his presence at the York Parliaments of 1319 and 1320 and it probably required the stirring news of Boroughbridge and Pontefract to draw him north to the restoration Parliament of May 1322.[3] No doubt it was the inconvenience of his absence which led to another attempt at a permanent settlement of the dispute, in so far as it concerned parliamentary attendance.

Some time in 1322 an agreement was certainly reached, though no first-hand record of it has yet been found. The terms of settlement are indicated in a letter written by Edward III in 1330, in which he stated that, in a Parliament held at York by his father, on the advice of the prelates and magnates of the realm, it was ordained that either archbishop might attend, without let or hindrance, Parliaments or councils held in the province of the other.[4] In proof of this decree he vouched the *memoranda cancellariae* of Edward II.[5] The disappearance of this document and the absence of all reference to it in the archbishops' registers suggests that it was not accepted by the chapters of Canterbury and York. Earlier references to the agreement occur in 1325, when the appointment of archbishop Melton as Treasurer (July 3) raised the whole question of the reverence due to him in the south. Archbishop Reynolds, even before the appointment

---

[1] *Lit. Cant.* I, 38.

[2] *Parl. Writs*, II, ii, 196. Conway Davies, p. 450, states that Reynolds was present, but this seems to be a misinterpretation of a list of magnates on the Parliament roll, Cole, *Documents*, p. 11.

[3] His writ ordering the summons of Convocation is dated *Acum* (Acomb) near York, May 4, 1322, *Parl. Writs*, II, ii, 259.

[4] *Report on the Dignity of a Peer*, IV, 399-400 ; Edward III to the archbishop of Canterbury, November 28, 1330. Another reference to the agreement reached under Edward II occurs in a royal letter, dated August 18, 1332, *ibid.*, p. 415.

[5] *Ibid.*, " . . . nobis per memoranda cancellariae dicti patris nostri satis constat . . ."

was made, had issued the usual threats of excommunication ; [1] he maintained, perhaps in Parliament, that no archbishop of York had ever erected his cross in the south, unless supported by armed magnates (as in 1315), or lately (*nunc*) in Parliament, lest private quarrels should impede public business.[2] The admission with regard to Parliament is new and significant.[3] In a mandate issued to protect his new Treasurer, Edward II reminded Reynolds that lately in Parliament at York, on the advice of the magnates, it had been determined that the archbishop of York should not impede him in carrying his cross, as he had come north by royal command ; a like protection had been promised to the archbishop of York, coming south for the same reason.[4] The last full Parliament at York was that of May 1322, and it seems probable that the agreement was then reached.[5] The date is important, as it helps to limit the brief period during which a working compromise between the archbishops was adopted.

The opposition of the lower clergy followed the same general lines. In 1318 the southern proctors suddenly seem to have realised the tactical advantage offered by the quarrel between the archbishops. On this occasion the provincial letter had not been issued, so they were forced to shift their ground to a new obstructive position. They refused to make a grant, except before their archbishop and within their own province.[6] Put

---

[1] Wilkins, II, 525, June 19, 1325, probably in connection with attendance at Parliament (June 25). Cf. Eastry's letter, *Lit. Cant.* I, 143-4, and a parliamentary petition from the archbishop and bishops of Canterbury, *Rot. Parl.* I, 418.

[2] *Vita Edwardii II*, p. 284. Cf. *Hist. Roffensis* (*Anglia Sacra*, I, 365), where there is a description of the bishop's indignation that the excommunication of Melton was a mere formality, since he was seen in Parliament speaking with Reynolds himself.

[3] Cf. Henry of Blaneforde's reference to *pax simulata* between the archbishops, *Chron.* (*Rolls Series*), *sub anno* 1323, p. 142.

[4] *Parl. Writs*, II, ii, Appendix, pp, 274-5.

[5] Another Parliament, without the lower clergy, met at York in November 1322, but, as archbishop Reynolds and the greater part of the southern prelates were absent, it seems very unlikely that an agreement was then reached (*Parl. Writs*, II, ii, 264 *seq.*). Alternatively, if the matter had been settled without him, Reynolds would certainly have used this as an argument, instead of admitting that some convention existed which allowed the northern archbishop to come to Parliament without challenge. Further, the royal order addressed to the archbishop of York, forbidding interference with Reynolds on his way to the York Parliament in November, seems to reflect a previous agreement (*Cal. Cl. Rolls*, p. 684, November 4, 1322).

[6] *Supra*, p. 137.

in this way, the refusal was almost tantamount to a claim that they had the right to secede from Parliament altogether. The same implication may be drawn from the archbishop's statement that he was unable to put through a grant of a subsidy without the convocation of the prelates and clergy of his province.[1] The southern clergy do not seem to have attended the Parliament of York in 1319 and the *premunientes* clause was omitted in the parliamentary summons to York in 1320.[2] When the clergy were again summoned to York in 1322 the southern proctors refused to transact any business, because the majority were absent and those present had not power to bind them. The bishops agreed to grant the king five pence in the mark, but it was necessary to summon Convocation, the archbishop of Canterbury admitting that the absent proctors could not be compelled to attend outside their territory and that the mandates given to them did not appear sufficient.[3] All this story is told in the archbishop's writ of summons and it is put in a way which suggests a certain sympathy with clerical obstruction. Edward II seems to have acquiesced in the implicit denial of his right and he did not attach the *premunientes* clause to the writs for the November Parliament at York (1322), though he was anxious for a subsidy from the clergy.[4] Instead, he requested the archbishops to sum-

---

[1] This statement is preserved in the archbishop's writ summoning Convocation to York, in which he reminded the bishop of Durham that he had said in Parliament " absque convocatione prelatorum et cleri nostrarum civitatis, diocesis et provinciae non poterit adimpleri " (Wilkins, II, 485 ; *Northern Convocations*, p. 69).

[2] Wilkins, II, 494-5.

[3] Wake, *op. cit.*, Appendix, pp. 47-8, from the Lincoln Register. " Cumque inter praesentes Tractatus super hoc habitus extitisset, ex parte Cleri extitit Allegatum quod cum Clerus quorundam Dioecesium, tunc abesset, a quo praesentes praedicti discrepare minime intendebant, circa hoc Responsum dare per se non valebant, praesertim cum ijdem Absentes reputari non potuissent in loco ipso, aut dici de jure Contumaces . . . ." The archbishop, on the advice of the prelates, decided to summon Convocation, " . . . quia magna pars Cleri a loco Tractatus tunc abfuit, ad quem venire tanquam extra suum Territorium, Provinciam, viz. Cantuar., compelli minime potuit de Jure, Mandataque Procuratoribus Cleri tunc praesentibus facta ad Actum de quo Agebatur sufficere minime videbantur . . . ." The grant of five pence in the mark was agreed to by Canterbury Convocation at London in June 1322 (Winchester Register of Rigaud de Asserio, ed. F. J. Baigent (*Hants Rec. Soc.*), pp. 488-90). Cf. Mortival's Register, liber II, f. 135^v-136^v, where the bishop's return is entered, stating that in a diocesan assembly he had secured the consent of all his clergy, except five, whose names he forwarded.

[4] *Parl. Writs*, II, ii, 261.

mon their Convocations, in order that a competent aid should be granted speedily.[1] Both provinces gave emphatic refusals, Canterbury after a long debate in which many grievances were aired.[2] After these failures the matter of ecclesiastical taxation was dropped for the rest of the reign.

In the first decade of Edward III's reign the king's pressing need of money and the unwillingness of the clergy to help him revived the obstruction of the previous reign. Confusion was increased by pressure of northern business, which made necessary a series of Parliaments (five) at York. The nuisance of delay and evasion became intolerable and the king was gradually forced to abandon his right to summon the clergy to Parliament. To understand how this came about attention must be turned, in the first place, to protests against the summons *extra provinciam* and, secondly, to the way in which the king was slowly brought to accept the procedure preferred by the clergy.

Edward III's first request for supply was brought before a great council at Lincoln (September 15, 1327), to which the clergy had been summoned by both forms of writ.[3] The attendance was so poor that no grant could be made. The few northern clergy maintained that they were not bound to go, or to make answer outside their province ; their archbishop, thinking the plea legitimate, with some difficulty won leave from the king and council to refer the grant to York Convocation.[4] This is the last record we have of the attendance of northern proctors as a body, at Parliaments or at great councils south of the Trent.

The southern clergy carried on the tradition of obstruction, stimulated by the revival of the quarrel between the archbishops.[5]

---

[1] *Parl. Writs*. II, ii, pp. 281 *seq*. The king also summoned certain abbots by separate writs, as if for a Parliament (*supra*, p. 139).

[2] Lincoln, January 13, 1323 (*Hist. Roffensis ; Anglia Sacra*, I, 362-3). For the refusal of York, see *Northern Convocations*, p. 70. I have used this collection as little as possible, as it is inaccurate, especially in dates.

[3] *Report on the Dignity of a Peer*, IV, 376.

[4] " . . . Per quosdam excusatores ipsius cleri nostri extitit responsum, quod idem clerus apud Lincolniam extra provinciam nostram non tenebatur comparere, nec debuit respondere. Nosque allegationem hujusmodi legitimam reputantes, cum difficultate tandem obtinuimus de dicto domino nostro rege et suo concilio, quod . . ." : archbishop Melton's writ summoning York Convocation (*Letters from Northern Registers*, p. 345).

[5] Cf. *Lit. Cant.* I, 348-9, 446 ; *Report on the Dignity of a Peer*, IV, 399, 415, 426, 446 ; *Rot. Parl.* II, 67.

There is no record of their presence at the first Parliament held at York (February 1328) ; though summoned by double writs, they probably did not attend, as they had made their grant in Convocation only three months earlier.[1] In November 1330 archbishop Mepham did not attend Parliament at Westminster, because he knew that the archbishop of York would be there ;[2] for the same reason he arranged to come late to another Westminster Parliament in 1332.[3] This Parliament of 1332 (March 16) is remarkable as the last occasion when we can be reasonably certain that the proctors were present as an estate of the realm. It is recorded on the Parliament roll that the prelates and the proctors of the clergy withdrew by themselves to take counsel on certain matters and, later, that the clergy were given leave to go home with the rest of the Commons.[4] We may also be fairly sure that the southern proctors never again attended a northern Parliament. Even the bishops were unwilling to go ; in 1332 the archbishop of York and the bishops of Lincoln and Carlisle alone were present at the Parliament of York (December 4), which was actually postponed for a month because of scanty attendance.[5] Supply was granted by the clergy in 1334, 1336 and 1337, each time in Convocation.[6] Signs of a curious attempt at a compromise on the territorial issue may be found in royal writs sent out in 1336. A great council was summoned to Nottingham on September 23, the clergy, both north and south, being summoned under the *premunientes* clause and the provincial letter ;[7] at the same time the archbishop of Canterbury was ordered to hold his Convocation at Leicester on September 30.[8] Nottingham and

---

[1] Canterbury Convocation had met at Leicester on November 4, 1327 (Wake, *op. cit.*, Appendix, p. 55).

[2] *Report on the Dignity of a Peer*, IV, 399. Cf. *Hist. Roffensis ; Anglia Sacra*, I, 370-1.

[3] *Lit. Cant.* I, 446. Cf. *ibid.*, pp. 348-9 (1331), for a letter from Eastry in which he strongly advises archbishop Mepham to attend Parliament, because all specially summoned, *per se vel per alios*, are bound to be present, to treat and to ordain *pro utilitate rei publicae*.

[4] *Rot. Parl.* II, 64-5. The proctors mentioned on the roll of the Parliament of York, 1332-33, are obviously the personal proxies of prelates, *ibid.* II, 69.

[5] *Ibid.* II, 67. The only prelates present were the archbishop of York, the bishops of Lincoln and Carlisle, and the abbots of Selby and York.

[6] Wake, App., pp. 58, 59, 61.

[7] *Report on the Dignity of a Peer*, IV, 460-1.

[8] *Ibid.*, p. 463. Both archbishops were sent additional writs to warn the clergy to come with sufficient powers, *ibid.*

Leicester lie less than thirty miles apart, one on each side of the provincial boundary ; the places of session were plainly designed to permit the archbishop of Canterbury to be present at both assemblies and to maintain a connection between them.[1] Though a variant of the old formula " quod omnes tangit ab omnibus approbetur " [2] appears in the writ to Canterbury, as if to revive memory of the first summons of the clergy to Parliament,[3] the clumsy make-shift was a sign that Edward I's plan of combining all estates in Parliament had been virtually abandoned.

In the same decade in which the barriers of provincial separatism were firmly erected, the clergy finally recovered their right to grant supply outside Parliament. The two questions were, in fact, closely associated. The issue underlying both the dispute over the provincial letter and that over extra-territorial summons was the royal right to demand attendance at Parliament. Edward II had been able to maintain his right in the conflict over the *venire faciatis* writ, but his victory proved barren, since provincial separatism was too strong for him. In admitting that the clergy could not be summoned outside their province (as he did implicitly in 1318 and 1322 and explicitly in 1327), the king accepted the doctrine that they could be summoned only by their archbishops and bishops, whose authority did not extend beyond the metropolitan boundary.[4] In other words, though the spiritual peers were bound to attend Parliament, *sicut barones*, the clergy were mesne tenants and the king had no direct authority over them. To Edward III it would seem wasted effort to go on struggling to bring the proctors to Parliament, since by their scant attendance they were able to postpone grants of supply. It is, therefore, not surprising to find that Convocation was steadily replacing Parliament, as far as the clergy were concerned.

---

[1] Earlier, though less complete examples, of the same experiment can be found ; e.g. in 1334 a Parliament was held at York (February 21), to which the clergy were summoned by double writs, but the king also required provincial Convocations to be held a month earlier (January 10 and 17) at Northampton and York respectively (*Report on the Dignity of a Peer*, III, 422-5 ; *Cal. Cl. Rolls, 1333-37*, p. 184, November 8, 1333).

[2] " . . . cum omnes tangant per omnes debeant pertractari . . . ."

[3] *Select Charters*, p. 480.

[4] As early as 1244, the king had admitted that *convocacio clericorum* pertained to the prelates, as *convocacio laicorum* pertained to himself (Cole, *Documents*, p. 356, no. XIII).

The writs of summons show plainly how this came about. In 1331 we have evidence of royal impatience in a strongly worded request for punctual attendance at a Parliament at Westminster (September 30).[1] In 1334 the archbishop of Canterbury summoned Convocation a week, and the archbishop of York over a month, after the date for which Parliament had been summoned to Westminster, thus clearly indicating that little would be done by the proctors outside the ecclesiastical assemblies.[2] Two other examples will serve to illustrate the way in which the archbishop of Canterbury was able to transform parliamentary business into Convocation business. The clergy were summoned by double writ to the Parliament of Winchester in 1330 (March 11).[3] Archbishop Mepham issued mandates, ordering the clergy to appear in Winchester cathedral before himself, to treat with the prelates on urgent business to be discussed in Parliament.[4] Again, six years later the king sent a writ to the archbishop of York, in which he stated that the clergy of Canterbury had granted him a tenth in his Parliament at Westminster (March 11, 1336).[5] The clergy had been cited to this Parliament in the normal way,[6] but the southern proctors had also been cited by their archbishop to appear before himself in St. Paul's, to treat of the affairs of Parliament.[7] We can hardly doubt that the grant was actually made in St. Paul's and merely reported by the archbishop to Parliament. If the king's writ to York be regarded as evidence for the parliamentary attendance of proctors, it might be argued that they played their part in Parliament as often as Convocation was summoned at the same time. It might even be urged that the Canterbury Convocation, sitting *coram archiepiscopo* at St. Paul's, was not essentially different from assemblies of the proctors under the *premunientes* clause, as they must always have sat apart as a separate *gradus* or estate. Such

---

[1] *Report on the Dignity of a Peer*, IV, 403.
[2] Wake, *op. cit.*, p. 283.
[3] *Report on the Dignity of a Peer*, IV, 391-2.
[4] " . . . compareant coram nobis in ecclesia cathedrali Winton . . . ad tractandum una nobiscum et ceteris prelatis super urgentibus ecclesie Anglicane et regni negotiis in Parliamento suis pertractandis . . . " (Wilkins, II, 557-8 ; Wake, *op. cit.*, p. 279).
[5] *Northern Convocations*, pp. 73-4 (wrong date) ; *Cal. Cl. Rolls, 1333-37,* March 26, 1336, pp. 660-1. The archbishop was ordered to summon his Convocation for the same purpose.
[6] *Report on the Dignity of a Peer*, IV, 457.   [7] Wake, *op. cit.*, p. 284.

arguments overlook altogether the absence of the northern clergy, who by their presence in the south transformed the session of a provincial Convocation into a coherent part of a session of Parliament.[1] The last phase of the transition may be rapidly illustrated. In 1337 the king, in urgent need of money for the French and Scottish wars, summoned a great council at Westminster (September 26), citing the prelates and clergy in the usual way.[2] On the same day he required the archbishops to summon their clergy to London and York respectively.[3] Here we have a plain recognition by Edward III that the shortest way to secure grants from the clergy was to consult them in their own assemblies. In the same month (August) special writs were issued to the bishops, ordering them to muster their clergy, to explain to them the justice and peril of the king's cause and to persuade them to grant him speedy aid.[4] We know that in one diocese at least (Coventry and Lichfield) the clergy, *post multos tractatus*, agreed to make a grant,[5] but local undertakings of this kind were afterwards superseded by grants in Convocation. The same method of particular bargains was applied to the laity, not only county [6] by county, but by separate negotiations with the merchants.[7] Edward III was working on the maxim *divide et impera* and it fitted exactly the deliberate policy of separatism followed by the clergy. His manœuvres over supply in 1337 are remarkable, not only, as Stubbs suggests, because the merchants " seemed likely to furnish the realm with a new estate," [8] but

[1] For example, proctors from Carlisle were present at the Parliament of 1309, Halton's Register, I, 314.
[2] *Report on the Dignity of a Peer*, IV, 479.
[3] *Ibid.* pp. 481-2 ; *Murimuth (Rolls Series)*, p. 80.
[4] Wake, *op. cit.*, p. 286, Appendix, p. 62 ; *Cal. Cl. Rolls, 1337-39*, August 21, 1337, pp. 254-5.
[5] Diocesan assembly at Stafford (September 15, 1337), Willard, *Eng. Hist. Review*, Vol. XXI, pp. 727 *seq.*
[6] *Cal. Cl. Rolls, 1337-39*, August 21, 1337, p. 254. For the answer given in the county court of Devon, see Grandisson's Register, I, 300, quoted by D. Hughes, *Early Years of Edward III*, pp. 24-5, where Somerset is put in error for Devon.
[7] Five special assemblies of merchants met in the course of the year 1337. For a list of assemblies of merchants in the fourteenth century, see *Interim Report of the Committee on House of Commons Personnel and Politics, 1264-1832*, 1932, pp. 109-10.
[8] *Constitutional History*, II, 398.

because they made it impossible for him to force the clergy into Parliament. The king was not prepared to contend for the royal prerogative of summons and was satisfied with establishing the practice of requiring the archbishops to call their Convocations at seasons convenient to himself. It is true, as Courtenay pointed out in 1384 (in a protest against a lay grant being made .conditional on clerical supply), that the archbishop had the right to refuse to assemble his clergy.[1] The king had let slip his right to compel the proctors to come to Parliament, without acquiring any coercive authority over the sessions of Convocation. Events proved that the weakness of his position was mainly theoretical, as his relations with the bishops were too close and secular public opinion too strong to admit of any formidable ecclesiastical resistance. The real losers were, in the first place, the clergy themselves, who were shut off from the political centre of the national life and, secondly, the lay commons in Parliament, who lost in the proctors men who would have brought to their deliberations another learning and another discipline to balance the narrow caution of the lawyers.

Thus by 1337 the proctors of the clergy had, for all practical purposes, ceased to be an estate of Parliament, a change finally underlined by the lapse of the provincial letter in 1340.[2] The conflict over their attendance had lasted for less than fifty years and was acute for a much shorter period. The obstructive tactics of the clergy had developed in two overlapping phases ; the first relating to the form of summons, the second to the place of session. The period of dispute over the summons lies between 1311 and 1322, or at the outside, 1323 ; that over the place of assembly between 1318 and, at latest, 1337. We find matter relating to both these disputes in the *Modus* and an examination of it makes it hard to believe that the relevant section

---

[1] Courtenay's Register, quoted by Wake, *op. cit.*, Appendix, pp. 77-8. Courtenay stated in full Parliament : " Quod nunquam de cetero cum Clero suo super aliquo Subsidio Regi concedendo tractaret, nec Convocationem faceret hac de Causa, donec dicta Conditio rejecta fuerit et deleta." The threat was sufficient to cause the obnoxious condition to be withdrawn.

[2] It should also be noted that the committee set up in the Parliament of 1341 contained thirteen knights of the shire and six citizens and burgesses, but no proctors, although one of its duties was to consider " les conditions et requestes touchaunt le clergie," *Rot. Parl.* II, 113.

of the document, at least, can be separated in time from the period of active controversy.

The matter of summons is dealt with in the first long chapter of the *Modus* (II). The whole body of the clergy ought to be summoned to Parliament, either separately and directly by the king, as prelates *qui tenent per comitatum vel baroniam*, or generally and indirectly, as proctors bearing warrants sealed by their superiors.[1] Should the king desire the presence of other clerks, either as members of his council or for some special reason, they ought not to be summoned like the prelates, but should receive royal writs requesting (*rogando*) their attendance. The whole orientation of the chapter is towards the king, whom he may summon and who must be called up through their ecclesiastical superiors. The title *Summonitio Parliamenti* emphasises the same ruling idea. A like concentration may be seen in the chapters on the lay Commons (III-VII), where the question of constituencies, notably for the barons of the Cinque Ports, is disregarded altogether. So strong was this intention of the writer that he forgot to make the section complete by exact definition of the proctorial constituencies and of the categories of ecclesiastical persons who ought to attend Parliament. He omitted altogether archdeacons and deans, who attended by reason of their dignities,[2] and also the proctors of cathedral chapters. His description of diocesan elections is confused and inaccurate : prelates and others having jurisdiction " for each deanery and archdeaconry of England, should cause to be elected, by the deaneries and archdeaconries themselves, two experienced and suitable proctors from their own archdeaconry to come and to be present at Parliament." Here the purpose of bringing in the deaneries is obscure and the inference plainly is that two proctors from each archdeaconry should attend Parliament. Such was the practice in the larger dioceses of the north and there are also traces of it in the province of Canterbury, though in an irregular way.[3] However, a scrutiny of the manner in which the elections were actually conducted will show that the writer

---

[1] The *premunientes* clause is indicated, though not specifically, in the phrase : " Rex solebat facere summonitiones suas archiepiscopis, episcopis . . . ."

[2] Deans are named only as among those exempt persons to whom the *premunientes* clause might be addressed ; archdeacons are not named at all.

[3] *Infra*, pp. 326-9.

was thinking rather carelessly of their primary stages.[1]   In some dioceses at least, the clergy of each rural deanery elected a proctor ; the proctors thus chosen in one archdeaconry together elected a representative to meet those from other archdeaconries ; by the proctors of archdeaconries the final choice for the diocese was made. The muddled and misleading summary of this procedure which we find in the *Modus* can be explained only by accepting the view that the author's interest was concentrated on the question of summons. Thus interpreted, the content and bearing of the chapter point clearly to the controversy over the *venire faciatis* writ and the provincial letter and so to a date between the years 1311 and 1322 or 1323.

The evidence from the dispute over the extra-provincial summons is less easy to disentangle. The quarrel was first taken up by the clergy in 1318 and was carried on into the early years of Edward III's reign. A temporary compromise on the honours due to the archbishops was reached in 1322, probably at the restoration Parliament in May, but perhaps not until the later Parliament in November of the same year. In 1325 the appointment of archbishop Melton as Treasurer caused the breakdown of the arrangement, which may never have been accepted by the chief parties concerned. Now in the *Modus* it is assumed that no difficulty will arise on the main issue of one archbishop's visit to the province of the other and attention is given only to details of precedence. The sermon shall be preached by a bishop or a clerk nominated by the archbishop in whose province Parliament meets (X) ; the archbishop of Canterbury shall sit on the king's right hand, the archbishop of York on his left (XIV) ; the archbishop in whose province Parliament meets shall act as one of the commissioners if the king be absent (XIII). The only period before the final settlement of 1353,[2] in which the main issue could have been ignored in this way and the details touched on so lightly, is the brief interval between the compromise of 1322 and the renewal of the quarrel in 1325. When this result is set beside the deduction from the dispute over the writs, we arrive at the conclusion that the sections of the *Modus* which relate to the summons of the clergy and to the rights of the archbishops in Parliament fit closely to the history

[1] *Infra*, pp. 326-9.
[2] *Historia Controversiae inter Sedes Cantuariensem et Eboracensem de Primatu* in *Anglia Sacra*, I, 75.

of the years 1322 and 1323 and to no other period. In addition
to the particular chapters under discussion, references to the
proctors appear throughout the document and it would be
impossible to withdraw them without destroying the unity of
the treatise. In their general bearing they conform to the
early date assigned to the particular chapters, as they belong to
a time when the clergy were still deemed to be an integral and
permanent part of Parliament, a time which cannot be later
than 1340 and is much more likely to be twenty years earlier.

CHAPTER VIII

THE COMMONALTY OF THE REALM IN PARLIAMENT

COMPARISON of the part played by the proctors in early Parliaments with the treatment of their rights and duties in the *Modus* has led us to the conclusion that the statements in the *Modus* correspond closely to events round about the year 1322 and to no other period. It remains to enquire whether other statements show a corresponding likeness to events in the latter half of Edward II's reign. Before proceeding to a close scrutiny of details,[1] it will be convenient to raise the general question of the Commons in Parliament in the first quarter of the fourteenth century. The author of the *Modus* was not exclusively concerned with the ecclesiastical estates and he in no way admitted that the rights of the laity ought to be overshadowed by clerical privilege. His ideal was the joint and harmonious co-operation of all the orders of the realm and this he hoped to secure by insistence on common responsibility and by application of the principle of representation or delegation within Parliament itself. The same ideas found concrete expression in the reign of Edward II, the time when the full significance of Parliament as a gathering of estates first began to be understood. In the statute of York and in the deposition of Edward II a striking likeness either to the general doctrine or to the procedure of the *Modus* may be discerned. It will, therefore, be useful to discuss both the statute of 1322 and the sequence of events in 1327 in some detail.

The meaning of the statute of York, enacted in May 1322 after the victory over Lancaster at Boroughbridge, has given rise to much controversy. The dispute turns on the clause which follows the repeal of the Ordinances : " But the matters which are to be established for the estate of our lord the king and of his

---

[1] *Infra*, Chapter X.

heirs, and for the estate of the realm and of the people, shall be treated, accorded and established in Parliaments by our lord the king, and by the assent of the prelates, earls and barons, and the commonalty of the realm, according as it hath been heretofore accustomed." [1] Even if the words do not, as Stubbs claimed, " embody in a very remarkable way the spirit of the Constitution," [2] they certainly appear to express the idea of common action by all the estates in Parliament, which is the burden of the *Modus*.

However, modern scholars have sought to impose a strict limit on the significance of the statute. Mr. Lapsley has maintained that the decisive words were intended to apply only to " fundamental constitutional changes," like the sanction clause of Magna Carta, the Provisions of Oxford or the Ordinances themselves. [3] In this opinion he has been supported by Tout [4] and, with considerable reserve, by Professor Pollard. [5] It is obvious that to read the statute in this way is to raise difficulties in the whole interpretation of the sensational events of 1322. We are asked to believe that when Edward II came to York, " bringing rebellion broached upon his sword," he at once put forward legislation to ensure the validity of " fundamental constitutional changes " in the future. In other words, a restoration Parliament prescribed the method which later revolutions ought to follow.

Further difficulties in accepting Mr. Lapsley's view become apparent when the passage in dispute is set out in its context.

(After a recital of the Ordinances) " . . . the which ordinances our said lord the king at his Parliament at York, in three weeks from Easter in the fifteenth year of his reign, did by the prelates, earls, and barons, among whom were the more part of the said ordainers who were then living, and by the commonalty of his realm, there by his command assembled, cause to be rehearsed and examined ; and forasmuch as upon that examination it was found, in the said Parliament, that by the matters so ordained the royal power of our said lord the king was restrained in divers things contrary to what

[1] *Statutes of the Realm*, I, 189. [2] *Constitutional History*, II, 369.
[3] " The Commons and the Statute of York," *Eng. Hist. Review*, Vol. XXVIII, pp. 118 *seq.*
[4] *Place of Edward II in English History*, p. 151.
[5] " . . . there is at least plausibility in the contention that it was only understood to apply to what would be called to-day constitutional changes or alterations of fundamental law " (*Evolution of Parliament*, p. 241).

ought to be, to the blemishing of his royal sovereignty, and against the estate of the Crown ; and, also, forasmuch as, in time past, by such ordinances and provisions, made by subjects against the royal power of the ancestors of our lord the king, troubles and wars have happened in the realm, whereby the land hath been in peril, it is accorded and established, at the said Parliament, by our lord the king, and by the said prelates, earls and barons, and the whole commonalty of the realm, at this Parliament assembled, that all the things, by the said ordainers ordained and contained in the said ordinances, shall from henceforth for the time to come cease, and shall lose their name, force, virtue and effect for ever ; the statutes and establishments duly made by our lord the king and his ancestors, before the said ordinances, abiding in their force. And that for ever hereafter, all manner of ordinances or provisions made by the subjects of our lord the king or of his heirs, by any power or authority whatsoever, concerning the royal power of our lord the king or of his heirs, or against the estate of our said lord the king or of his heirs, or against the estate of the Crown, shall be void and of no avail or force whatever ; but the matters which are to be established for the estate of our lord the king and of his heirs, and for the estate of the realm and of the people, shall be treated, accorded, and established in Parliaments, by our lord the king, and by the assent of the prelates, earls and barons, and the commonalty of the realm ; according as it hath been heretofore accustomed." [1]

The clause which deals with the royal power and the estate of the Crown was designed to protect the monarchy in perpetuity from all limits imposed by subjects. The phrase *estate of the Crown*, which occurs twice in the statute, was a new term, prominent in the disputes at the beginning of the reign. It was used to express the doctrine of the king's two capacities, which was formulated by the barons to defend their attack on Gaveston in 1308. " . . . Before the estate of the Crown hath descended (i.e. is inherited), no allegiance is due to the person. Wherefore, if the king by chance be not guided by reason . . . his lieges are bound by oath made to the Crown to guide him and the

---

[1] *Statutes of the Realm*, I, 189. The original words of the disputed clause run : " Mes les choses que serrount a establir pour lestat de nostre seigneur le roi et de ses heirs, et pour lestat du roialme et du poeple, soient tretes, accordees, establies, en Parlementz, par nostre seigneur le roi, et par lassent des prelatz, countes et barouns, et la communalte du roialme ; auxint come ad este acustume cea enarere."

estate of the Crown back again by reason."[1] Here *estate of the Crown* plainly means the monarchy as distinct from the person of the king. The words appeared again in the first attack on the Despensers in 1321. The Despensers were branded as "disinheritors of the Crown"[2] and the doctrine of capacities was re-stated in the form of an accusation.[3] The Doncaster petition (November 29, 1321), drafted by Lancaster and his confederates, used the term seven times and gave to it the general meaning of the prestige and authority of the monarch.[4] In this sense it was taken up and applied in the statute of York, closely attached to the phrase " the royal power of our lord the king and of his heirs." Thus the hereditary and permanent prerogative of the Crown was associated with the personal authority of the king himself. A phrase, forged and popularised by rebellion, was adapted to express the inherent and sacrosanct character of the monarch.

The clause, directed in the first place against the Ordinances of 1311, was thus worded in such a way that it covered all the restrictions imposed on the Crown from below. This must certainly include, if not the restraints of Magna Carta at least those of the Provisions of Oxford, which Mr. Lapsley cites as examples of fundamental law. If this be so, it is impossible to suppose that the following clause gave back, by means of the phrase " matters which are to be established for the estate of . . . the king . . . and for the estate of the realm and of the people," the right of fundamental change, emphatically abolished in the preceding sentence. The second provision must not contradict, but supplement the first. This interpretation is adopted by Mr. Conway Davies. Matters to be established for the estate of the king, the realm and the people are matters which concern both monarch and subjects ; they must on that account,

[1] *Annales Londonienses* in *Chronicles of Edward I and Edward II*, Vol. I (*Rolls Series*), p. 153 ; Bridlington, p. 33.
[2] *Exheredatores coronae*, arraignment of the Despensers (Bridlington, p. 69 ; *Statutes of the Realm*, I, 184).
[3] In the full text of the process the younger Despenser was accused of using the doctrine of two capacities to further a league with Giffard, Grey and others, to constrain the king (*ibid.* I, 182 ; *Cal. Cl. Rolls, 1318-23*, p. 492). In the version preserved by Bridlington (p. 65 *seq.*), which was probably for popular circulation, this accusation is omitted, and the passage reads like a justification of the proceedings.
[4] *Infra*, pp. 164-6.

share in their establishment, that is, share in the general business of law-making and government.[1]

Even apart from the difficulties of the context, the distinction between fundamental and ordinary law lacks the warrant of contemporaries. In an age when legal theorising was strictly confined by precedents and texts and when every jot and tittle of evidence seemed to carry equal weight, it is scarcely conceivable that a line should be drawn between two kinds of statutes. Not only was the idea too subtle for lawyers and law-makers, who were as yet unable to distinguish between statute, ordinance and provision,[2] but also the concept of fundamental change was altogether alien to medieval statesmen. When the barons laboured to impose restraints upon the Crown, they believed themselves to be acting as conservators of immemorial custom, enforcing the principle of *rex sub lege*. Throughout the English constitutional conflict we can always hear two voices and each is mighty ; one from the monarch maintains the inviolability of royal power and the other from the magnates asserts the indefeasible rights of their order. The statute of York cannot be used to force the two into unison and no subtlety of interpretation will reconcile it with the deposition of Edward II.

If we interpret the disputed clause in the wider sense, as a reference to general legislation and administration, it is still necessary to decide what significance may be given to the words " in Parliaments, by our lord the king, and by the assent of the prelates, earls and barons, and the commonalty of the realm." Though the direct object of the statute was certainly the revocation of the Ordinances, this cannot be regarded as its sole purpose and it is, therefore, impossible to divorce commentary on the statute from a discussion of contemporary opinion and practice. The reign of Edward II was remarkable for assemblies which in number, composition and variety illustrate the diverse influences at work in shaping the growth of Parliament. The great legal development of the thirteenth century rendered regular meetings

---

[1] *Baronial Opposition to Edward II*, p. 515. Cf. *ibid.*, Appendix no. 93, pp. 582-3, for the king's instruction to his council to draft the statute, showing that the initiative came from above. A similar view is expressed by Professor McIlwain, *Cam. Med. History*, Vol. VII, p. 678.

[2] Cf. Plucknett, *Statutes and their Interpretation in the First Half of the Fourteenth Century*, p. 34.

of the Curia essential, both to deliver judgement and to declare the law ; Mr. Richardson and Mr. Sayles have reckoned that Parliament, in this sense of the word, sat thirty-two times between 1307 and 1322.[1] The king's need of money compelled him to consult his subjects frequently in order to bargain with them for grants of supply. Representatives of the Commons were summoned regularly to Parliament from 1311 ; the merchants were called together in special assemblies in 1316 and, twice, in 1319 ;[2] almost every year the Convocations of Canterbury and York met for a fiscal purpose. In 1307 it was still uncertain whether the sessions of the Curia and the assemblies granting supply would permanently coalesce, or even whether representatives of all, or of the greater part of the estates would meet together regularly as a single body. The compulsion towards unity was derived less from the normal routine of business, judicial, legislative or fiscal, than from the growing rivalry for power between the king and his contrariant magnates. It was the baronial opposition to the Crown, pressing hard on royal administration, which gave peculiar significance to all public assemblies. Not only were the Commons in Parliament coveted as possible allies, but the principle of representation was applied by critics and malcontents, as a means of organising resistance to the Crown.

At the beginning of the reign the political importance of the Commons was not yet understood. Though summoned to Parliament in 1307, 1308 and 1309, they were allotted no part in the quarrel between king and magnates. The Ordinances of 1311 are clear evidence that the barons set no value on their co-operation.[3] The annual or half-yearly parliaments prescribed in the twenty-ninth Ordinance were intended to be baronial assemblies, which should meet to transact judicial business, to appoint royal officials, with the counsel and consent of the baronage,[4] and to assent to royal gifts.[5] In short, the Ordinances were devised to expel Gaveston and to secure aristocratic control of the administration. They contain no reference whatever to the share of the Commons in granting

---

[1] *Bulletin*, Vol. VI, pp. 85-7.   [2] *Ibid.*, p. 84.
[3] Evidence for the baronial attitude is clearly summarised by Conway Davies, *op. cit.*, pp. 511-13.
[4] *Statutes of the Realm*, I, 160, Ord. 14.
[5] *Ibid.*, p. 158, Ord. 7.

taxes, or to their right to present petitions. Though the king had authorised the appointment of prelates, earls and barons *et des autres*,[1] the Ordainers chosen were all magnates and there is, at first, no evidence that the Commons were deemed to be directly concerned.

The king stood to lose both his authority and his minion. The double danger roused him to resist the baronial demands with an unexpected obstinacy. To compel his assent to the Ordinances the magnates were driven to search for new allies and to appeal for wider support. The Ordinances were published in a Parliament of estates on September 30, 1311.[2] Edward II delayed his assent for five days longer[3] and it was probably on that account that a demonstration was organised in the city to show that popular approval was neither silent nor informal.[4] The Ordinances were read at St. Paul's Cross, in the presence of archbishop Winchelsey, Lancaster, Pembroke, Hereford, Warwick and many other prelates and magnates.[5] Not only were the great men sworn to maintain the Ordinances, but like oaths were taken on the archbishop's cross by men from each city and borough in the realm.[6] These representatives of the towns must have been members of Parliament and it can hardly be doubted that the knights of the shire were also sworn. Copies of the Ordinances were sent to every county and to each cathedral city.[7] The archbishop issued orders that they should be read annually in each diocese ; they had been drafted, he explained, by the prelates, earls and magnates and, after publication, *quasi ab omnibus communiter accepta sunt et approbata*.[8] In the same

[1] *Annales London*, p. 169.

[2] Bridlington, p. 39. Writs *de expensis* show that the lay Commons were present from August 9 to October 9.

[3] October 5, *Statutes of the Realm*, I, 167.

[4] Cf. Tout, *Place of Edward II*, pp. 88-91, where a different view of the ratification of the Commons is expressed.

[5] *Annales Paulini*, p. 270. Cf. Rob. of Reading, in *Flores Historiarum*, p. 147 ; Walsingham (I, 124) refers to the presence of prelates, magnates *et communium totius regni*.

[6] " Et des chescune cite et burghe par my la terre furent gens iurez a Loundres sur la crois lercev⟨e⟩sche Robert de Winchelse ; et aussint touz les graunz de la terre iuserent (*sic.* iurerent) de sauvement garder et maintener les dites ordeignaunces " (Pipewell Chronicle, Cotton MS., Julius A, I, f. 51*b* ; see Note A, *infra*, Chapter IX).

[7] *Vita Edwardi II*, p. 171 ; Rob. of Reading, p. 147 ; Murimuth, p. 15.

[8] Mandate dated October 18, 1311, Register of Sim. de Gandavo (Salisbury), Vol. I, pp. 412-13.

connection the chronicler of Malmesbury cites the famous tag *quod omnes tangit ab omnibus debet approbari ;* though he was, perhaps, telling the story in a form more in harmony with ideas at the end of the reign, he was the first to read a wider political application into the doctrine of consent.[1] Thus it seems that the year 1311 may well be taken as a turning-point in the history of the Commons. It is from that date that their regular summons to Parliament can be traced and, from that time, as the personal struggle for power grew more dangerous, both king and barons steadily competed for their support.

Nothing illustrates more clearly the new estimate of their relative value than the pseudo- or counter-parliaments which met in the north between 1315 and 1321. Just as the inquest procedure was borrowed by seignorial courts in the thirteenth century, until declared a royal monopoly by the Provisions of Westminster, so the idea of representation was borrowed by political malcontents in the reign of Edward II. The originator of the plan may have been William de Greenfield, archbishop of York (1306-15).[2] On April 13, 1315, he issued summons for an assembly of clergy to be held at Doncaster on May 5 ; to the dean and chapter of York he explained that he was acting on the urgent request of Lancaster and other magnates.[3] To assemble the clergy was altogether within his rights, but he did not stop short there. The meeting at Doncaster was intended to be something more than a session of the northern Convocation, since he also issued special summons to John de Mowbray and fifty knights, requesting them to come to Doncaster on the same day. He stated that the prelates, other ecclesiastical dignitaries

---

[1] *Vita Edwardi II*, p. 170. Stubbs considered that the chronicler was writing at the end of Edward II's reign, not much later than 1325 (Introduction, p. xliv).

[2] Greenfield was closely attached to the Giffard family, and, as a young man, had been sent to Oxford by Walter Giffard, then archbishop of York. In July 1315, during an outbreak of the perennial quarrel with Canterbury, Greenfield stated that he had the support of John Giffard, lord of Brimpsfield, Alexander de Freville of Tamworth, and his son, Baldwin, and John de Wylington (Greenfield's Register, I, 278). It is significant that all these supporters, except Alexander, rebelled against the king in 1321-22. There seems little doubt that, unlike Reynolds of Canterbury, and in spite of his training in the royal service, Greenfield was on the side of the barons.

[3] " . . . ad instantem requisicionem nobilis viri domini Thome comitis Lancastrie et quorumdam aliorum procerum ac magnatum," *ibid.*, no. 359, pp. 158 *seq.*

and the great lords of the north were about to meet to provide for the defence of the province ; that the plan was the outcome of an accord between Lancaster and himself ; and that they would act for the honour of the Church and of the king and for the safety of the realm.[1] The year 1315 was the time of full Lancastrian ascendancy and it is not surprising that the king made no protest against this assumption by a subject of his own prerogative of summons.

The provincial separatism implicit in the summons to Doncaster was typical of Lancaster's idea of government. His purpose, so far as it can be discerned, was not to co-operate with the king in the task of government, but to maintain his own independence at the expense of royal authority. With the help of Pembroke's middle party, Edward II slowly recovered power, and in 1317 he was strong enough to rebuke Lancaster for holding private and unlawful assemblies of magnates and commons.[2] Lancaster pleaded in defence that he had made no assemblies against the king's peace and that he was merely gathering retainers in accordance with the royal writ of military summons. At the same time he refused to attend a meeting of the Great Council at Nottingham, on the ground that the business for which it had been summoned ought to be treated *en pleyn Parlement, en presence des peeres de la terre ;* this he and all who had sworn to the Ordinances were bound to maintain.[3] It is difficult to see how the Great Council differed from the Parliament of magnates provided for in the Ordinances. Three years later Lancaster refused to attend a council of barons at York (1320), because it was not fitting to hold Parliament *in cameris ;* [4] this suggests that his break with the middle party had led him to distrust his peers and to prefer a Parliament of estates to an aristocratic council. If this were his meaning in 1317, the phrase

---

[1] Greenfield's Register, I, 158-9.

[2] The royal prohibition is referred to in Lancaster's letter, written in justification (French version, Cotton MS., Claudius *E*, VIII, f. 256, printed in Murimuth, Appendix, pp. 271-4 ; Latin version, Bridlington, pp. 50-2). Edward II had already (March 8, 1312) forbidden the mayor and bailiffs of Bristol to appear before an assembly of prelates, earls and barons, to answer for certain contempts, since their appearance might prejudice the king and his royal dignity (*Cal. Cl. Rolls, 1307-13*, p. 450, quoted by Conway Davies, *op. cit.*, p. 353).

[3] Lancaster's letter, cited in the previous note.

[4] *Vita Edwardi II*, p. 250.

peeres de la terre must bear an enlarged significance, comparable to that in the *Modus*.[1]

In the grand struggle against the Despensers (1321-22), Lancaster followed a line of action more subtle than the defiance and appeal to arms of the Welsh Marchers. Perhaps with some confused idea of his rights as High Steward of England,[2] he seems to have relied mainly on the irregular counter-Parliaments that he organised in the North. In May 1321 he held a council at Pontefract, at which he and fifteen barons and bannerets formed a solemn league of defence and agreed to appeal to a more representative assembly at Sherburn in Elmet.[3] According to Bridlington, the prelates, abbots and priors of the northern province met Lancaster, Hereford and many barons, bannerets and knights from north and south at Sherburn on June 28.[4] Another chronicler states that three clerical and twelve lay magnates, thirty-seven barons and bannerets and many elected knights (*militibus electis*) were present.[5] Business was carried on with some formality. Bartholomew de Badlesmere appeared with a message from the king.[6] In a statement of seven grievances, read out by John de Bek, the stock complaint against evil councillors was followed by a demand for specific administrative reforms. The prelates and clergy, sitting apart in the rector's house, drafted a reply to the statement of grievances. While ready to help in defence of the Border, they refused to identify themselves with a policy of separatism or rebellion ; all matters in dispute, they declared, ought to be discussed by the king and his subjects in the next Parliament.[7] Probably while the clergy were conferring, an indenture, perhaps drawn up in advance, was sealed by about sixty magnates, in which they bound themselves to achieve the destruction of the Despensers.[8]

[1] Cf. *infra*, pp. 199-200.
[2] Cf. *infra*, pp. 241-2.
[3] May 24, Bridlington, pp. 61-2.
[4] *Ibid.*, p. 62.
[5] *Flores Historiarum*, III, 197.
[6] *Brut*, Part I, 213-14, an authority in which some interesting northern evidence is preserved. Its provenance appears from internal evidence to be somewhere in the neighbourhood of Pontefract.
[7] Bridlington, pp. 62-5.
[8] An English translation of the indenture is printed in R. Brady's *Continuation of the Complete History of England*, p. 128, from a French document in a register of Christ Church, Canterbury. Cf. transcripts in the Bodleian : Tanner 12, f. 50, contains the Latin preamble, the text of the indenture in French and sixty-one names ; Ashmole 860, ff. 375-6, has a Latin summary and fifty-seven names. Brady prints only thirty-four names.

Though the Sherburn indenture seemed to commit Lancaster to the cause of the Welsh Marchers, he gave them no active support. He failed to take effective action in the north while the Marchers army was in London, compelling the king to banish the Despensers (July-August, 1321). No doubt his absence encouraged Edward II to plan his *coup-d'état* with the younger Despenser and the Cinque Ports [1] and to raise the Londoners against Badlesmere in Kent. Instead of joining the Marchers in their second rising, Lancaster summoned (October 18) another pseudo-Parliament at Doncaster for November 29. One letter of summons, addressed to John Engayne, has been preserved in a contemporary manuscript.[2] Engayne was required *santz nule excusation*, to come to Doncaster on the appointed day, together with *touz noz . . . pieres parmy la terre*. On November 12 the king issued letters close to Lancaster and 107 others, forbidding them to attend the meeting.[3] Not only was the Doncaster assembly proclaimed, but it was definitely asserted that " by the consent and advice of the prelates, magnates and nobles of the realm, it had already been forbidden that anyone, of any estate or condition whatsoever, should presume to make *congregationes seu conventicula* within the realm, without the special permission of the king." Thus Edward II definitely declared that the prerogative of summoning assemblies of subjects belonged to the Crown.[4]

Though there is no direct evidence that the meeting at Doncaster was ever held, it is unlikely that Lancaster and his confederates showed any regard for the royal command. A petition addressed to Edward II, preserved with the Engayne summons and the king's letter of prohibition, was probably the

[1] September 5-18. Between these dates the king visited both Sandwich and Harwich, making agreements with the men of Winchelsea on the water (*Cal. Cl. Rolls, 1318-23*, March 26, 1322, p. 533), and with the younger Despenser at Harwich (Murimuth, p. 33).

[2] MS. Cotton, Cleopatra *D*, IX, f. 81*b*.

[3] *Ibid.*, ff. 81*b*-82 ; *Cal. Cl. Rolls, 1318-23*, November 12, 1321, pp. 505-6.

[4] Cf. an earlier prohibition addressed to all the sheriffs (except those of Cumberland, Northumberland and Westmoreland), and to Hereford and twenty-eight other persons, January 30, 1321 (*Cal. Cl. Rolls, 1318-23*, pp. 355-6), in which it is asserted that assemblies ought not to be held without the king's special order, nor treaties made without his presence, or that of councillors appointed by him. There is nothing to suggest that assemblies of ecclesiastics were brought under these prohibitions.

outcome of the proclaimed *conventiculum*.[1] It certainly represents the formal deliberations of the party, meeting at some time in November, and it is reasonable to suppose that it was drafted at Doncaster on the appointed day. The evidence for this conclusion may be briefly stated. The document contains eight articles, directed against the younger Despenser and other evil councillors. It bears no names, but the petitioners style themselves " the good people, lieges and peers of the land," a style more suited to a meeting formally convened than to a small group of contrariants. It is certainly of northern provenance, as the last sentence justifies the demands for redress on the ground that it is urgently necessary for the defence of the northern March. The date can be fixed within fairly narrow limits. On the one hand, reference is made to the operations of a commission of enquiry into unlawful confederacies, granted to Robert Ewer on October 19, 1321 ;[2] on the other, the king is requested to provide à remedy before the Sunday after the feast of St. Lucy (December 20). Allowing time at both ends—for news of Ewer's activities to reach the north and for due warning to the king—we arrive at a date in the second half of November, that is, within a short period which includes November 28, the day ordained for the Doncaster meeting.

Like the articles and indentures drawn up at Sherburn, the Doncaster petition goes to prove that the Lancastrian meetings in the north had an ambitious constitutional purpose. They cannot be disregarded in a review of events leading up to the statute of York. The Doncaster petition has a special interest, because its emphasis on the estate of the Crown and on the estate of the realm recalls the phrasing of the statute itself.[3] The petition was directed against grievances *en blemisement de lestat du realme et de la corone ;* the statute declared that " all manner of ordinances or provisions made by subjects of our lord the king or of his heirs, by any power or authority whatsoever, concerning the royal power . . . or against the estate of the Crown, shall be void and of no avail or force whatever." It is difficult to

---

[1] MS. Cleopatra *D*, IX, ff. 82-3, immediately following the Engayne letters, and obviously associated with them.

[2] *Cal. Pat. Rolls, 1321-24*, p. 28.

[3] *Estat de la coroune* occurs seven times, and *estat du realme* three times in the petition.

escape the conclusion that in one we have an answer to the other. There can, at least, be no doubt that the king's council and Parliament, sitting at York in May 1322, had the high claims of these pseudo-Parliaments in their minds. The form of words in the statute was probably intended to cover assemblies which had no royal summons as much as legislation which was not " treated, accorded and established by our lord the king."

However, the most significant phrase in the statute is that associating *la communalte de roialme* with the prelates, earls and barons in assent to legislation. In itself it was not a novelty and we cannot be certain whether the words were deliberately chosen, or whether they were merely an unconscious crystallisation of current opinion.[1] The assemblies in the north and Lancaster's appeals to *pleyn Parlement* in 1317 and in 1320 are not the only signs of change. When the Ordinances were confirmed in 1315, oaths to observe them were taken by the king and *tota communitas Anglie tam cleri quam laici*.[2] The Treaty of Leake was accepted by the prelates, earls and barons in the Parliament of York (1318) and the king pardoned Lancaster with their assent and with that of *la communaute de son roialme*.[3] It was also ordained *in pleno Parliamento*, by the prelates, earls and barons, and *totam communitatem eiusdem regni* that all gifts to Gaveston and his wife should be revoked.[4] Edward II had come to understand that his own Parliaments were less dangerous than baronial assemblies. In fact, throughout the year of parley, conspiracy and war that went before the statute of York, both king and magnates looked to Parliament to give the final decision. When the Welsh Marchers rose against the Despensers in the spring of 1321, Edward appealed to parliamentary authority in a remonstrance sent to Hereford and Mortimer of Wigmore. He reminded them that the younger Despenser had been appointed Chamberlain in full Parliament ; that no complaint had been brought against him then or in any later Parliament ; and that he was ready to meet a public enquiry in Parliament or elsewhere.[5]

---

[1] See *infra*, pp. 170-1, for a discussion of the term *communalte de roialme*.
[2] MS. Laud 529, f. 105 (Bodley). Cf. *Annales London*, p. 237 ; Bridlington, p. 47.
[3] Cole, *Documents*, pp. 2-3. Cf. the petitions of prelates, earls and barons and *tute la communalte du roiame, ibid.*, p. 6.
[4] Parliament of York, May 1319, *ibid.*, p. 49.
[5] April 23, 1321, *Cal. Cl. Rolls, 1318-23*, pp. 367-8.

The Marchers, on the other hand, had already demanded that a Parliament should be summoned, in which their grievances might be heard. At the same time, at least for purposes of judgement, they still thought that power was vested exclusively in their own order. In their arraignment of the Despensers (July 15, 1312), a remedy was demanded by the prelates, earls, barons and other peers of the realm ; the verdict of banishment was delivered by the peers of the realm, earls and barons, with a rider that it should not be reversed without the consent of the king and magnates in a Parliament duly summoned.[1] Though judgement was thus exclusively baronial, the magnates showed deference to the commons where their own safety was concerned. They required that their pardon should be decreed " in full Parliament by the king, prelates, earls, barons and the commonalty of the realm." [2]

The Despensers were quick to seize upon the flaws in the procedure of the Marchers. In their nine articles of protest they declared that sentence had been passed on them *absque clero* and that no judgement in *diversitate legum cadens* ought to be given *absque assensu communi*.[3] In another protest it was stated that the award had been made without the assent of the prelates, who are peers in Parliament.[4] Further details of the irregularity of the procedure were rehearsed in the Parliament of York.[5] The king had summoned Parliament to Westminster in due form (July 15, 1321). Against the royal order, the magnates had come armed to London, where they held their council and assembly. They had disobeyed the king's command to come to Parliament at Westminster, as they had been summoned ; they told him nothing of their proceedings against the Despensers until they had been sitting for fifteen days and more. The king had caused to come before him the prelates, other earls and barons, the knights of the shire and others who came for the

---

[1] Process against the Despensers, July 15, 1321, *Statutes of the Realm*, I, 184.

[2] August 20, 1321, *Cal. Cl. Rolls, 1318-23*, pp. 494-5.

[3] Bridlington, p. 70. Later the king stated that the prelates had not consented to the judgement, but that each of them *protestabatur in scriptis se nolle nec posse eidem consentire* (letter to Stapeldon, cited *infra*, p. 168 ; cf. Stapeldon's reply, *infra*, p. 169).

[4] Revocation of the judgement on the Despensers, Parliament of York, 1322 (*Cal. Cl. Rolls, 1318-23*, p. 543).

[5] *Ibid.*, pp. 544-5.

commonalty of the realm and he had proclaimed that all who had petitions should cause them to be delivered. No petition or complaint was made against the Despensers, until the magnates came to Westminster with force and arms and unduly. Then they had made their award, against reason, as of a matter treated and agreed among themselves, by their own authority and in the king's absence. By these actions the magnates had accroached the royal power, jurisdiction and cognisance of making process and judgement, on matters pertaining to the royal dignity. This important statement and the protests of the Despensers themselves show plainly that the action of the Marchers had raised the whole question of the composition, powers and procedure of Parliament.

The first answer was given in a strangely constituted assembly, held in London on December 1, 1321, after Edward had recovered his authority in the home counties. It consisted of the Convocation of Canterbury, afforced by those magnates and officials who remained loyal to the king. Its procedure was succinctly described in letters sent by Edward to those bishops who were absent.[1] The archbishop, bishops, other prelates and the clergy of Canterbury were ordered to examine the process against the Despensers. The prelates and their proctors declared it to be totally and unjustly erroneous and they advised that, with the full assent of the peers of the realm, it should be revoked. This assent was given to the king by the prelates and clergy, the four earls of Kent, Richmond, Pembroke and Arundel[2] and other nobles present. The judges and other members of the council pronounced the process to be against the laws and customs of the realm. In a mandate issued on the same day, ordering the news to be made public, archbishop Reynolds stated that the process had been examined by the prelates and *omnes gradus ceteros cleri* and was declared by them to be revocable and erroneous.[3]

The irregularity of the whole procedure roused protests both at the time and later. The monks and their proctors, who were

---

[1] Stapeldon's Register (Exeter), pp. 441-2 ; Cobham's Register (Worcester), p. 117. The letters bear the date January 4, 1322.

[2] It was added that Richmond, Pembroke and Arundel had previously agreed to the judgement *pro timore*.

[3] Mortival's Register (Salisbury MS.), liber II, f. 129.

probably sitting as a separate estate,[1] advised that the revocation should be made *per illos per quos fieri debet, locis et temporibus ad hoc opportunis.*[2] Ten bishops were absent and the king wrote to them for their personal consent.[3] Fortunately, the replies of Stapeldon of Exeter and Cobham of Worcester have been preserved in their registers. Cobham acknowledged that the king, in the plenitude of royal power, might revoke the process when and how he pleased. None the less, he advised that the revocation should be carried out *modo legitimo evidenter . . . in pleno Parliamento, propter hec et alia convocando*, in order that the Despensers, *saltem apparenter*, might be absolved and restored to honour by the same authority which had condemned them.[4] Stapeldon's reply was stiffer and more specific in its demand for action through Parliament. He wrote that he did not wish to oppose the revocation, but that it did not seem right or proper to him and his council that he should give his express consent without common deliberation and fuller discussion ; it was not fitting to give advice on grave matters by letter, instead of by word of mouth (*viva voce*). He advised that, as judgement had been given during the session of Parliament, it would be more honourably, usefully and securely revoked in a Parliament convoked for that and other purposes in a suitable place.[5] The king answered sharply, demanding Stapeldon's express consent and summoning him to the royal presence.[6] The bishop replied that he believed the judgement to be erroneous and unjust and, therefore, consented to its revocation. He refused to retract his advice that what Parliament had done, Parliament should undo, repeating his former argument as follows :

" Quantum, vero, ad consilium quod a nobis expetitur in premissis, videtur nobis, absque preiudicio consilii sanioris, quod

---

[1] Cf. *infra*, p. 323.   [2] Bridlington, p. 71.
[3] *Rymer*, II, Part II, 470 ; also in the registers, as cited below.
[4] Cobham's Register (Worcester), p. 119.
[5] " . . . quia, tamen, dicta consideracio tempore Parliamenti facta fuit, videtur nobis, absque preiudicio melioris consilii, quod revocacio predicte consideracionis honorificencius, utilius et securius fieri poterit in Parliamento quam alibi, si tempus permiserit et vestre celsitudini placuerit—utinam pacifico et pacifice—in loco competenti, propter hec et alia, convocando," January 31, 1322, Stapeldon's Register (Exeter), no. 409, p. 442. There is a close resemblance between parts of this letter and that of Cobham ; in his second letter Stapeldon repeated this passage *verbatim*, see below.
[6] *Ibid.*, pp. 442-3, no. 410, February 10, 1322.

finalis revocacio consideracionis predicte, que tempore Parliamenti, licet absque consensu et presencia prelatorum, facta extitit, honorificencius, utilius, et securius in Parliamento fieri poterit quam alibi, si tempus id permiserit et vestre celsitudini placuerit—utinam pacifico et pacifice !—in loco competenti propter hec et alia convocando. Et, si discrecioribus et in legibus Anglie magis expertis expediens videatur, per securitatem ydoneam de stando recto in proximo Parliamento, dicta consideracio forsitan revocari poterit interim vel suspendi ; licet enim consideracio predicta per iniusticiam facta fuerit et errorem, non tamen videtur expediens quod iniusticia seu error aliquis interveniat in revocacione ipsius quomodolibet facienda." [1]

Cobham and Stapeldon, like the northern clergy at Sherburn, insisted on the exclusive competence of Parliament, at least for the matters under consideration.

Yet we must be careful not to read too much either into this new emphasis on Parliament, or into the statute itself. It is hard to be certain what exactly contemporaries meant by Parliament, or what parts they cast for the Commons to play on its stage. One thing, however, the evidence plainly shows : prelates and magnates alone were no longer deemed sufficient to constitute a full Parliament and a sharp line was beginning to be drawn between wholly aristocratic assemblies and those at which the Commons were present. This line appears clearly in a royal order sent to the judges immediately after the statute was passed. The Ordinances, which had been ordained *per quosdam prelatos, comites et barones regis*, have lately, in the Parliament at York, been duly examined *per prelatos, comites, barones et communitatem dicti regni ;* by them and by the king it has been determined that they should be cancelled altogether.[2] A distinction was thus drawn between two kinds of enacting bodies ; on the one hand, we have the magnates and, on the other, the magnates and the commonalty of the realm in Parliament.

We must regret that the drafters of the statute preferred the phrase *communalte de roialme* to a precise enumeration of the

---

[1] Stapeldon's Register (Exeter), pp. 443-4, no. 412, February 20, 1322.

[2] The king to Geoffrey le Scrope and his colleagues on the Bench, York, May 19, 1322 ; order for the publication and enrolment of the statute (*Placita coram domino rege apud Westmonasterium de termino sancte Trinitatis, anno regni regis Edwardi filii regis Edwardi decimo septimo, rotulo XXV :* transcript in Bodley MS. Eng. Hist., b, 134, f. 51).

estates of the commons. The words *communalte, communitas* and *commune* were still highly ambiguous and almost every example of their early usage ought to be separately interpreted.[1] In the first decade of the century the phrase was used in a general sense to convey a consensus of opinion, expressed by the magnates on behalf of society as a whole. The *billa* of 1301 was presented by the prelates and *proceres* of the realm *ex parte tocius communitatis*[2] and a protest, addressed by the magnates to the pope in 1309, was sealed *tam pro nobis quam pro tota communitate regni et terrarum predictarum.*[3] But it is not necessary, for this reason, to empty the words of all meaning when employed in a different form and at a later date,[4] especially as they were afterwards certainly used to express the consent of the Commons in Parliament. In the famous statute abolishing tallage (1340) the formula runs : " the common assent of the prelates, earls, barons, and other magnates and commons of our said realm of England and that in the Parliament."[5] The wording is virtually the same as that of the royal order to the judges in 1322 and we have no warrant for supposing that another meaning, or no meaning at all, was then intended. On the contrary, a general definition, in this sense, is contained in the statute itself. It is stated that the king had caused the Ordinances to be rehearsed and examined in the Parliament of York " by the prelates, earls and barons, among whom were the more part of the Ordainers then living, and by the commonalty of his realm, there by his command assembled." Further, in an account of the procedure in the Parliament of 1321, also drafted in May 1322, " the knights of the shires and others who came for the commonalty of the realm " are described as attendant on the king, with the prelates, earls and barons.[6] In both these examples the distinction between the magnates and the commonalty is drawn even more clearly

---

[1] Cf. Stubbs (*Constitutional History*, II, 175-6, n. 3) : " . . . it is extremely difficult to distinguish the passages in which ' le commun ' is used discretively for the commons from those in which it is used comprehensively for the whole body."

[2] *Parl. Writs*, I, 104, cited *Bulletin*, VI, p. 77, as in note 4 below.

[3] Swinfield's Register (Hereford), pp. 472-5, cited Conway Davies, *op. cit.*, p. 513.

[4] For another view, compare H. G. Richardson and G. O. Sayles, *Bulletin*, Vol. VI, pp. 76-7.

[5] *Statutes of the Realm*, I, p. 290.

[6] *Cal. Cl. Rolls, 1318-23*, pp. 544-5.

than in the order to the judges. It is possible that the phrase " commonalty of the realm " was adopted deliberately when the statute was drafted. We have already seen that the position of the clerical proctors in Parliament was far more dubious in 1322 than the writs of summons would lead us to suppose. To define the estates of the commons precisely would have drawn attention to a controversy which was irrelevant to the main issue. Either for that reason, or in unconscious evasion of the difficulty, a general formula was chosen which afterwards passed into normal parliamentary usage. The commonalty of the realm became the Commons in Parliament.

We may conclude, therefore, that Edward II's long drawn-out conflict with the contrariants had endowed the Parliament of estates with a new significance. In his reign the commonalty, or the Commons in Parliament, began to exercise political functions, hitherto the monopoly of the magnates. The king himself was recognising this when he summoned representatives of his allies in the Cinque Ports and in Wales to the Parliament of York (1322). The opinions of all parties, from right to left, were converging in the same direction ; in great matters, both legal and political, the final decision must rest with Parliament. Parliament must be summoned in due form by the king himself ; it must include the commonalty of the realm as well as the magnates ; the king must enact, but the common assent of the estates is essential to the validity of enactments. The sum of these opinions was expressed succinctly in the statute of York. Henceforth " matters which are to be established for the estate of our lord the king . . . and for the estate of the realm and of the people, shall be treated, accorded and established in Parliaments, by our lord the king, and by assent of the prelates, earls and barons, and the commonalty of the realm." It is true that the principle thus stated was in some ways premature and that its full implications could be worked out only very slowly. The main point, for our purposes, is that the clear intention of the statute was to assert the authority of the Parliament of estates. It maintained, therefore, in general terms, the same doctrine of common responsibility which we find in the *Modus*.

CHAPTER IX

COMMITTEES OF ESTATES AND THE DEPOSITION OF
EDWARD II

LIKE the *Modus*, the famous sentence in the statute of York
(1322) ("matters which are to be established for the estate of
our lord the king . . . and for the estate of the realm and of the
people, shall be treated, accorded and established in parliaments
by our lord the king, and by the consent of the prelates, earls
and barons and the commonalty of the realm . . .") represents
an ideal of the harmonious co-operation of all the estates. The
narrow circle of authority round king and magnates was being
slowly forced open by the equal pull of forces within it. How
that enlargement was realised in action may be seen in the final
trial of strength between Edward II and his barons. In January
1327 an embassy representing all the estates was sent to Kenilworth and homage to the king was formally renounced by a
prolocutor in the name of the whole realm. The general phrase
commonalty of the realm was invested with a precise meaning
by the presence of the commons acting through representatives
chosen from the clergy, the Cinque Ports, the shires, the cities
and the boroughs. This procedure will require examination
in some detail, as its significance has hitherto been obscured by
confusion of evidence.

The procedure of the deposition cannot be considered apart
from the earlier history of committees of estates, familiar instru-
ments of arbitration and of action in the early fourteenth century.
These committees have, for us, a double interest, as they are also
highly characteristic of the *Modus* (XIII and XVII). The evidence for their history thus gives us a direct bearing on the date
of the document. It may even carry us further and be interpreted to mean that the *Modus* itself exercised an influence on
the course of events in 1327.

In 1327 there was nothing novel in the idea of estates or orders representing the whole realm, though it had grown up slowly and for a time had evaded generalisation. Edward I's writs of summons to his Parliaments of estates were a tacit recognition of the cellular organisation of English society and the discussions of the clergy, divided into separate orders or *gradus*,[1] illustrate the same principle more clearly applied in the Church. However, both in ecclesiastical and secular matters the idea of hierarchy for long overshadowed that of equal co-ordination. In the body politic described by John of Salisbury all members are bound to fulfil their several functions under the rule of the king as head and the Church as soul. Friction between Church and Crown was in itself sufficient to make the hierarchical theory unworkable and in the thirteenth century the magnates began to put themselves forward as partners with rights at least equal to the monarch's.

The process of change to a new conception of social order can be traced, intermittently and through the dust of conflict, in the constitutions and committees thrust on the Crown from 1215 to 1327. The idea of distribution of power slowly emerged, though for a time it halted at the stage of a balance between monarchical and aristocratic government. The twenty-five appointed by Magna Carta to restrain the king were styled *barones electi* without further classification.[2] Under Henry III new groups began to form within the circle of the magnates. In 1244 the king's request for a subsidy was debated by the Great Council, divided into three orders, prelates, earls and barons ; the bishops advised that nothing should be done without common consent (*sine communi universitate nihil facerent*), and proposed that a committee of twelve, four drawn from each order, should be appointed to draw up a plan of reform.[3] The committee,

---

[1] E.g. at the Parliament of Bury St. Edmunds, 1296 (Cotton (*Rolls Series*), pp. 314-15).

[2] *Select Charters*, pp. 301-3. That the Mayor of London is named among the twenty-five may perhaps be taken as an indication that London was deemed to be a corporate tenant-in-chief.

[3] Matt. Paris (*Rolls Series*), IV, 395 ; *Select Charters*, p. 327. Two of the barons chosen were the abbots of Bury St. Edmunds and Ramsey. Cf. the committee of twelve *pares* appointed by the Parliament of Scotland to advise John Balliol in 1294 : it consisted of four bishops, four earls and four barons (Conway Davies, p. 349 ; *Chronicle of Lanercost*, ed. J. Stevenson, Edinburgh, 1839, pp. 161-2 ; Hemingburgh's *Chronicle*, ed. H. C. Hamilton, (*Eng. Hist. Soc.*), 1848-49, II, 78).

pledged to put forward nothing which lacked the consent of all, demanded that the justiciar, the chancellor and the itinerant justices should be controlled by the Council.   This first committee of estates, narrow though it was according to later ideas, thus recognised, not only the principle of ministerial responsibility, but the coercive force of a representative body in which diverse elements were represented.

During the experiments of the Barons' Wars the idea of entrusting power to committees was developed, though neither the complicated constitution of 1258 nor the committees of three and nine established by Parliament in 1264 drew a distinction between separate estates within the baronage.   Little is heard of the committee under the strong rule of Edward I, as it was essentially the weapon of revolution.   At the turn of the century, however, a group within the aristocratic circle began to act together as leaders of their order.   Though at first it was the Constable and Marshal who claimed peculiar authority, these great hereditary officers were too small a unit to form a permanent estate.   Instead, the claim was shifted to the earls who, as Mr. Conway Davies has pointed out,[1] began to be regarded as a separate order upon whom a special responsibility for the good government of the realm devolved.   The ideal of government in the *Mirror of Justices* was the rule of the earls, and in a famous gloss on Bracton Longuevill argued that the king had earls, associates, masters and superiors.[2]   No doubt the theory grew up to match the facts, as at that time the earls were in wealth and in personality the natural leaders of the whole baronage.

The effect soon showed itself in the constitutional devices used in the struggle over Gaveston and the Ordinances, when the plan of committees of estates within the baronage was revived. Its virtue lay in a nice distribution of responsibility without loss of expert leadership, a subtle compromise between aristocratic control and the general will of the commonalty of magnates. In 1310 the Ordainers were chosen in accordance with a plan of indirect or cross elections, worked out on the basis of the three estates of prelates, earls and barons.   The prelates chose two earls and the earls two prelates ; these four elected two barons ;

---

[1] Pp. 16 *seq.*

[2] *Rex habet . . . comites . . . socios . . . magistros . . . superiores*, my adaptation from Longuevill's syllogism, cited by Conway Davies, p. 16.

the six then co-opted fifteen, making a committee of twenty-one in all. On this committee sat seven bishops, eight earls and six barons.[1] The same idea of a division of power among the estates was expressed in Ordinance Forty, where it was ordained that in each Parliament one bishop, two earls and two barons should be assigned to hear complaints against royal officials who broke the Ordinances. It is significant that this committee was the only machinery devised to enforce the rules laid down by the Ordainers. In the Parliament of Lincoln (1316) another committee of three orders was appointed; five bishops, five earls and one baron were appointed to take order with the Council for the better governance of the realm and of the royal household.[2] The same plan was adopted in the Treaty of Leake (August 1318) when eight bishops, four earls, four barons and one banneret nominated by Lancaster were appointed to remain with the king until the next Parliament. Two bishops, one earl, one baron and the banneret were to be in constant attendance.[3] The symmetry of the Leake arrangement was destroyed in the Parliament of York (October 1318) when two bishops and seven barons were added to the committee of estates.[4] In other words, an academic agreement as to the distribution of power broke down under pressure of the claims of individuals.

Thus the idea of a committee of estates representing the orders within the baronage was fully developed during the first phases of the conflict between Edward II and his subjects. Up to 1318 it remained an aristocratic monopoly. Though the worth of the commons was recognised in general assemblies, there was as yet no move to share with them executive responsibility. However, once the statute of York had recognised their permanent place in Parliament, no distributive scheme could ignore the orders outside the baronial circle. It was natural that the heavy burden of responsibility for the deposition of Edward II should be laid by Parliament on a committee which included all the estates of the realm.

When Parliament met in January 1327 the deposition of the

[1] *Parl. Writs*, II, ii, Appendix 27.   Cf. *Annales London*, pp. 171-2.
[2] Lancaster's letter, July, 1317, Murimuth, pp. 271-4.
[3] Cole, *Documents*, pp. 1-2 ; *Cal. Cl. Rolls*, 1318-23, pp. 112-14.
[4] Cole, *loc. cit.*, p. 12.   The new members were the bishops of Winchester and Coventry, the younger Despenser, Badlesmere, Mortimer of Chirk, Martin, Somery, Giffard and Botitourt.

king was a foregone conclusion, as the queen, Mortimer and their supporters held an impregnable position. Edward II had been hunted across England and taken prisoner in Wales. His chief friends and advisers—the Despensers, Arundel and bishop Stapeldon—had been put to death. The Londoners had murdered Stapeldon without any show of trial and were thus deeply committed to the queen's party. No compromise with the king was possible, nor was it desired by any of the leaders. Parliament was summoned to justify rebellion and to authorise the substitution of one king for another. Interest, therefore, lies less in the decision itself than in the legal forms adopted to carry it out. As no one complete or reliable account of the procedure has been preserved, it is necessary to set out the sequence of events in some detail.[1]

No doubt the queen's supporters were deeply concerned as to the procedure to be followed. There were no precedents and it was essential to make their legal position as secure as possible. A letter has been preserved which suggests that a chief adviser in the business was the archbishop of Canterbury, Walter Reynolds. His friend, Henry Eastry, the venerable Prior of Christ Church, Canterbury—he was then over eighty—had been sending him advice since the first rumours of an open quarrel between the king and queen. At a date shortly before the meeting of Parliament he sent a letter, probably the last of a series, in which he outlined the line of action which was afterwards followed, at least in part. It ran as follows :

" . . . Two bishops were lately sent to the king to beg him on behalf of the commonalty that he would please to come to the Parliament about to meet in London to ordain and to dispose of certain arduous business. . . . The king refused to consent. . . . Therefore, it seems expedient that he should again be required to attend Parliament by an embassy of two earls, two barons, four citizens and burgesses and four knights of the shire, specially elected

---

[1] No Parliament roll is extant, and it is possible that no official account of the proceedings was ever drafted (The Parliaments of Edward III, *Bulletin of the Institute of Historical Research*, Vol. IX, pp. 16-17). However, a passage in Knighton (II, 217) suggests that an account *ex antiquo statuto* of the deposition was shown as a threat to Richard II during the session of the Parliament of 1386. Perhaps at this time it was lost, or even destroyed, at Richard's command. Cf. the questions put to the judges referring to the statute by which Edward II was condemned in Parliament (*ibid.*, p. 239, question nine).

to represent the whole commonalty of the realm. This ought to be done in order that not only the prelates, but the magnates, nobles and chief persons of every estate and condition in the realm may be involved in the business. All this should be done formally before proceeding any further. *Valete.*

"[Postscript.] Let no other eye see this letter. I am anxious to know rather than to see whatever is done."[1]

Eastry was afraid that the archbishop would allow the main responsibility to be laid upon himself and the bishops. His advice evidently left a strong impression and his plan of a representative embassy was used, though not for the purpose for which it was proposed. It seems probable that archbishop Reynolds was the man to whom the details of the procedure were entrusted.[2]

Writs were issued on December 3 for a Parliament to be held on January 7.[3] Fairly full returns are extant and they show two unusual features. Twenty-four persons, English and Welsh, were summoned from North Wales through the justice ; this was, no doubt, in imitation of a similar summons, issued by Edward II in 1322 and now used to bring in Mortimer's supporters.[4] London elected six persons, of whom two were to act as members of Parliament, with full power to represent the community.[5] This indirect election reflected the disturbed state of the city.

When Parliament met (Wednesday, January 7) the London mob crowded into Westminster Hall,[6] about which we may suppose that the soldiers of Mortimer and Lancaster were already drawn up. Orleton, bishop of Hereford, addressed the assembly. He explained that the king was absent because the queen was afraid of him and asked whether Parliament wished to be ruled by him any longer. Probably on the same day, archbishop Reynolds brought a series of charges against the king, as grounds for his

---

[1] *Lit. Cant.* I, 204-5. Letter from the Prior to the Archbishop, January 1327 : " . . . per duos comites, duos barones, quatuor personas de civitatibus et burgis et quatuor militis de comitatibus, per communitatem totius regni ad hoc specialiter electos." Postscript: "Istam cedulam non aspiciat oculus alienus. Quid autem actum est super praemissis scire desidero potius quam videre."

[2] See *infra*, pp. 184, 189.

[3] *Parl. Writs*, II, ii, 350-2 ; *Cal. Cl. Rolls*, 1323-27, p. 626.

[4] *Cal. Cl. Rolls, 1318-23*, p. 539.

[5] *Parl. Writs*, II, ii, 359.

[6] *Historia Roffensis* in *Anglia Sacra*, I, 367. Cf. *Cal. Plea and Memoranda Rolls, 1323-64*, ed. A. H. Thomas, Cambridge, 1926, p. 11, n. 3.

deposition. On the following day (Thursday, January 8) Parliament was again asked to choose between father and son and apparently the great majority declared for the young prince. Homage was sworn to him forthwith and Reynolds preached on the text *Vox populi, vox Dei.*[1] The archbishop of York, three bishops and certain others whose names are unrecorded refused to consent ; one recalcitrant, the bishop of Rochester, was badly hustled and threatened with death.[2] Thus a new king was chosen before the old king was deposed.

We have no reliable evidence for what happened during the rest of the week. Several chroniclers say that two bishops, Stratford and Orleton, were sent to Kenilworth to request the king to come before Parliament " to concur in some just and suitable arrangement with regard to the Crown." He refused to attend and the bishops were back in London to report his answer by Sunday, January 12.[3] The story does not tally with Prior Eastry's letter which implies that the bishops' mission was sent before the session of Parliament. Also it was hardly possible for the distance to Kenilworth and back (about eighty miles) to be covered between Wednesday evening and Sunday. It is more probable that the second half of the week was spent in negotiations to secure unanimity. We know that four prelates had refused their homage to the prince and that they had some support from others. Resistance was at least sufficient to make the queen's party hesitate to proceed to the formal act of deposition.

The technical difficulty in the way was probably not so much the wish for a unanimous verdict as the absence of the king. The medieval idea of a fair trial had its centre in judgement rather than in proof. There was no close scrutiny of evidence and no presumption of innocence. Arraignment in due form, coupled with a reference to matters notoriously believed, virtually established a presumption of guilt and the accused had little chance of escape save on a point of law. At the same time justice required that the criminal should be brought to trial. It was a grave wrong to punish " unjustly and without a judgement,"

---

[1] *Historia Roffensis ; Anglia Sacra,* I, 367. Reynolds apparently preached again on this theme on January 15. Cf. *infra,* p. 184.
[2] *Ibid.,* p. 367.   [3] *Chronicle of Lanercost,* p. 257.

to act without due formality of procedure ; the procedure must include the personal appearance of the accused party and an opportunity for him to state his defence. In the eyes of contemporaries the charges brought against Edward II were unjust, not because they were vaguely worded and unsupported by witnesses, but because he himself was not present to hear them. Here lay the dilemma of the magnates in 1327. They lacked the courage to produce the king in Parliament and they had betrayed their fear by giving contrary reasons for his absence. Eastry and certain chroniclers state that he had refused to attend, but Orleton in Parliament defended his absence by saying that the queen was afraid of her husband.[1] It is possible that for a few days the archbishop of York and others demanded that the king should confront Parliament and thereby created a deadlock, as the queen's party were determined not to risk a loyalist reaction.

The delay naturally gave rise to growing uneasiness and suspicion. On Monday, January 12, the citizens of London forced the issue by sending a letter to the magnates which was in fact an ultimatum.[2] The mayor, aldermen and commonalty of the city requested the magnates to agree to certain conditions : to make an accord with London ; to swear to maintain the cause of the queen and her son ; to crown the new king and to depose Edward II. It may be that the Londoners took the initiative as part of a preconcerted plan. Two months earlier (November 15) the queen had sent Stratford, bishop of Winchester, to London to grant the citizens permission to elect a mayor, a right which they had forfeited in 1321.[3] They had at once chosen Richard of Bethune, the man who had helped Mortimer to escape from the Tower in 1322.[4] At the same time the bishop swore to guard the liberties of the city. The Londoners were resolute against Edward II. In the Lichfield Chronicle it is stated that every great man—bishop, earl, abbot, baron or any other in England—who entered the city, was compelled, even against his will, to swear on holy relics that he would defend and

---

[1] Orleton's *Apologia* in Roger Twysden, *Historiae Anglicanae*, 1652, § 2767.
[2] *Cal. Plea and Memoranda Rolls, 1323-64*, pp. 11-12.
[3] *Chronicle of London (Camden Society)*, p. 55.
[4] *Parl. Writs*, II, ii, Appendix, 249.

maintain the commonalty in their undertakings.[1] The queen's party had probably from the first intended to make use of the political excitement in the city and, whether the message was provoked by them or not, they were certainly ready to act upon it.

On the following day (Tuesday, January 13) the prelates and magnates rode to the Guildhall.[2] Stratford made a public declaration of the articles of accusation which had been laid before Parliament. On the text *Rex insipiens*, Orleton preached so hotly against the king that the crowd shouted " we will no more have this man to reign over us."[3] Later in the day another great public meeting was organised by Mortimer and archbishop Reynolds. Stratford preached an inflammatory sermon on the text " my head, my head " (*caput meum doleo*) and an oath of confederacy was sworn by the prelates and magnates. The oath was a solemn undertaking to support the queen and her son to the death, to keep the ordinances made or to be made in Parliament and to guard and to maintain the franchises of the city.[4] Its purpose was obviously to compel as many as possible to commit themselves beyond withdrawal in support of the final decision to be reached in Parliament.

The London memoranda rolls have preserved a list of persons who took the oath.[5] The names are grouped in eight categories or estates as follows : four earls [6] and all the knights of their retinue ; twenty-four barons with Mortimer at their head ; sixty-two knights, six serjeants-at-law and four judges ; thirteen persons called knights of the shire ; the archbishops of Canterbury and Dublin and twelve bishops ; four abbots

[1] " . . . non erat aliquis magnus dominus, episcopus, comes, abbas vel baro, seu aliquis alius tocius Anglie qui civitatem Londoniensem intravit, quin communitas Londoniensis compulsit ipsum, licet invitum, iurare tactis sacrosanctis ut ipsam communitatem in suis inceptis defenderet et manuteneret " (Lichfield Chronicle, MS. Bodley 956, f. 205, col. 2). Cf. the statement in *Gesta Abbatum* (*Rolls Series*), II, 156, that the Londoners " compelled all prelates and lay magnates, who were in the city for any reason whatsoever, to bind themselves by oath, *nolens volens*, to maintain I know not what liberties."

[2] *Cal. Plea and Memoranda Rolls, 1323-64*, p. 12.

[3] *Chronicle of Lanercost*, p. 257.

[4] *Annales Paulini*, p. 323. Cf. *Cal. Plea and Memoranda Rolls, 1323-64*, p. 12.

[5] *Cal. Plea and Memoranda Rolls, 1323-64*, pp. 12-14.

[6] Thomas earl Marshal, Edmund earl of Kent, John earl of Hereford, John earl of Warenne.

and three priors ;[1] twenty-one priests and clerks ; thirty barons
of the Cinque Ports, five burgesses from Bury St. Edmunds
and thirteen from St. Albans. Thus all the estates of the realm
were represented—prelates, secular magnates, lower clergy,
knights of the shire and burgesses—though in an irregular way,
altogether distinct from representation in Parliament. The list
is a guide to the strength of the queen's party outside Parliament
as well as within, but it can also be read as evidence that there
was still a party for the king. Fifty-four secular magnates had
been summoned to Parliament,[2] but only twenty-eight took the
London oath. Three of the prelates who had refused homage
to the prince did not swear ; the fourth, Hamo of Rochester,
swore saving his order and the liberties of Magna Carta.[3] Fourteen out of nineteen abbots summoned to Parliament were not
sworn.[4] One of the thirteen called knights of the shire was not
in fact a member of Parliament [5] and the other twelve all came
from counties south of the Trent.[6] The boroughs were cap-
riciously represented by the men of Bury and St. Albans, towns
then on the eve of revolt against their monastic overlords.[7] It
may, perhaps, be inferred that Parliament was not yet prepared
to depose the king.

The swearing-in of all these people [8] seems to have lasted for
at least three days ; we know, for example, that the earls did
not take the oath until Thursday, January 15.[9] In the mean-
time events had moved quickly in Parliament, running concur-

---

[1] The abbots of Westminster, St. Albans, Bury St. Edmunds and Peterborough and the priors of three London houses.
[2] *Parl. Writs*, II, ii, 351.   [3] *Historia Roffensis, loc. cit.*, p. 367.
[4] *Parl. Writs*, II, ii, 351.   [5] Brian de Bowyz.
[6] Norfolk, Somerset, Bucks, Cambs., Hunts, Hants, Northants, Salop,
Glouc., Devon and Hertfordshire (two knights).
[7] Four out of the five burgesses of Bury were concerned in disputes with,
or attacks on, the Abbey (*Memorials of Bury St. Edmunds (Rolls Series)*, II,
332, 339 ; III, 42-3) ; eight of the thirteen men from St. Albans were involved
in a similar way (*Gesta Abbatum*, II, 233, 234, 235, 240, 243, 249, 259-60).
[8] The importance of these oaths is shown by a petition, presented by the
commons in the first Parliament of Edward III, in which they asked that oaths
should be taken throughout the realm to maintain the queen's party (*Rot. Parl.*
II, 10*b*-11). The demand is put more specifically in the unprinted version of
the Parliament Roll—" et qe homme face en chescun counte la comune iurer
auxi com nous avoms iure de meintenir lenprise ore encomence, et auxi soit
maunde a les Eveks de faire la clergie en mesme la manoir " (P.R.O., Parliament and Council Proceedings (Chancery), Roll 11, m.2).
[9] *Cal. Plea and Memoranda Rolls, 1323-64*, p. 12.

rently with the movement in the city. Sessions were resumed either on Monday or on Tuesday (January 12-13) and probably the first business dealt with was the legal objection to judgement *in absentia*. According to the *Lanercost Chronicle*, the bishops of Winchester and Hereford reported that Edward II had refused with angry contempt to come among his enemies who were traitors to him.[1] Another authority states that the bishops described the king as filled with the same cruelty and evil intent as he had been in the past.[2] Though it is improbable that a special message had been sent to the king, Parliament was certainly given the impression that he had definitely refused to appear. In this way the legal defence made on his behalf was undermined and the way was clear for the final verdict.

The fullest and most reasonable account of the proceedings in Parliament on Tuesday, January 13, is contained in the hitherto unpublished chronicle of Pipewell[3] :—

" And on the feast of St. Hilary [1327], there came to the great hall at Westminster the archbishops and bishops, earls and barons, abbots and priors, and all others from the cities and boroughs, together with the whole commonalty of the land. There, by common assent of all, the archbishop of Canterbury declared how the good king Edward when he died had left to his son his lands of England, Ireland, Wales, Gascony and Scotland in good peace ; how Gascony and Scotland had been as good as lost by evil counsel and evil ward ; how, further, by evil counsel the son had destroyed the greater part of the noble blood of the realm, to the dishonour and loss of himself, his realm and all the people ; and how he had done many other marvels. Therefore, it was agreed by all that he ought not to reign but that his eldest son, the duke of Guienne, should reign and wear the crown in his stead. For since the bishops of Hereford and London [*sic*], who had been sent to him at Kenilworth as messengers for the commonalty of the land . . . bore witness in Parliament that he still had the same cruelty and ill intent towards them that had moved him in the past,[4] thereupon it was ordained and agreed that great persons—bishops, abbots, priors, earls, barons, knights, justices and others—should go to him and renounce their

---

[1] *Chronicle of Lanercost*, p. 257.

[2] Pipewell Chronicle, see *infra*, p. 194.

[3] MS. Cotton, Julius A 1, ff. 56-56b. See *infra*, Note A, pp. 193-5, for a short account of this chronicle, and the text of the translated passage.

[4] This probably was reported on the previous day. Cf. *Chronicle of Lanercost*, p. 257.

homage and that of all the land. It was also ordained that, because of the burdens and anguish that she had suffered as well this side the sea as the other, our lady the queen should continue to reign all her life and that our lord the new king should wed the daughter of the count of Hainault."

The substantial accuracy of this account is confirmed by other writers. Higden,[1] his imitators [2] and the Lichfield Chronicle [3] agree that the date of deposition was Tuesday, January 13. Lanercost alone drags out the whole proceedings for three days during which the assembly was gradually worked up to the highest pitch of excitement and anger against the king.[4] On Tuesday Hereford preached on the childish folly of Edward II, taking as his text *Rex insipiens perdet populum suum* ; [5] on Wednesday Winchester spoke on the same theme with the text *Caput meum doleo* ; [6] and on Thursday archbishop Reynolds boldly proposed the deposition with the warrant of the old Latin tag *Vox populi, vox Dei*. It is not specifically stated that these speeches were made in Parliament, and it seems much more likely that they were delivered in the city and that the whole business of deposition was carried through on Tuesday. The delegates appointed by Parliament had reached Kenilworth by Tuesday, January 20.[7] The unwieldy cavalcade of lords and

[1] *Higden*, VIII, 322-3.
[2] E.g. Knighton, I, 441 ; *Vita Edwardi II*, p. 289.
[3] MS. Bodley 956, ff. 205-6. The whole passage is worth quoting. " . . . convocatum est concilium generale tocius cleri et populi Anglie apud West-monasterium ad diem mercurium in crastino Epiphanie domini anno eodem, videlicet, de qualibet civitate et de quolibet comitatu et burgo certus numerus personarum ad tractandum et ordinandum cum magnatibus de statu regis et regni. In quo concilio ad clamorem tocius populi unanimiter in ipso clamore perseverantis ut rex Edwardus quintus regni solio omnino deponeretur, eo quod ab initio regni sui huc usque in regimine male se habuerat, populum suum nequiter vex⟨av⟩erat, terras castra et alia ad coronam pertinencia dissipaverat, nobiliores regni perverso iudicio iniuste morti adiudicaverat, ignobiles sublima-verat, ac alia quamplura mala contra sacramentum suum in coronacione sua prestitum fecerat. Sicque Waltero Cantuariensi archiepiscopo huiusmodi articulos pronunciante, assensu et consensu omnium rex Edwardus, quintus die Martii in festo sancti Hillarii anno eodem, a regni gubernaculo omnino depositus est et Edwardus primogenitus suus in regem Anglie est sublimatus, ordinatumque est quod ex tunc non *rex* sed *Edwardus de Karnarvan pater regis* amodo vocetur."
[4] *Chronicle of Lanercost*, pp. 257-8.
[5] Ecclesiastes x, 16, " Woe to thee, O land, when thy king is a child."
[6] 2 Kings iv, 19, " My head, my head."
[7] Pipewell Chronicle, f. 56ᵛ, see p. 194 ; *Chronicle of Geoffrey le Baker*, ed. E. Maunde Thompson, Oxford, 1889, p. 27.

commons can hardly have ridden much more than a dozen miles a day, and we must suppose that they left Westminster on Wednesday, January 14. The conclusion is that Parliament deposed Edward II and appointed delegates to go to Kenilworth on the previous day.

The pitiful scenes at Kenilworth are well known.[1] The bishops first saw the king by himself; by the threat that a successor outside the royal circle would be chosen instead of his son [2] they forced from him a promise to abdicate. The delegates were then ranged in the audience chamber in order of rank and the king was led out to them by Lancaster and the bishop of Winchester. After a railing speech from Orleton, Edward, half-fainting and with groans and tears, abdicated in favour of his son. On the following day allegiance and homage were solemnly renounced in the name of the whole realm. This was done by William Trussel, a Lancastrian knight,[3] who was styled proctor or *procurator* " of all in the land of England and of the whole Parliament." [4] News of Edward's abdication was reported to Parliament on Saturday, January 24, and the new king's peace was at once proclaimed.[5]

All authorities agree that the deposition was carried out by common consent. The Lichfield Chronicle states that it was done " by clamour of the whole people, unanimously persisting in that clamour." [6] The clamour was, no doubt, the work of armed retainers and the London mob, but the leaders were determined to distribute responsibility throughout all the estates of the realm. For this reason it was decided to send to Kenilworth a parliamentary deputation, formed on the lines suggested by Prior Eastry though for an entirely different purpose. As this deputation marks the climax of the long process of change from hierarchical control to co-operative action, it is necessary to examine its composition as closely as the evidence permits.

---

[1] The most detailed account is given by Baker (pp. 26-8), who used a narrative written by Thomas de la More, an eyewitness who came in the train of the bishop of Winchester.

[2] Perhaps Mortimer.

[3] He fought with Lancaster against the king in 1322, forfeited and fled abroad to return in the queen's train in 1326.

[4] Cotton MS., Nero, D II, f. 204b. There are a number of variants of Trussel's title.

[5] *Rymer*, Vol. IV, 243.   [6] *Supra*, p. 184, n. 3.

The chronicles differ in their accounts of the deputation, but it is possible to simplify and to compare their evidence by considering them in groups. In the *Polychronicon* it is stated that by common agreement three bishops, two earls, two barons and two judges were sent as solemn messengers to the king to renounce the homage which had been given to him.[1] The statement is repeated by the chroniclers, who depend on Higden,[2] but it carries no more weight on that account. A second version occurs in the Lichfield Chronicle ; the bishops of Hereford and Winchester, earl Warenne, two abbots, barons and many knights were sent to Edward II to tell him what had been done and to read to him the articles of deposition.[3] If the evidence stopped here, we might suppose that the deputation was limited to the estates who had sworn fealty and that its main business was the renunciation of homage. This, in fact, is the view presented in the popular *Brut* Chronicle, where the delegates are reduced to earl Warenne, the bishop of Ely, Henry Lord Percy and Sir William Trussel, a knight of Lancaster's household.[4]

However, four other accounts, which appear to be independent of each other, emphasise the presence of the commons in the embassy, showing that it was, in effect, a committee of estates. Murimuth states that three bishops, two earls, two abbots, four barons, two knights from each shire in England and a certain number of persons from London, other cities and great towns, especially the [Cinque] Ports, were sent to Kenilworth to require the king to abdicate.[5] Baker's version is substantially the same, except that he substitutes two burgesses from each borough and the Cinque Ports for the *certus numerus* of Murimuth.[6] Baker and Murimuth are both good witnesses. Murimuth was a

[1] Vol. VIII, 322-3.

[2] For example, Knighton, I, 441 ; *Vita Edwardi II*, p. 290 ; Cotton MS., Nero, D. II, f. 209, col. 2. It is also worth noting that Higden, writing at Chester, had little opportunity to collect exact information.

[3] MS. Bodley, 956, f. 206. Another version of this Chronicle, with certain omissions, occurs in MS. Cotton, Cleopatra D. IX, no. 6, f. 71ᵛ.

[4] *Brut*, I, 241-2.

[5] Murimuth, p. 51. The phrase describing the burgesses is ambiguous— " de quolibet comitatu Angliae duo milites, item de Londoniis et aliis civitatibus et magnis villis, et praecipue de portubus, de qualibet certus numerus personarum." The meaning is made clear in the passage (otherwise identical), in *Flores Historiarum* (III, 235)—" de civitatibus autem et magnis villis, praecipue de portibus, certus numerus personarum."

[6] Baker, pp. 26, 204.

skilled canonist and had served in Parliament both as a personal proxy and as proctor of the clergy ; [1] Baker drew his information from Thomas de la More who went to Kenilworth in the train of the bishop of Winchester.[2] At the same time it is not credible that all or even a considerable number of the lay Commons in Parliament formed a part of the embassy and we may adopt without hesitation the drastic reduction of its size which appears in the chronicles of Pipewell and Lanercost. The Pipewell chronicler states that the delegation consisted of the bishops of London, Winchester and Hereford, the abbots of Glastonbury and Dover, earl Warenne and the earl of Lancaster, the barons Hugh de Courtenay and Richard de Grey, the judges Geoffrey le Scrope and John de Bourser (?), two barons of the Cinque Ports, four burgesses of London and four knights for the commonalty of the realm.[3] The *Lanercost Chronicle* has a longer and rather different list : the bishops of Winchester and Hereford, earl Warenne and the earl of Lancaster, the barons of Ros and Courtenay, two abbots, two priors, two judges, two Dominicans, two Carmelites, two knights from north of the Trent and two from the south, two citizens of London and two men from the Cinque Ports.[4]

Thus a brief analysis of the chronicles shows that the difficulty about the composition of the embassy is almost altogether restricted to the commons. The numbers and even the names of the magnates are for the most part clear. The two earls were certainly Warenne and Lancaster. There is also no doubt that two judges were delegates ; the names Geoffrey le Scrope and John de Bourser (?), given in the Pipewell Chronicle, are probably correct. The bishops were Stratford of Winchester and Orleton of Hereford with either Hotham of Ely or Gravesend of London as the third. Baker and Murimuth both mention four barons, and as four names in all—Courtenay, Grey, Ros and Percy—are recorded by various authorities, it seems probable that the representation of the barons was double that of the earls. Nearly all the chronicles mention two abbots and only Lanercost adds two priors. The abbots are named in the Pipewell Chronicle as Glastonbury and Dover. Now Dover had

[1] E.g. he was proctor for the chapter of Canterbury in the Parliament of York in May 1319, *Parl. Writs*, II, ii, 199.
[2] Baker, p. 27.   [3] For the text, see *infra*, Note A, p. 194.
[4] *Chronicle of Lanercost*, p. 258.

no abbey, but its priory was important [1] and it may be that the religious houses were represented by one abbot and one prior. Reference to the attendance of two preaching friars and two Carmelites occurs only in Lanercost, though the remark that the Franciscans were excused at the queen's request serves to corroborate the unexpected addition.[2] The representation of the lay commons is less certain. The best authorities agree that two barons came from the Cinque Ports and that the knights were represented by four, probably, as Lanercost states, two from north of the Trent and two from the south. The greatest difficulty rests with the men from the cities and boroughs. Pipewell and Lanercost agree in limiting attendance to the citizens of London, though they differ as to the number of persons sent. In the London records we find a note of the payment of £50 to John de Gisors, Reginald de Conduit, John Hauteyn and others " elected by the commonalty to go to the late king at Kenilworth." [3] Perhaps the three men named were the official representatives [4] and the presence of others was merely a sign of the great excitement in the city. As both Baker and Murimuth emphasise the representation of other cities and boroughs, we probably ought to add one or more burgesses to the London quota. The men of Bury and St. Albans were prominent among those who had sworn to support the queen's party, and it is possible that burgesses from these towns were sent with the London citizens to Kenilworth, thus increasing the number to four or six.

Though we have thus a fairly clear idea of the composition of the embassy, it is impossible to fix it at an exact figure. Probably it contained about thirty persons—twenty-seven at least and thirty-one at most.[5] The irregularity of the numbers is rare

[1] The prior was John de Scholdon (1321 c. 1330) (C. R. Haines, *Dover Priory*, Cambridge, 1930, p. 261). Adam de Sodbury (1322-35) was then abbot of Glastonbury (Dugdale, I, 6-7).

[2] " . . . fratres autem Minores ad preces dominae reginae non sunt missi, ne essent bajuli nuncii tam displicentis, quia Minores multum amabat," *Chronicle of Lanercost*, p. 258. It will be remembered that the Chronicle was mainly the work of the Franciscans of Carlisle.

[3] *Calendar of the Letter Book E*, p. 222. Cf. *Cal. of Plea and Memoranda Rolls, 1323-64*, p. 30.

[4] Reginald de Conduit was one of the members of Parliament for London (*Return of Members*, I, 1, 76).

[5] These figures assume that the embassy was composed as follows : two earls, three bishops, four barons, two judges, one abbot and one prior *or* two

in medieval schemes of representation, which invariably aimed
at a symmetrical balance of interests.   We have already seen how
the symmetry of the paper plan agreed to at Leake was marred
by pressure of personal interests in the Parliament of York [1]
and we may suppose that something of the same kind happened
in 1327.   At first it was probably intended that the estates in
Parliament should be represented in due proportion, but when
a choice of delegates came to be made it was found necessary
to include persons and categories outside the original plan.

It remains to enquire what was the original plan from which
the delegation, as we know it, diverged.   We have suggested
that the idea of sending a committee of estates to the king was
first put forward by Prior Eastry.   His proposal that it should
consist of two earls, two barons, four citizens and burgesses and
four knights was devised to shift responsibility from the bishops
to the laity.   It was, therefore, not a proper basis for a scheme
of common parliamentary action.   Archbishop Reynolds, we
may suppose, brought forward Eastry's plan with the suggestion
that it should be adapted in such a way that all estates were equally
implicated.   Is it not possible that the machinery, devised for
use in a grave emergency, lay ready at his hand ?   Chapter XVII
of the *Modus Tenendi Parliamentum* (*de casibus et iudiciis difficilibus*)
provided a remedy, " if through discord between the king and
certain magnates . . . the peace of the land should be disturbed."
The Steward, the Constable and the Marshal, or two of them,
should choose twenty-five persons, a committee of estates consisting of two bishops and three proctors, two earls and three
barons, five knights of shires, five citizens and five burgesses.
In 1327 Henry of Lancaster was Steward and Thomas of
Brotherton was Marshal, while the office of Constable was in
abeyance.   Lancaster was set on vengeance for Boroughbridge
and Pontefract and he and Thomas, the king's half-brother, had
been the first of the earls to welcome the queen and Mortimer.[2]

---

abbots and two priors, two preaching friars, two Carmelites, two barons of the
Cinque Ports, four knights of the shire, four *or* six citizens and burgesses,
including three from London = twenty-seven *or* thirty-one.

[1] *Supra*, p. 176.

[2] The queen and Mortimer had landed *in terra comitis Mariscalli apud
Waltoniam* and straightway " idem comes Mariscallus et comes Leycestriae et
alii barones et milites illarum partium adhaeserunt eisdem " (Murimuth,
p. 46).

No board of nominators could have been more convenient for the occasion.

The following table brings out the way in which the committee in the *Modus* resembles and differs from the Kenilworth deputation :

Modus.	Kenilworth deputation.
2 bishops	3 bishops
3 proctors of the clergy	none
2 earls	2 earls
3 barons	4 barons
5 knights of shires	4 knights
5 citizens	3 (at least) citizens of London
5 burgesses.	1-3 (?) burgesses
	2 judges
	1-2 abbots
	1-2 priors
	2 preaching friars
	2 Carmelites
	2 barons of the Cinque Ports.

Once the hypothesis is accepted that the *Modus* was the working basis of the deputation, divergences from the original plan can easily be explained. The interval (January 7-13) between the opening of Parliament and the final act of deposition was long enough to allow full consideration of the claims of particular persons and estates. No doubt some, like the Londoners, out of zeal clamoured for places, and others, like the judges or, perhaps, the friars, were compelled to serve that they might bind their orders with the rest. The controlling part played by the bishops left no room for the politically insignificant proctors of the clergy ; their place was taken by a third bishop, two or four heads of religious houses, and four friars. Probably for territorial reasons, a fourth baron was added, so that Percy and Ros stood for the north, north-east, and east midlands, Courtenay for the south-west and Grey for the Welsh Marches. Fifteen was perhaps deemed to be an excessive representation of the lay commons ; their number was reduced to eight or ten and the ratio was altered in order to represent London and the Cinque Ports. Though the deputation was appointed in Parliament to carry out a parliamentary decree, formal membership of the assembly was not considered essential.

The deputation was neither exclusively a committee of parliamentary estates nor even (because the proctors were left out), fully representative of all the orders in Parliament. It was no time for the scrupulous fulfilment of an academic design. The leaders well knew that, in Marlowe's words :

> ". . . now we hold the old wolf by the ears,
> That, if he slip will seize upon us both,
> And gripe the sorer, being griped himself."

The queen's party made no mistakes. If the *Modus* were indeed the basis of their plan, they took from it exactly what they required and no more. The same convenient looseness in the application of the idea of representation was shown in the choice of William Trussel to renounce allegiance to the king, as *procurator* " of all the land of England and of the whole Parliament." He was probably one of the two knights from north of the Trent, but he was not a knight of the shire. His duty is put in a few words in a Winchester chronicle roll : " the king, as *regni delapidator*, was renounced by all in Parliament, by William Trussel, knight, in whose mouth Parliament as a whole put their words." [1] There was, of course, nothing new in the use of a *procurator* or *prolocutor universitatis* who had *verbum commune in ore*.[2] It was an accepted practice in ecclesiastical assemblies in the thirteenth century, as a natural development of the functions of an attorney or proctor.[3] It is, however, possible that Trussel was regarded in a special sense as the speaker of the committee of estates, reduced by stages to the single person " who cannot disagree with himself and, [therefore], shall ordain for all." [4] If the idea were indeed borrowed from the *Modus*, there was a sharp divergence from the original, since the Committee of

---

[1] " . . . tanquam regni delapidator ab omnibus in Parliamento diffidatus est per Willelmum Trussel, militem, in cuius ore universitas Parliamenti sua verba posuerat " (MS. Bodley, Roll 23).

[2] For example, 1256, Master Leonard " quasi cleri advocatus et prolocutor universitatis, verba faceret pro episcopis " (Matt. Paris, V, 539). Cf. Leonard, " verbum pro universitate faceret " (Cotton, p. 135) and Henry of Cornhill in 1244, who had " verbum commune in ore " (Matt. Paris, IV, p. 374).

[3] Cf. the eleven barons who sealed a letter to the pope in 1258 " vice totius communitatis " (*Annales de Burton (Rolls Series)*, p. 460).

[4] XVII, " . . . et ita condescendo . . . in unam solam personam . . . tandem sola persona . . . pro omnibus ordinabit, que cum se ipsa discordare non potest." A William Trussel, probably the same man, was speaker and clerk of the Commons in 1343, though not an elected member of Parliament.

twenty-five could not diminish itself to less than three without the consent of the king. Once again a doctrinaire rule was abrogated by necessity.

The procedure at the deposition of Edward II was the work of cunning minds. The shifts and experience of twenty years of political friction had been freely drawn into service. The rights of the commons, guaranteed in the statute of York, were neatly exploited and the idea of a committee of estates, hitherto the monopoly of the magnates, was extended to include the lesser orders of the realm. It was, however, an extension not so much of power as of responsibility. On the one hand, all were equally involved in the rejection of Edward II ; on the other, the committee of regency was formed on the old lines and consisted of four prelates, four earls and six barons.[1] Yet the Kenilworth embassy was by no means an empty gesture. It was an act of necessity, forced upon men too proud and too greedy for power to make a single generous or needless concession. Men outside the circle of the magnates had by degrees been admitted to a share in the king's business ; they served on his juries, were suitors in his courts, granted his taxes and gave assent to his laws. These duties gave them strength throughout the realm and, though they did not yet ask to lead, they must know why and where they were moving. The pyramid of authority rested on a broad base. Recognition of this was the key to the whole line of action followed in Parliament, in London and at Kenilworth. Renunciation of allegiance was transmuted from feudal defiance to the will of the commonalty and the king was rejected not by vassals but by subjects.

What has been done is to set the procedure of Edward II's deposition beside Chapter XVII of the *Modus* and to mark how they seem to dovetail into each other. In the *Modus* we have a plan of the study, worked out in accordance with the general principles of equality and harmony which characterise the whole document. The procedure of deposition was conceived in rebellion and blood by men to whom a false step would mean death as traitors. In government, as in any other process above the lowest plane of material needs, habit, equipment and the infinite range of human talent and stupidity are always translating abstract

[1] *Rot. Parl.* II, 52. A bishop, an earl and two barons were appointed to be in constant attendance upon the young king.

notions of harmony and equity into dominance and subordination. Against the assumption of equality in the *Modus* must be set a long tradition of aristocratic leadership ; against the assumption of harmony, the rancours of civil war and judicial murder, the strength of armed retinues and the passionate partisanship of the capital. The difference between the two is, therefore, less remarkable than the likeness. If it were established that in 1327 the *Modus* was already known to men in public life, few would hesitate to admit that it was the natural origin of the procedure of deposition. The idea of a committee of estates was, as we have seen, fully developed by the magnates, for themselves, in the first half of the reign ; in the final struggle it was suddenly extended to include the commons. Between its two forms stands the statute of York, the outward and visible sign of the change in the balance of power. The change, thus openly acknowledged, cannot have missed the attention of contemporaries, and it is not surprising to find in the *Modus* an attempt to elaborate and to fix it in a permanent form. Whether or not this attempt was coeval with the change itself still remains to be proved. Here it is enough to emphasise the likeness between Chapter XVII and the procedure at the deposition and to note that the confident assumptions of the one were ill-matched to the dangerous realities of the other. In short, the chapter *de casibus et iudiciis difficilibus* bears all the marks of a theory of government untested by experience.

NOTE A

The following extract is taken from a short French chronicle of the reign of Edward II (1307-27) which is preserved in Cotton MS. Julius A 1, ff. 51-52. It is described in the catalogue as : " Historia de rege Edwardo II et de initiis regni R. Edward III, Gallice. Epistolae nonnullae inseruntur." It appears to be written in a hand of the first half of the fourteenth century. The ink on ff. 51-2 and 56 is very faint, but with the help of ultra-violet ray photographs it is fairly legible, though some words are too much blurred to be read at all. The chronicle is immediately followed (ff. 63-72) by extracts from the register of Pipewell, a Cistercian abbey in Northamptonshire, and it may have been written in that house. It was certainly the work of some one who had access to official documents, as it contains the indictment of Hugh Despenser, ff. 54-6 ; the renunciation by Trussel,

f. 57 ; the statute against the Despensers, ff. 57-9*b* ; an account of the coronation of Edward III, ff. 60-2 ; two letters to Queen Isabella, the second dated June 30, 1321, warning her of a conspiracy of lepers in France, ff. 62-3. The passage printed below concludes the Chronicle proper [1]:—

Cotton MS. Julius A 1, ff. 56-6*v*.

Et sur la fest de seint Hilleir [January 13], lan de nostre seignur mille CCCXXVI, vindrent en la grant salle de Weymustre les ercevesqes, evesqes, countez, et barons, abbeez, et prieurs et touz altres auxi bien des citeez comme des burghes ensemblement oue toute la communaltee de la terre. Illoqes par commun assent de touz pronuncie fu par lercevesqe de Cantuarbires coment le bon roy Edward a son decees avoit lesse a son filz en bone pees les terres dEngleterre, Irland, Gales, Gascoigne et Escoce, et coment les terres de Gascoigne et dEscoce sount sicom perdu de ly par malveis conseile et mauveis garde, et ensement coment par malveis conseille il ad fait destur grand partie del bon saunk de la terre, a deshonur et damage de ly et de son reialme et de tute le pople, et multz des altres mervelles fait. Parqei assente fust par trestouz les avauntdiz qe meis ne devereit regner, mesqe son filz eyne, duke de Guyenne, deveroit regner et coroune porter pur ly. Car sicom levesqe de Herford et levesqe de Loundres qe furent a ly message de par la communalte de la terre a Kenylworth de prieser le (?) au parlement testmonerent qil fust demorant en mesmes la cruealtee et malevoluntee qe devant,.sus ceo ordine fu et assentu qe triorys [2] granz com de evesqes, abbes, priores, countes, barouns, chevaleres, justices et altres irrerent a ly, et ly rendere[nt] en grande (?) lour homage, et pur tut la terre et ensi fu fait. Derechef ordine fu pur graunt travaux et anguisses qe nostre dame la reine aveit suffert auxi bien de sa la meer com de la, qelle demorge reyne toute sa vie. Et qe nostre seignur le rey qor est prenge la feille le count de Hanaud en feme.

f. 56v.

En la feste de seinz Fabian et Sebastian [January 20] lan avantdit solom la manere de le esglise dEngleterre D lettre dominical, vindrent a Kenilworch les seuz (sic) diz, fait asaveir, les eveuqes de Loundres, Wyncestre et Herfordh, les abbeez de Glastenbires et Dovere, les countz Warenne et de Lancastre, les barones monsieur Hugh de Courteney, monsieur Richard de Grey, les justices monsieur Geffrey Lescrope et Johan de Boursier (?) [3] d(eux ?) barouns des Portez, quatre burges de Loundres et quatre chivalers pur la communalte de la terre.

---

[1] My thanks are due to Professor M. K. Pope and Miss D. M. Legge for help in deciphering and fixing the text.

[2] This may be translated *the triers*.

[3] This word is almost illegible in the MS., but the first letters appear to be *Bou*. John Bourser was one of the judges sworn in London on January 13, 1327 (*Cal. Plea and Memoranda Rolls*, 1323-64, p. 13).

Et disaient a nostre seignur le Roy les defautes susdites si come il furent chargeez et il devant eaux touz granta de sa pure voluntee qe il avoit malement governe eaux et la terre et de ceo lermant et seant a genulz les cria il merci et pria qeaux le voleient pardoner et qil priassent en pleyn parlement, qeaux ly pardonassent ceo qil avoit trespasse contre eaux.   Et auxi granta il et ordina qe monsieur Edward son filz eyne fust roy en son lieu et portast coroune le dymange cest a savoir la veille de la Purificacion [February 1], et qe toutes maners des homage et services fuse nent faitz a ly — furent a ly.   Et sus ceo vint monsieur William Troussell de Petlyng et sassist a genulz devant nostre seignur le roy et le cria merci en priant qili voleit pardoner ceo qili avoit trespasse et ili pardona devant trestouz et ly dona signe de pees.

CHAPTER X

THE COMPOSITION AND PROCEDURE OF EARLY PARLIAMENTS IN ENGLAND

WE have seen that the position assigned to the proctors in Parliament can hardly have any historical basis after 1340 and that the particular chapters on the summons of the clergy and on Canterbury and York may be assigned respectively to the years 1311-23 and 1322-25. We have also seen that the great statute of York, passed in May 1322, expressed in succinct form the doctrine of parliamentary authority set out in the *Modus* and that the procedure at the deposition of Edward II appeared to follow the procedure *de casibus et iudiciis difficilibus* prescribed for a parliamentary crisis. This evidence, coming from directions so different, is sufficient to justify the adoption, at least as a working hypothesis, of the idea that the *Modus* was written as an honest, though tendentious, description of Parliament at some time in the second half of Edward II's reign. In order to test this hypothesis it is necessary to return to the text and to examine it in detail for particular indications of date and meaning. The examination may be divided into two parts : the summons and composition of Parliament, both political and official ; its formal and constitutional procedure.

I

The composition of Parliament as described in the *Modus* is based upon two simple principles. Members are summoned for two reasons and two reasons only ; either they come for reasons of tenure as individuals (*pro sua propria persona*) [1] or else

[1] II, III, XXIII. This applies to prelates as well as to the lay magnates. Cf. Glanville, liber VII, cap. I (ed. Woodbine, p. 101) : " Notandum autem quod nec episcopus nec abbas, quia eorum baroniae sunt de elemosina domini

196

they come as representatives of communities. Other persons come to Parliament by reason of office or service ; though the king requires their presence, they are said to attend *sine summonitione*.[1] These persons are the great officers of state—the chancellor, the treasurer, the chamberlains and barons of the Exchequer and the judges ; serjeants at pleas and those of the lower clergy who belong to the king's council or whose presence is deemed useful ; and the ushers, criers and clerks who are the officials of Parliament itself.[2] The inclusion of lesser servants, like the usher and the crier, in the same category as the chancellor and treasurer serves to bring out the sharp distinction between the king's council or royal executive, and Parliament as the political assembly of the nation. Before considering this general distinction it is necessary to examine the constituent details of each group of persons who come to Parliament for any reason whatsoever.

The lay magnates summoned by special writ are " *omnes et singuli comites et barones et eorum pares* " (III). The omission of dukes is significant and at once points to a date before the creation of the duchy of Cornwall for the king's son in 1337. The only general titles of rank named are earls and barons, but their status is put so definitely on a tenurial basis that the right of attendance is extended to the *pares* or men of the same condition. The qualification for an earl is lands and rents to the value of twenty knight's fees, each worth £20 and making a total value of £400 ; for a baron, thirteen and a third fees, amounting to a total value of 400 marks (III). These figures give us a clue to the date of the classification. They derive ultimately from Magna Carta (§ 2), where the relief paid for a knight's fee is fixed at 100 shillings and that for an earldom or barony at £100. This ratio carried with it the implication that twenty fees made up an earldom or a barony and, when the baron's relief was reduced to 100 marks at the end of the thirteenth century, it was natural to conclude that a barony consisted of thirteen and a third fees. The rate of 100 marks for a baron appeared in the

regis et antecessorum eius, non possunt de dominicis aliquam partem dare ad remanentiam sine assensu et confirmatione domini regis." Cf. the statement of archbishop Stratford in 1341, that only those who hold *per baroniam* were bound to attend Parliament (Grandisson's Register (Exeter), pp. 937-9).

[1] VIII.   [2] II and VIII.

new relief clause in Edward I's re-issue of Magna Carta (1297) and, though the practice was certainly earlier, the valuation in the *Modus* seems to be based upon it.[1] On the other hand, the value of an earldom went up in the first half of the fourteenth century and, at least from 1337, was reckoned at 1000 marks.[2] The change seems to have begun in 1322 when Andrew Harclay was granted 1000 marks in land and rents to maintain his dignity as earl of Carlisle.[3] That the new value was not then fixed is indicated by the absence of reference to it in the charter, granted at the same time, by which the elder Despenser was made earl of Winchester.[4] Before Mortimer was made earl of March in 1328, he was given land and rent worth £1000, which, while in France before his succession, the king had promised him as soon as he should obtain the realm.[5] It seems reasonable to suppose that Mortimer had been promised an earldom and £1000 to maintain the dignity. We may conclude that the valuation of an earldom went up at some time between 1322 and 1337, a conclusion which seems to make it impossible that the omission of dukes from the category of lay magnates was accidental.

The phrase *et eorum pares* obviously refers to the tenurial qualification [6] and points to a time when a magnate might be summoned to Parliament who was not styled either earl or baron. *Baro* was not used as an official title of dignity until the reign of Richard II ; in legal proceedings it was not necessary to sue a baron under his name of dignity and even in the records of Parliament the title was often omitted.[7] In 1316, for example, at the Parliament of Lincoln, not one of the magnates who acted as mainpernors [8] for the younger Despenser were styled barons,

[1] Pollock and Maitland, *History of English Law*, 2nd ed., Cambridge, 1911, I, 260, 309.
[2] L. O. Pike, *The Constitutional History of the House of Lords*, 1894, pp. 75-6.
[3] *Cal. Charter Rolls*, III, 442, April 30, 1322.
[4] *Ibid.*, p. 444, May 10, 1322.
[5] *Ibid.* IV, p. 55, September 13, 1327.
[6] Cf. XXVI : " Quartus gradus est de comitibus, baronibus et aliis magnatibus et proceribus " and cap. IX, " pares comitibus et baronibus."
[7] Pike, *op. cit.*, pp. 100-2.
[8] *Rot. Parl.* I, 352.   The magnates were Roger Mortimer of Chirk, Theobald de Verdon, Ralph Basset, William de Ferrers and Robert de Hastings. Earl Robert de Umfraville was also a mainpernor.   For their summons see *Parl. Writs*, II, ii, 153-4.

though four of them had come to Parliament with a special summons. The term peer, used generally throughout the *Modus* to mean any member of Parliament, bears here the special sense of an equal in tenure and thus corresponds closely to its later use to denote a peer of the realm. The beginning of this modern use cannot be traced beyond the reign of Edward II,[1] but it seems to have had a vogue as a party catch-word from the time of the quarrels over Gaveston and the Ordinances. It appears in 1312 in two semi-official documents, the terms of peace, proposed between the king and the earls, and the articles of accord put forward by Lancaster, Hereford and Warwick later in the year.[2] In 1317 Lancaster wrote to the king protesting that affairs of state ought to be honestly explained and discussed " in parliamento, paribus terrae presentibus "[3] and he used the same term in his answers at the Leicester conference in 1318.[4] Finally, the word gained full official sanction in the Treaty of Leake in the phrase " en parlement par agard des piers."[5] Judgement against the Despensers was given in 1321 by " pares terrae, comites et barones "[6] and was finally incorporated in the statute of York when the judgement was revoked by the " peers of the land, earls and barons, in the presence of the king."[7] From 1322 onwards it became increasingly difficult to employ the word *pares* in any other sense than that given to it by the statute.

Earls, barons and their peers, according to the *Modus*, came to Parliament by reason of their tenures, that is, they were *piers de la terre*, summoned by right and not by the king's grace. There is no suggestion that the king could issue or withhold summons at his pleasure, or that the status of a baron depended on his writ rather than on tenure. We may suspect that emphasis on the form of special summons and on the exclusively tenurial basis on which it rested, was no more accidental than

---

[1] When Peter des Roches said in 1233 that there were no peers in England, he was thinking of the twelve peers of France, not of feudal equals ; he came near the truth, though by the wrong route (*Matt. Paris*, III, 252). Cf. the statement made in 1260 by Edmund, son of Henry III, that " omnes alios barones et comites sibi de iure non esse pares " (*Flores Historiarum*, II, 448).

[2] *Annales London*, pp. 211, 227.

[3] Bridlington, p. 51.   [4] Knighton, I, 414.

[5] *Rot. Parl.* I, 454. Conway Davies (*Baronial Opposition*, p. 19) sets the date of the first use of the term in 1321 ; Pike (*House of Lords*, p. 157) in 1322.

[6] Bridlington, p. 69.   [7] *Statutes of the Realm*, I, 184.

the emphatic treatment of the summons of the proctors through the prelates. We know that the leaders of the baronage were concerned about the mode of summons early in Edward II's reign. In 1312 the earls of Lancaster, Hereford and Warwick protested that they had not been cited to a Parliament at Westminster on February 27, in accordance with the ordinary formula in the register of the chancellor and, therefore, that they had neither gone in person nor sent proxies.[1] The grounds of complaint are obscure. The earls were summoned in the usual way to a Parliament at Westminster on February 13, but this assembly was postponed because of the king's absence ; no earls were summoned to a council held at York on February 27.[2] Possibly the earls were aggrieved because the king had not held a Parliament at Westminster on February 27 instead of a council at York. However, for our purposes the main point is the form of the complaint and it shows clearly that the magnates in the reign of Edward II maintained their right to be summoned to Parliament, according to the formularies of the Chancery. They were, in short, determined that control of the composition of Parliament should not lie with the king.

The chapters relating to the lay commons (IV-VII), like that on the commons of the clergy, are written altogether from the point of view of the central assembly and are not concerned with details of elections or of constituencies. The core of each section is the writ of summons, expanded or paraphrased to emphasise the need of sending to Parliament competent persons with full authority to act for the communities that they represent. The descriptive formula of the writs—" milites de discretioribus et ad laborandum potentioribus "—is replaced by the adjectives " idoneos, honestos et peritos " and " ad faciendum " is expanded into " ad respondendum, subeundum, allegandum, et faciendum." The elected members are even described as attorneys (*attornati*), so strong is the emphasis on their appointment with full power to act for others.[3] The idea was not a novelty at any time in

---

[1] *Annales London*, pp. 225, 227.

[2] *Parl. Writs*, II, ii, 70. The bishops of Norwich and Salisbury and fifty-four other persons were summoned to the council at York on February 27.

[3] Mr. J. G. Edwards has shown that the *plena potestas* of the Commons and the judicial authority of the High Court were the double roots of the legal sovereignty of Parliament (*Oxford Essays in Medieval History*, ed. F. M. Powicke, 1934, pp. 141 *seq*. Cf. *infra*, Chapter XIV, p. 314).

the fourteenth century; it had been developed in the reigns of Henry III and Edward I and was formulated definitely in the writs of summons to the Parliament of 1294. For purposes of dating, we can say no more than that the emphatic expression of the principle of representation suggests an early rather than a late stage in parliamentary development.

The careful directions for payment of wages to elected members—ten shillings a day to a baron of the Cinque Ports, half a mark to a knight or a citizen and five shillings or a quarter mark to a burgess—do not correspond to actual practice at any known period. No official rate for the Ports was ever laid down ; from early in Edward III's reign that for knights was four shillings and for burgesses two shillings a day.[1] The same rate was prescribed in 1315,[2] but in 1322 the king ordered that knights should be paid a daily wage of three shillings, and burgesses (for five towns only) one shilling and eight pence.[3] The problem is more complicated than the official records suggest. Miss McKisack has shown that the wages paid by the boroughs varied with their wealth and prestige, ranging from London, where ten shillings a day was paid when Parliament met away from the capital, to the poorest boroughs which paid nothing at all.[4] The rates in the *Modus* (VII) admit of variation between 5s. and 3s. 4d. for the boroughs, but there is no suggestion that the official rate was totally ignored. The *Modus* rates seem to be worked out to a schedule, without any relation either to official orders or to actual practice. We may suppose that the object of the author was to render attendance at Parliament more attractive and important by fixing the wages high and that, as elsewhere, he was not concerned with the point of view of the constituents. His rates bear a close resemblance to the daily wages paid to members of the council in 1378—half a mark for a knight, one mark for a banneret and two marks for a bishop ;[5] the council rate was either built up from the allowance in the *Modus* (V) of

[1] Prynne, *Fourth Register*, pp. 1-608, quoted by Stubbs, *Cons. Hist.* III, 501.
[2] *Parl. Writs*, II, ii, 149-50, March 9, 1315.
[3] *Cal. Cl. Rolls*, 1318-23, pp. 555-6, expenses for the Parliament of York, May 1322.
[4] *Parliamentary Representation of English Boroughs*, Oxford, 1932, Chapter V.
[5] J. F. Baldwin, *King's Council*, Oxford, 1913, p. 123, from the Issue Roll of 3 Richard II.

half a mark for a knight or both were derived from a common source. As to date, all we may conclude is that rates of this kind would not have been put forward as customary after the official rate was stereotyped early in Edward III's reign.

The *Modus* discusses the summons of barons from each Cinque Port with special emphasis (IV). They are placed first of all elected lay members and their wages are fixed at a higher rate than knights of the shire ; [1] for fines for non-attendance they are equated with the barons by tenure (IX). The Cinque Ports were not regularly represented in Parliament until 1322.[2] Their inclusion from that date was probably a reward for the valuable services they rendered to Edward II in protecting the younger Despenser and in aiding the royal campaign against the Marchers and Lancaster.[3] It must be admitted that there is no clear evidence associating Chapter IV of the *Modus* with these events, as it might have been composed long after the summons of the barons to Parliament. It is, however, unlikely that it was written earlier than 1322, as the absence of the Ports from Parliament must have been well known. It is significant that one of the better copies of the *Modus* occurs in a Cotton manuscript which deals with the rights and liberties of the Ports.[4] It is immediately followed by a note on the judicial privileges of the Ports, in which the claim is made that none of their officers should answer except before the Warden in Shepway or before the king himself (*coram corpore ipsius regis et consilii sui*).[5] The

---

[1] Miss K. M. E. Murray, to whom I am much indebted for information about the Ports, tells me that there was no fixed rate of wages, the payments varying from port to port between about 1s. 3d. and 2s. 6d. a day.

[2] Representatives were summoned at irregular intervals from 1264. The first Parliament that they attended under Edward II was that of 1322.

[3] *Cal. Cl. Rolls, 1318-23*, pp. 524 and 533, cf. Murimuth, p. 33, and *Rot. Parl.* II, 413. Note (p. 524) the letter of March 1 in which the king reminded Winchelsea that when he was lately on the water with them he had begun by their counsel what was now finished to the confusion of the contrariants. His itinerary shows that the conference on the water must have been held about September 6-8, when he was at Sandwich (*ibid.*, pp. 400, 402).

[4] MS. Julius B, IV, see *infra*, Chapter XV, p. 359.

[5] F. 24. The *Modus* covers ff. 21-4. The full phrase runs : " . . . vel in curia de Shapwaya coram ipso custode et combaronibus suis quinque portuum, vel coram corpore ipsius regis et consilii sui, ubi ipse dominus rex sit presens, non coram aliquo justiciario, thesaurario vel aliis ministris domini regis. . . ." The passage is repeated twice in the same MS. on ff. 14 and 89. Cf. the claim made by the Ports in 1299 to be tried in the king's court " at the hands of their peers, earls and barons " (R. G. Marsden, *Law and Custom of the Sea* (*Navy Record Soc.*), 1915, I, 56).

reason given for this privilege is that barons of the Ports ought not to be judged except by their peers and combarons, who are the archbishops, bishops, abbots, earls and barons of England. The document in which these high claims are made cannot have been drafted later than the reign of Edward II and may be rather earlier.[1] Its association with the *Modus*, in which the special position of the Ports is recognised, suggests an early date for that document also.

Turning from the members of Parliament, both magnates and commons, we find opposed to them in the *Modus* the heterogeneous group of officials and servants enumerated in Chapter VIII. It will be convenient to discuss them separately before considering the general interest of the hard line drawn between Parliament and the executive. In addition to the obvious division between councillors and servants, the council itself may be divided into the great officers of state, the judges and the ordinary councillors, either permanent or summoned for a special purpose. Each category will require separate treatment in order to bring out the significance of their appearance in the *Modus*.

The great officers of state named are the chancellor, the treasurer, the chamberlain and barons of the Exchequer and the judges (VIII, XIV). This selection is interesting in itself, as defining a particular period. The " public, ministerial character " of the chancellor and treasurer was well established in the first half of the thirteenth century and as such had special treatment in the Provisions of Oxford.[2] From early in Edward III's reign the keeper of the Privy Seal was regarded as the third minister of state.[3] An exact date can hardly be assigned to his public association with the chancellor and treasurer : Tout puts it in the keepership of Richard of Bury (1329-31) ;[4] Baldwin cites a statute of 1340 in which the officers to take oaths are enumerated as the chancellor, the treasurer, the keeper of the Privy Seal and the judges, as an indication that by that time the keeper was " regularly given a rank in the council next to

---

[1] Reference is made to four magnates of whom the latest in date is Walter Langton, bishop of Coventry and Lichfield, 1296-1321.

[2] Tout, *Chapters*, I, 8 ; *Select Charters*, p. 382.

[3] Tout, *Chapters*, III, 54-5.   [4] *Ibid.*, p. 54.

the chancellor and the treasurer."[1] His omission from the list in the *Modus* is a definite indication of an early date.

After the treasurer, the best manuscripts name the *camerarii et barones de scaccario* (XIV), but others, including the text hitherto printed, read *camerarius*, meaning the king's chamberlain.[2] It is tempting to adopt the less authoritative reading, as the king's chamberlain was a household officer who never officially came " out of court " and his appearance as third in the council would point to a time when he was unusually important. The work of Tout has made it easy to see in the younger Despenser the only chamberlain whose use of his office and personal authority would account for this remarkable elevation of a lay officer of the Household.[3] Despenser was chamberlain from 1318 and, except during his brief exile in 1321, continued to act until his death in 1326. However, it is difficult to press this interpretation against the better reading, even though to name the chamberlains before the barons of the Exchequer and the judge may surprise us. The two chamberlains of the Exchequer were " jointly second in command over the receipt, ranking immediately after the treasurer."[4] Apparently an order of association rather than an order of precedence was followed in the *Modus*. Their inclusion among the great officers of state must belong to a time when the distinction between ministers and technical officials was not fully understood ; in the reign of Edward II the chamberlains and the remembrancers were sometimes summoned to serve on the king's council.[5] It is possible that the variations in the

[1] Baldwin, *King's Council*, p. 74 ; *Statutes of the Realm*, I, 283.

[2] Cf. *infra*, Chapter XV, and textual notes on *Modus* IX and XIV.

[3] Tout, *Place of Edward II in English History*, pp. 168-75 ; *Chapters*, Vol. II, Chapter VIII, Section V, pp. 314 *seq.* Cf. Conway Davies, *Baronial Opposition*, pp. 67 *seq.* Mr. Richardson and Mr. Sayles have drawn attention to the important part played by the chamberlain in certain parliaments of Edward III's reign (*Eng. Hist. Review*, Vol. XLVII, pp. 391-2), but these activities were due to his special knowledge rather than to official pre-eminence. The precedence given to the chamberlain over the keeper of the Privy Seal on the Parliament Roll of 1346 (*Rot. Parl.* II, 157b, 158) is clearly not official, as Bartholomew de Burghersh is put above them both, though he was then not in royal service, being the master of the Black Prince's household (Tout, *Chapters*, V, 319, 433).

[4] Tout, *Place of Edward II*, p. 350.

[5] Conway Davies, *op. cit.*, p. 282. Cf. Tout's remark of a later period—" Technical knowledge, not politics, was what was required from an exchequer officer " (*Chapters*, III, 451). He also noted that " no officer of the receipt " was reckoned as a chief minister in a petition of the Commons in 1381 (*ibid.*). The early dependence of the offices on great hereditary mag-

manuscripts may arise out of some original confusion between the two kinds of chamberlain, since in the Sherburn indenture (1321) the same alternative readings occur.[1] However, the interest of the problem is mainly technical, as neither the king's chamberlain nor the chamberlains of the Exchequer would appear in the place of the keeper of the Privy Seal, except at an early period of the fourteenth century.

The barons of the Exchequer and the judges are named after the great officers of state. Their position as mere assistants or assessors is made explicit by the statement that the clerks are not subject to them and that no judge of England is judge in Parliament, nor is able to have his own records there (XV). It has been suggested that the judges lost their right to share in the functions of Parliament because they could not try peers of the realm,[2] but it seems more probable that their disability arose, as the *Modus* indicates, from the fact that they had no right to membership, either by tenure or as representatives of communities. Stubbs noted that the omission of the word *ceteris* before *prelatis, magnatibus et proceribus* in the writs of summons had " the great legal force " of excluding them from claiming peerage.[3] Hence their remarkable position as " assistants " with a voice but not a vote, a position which is a warning against over-emphasis on the judicial functions of the Parliament of estates.

The other members of the council are described as king's clerks and knights and serjeants at pleas. The king's clerks and knights were men in close personal attendance on the king, members of the royal household. The clerical element in the council was strongest under Edward II, though already under Edward I there were frequent references to " clerks of the council."[4] To the Model Parliament were summoned the judges, *decanis, iuratis de consilio*, the barons of the Exchequer, *et aliis clericis de consilio;*[5] the summons to the council of

nates, who held them in fee, probably gave them formal importance for a time. One lapsed to the Crown in 1293 and the other was in the king's hand during the minority of Warwick's heir from 1315.

[1] Bridlington, p. 63.
[2] Pollard, *Evolution of Parliament*, pp. 97, 291-2.
[3] *Constitutional History*, III, 406. Cf. *ibid.*, p. 461, where Stubbs points out that the judges did not succeed " in obtaining recognition as peers, or the right of voting. They were not regular or essential members . . . they were summoned in varying numbers, and they had no power to appear by proxy."
[4] Baldwin, p. 79. [5] *Parl. Writs*, I, 29.

September 1297 was issued to eight persons called *clerici de consilio*, as well as to the archdeacons of Chester and East Riding and to two friars.[1] Under Edward II much administrative work was carried on by the king's clerks and they were summoned steadily with the judges to the council. The king's knights are less often specifically named in the councillor's summons. In 1297 nine knights were summoned of whom eight were judges ;[2] the ninth, Bogo de Knovil, was constable of the castle of Montgomery.[3] Maitland has noticed the presence of twenty-four knights, as councillors at the Parliament of 1305 ; of these ten had received the baronial summons, eight were judges and had received the councillor's summons and the rest were for the most part constables and captains in the service of the crown.[4] The more important lay members of the royal household, like the chamberlain, Peter de Champvent, who was summoned to Parliament in 1300 and 1301,[5] were probably reckoned among the king's knights. Under Edward II few persons specifically described as knights were summoned,[6] though the term certainly covered those judges who were knights and also the chamberlains and steward of the Household.[7] There seems no doubt that laymen were in a substantial majority among the professional councillors. The king's serjeants, judges in the making, were necessarily few in number, but at least three lawyers of some eminence, Herle, Stonor and Geoffrey le Scrope, were Edward II's councillors before they were raised to the Bench.[8] We know also that serjeants at law acted as advocates for the king in Parliament in 1316 and 1320.[9]

Baldwin has noted that the list of councillors in the *Modus* " bears the stamp of the earlier part of the century,"[10] the time

[1] *Parl. Writs*, I, 55.   [2] *Ibid.*, p. 52.
[3] *Cal. Cl. Rolls, 1288-96*, October 15, 1290, p. 104.
[4] *Memoranda de Parliamento*, 1305, *Rolls Series*, p. xliii.
[5] *Parl. Writs*, I, 82, 90.
[6] E.g. " tres milites de consilio domini regis," 1309, Wilkins, II, 312, cited by Conway Davies, p. 253, n. 9.
[7] See Tout's list of judges under Edward II, *Place of Edward II*, pp. 370 *seq.* Tout notes that by the end of the reign lay judges were " in a substantial majority " (*ibid.*, p. 368).
[8] Tout, *ibid.*, p. 372 ; *Parl. Writs*, II, ii, 179, 183, 198.
[9] *Rot. Parl.* I, 352, Nos. 2 and 3 ;   370, No. 3, cited in *Eng. Hist. Review*, Vol. XLVII, p. 389.
[10] *Op. cit.*, p. 70 n.

when, as Maitland puts it, " we have to picture to ourselves the council as being in the main a body of officers, of ministers, of men who in one capacity or another are doing the king's work and receiving the king's pay." [1] By the reign of Richard II, at latest, most of this strong professional element had been excluded from the council. Even the judges ceased to be sworn councillors before the middle of the reign of Edward III.[2]

Under Edward I and Edward II it was characteristic of the king's council, both within Parliament and without, to contain all the categories enumerated in the *Modus*. Though what may be called the professional element—judges and civil servants —remained in the council until the minority of Richard II ; [3] it declined both in strength and in importance under Edward III. The evidence of the councillors' writs of summons may be taken as a rough indication of the way in which the size of the professional council was reduced. In the last years of Edward I the number of officials specially summoned varied between thirty-nine and fifteen (1295-1307).[4] Under Edward II the largest number thus summoned was forty-three in 1313, thirty-eight in 1318 and 1321, thirty-seven in 1308 and 1318, thirty-five in 1308, and thirty and thirty-two in 1307, 1312, 1318 and 1320 ; in 1315, 1316 and 1322 thirty-three councillors' summonses were issued.[5] In the first decade of Edward III the highest numbers reached were twenty-one and twenty-three in 1333-35 and in the second decade the average number cannot be put much higher than a dozen.[6] There seems no doubt that the large professional council was an outstanding feature of Edward II's government, and it cannot be found at full strength after that date.

The hostility between this professional council and Parliament is clearly indicated in the *Modus* and it is hardly necessary to recall how closely this attitude represents the great conflicts of the reign. These conflicts were the outcome of the strong, royal administrative system on the one hand and of the financial and military strength of the magnates on the other. The pre-eminence in Parliament of the trained servants of the king was so marked at the beginning of the century that Tout declared that

[1] *Memoranda de Parliamento, 1305*, p. xlvii.
[2] Baldwin, *op. cit.*, p. 76.
[3] *Ibid.*, Chapter VI.
[4] *Parl. Writs*, I, *passim*.
[5] *Ibid.* II, ii, *passim*.
[6] *Report on the Dignity of a Peer*, III, 378 *seq*.

they seemed to him " as much ' members of Parliament,' if you will ' members of the house of Lords,' as any of the summoned magnates, even if the terms of their summonses to attend the council may vary in phraseology from the summonses directed to the ' barons ' or knights or burgesses." [1] He considered that the main business of Parliament rested on their shoulders and that their weight was altogether out of proportion to their numbers.[2] The situation in 1307 was disturbing to the magnates, who had recently shown their restlessness in the crisis of the *confirmatio cartarum*. No doubt it was as much for this reason, as from hatred of Gaveston, that they forced on Edward II an addition to the coronation oath, by which the king bound himself to maintain the laws and rightful customs as the commonalty of the realm shall ordain (*les quiels la communaute de vostre royaume aura esleu*).[3] The interpolated clause was a declaration of war on the professional council, announcing a resolve on the part of the commonalty of magnates to capture from it the agenda of " Parliament." Edward II, as Mr. Wilkinson has shown,[4] began his reign tied by a pledge to accept the ordinances of the magnates, put forward either in the great council or in the new Parliament of estates.

It is sometimes said that the centre of constitutional conflict in the thirteenth and fourteenth centuries was a struggle for the control of the council, a statement which conceals the deeper divergence of opinion over what the council was and how it ought to be composed. The royal conception of a strong executive was a body of skilled, docile servants, afforced by those prelates and magnates whose knowledge and opinions were useful in putting the king's policy into action ; to this permanent body, organised in close connection with the household and the great departments of state, sessions of the great council and the Parliament of estates should be ancillary and subordinate. The barons, on the other hand, in the reign of Henry III had gradually formulated the rival conception of a council, composed of their own order, assisted by the civil servants as technical experts, and supported, if need be, by gatherings of the commons. Their

---

[1] *Chapters*, II, 149, n. 1.   [2] *Ibid.*, pp. 148-9.
[3] *Rymer*, III, 63.
[4] " The Coronation Oath of Edward II " in *Historical Essays in Honour of James Tait*, M.U.P., 1933, pp. 405 *seq.*

conception lay dormant under the strong rule of Edward I, but revived at full strength in the resistance to his son. Throughout the first eleven years of the reign (1307-18) we see the royal and baronial plans of government abruptly confronting each other, in the shape of large professional groups of councillors summoned by the king, and in the series of baronial councils set up by the Ordainers, by Lancaster and by the Middle Party. The lesson of hard-won tactical victories, which made no permanent impression on the structure of the king's government, was gradually learnt by the opposition and they slowly abandoned their belief in the efficacy of baronial councils. It is remarkable that in the crisis of 1321 the issue of the council was forgotten ; the Marchers used Parliament to expel the Despensers as evil councillors and then retired, leaving the king in full control of the machinery by means of which a revenge could be organised. As we have already seen,[1] a new solution was gradually finding favour, both with the king and with the magnates, and each began to look to Parliament for support. The statute of York, formulated on the morrow of Boroughbridge, expressed a new royal confidence in the authority of Parliament. The other side of the shield is shown in the *Modus*. There the authority of Parliament is exalted at the expense of the council ; councillors are mere technical advisers, without rights of attendance or membership ; power is vested exclusively in the six *gradus*, the king in Parliament. It seems as if the baronial plan of government, first set out under Henry III, had at last gained substance. For magnates to carry on the government, to be the council, had proved impossible, since they lacked the wish, the time or the training to fit themselves for continuous service ; to control the council through Parliament was, by reason of the king's fiscal dependence, practicable and to this end their energies were thenceforth directed. As the king's expert councillors had failed to establish themselves as members of Parliament, their political value rapidly declined and they soon lost their seats at the council board and were elbowed out of Parliament. In the *Modus* we have a picture of a large body of councillors in, but by no means of, Parliament ; a representation, in short, of the first stage of the transition from bureaucratic to parliamentary government, which corresponds

[1] *Supra*, pp. 159-72.

to no other period than that of the failure of the Ordinances, the rise of the Middle Party and the statute of York.

II

We are relatively well informed as to the composition of early parliaments, but it is much more difficult to discuss their procedure. Contemporary evidence is not only scanty, but irregular and broken in such a way that it is impossible to discover what was the normal routine for a session of a Parliament of estates. It will be convenient to consider first the evidence itself, as we find it on the Parliament rolls, since in the *Modus* we have interesting remarks about these records and their custody. Two principal clerks of Parliament shall sit among the judges [1] and shall enrol all the pleas and business of Parliament. They shall not be subject to the judges, but to the king and Parliament jointly, unless one or two judges be assigned to examine and amend their enrolments. Unanimous judgements on petitions assigned to be heard by peers of Parliament shall be recited in full Parliament and enrolled *in principali rotulo Parliamenti*. These rolls shall be delivered to the treasurer and shall be deposited in the Treasury before Parliament is dissolved, though the clerks themselves may keep the transcript or counter-roll if they wish. The clerks shall receive as wages half a mark a day and their board, unless they are already creditably provided for in the king's service. They shall be assisted in the work of enrolment by the five clerks, assigned one to each *gradus*, when they are at leisure.[2] The clerks of Parliament are bound to give to anyone asking for it a copy of his process, charging fees at the rate of ten lines a penny ; those who declare on oath their inability to pay shall be charged nothing. Finally, the rolls of Parliament shall be ten inches in width.[3]

These passages read less like a description of a working system than a scheme of reform, an attempt to devise for Parliament an indepenuent and expert staff of clerks responsible for its records. They seem to point to a time when Parliament was sufficiently burdened with business to require regular and

---

[1] It does not seem necessary to assume from their position that the clerks were equal in rank to the judges (B. Wilkinson, *The Chancery under Edward III*, M.U.P., 1929, p. 81, n. 2), as the place was probably allotted to them in order that they might hear easily.

[2] XV-XVI.   [3] XXV.

competent officials, yet before any clear tradition of service had been established.[1] Emphasis falls mainly on the clerks and the rolls in their care. They should be independent, properly paid [2] and exclusively occupied with the business of enrolment, at least as far as Parliament is concerned, though their employment on other duties at other times is permitted. This does not correspond to what we know of the clerks of Parliament at any period, though some of the implications of the scheme are significant. The early history of these officials shows that the first clerks, John of Kirkby and Gilbert of Rothbury, were important royal servants, well trained in technical knowledge of the king's business.[3] Rothbury, who served from 1290 to about the year 1314, was a household officer who was later connected with the king's bench ; he had never any connection with the Chancery. To his successor, Robert of Ashby or Askelby [4] (1315), we may trace the beginning of the tradition of drawing on the Chancery for clerical service, but it was hardly fully established before the reign of Edward III. The fact that the *Modus* does not refer to the Chancery as the place of training for the clerks suggests an early date, and this suggestion is confirmed by the ruling that the rolls should be deposited by the treasurer in the Treasury.

To name the Exchequer or Treasury as the place of deposit is tantamount to an acknowledgement that it was the first great office of state, an admission characteristic of the end of the thirteenth or the early fourteenth century [5] The classification of the Parliament rolls themselves reminds us that between 1290 and 1321 certain of them were in the custody of the treasurer.[6] Though the

[1] Nothing is said, for example, about the duty of clerks to act as receivers of petitions.

[2] The rate of wages seems to be that paid to chancery clerks of the first grade (Wilkinson, *Chancery*, p. 81, n. 2).

[3] What is known of the early clerks has been carefully collected by Mr. Richardson and Mr. Sayles in " The King's Ministers in Parliament " (*Eng. Hist. Review*, Vols. XLVI and XLVII. Note especially Vol. XLVI, pp. 532 seq. ; Vol. XLVII, pp. 194 seq.).

[4] *Ibid.*, Vol. XLVII, p. 194 ; Tout, *Chapters*, II, 218, n.

[5] This was first pointed out by A. Hughes, "The Parliament of Lincoln, 1316 " (*Transactions of the Royal Historical Society*, New Series, Vol. X, pp. 41 seq.).

[6] " The Exchequer Series of Parliament Rolls " (*Bulletin*, Vol. VI, pp. 146 seq. I have followed closely the learned investigation published in " The Early Records of the English Parliament," and in " The Parliaments of Edward III " (*ibid.*, Vols. V, pp. 129 seq., VI, pp. 71 seq., 129 seq., VIII, pp. 65 seq., and IX, pp. 1 seq.).

" Exchequer series " of rolls, 1290-1321, is a modern collection, it has, as Mr. Richardson and Mr. Sayles point out, " a medieval nucleus." We know that the originals of rolls 3 and 4 were ordered by the king in 1290 to be deposited in the Exchequer,[1] and further references to rolls in the Exchequer come from the years 1305, 1308, 1310, 1319, and 1323.[2] Other rolls were in the Wardrobe or were in the hands of the clerk of the council, but in no case have we evidence of rolls in the Chancery.[3] There are indications that the early rolls outside Exchequer custody were transcripts [4] and it may be that the originals were deposited with the treasurer and the transcripts were kept rather at haphazard by the officials who found them useful. Such a practice would be in harmony with the statement in the *Modus* that the clerks may keep the transcript or counter-roll if they wish.

An alternative explanation may be deduced from certain entries on the Parliament rolls of 1318 and 1319. At the Parliament of York (October 1318) it was ordered that the Treaty of Leake should be entered on the Parliament roll, sent to Chancery and there enrolled, and then sent to the Exchequer and both Benches to be enrolled there also. The transcript of the enrolment should also be sent to Chancery.[5] In the following year (May 1319) it was ordered in Parliament that the judgement in Audley's case should be entered on the Parliament rolls and in Chancery and thence sent to the Exchequer and the Benches to be enrolled in the same way.[6] These entries suggest that separate enrolment in each great department of state was still considered necessary and that the place of custody for the Parliament rolls themselves was not in any of them. It was, perhaps, still neither fixed nor permanent. Whichever explanation be accepted, at least it is clear that the rolls were not at that time kept in the Chancery. The " Chancery series " of Parliament rolls does not begin until 1327 [7] and, though the classification is modern, we have evidence that they were written by Chancery

---

[1] *Bulletin*, VI, p. 136, n. 4, citing *Rot. Parl.* I, 16.
[2] *Ibid.*, pp. 136-7.   [3] *Ibid.*
[4] " The clear uncorrected writing of these rolls (i.e. *Exch. Parl. Rolls*, nos. 3 and 4) shows unmistakably that they are transcripts " ; the originals were those ordered to be deposited in the Exchequer in 1290 (*ibid.*, p. 136).
[5] Cole, *Documents*, p. 3.
[6] *Ibid.*, p. 49.
[7] *Bulletin*, Vol. IX, pp. 15 *seq.*

clerks and kept in the Chancery.[1] The reference to the Treasury in the *Modus* can hardly be accidental or without significance. It may be concluded, therefore, that to name the Treasury as the place of deposit, not only points to a period before 1327, but also indicates, by implication, a time when the Chancery was beginning to be regarded as a possible alternative, that is, when Robert of Ashby (1315) and William Airmyn (1316) succeeded Rothbury as clerks of Parliament.

The nature of the early Parliament rolls is a useful guide to the nature of Parliament itself. It has been fully investigated by Mr. Richardson and Mr. Sayles.[2] They explain why "we should not postulate a single bulky continuous roll for each Parliament "[3] and show that the early roll was not a journal but a " putting together of odds and ends,"[4] sometimes on no more than a single membrane. Rolls called by contemporaries *rotuli de parliamento* are extant, but they are neither complete nor homogeneous, either leaving out what we should expect to go in, or else breaking up into separate rolls records belonging to the same session. The first impression conveyed by these records is one of Parliament as an improvisation, something growing without a set plan or any definite centre, something that, in Mr. Plucknett's apt phrase, was still " an event rather than an institution."[5] The prevailing uncertainty, or even confusion, may be illustrated by the early enrolment of petitions, later seen to be unnecessary;[6] this could hardly have happened if the officials had in mind any clear idea of the purpose for which the record was required. The tradition of roll-keeping was already well established and, if Parliament were indeed little more than the regular sessions of a great or high court, as some historians would have us see it, then why did it not at once fall into line with other courts and have its own roll, complete and conforming to its main sphere of action ? The governing factor

---

[1] *Bulletin*, Vol. IX, p. 17. For example, one membrane of the roll of the Parliament of November 1330, is headed : " Rotulus iste de Parliamento . . . liberatus fuit in cancellaria Regis per Henricum de Edenestowe, clericum de Parliamento . . . ." A similar note is on the roll of the Michaelmas Parliament of 1331.

[2] *Ibid.*, Vol. VI, pp. 132 *seq.*   [3] *Ibid.*, p. 132.

[4] Tout, *Place of Reign of Edward II*, p. 185.

[5] Plucknett, *Statutes and their Interpretation*, p. 20.

[6] Cf. *Memoranda de Parliamento*, 1305, p. lxv. " The enrolment of the petition and its response is all along somewhat of a luxury. . . ."

in its growth must be looked for in the miscellany of business which came before it, partly overlapping with and supplementing that of other courts and partly breaking new ground for public service. Because Parliament was concerned with finance and law-making as well as judicial business, it was difficult to summarise its activities for purposes of record. Analysis of the rolls proves that it was found necessary to enter on them much general business —legislation, finance, administration and procedure—in addition to the pleas and judgements of the court. We must not only think of early Parliaments as so many *ad hoc* improvisations, but also admit that comprehensive and general business might and did come before them. A hard and fast theory of Parliament as a high court will explain neither the facts in the records nor the failure to apply a selective principle to their make-up and content.

The references to the Parliament rolls in the *Modus* do not conform to the later plan of the record as journal, but they correspond fairly closely to the older, less orderly system. Mr. Richardson and Mr. Sayles have noted that the description of the records as we have it in the *Modus* is in accordance with the early records themselves.[1] They point, for example, to the instruction in Chapter XVII that difficult cases should be set down in writing in order that they should be brought before Parliament, and they show that this practice was followed under Edward II, citing royal orders issued before sessions of Parliament in 1309, 1311 and 1316. It was the duty of the clerks in the *Modus* to enrol the pleas and business of Parliament ; judgements by peers of Parliament ought to be entered *in principali rotulo parliamenti* (XV). The phrase " principal roll " implies the existence of others,[2] the rolls of *dubitationes et responsiones* written by the secondary clerks (XVI). The author had still no idea of one comprehensive roll for each session and the term he employed indicates a stage of transition. On the one hand, we have the time when business was recorded not on any set plans but as seemed most convenient, as, for example, in the two separate rolls for the Easter Parliament of 1290 ;[3] on the other,

---

[1] *Bulletin*, Vol. VI, pp. 130-1.

[2] " Principal roll " may, however, mean no more than the " master copy " or official record, though the reference to the *dubitationes et responsiones* makes this less likely.

[3] *Ibid.*, pp. 146-7.

the time when the journal was adopted and the ordinary petitions dropped out of the roll altogether. Such a transition is clearly indicated in the records of the Lincoln Parliament of 1316.[1] We have, in the first place, a roll of nine membranes consisting mainly of petitions and their answers ; the entry of the statute of sheriffs shows that restriction of enrolments to one kind of business was not yet clearly understood. There is also another roll of eight membranes, on three of which we find the first attempt at a journal or orderly summary of the business from day to day. No doubt the plan was adopted on account of the long delay and confusion caused by the absence of Lancaster, but the details enrolled [2] indicate that something more was intended than " a sort of protocol to record the steps leading to the agreement between the earl of Lancaster and the king." [3] The matter recorded on the other membranes consists mainly of judicial business, which came up before the council at Westminster, and also details of negotiations with the count of Flanders in the previous year. Though there is still confusion in the division of subjects, someone certainly had the idea of one roll for petitions and answers and another, the principal roll, for an orderly record of proceedings. It may also be significant that just at this time the rolls increase slightly in width and that the first rolls in which the membranes are approximately ten inches wide are those of 1315 and 1316.[4] The rolls earlier than 1315 are never as wide and scmetimes they are no more than seven inches across.[5] As they grew longer, the practical inconvenience of narrow membranes became clear, and no doubt it was for this reason that the width is fixed at ten inches in the *Modus* (XXV).[6]

---

[1] *Rot. Parl.* I, 337-49, 350-64.

[2] For example, the statute of sheriffs is mentioned once, and once entered in full (*ibid.*, pp. 351, 353). Cf. *ibid.*, p. 343*b*, for a reference on the other roll.

[3] *Bulletin*, Vol. VI, p. 141.

[4] The roll of 8 Edward II (P.R.O., Parliament Rolls, Exchequer Series, S.C. 9/18) has membranes varying in width from 10½ to 11 inches wide ; those of 8 and 9 Edward II (S.C. 9/19, 9/20) from 10 to 11¼ and 10 to 10¼ respectively, the second being the journal roll.

[5] The average width of the rolls of Edward I is 8 inches.

[6] The roll of 1 Edward III (P.R.O., Parliament Rolls, Chancery, C. 65/1) has two membranes, one 11½ inches wide and the other 10½ ; the roll for 4, 5, 6 Edward III (C. 65/2) has an average width of over 11 inches ; that for 6 Edward III (C. 65/3) is only 9 inches wide, perhaps because it has only one membrane.

We may suppose that the new plan, and, perhaps the greater width, were the work of William Airmyn, who drew up the journal of 1316 ; it is also reasonable to imagine that he explained its advantages to other officials and that the change was known within that limited circle. However, so far as we can tell, nothing similar was attempted until the reign of Edward III, when the journal or narrative summary of parliamentary business began. The author of the *Modus* tried to expound the plan of 1316, though only in a general way ; if he had understood that his *principalis rotulus* ought to be a journal of events he would certainly have said so. It seems, therefore, that his brief description of the records was probably written after the Lincoln Parliament of 1316 and certainly before the narrative rolls, without petitions, of Edward III.

We know little enough of parliamentary procedure at any time during the middle ages, but least of all about the period before the narrative rolls begin. For this reason it is difficult to find evidence to compare with the formal rules laid down in the *Modus ;* what has come to light is drawn from a variety of sources, unequal in authority. It will be convenient to take the regulations in order, and to try to set beside them what we know of parliamentary practice early in the fourteenth century.

Parliament, according to the *Modus* (XIX), shall be held *in loco publico* and not in a private or secret place. The prohibition recalls the ordinance of 1311, which declared that Parliament should meet *en lieu covenable*.[1] From an early date the idea prevailed that Parliament should meet at Westminster. In 1261 the magnates refused to attend when summoned to the Tower, saying that they would go to Westminster, where they were wont to hold Parliament, and to no other place.[2] Parliaments held away from Westminster were relatively few and usually there was an obvious reason of convenience. There are no English precedents to suggest the danger of holding Parliaments in remote villages, as the Irish Parliament was held in 1371,[3]

---

[1] *Rot. Parl.* I, 285, no. 29.
[2] *Annals of Dunstable (Rolls Series)*, p. 217 (*s.a.* 1260), cited by Stubbs, *Constitutional History*, III, 396.
[3] At Ballyduagh, near Cashel, a place where there were no buildings nor any provision for hospitality (*Windsor Documents, op. cit.*, p. 115).

and it seems likely that the author of the *Modus* feared, not so much a session in an isolated place, as the withdrawal of certain members in secret conclave. We have evidence that such practices were resented in the reign of Edward II. In 1311, referring to the Parliament which met after Gaveston's murder, the bishop of Salisbury wrote to archbishop Reynolds, protesting against the secret debates of certain prelates and magnates first for two, then for ten and again for two days, so that the proctors of the clergy withdrew, either from boredom or from lack of money to stay idle in London.[1] Later in the reign Lancaster several times refused to attend Parliament because he feared that its sessions would be neither full nor public ; in 1320 he said " non enim decebat habere parliamentum in cameris. . . ." [2] The prohibition of secret meetings in the *Modus* points definitely to the reign of Edward II.

The days of parliamentary session are defined in the *Modus* with exactitude. The summons shall be issued forty days in advance (I), the time ordained for summons to the Great Council in Magna Carta.[3] Sundays and three *dies nefasti*—All Saints, All Souls and the Nativity of St. John the Baptist—are named as days on which Parliament ought not to meet ; on all other feast days Parliament ought to begin early, on account of divine service (XIX). The selection of these three feasts at first seems strange, since there were other feasts more sacred, long regarded as *dies non juridici*. The choice was evidently made on the assumption that Parliament would sit only in the four law terms of Hilary, Easter, Trinity and Michaelmas,[4] thus excluding the greater festivals of the Christian year. The selection, therefore, recalls a time when Parliament, closely associated with the courts of Common Law, met normally within the legal terms. A rough

[1] Register of Simon de Gandavo, pp. 417-18.

[2] *Vita Edwardi II*, p. 250. In October 1309 the five earls of Lancaster, Lincoln, Warwick, Oxford and Hereford refused to attend a *secretum parliamentum* at York, because of their hostility to Gaveston (Hemingburgh, II, 275). There is no evidence that this meeting was a parliament in any technical sense.

[3] Cf. forty days for an essoin *ultra mare*, Glanville, I, 25 (ed. Woodbine, p. 50). Mr. A. G. Little tells me that the notice given for a university summons in the thirteenth century was forty days.

[4] W. Holdsworth, *A History of English Law*, 1923, III, 674 *seq.* ; J. Reeves, *History of English Law* (ed. W. A. Finlason, 1869), I, 232-3. Cf. N. Harris Nicolas, *Chronology of History*, 1833, pp. 383-5.

calculation from the records shows that Parliament did not often meet out of term before the reign of Edward III.[1]

The *Modus* (XIX) also fixes exactly the time at which parliamentary business should begin—at mid-prime on each day, except on festivals, when it should begin at prime, on account of divine service. Mid-prime was the middle of the first hour, which began either at six o'clock in the morning or, in summer, at sunrise. We know that the Parliament of Carlisle met at prime on January 25, 1307 ; as it was the feast of the Conversion of St. Paul, we may suppose that the normal time of meeting was half an hour later.[2] We have no further indication of the time when Parliament met until the last quarter of the century. In 1376 the Good Parliament assembled at eight o'clock : [3] in January 1397 the Lords were ordered to attend at nine o'clock at latest ; [4] in 1406 the Commons were enjoined to attend at eight o'clock each day and the Lords at nine.[5] Within a century from 1307 the time of assembly had been pushed forward from half past six to eight or nine o'clock, but unfortunately we have no direct evidence as to the period when the change began. There is, however, a clue in the special insistence that the king himself should be present at mid-prime (" qua hora rex Parliamentum tenetur interesse ") ; the injunction occurs again in Chapter IX and, in the section on the king's absence (XIII), the implication that he might stay away from idleness or sloth is fairly clear. We have evidence in a letter written by Cobham of Worcester to the Pope that Edward II was known to lie in bed in the mornings. Describing the Michaelmas Parliament of 1320, he wrote that the king had borne himself magnificently, prudently and discreetly, rising early, contrary to his ancient

---

[1] Cf. Stubbs, *Constitutional History*, III, 391-3, for the coincidence of legal and parliamentary terms.

[2] *Rot. Parl.* I, 189. The purpose of the earlier time was to allow attendance at the procession and high mass before the hour of sext.

[3] *Ibid.* II, 321.

[4] *Ibid.* III, 338.

[5] *Ibid.* III, 568. Cf. an adjournment to nine o'clock in 1402 (*ibid.* III, 485), and an order in 1404 that the speaker should be presented in Parliament at nine o'clock at the latest (*ibid.* III, 522b). John Hooker, writing under Elizabeth, states that the time of beginning was " at eight of the clock in the morning, and doth continew until XI of the clock. They doo not sit at after noones, for those times are reserved for committiees and the convocation house," *The order and usage of the keeping of a Parlement in England*, p. 30.

custom, and showing a noble and joyful countenance to the prelates and magnates.[1] The retrospective criticism implied in the phrase *contraque antiquam consuetudinem mane surgens*, that is, unwonted early rising, may be compared to a chronicler's record of the exasperation caused by Edward II's unpunctual habits : " Sed quid prosunt regi procrastinationes assiduae ? "[2] The marked emphasis on early royal attendance in the *Modus* certainly suggests that the author had a special intention directed towards Edward II.

In Chapter IX we have a detailed description of the way in which members ought to appear for the work of the session. On the first five days a roll-call of estates should be held, in an ascending order of precedence, from citizens and burgesses on the first day to the prelates on the fifth day. A detailed table of fines for default is set out, which illustrates a resolute intention to secure punctual attendance. The records have little evidence to show what actually happened, though it is obvious that a call-over of some kind must have been held, at least for the Commons who were granted writs *de expensis*. The long list of proctors at the Parliament of Carlisle may have been compiled at a ceremony of this kind.[3] At the Parliament of Lincoln (1316) the king ordered a list of proxies and excuses for non-attendance to be drawn up and a report made to him of the names of the absent.[4] The first definite evidence of a call of the Commons occurs on the Parliament roll of 1379,[5] though the practice was probably of long standing ; in 1384 it was referred to as " nominatim invocatis, prout moris est."[6] Throughout the whole of the fourteenth century there is ample evidence of unpunctuality and failure to attend, but no mention of a scale of penalties before the statute of 1382 ;[7] in fact, the statement on the roll of 1344 that the names of absentee lords should be sent to the king, in order that he might ordain what punishment he pleased, suggests that there was then no fixed rule to be followed.[8] The statute of 1382 decreed that absentees should be amerced and otherwise punished, " selonc ce que aunciene-ment a este usez deinz le roialme . . . en dit cas " ;[9] this may

[1] Cobham's Register, p. 97.
[2] *Vita Edwardi II*, p. 194 ; cf. pp. 170, 190, 258, and *infra*, p. 237.
[3] *Rot. Parl.* I, 180-91.   [4] *Ibid.* I, 350.
[5] *Ibid.* III, 55.   [6] *Ibid.* III, 184.   [7] *Ibid.* III 124b.
[8] *Ibid.* II, 147.   [9] *Ibid.* III 124b.

refer to an early tradition, but, as we have no evidence of the collection of fines, it is more likely that " ancient usage " is either a figure of speech or, more probably, an echo of the *Modus* itself.

The description in the *Modus* (XIV) of a formal grouping of the estates in Parliament has certain striking features. The king shall sit in the middle of the greater bench, with the archbishops of Canterbury and York on his right and left ; at his right foot shall sit the chancellor, the chief justice and his associates and at his left the treasurer, the chamberlains [1] and barons of the Exchequer and the justices of the bench, each with the clerks allotted to them. Members of Parliament shall sit among their peers, the prelates ranking first ; the steward of England shall see that this is done. The interest of the unobtrusive reference to the superior place occupied by the archbishop of Canterbury has already been discussed ; [2] the large size of the professional council in Parliament also requires no further comment, though the specific mention of the chamberlains should again be noted.[3] The phrase describing the king as sitting *in medio loco maioris banci* has an archaic flavour, as we are accustomed to think of him on his throne confronting the whole assembly. In a miniature of the fifteenth century representing the deposition of Richard II, the empty throne is depicted in the centre, with the spiritual and temporal peers to right and left ; [4] the later and more reliable pictures reproduced by Professor Pollard show the throne in the same position.[5]

It seems unlikely that, as late as any date when a Parliament of estates was held, the king would sit, even on the greatest bench, cheek by jowl with his subjects, yet there must be something behind the express statement in the *Modus*. It cannot merely refer to a time when Parliament often met away from Westminster, where there was certainly a chair of estate, because in any chapter house or cathedral it would be easy to find some

---

[1] Here the best MSS. agree in the plural reading *camerarii* (or *camerariis*). Cf. *supra*, p. 204.

[2] *Supra*, p. 152.

[3] Their seats, between the treasurer and the barons and opposite the judges, is some confirmation of the reading adopted.

[4] Reproduced in *Archaeologia*, XX, 191.

[5] *Evolution of Parliament* ; the earliest picture shows the Parliament of 1523.

dignified piece of furniture, the seat of a bishop or an abbot. An explanation is suggested by the use of the word *scamnum*, which appears in the Irish version as a synonym for *bancus*.[1] *Scanna* is the word used for benches in the famous account of the sessions of the Exchequer in the *Dialogus*,[2] and when the whole passage is examined a striking parallel between it and that in the *Modus* is apparent. The officers of the Exchequer were grouped round the board on which the chequered cloth was spread. This table, ten feet by five, was set across the upper end of the chamber, like the high table in a college hall ; its head and foot were the short ends, each accommodating three people. There were four *scanna*, *sedilia* or benches at the table, the two at the ends being prolonged beyond the board. The bench at the head of the table was called *primum sedile ;* there the justiciar sat, not at the middle of the bench but at the middle of the board (*in medio non sedilis sed scaccarii loco*). The chancellor sat on his left hand and the bishop of Winchester on his right ; beyond the chancellor and off the board, sat in order the constable, the two chamberlains and the marshal. At the foot of the table sat the sheriff, his clerk and Thomas Brown ; on the lower side, with their backs to the rest of the room, sat the calculator and his assistants and on the upper side those who kept the rolls, with the treasurer on the bishop's right. The justiciar was the king's representative, and on the occasions, probably rare, when the king came tó preside at the Exchequer he would certainly sit *in medio scaccarii* with his chief officials at his right and left hand. The description in the *Modus* of the king sitting *in medio loco maioris banci*, with an archbishop on either side and his other officers and councillors before him, to right and left, as if at a table, closely resembles his position at the Exchequer, though we must imagine the board swung round, so that its head is, not at one side, but against the end wall of the chamber. If we equate the *locus in medio* of the *Dialogus* with the *in medio loco* of the *Modus*, we have an explanation of the phrase *maioris banci*, otherwise not intelligible, as no other benches are mentioned. The suggestion then is that the king in Parliament originally sat

---

[1] *Infra*, p. 387.
[2] *Dialogus*, p. 69, ed. by A. Hughes, C. G. Crump and C. Johnson. For a discussion of the passage see *ibid*., pp. 46 *seq*., and R. Lane Poole, *Exchequer in the Twelfth Century*, Oxford, 1912, pp. 101 *seq*.

after the manner of the justiciar in the Exchequer, an arrangement at first conditioned by the need to sit at the chequered board.
As the Exchequer was the first special court to take shape, it was
naturally the model for others ; first the court *de banco*, then
coram rege (later known as the king's bench), and finally the
council in Parliament followed its tradition, either in actual
arrangement or at least in naming the place of dignity.   The
force of the comparison can be seen more clearly if the pictures
of Parliament in the sixteenth century are examined.   They
show the councillors sitting facing each other, as if at a table ;
the chancellor's woolsack is immediately in front of the throne,
showing what happened when the archbishop took over his place
at the left of the seat of dignity.[1]   The direct interest for our
immediate purpose is that the phrase in the *Modus*, preserving
as it seems to do, vestiges of the first formal sessions of an English
royal court, takes us back to a time which cannot be far removed
from the origin of Parliament itself.   In the context it would
have been pointless to invent, or even to revive a terminology
which had lost its meaning ; therefore, the use of the phrase
helps to give us confidence in the age and general value of the
whole document.

Turning to the position of the rest of the estates in Parliament,
we find that the *Modus* merely says that they should sit in rows
(*linealiter*), in such a way that no one should sit except among
his peers.   *Linealiter* does not help at all in determining their
exact place in the hall, as the seats either might be arranged in
rows facing the king, or else facing each other, like the stalls of
a choir or a college chapel.   What we know from other sources
leaves no doubt that the second is the correct interpretation.
The later pictures show plainly that the estates were arranged
four-square, the spiritual and temporal peers confronting each
other and the lay commons standing at the end of the hall, confronting the king.[2]   This was the ancient order of the communal
courts, where the doomsmen gave judgement " within the four

---

[1] The English translation of the fifteenth century adds that the bishops of
London and Winchester shall also sit at the king's right and the bishops of
Durham and Carlisle at his left (MS. Harley 930, printed in *Eng. Hist. Review*,
Vol. XXXIV, pp. 219-20).

[2] The account of the stations of the estates in the Irish version (§ 10) adds
that the proctors sat on the ground, no doubt in front of the lay commons,

benches."[1]   In Parliament, therefore, was stereotyped the traditional form, not only of the Exchequer, but of the far older grouping
of free doomsmen, seated on the ground, or on four *scamna*,
making a hollow square. For purposes of dating, the passage
has no special value, as the description covers any session of all
the estates in Parliament down to modern times.

After a discussion of fines for non-attendance or unpunctuality,
the *Modus* (IX) goes on to describe the formal opening of Parliament. The roll-call and business arising out of it should last
for five days, but on the first day proclamation should be made,
both within the place of session and without, that all petitions
should be delivered on the five days following.[2] Proclamations
of the kind were issued at least from the beginning of the fourteenth century[3] and the time allotted for the filing of petitions
was usually six days.[4] According to the *Modus* (IX), the formal
opening was delayed until the sixth day, when the king came
at prime. This does not correspond to recorded practice at
any time and it has the look of a plan devised to secure a more
orderly procedure. Delays in setting to work, such as characterised the Lincoln Parliament of 1316, would naturally suggest
a reform of this kind.[5]

The king was not bound to be present until the sixth day,
but the sermon (*predicatio*), preached by one of the two archbishops
or his nominee, might be delivered before the king and the
majority of the estates on one of the previous five days (X). The
sermon ought to take the form of intercession with God for
the peace and quiet of the king and the realm. It was one of the
three formal orations with which the proceedings began, the
others being a rehearsal of the causes of summons (*pronuntiatio*) and the king's speech (*loquela regis*). This account of the
parliamentary sermon raises some difficulties. Though we may

---

[1] Pollock and Maitland, I, 556, n. 1, where it is noted that proceedings in
the boroughs took place *inter quatuor scamna gildhallae*.

[2] Cf. *infra*, pp. 231-5, for a fuller discussion of petitions.

[3] Edward I ordered proclamation to be made about the presentation of
petitions to the Parliament of February 1305, *Memoranda de Parliamento*,
1305, p. lvii. Cf. *Ibid.*, p. 3, no. 1, for the text of the proclamation.

[4] For example, in the Parliaments of September 1305, January 1316, April
1343, and January 1348 (*Rot. Parl.* I, 182, 350; II, 135, 164). In the proclamation of 1346 only three days were allowed (*ibid.* II, 157).

[5] We see again the indifference to the constituencies, upon whom the
expense of the extra wages would fall.

suppose that the custom of opening ceremonial councils or Parliaments with a sermon went back at least to the great crown-wearing courts of the Norman kings, we have traced no early reference to the practice in England. Something is known of the type of discourse thought to be suitable on the occasions from the headings of a sermon prescribed to be preached before Parliaments in the middle of the thirteenth century.[1] The author was Humbert de Romans, Master General of the Dominican Order (1254-63), author of *Instructiones de Officiis Ordinis* and probably the greatest expert of his day on sermons for all occasions.[2] The sermon that he outlines for Parliaments is severely penitential in character and had no direct secular purpose. In marked contrast to the Dominican's advice are the first English parliamentary sermons of which we have knowledge, —those preached by the archbishop of Canterbury and the bishop of Hereford in the debates on the deposition of Edward II.[3] Orleton of Hereford apparently opened the proceedings by a sermon, in which he asked if Parliament wished to suffer Edward to rule any longer, a discourse which seems to combine preaching with the rehearsal of the causes of summons. Perhaps the two orations, so carefully distinguished in the *Modus*, were run into one, when it fell to an ecclesiastic to introduce the main business of Parliament. In 1331 [4] and in the autumn Parliament of 1332 [5] the bishop of Winchester, who was then chancellor, delivered the *pronuntiatio*, which may also have been the opening sermon ; in an early Parliament of 1332 it was delivered by the archbishop of Canterbury and the bishop of Winchester " en fourme de predication." [6] This form was probably the same as that of the political sermons which begin to be summarised fairly regularly in the reign of Richard II, though earlier examples are recorded on the rolls for 1365 and for the Good Parliament.[7] It is remarkable that nearly all the opening speeches of ecclesiastics in Edward III's Parliaments are reported as wholly secular, and that there is no evidence whatsoever for an intercession

[1] Summarised by Mr. Richardson, *Transactions of the Royal Historical Society* (fourth series), XI, 150-1, from La Migne, *Maxima Bibliotheca Veterum Patrum*, 1677, XXV, 559.
[2] See G. R. Galbraith, *Constitution of the Dominican Order*, M.U.P., 1925, pp. 166 *seq.*, for a summary of his general advice to preachers.
[3] *Supra*, p. 184.   [4] *Rot. Parl.* II, 60.   [5] *Ibid.* II, 66.
[6] *Ibid.* II, 64.   [7] *Ibid.* II, 283, 361-2,

sermon of the type described in the *Modus*. It may be that Orleton's sermon in 1327 marked a change from the original address, entirely religious in subject matter, to the political oration, ingeniously built round a text. This second type became common at a later date.[1] If this be so, the sermon in the *Modus* represents an older tradition which failed to survive the shock of political conflict or the strain of royal pressure.

According to the *Modus* (XI and XII), the sermon should be followed by the declaration of the causes of summons, both general and particular, delivered by the chancellor, the justiciar or a clerk appointed by one of them. Afterwards the king himself should entreat each *gradus*, by name, to labour for the honour of God and for the honour and welfare of himself and the realm. We need not delay over the king's speech, as few examples are recorded;[2] if it were ever a regular practice, as the *Modus* states, it must always have been purely formal. The declaration of royal needs was not made personally, but was entrusted to a minister of state, who understood the details of the king's business. The *pronuntiatio* can be traced back to 1275, when the chief justice of the common pleas explained to the Parliament how Edward I had toiled in his youth, especially in the Holy Land, spending his own substance and that of his father, so that it was necessary that his subjects should grant him an aid.[3] The first speech on the rolls is that made in the Lincoln Parliament of 1316 by William Inge, then probably chief justice elect.[4] Under Edward III, when the names are usually recorded, we find that the *pronuntiatio* was nearly always delivered either by the chancellor or by the chief justice ; in some parliaments speeches by both are recorded.[5] It may be said that, on the

---

[1] The most famous example of the fourteenth century is the sermon preached by the bishop of Exeter at the opening of the Revenge Parliament of 1397, *ibid.* III, 347. Cf. the remarks on it by J. N. Figgis, *Divine Right of Kings*, 2nd ed., Cambridge, 1924, pp. 77-8.

[2] Cf. Stubbs, *Constitutional History*, III, 495-8.

[3] *Continuation* of Gervase of Canterbury, II, 281, cited by Stubbs, *op. cit.* III, 442.

[4] *Rot. Parl.* I, 350. Inge succeeded Brabazon as chief justice, who retired on February 23, 1316.

[5] See *infra*, pp. 237-8. The few exceptions noted are—an order from the king in 1325 to the chancellor and treasurer, commanding them to open Parliament on his behalf and to declare the causes of summons (cited in *Eng. Hist. Review*, Vol. XLVII, p. 389, n. 5) ; speeches by the archbishop of Canterbury in 1332 and

whole, the description in the *Modus* is confirmed by evidence, at least for the reign of Edward III, but too little is known of early practice to justify a definite conclusion.

There is, however, an omission in the *Modus* which helps us a little further. In the rolls of Edward III's Parliament we can trace the development of another formal speech in the shape of the charge particularising the royal needs, which was addressed to the Lords or, more often, to the Commons. Perhaps it arose out of the joint responsibility of the chancellor and the chief justice, seen in 1332 and 1333, when they both addressed Parliament.[1] The action of chief justice Shareshull, who gave a special charge to the Commons on three separate occasions (1351, 1352 and 1355), may have helped to standardise a half-grown custom.[2] By the second part of Edward III's reign it had become definitely a part of Parliamentary procedure to divide the declaration of the causes of summons into the *pronuntiatio* and the charge, that is, into general and particular appeals for support. The absence of reference to the charge in the *Modus* suggests that its description of the opening ceremonies belongs to the first stage of its development.

The chapter (XVIII) in which parliamentary business is defined has in the B version the title *de negotiis Parliamenti*, but that of the A text, *de ordine deliberandi negotia Parliamenti*, is a better description of its content. The order, or *kalendarium*, is as follows :

1. War and business touching the king, the queen and their children.

2. The common business of the realm, such as legislation correcting the defects of the common law, after judgement has been given.

3. Private business, that is, petitions. These must be heard strictly in the order in which they have been filed, on the principle that he who first proposes shall first act.

The order is interesting in itself, as it emphasises that the purpose of the assembly was not primarily judicial, but royal, political

1339, though he was not the sole speaker on either occasion (*Rot. Parl.* II, 64, 107) ; a speech by Sir Walter Manny in 1355, introduced by Shareshull, chief justice (*ibid.* II, 264). Several times the name of the man who made the *pronuntiatio* is not stated.

[1] *Ibid.* II, 66, 69.

[2] *Ibid.* II, 226, 237, 264b-5. In 1344 the king's needs were explained to the commons by the council (*ibid.* II, 148).

and national. It should also be noted that supply was included in the first category of business and that there is no suggestion of the claim, made in 1401, that it should follow the redress of grievance.[1]

It is difficult to determine from the records what order was actually followed and it seems probable that the variety of business made a stereotyped time-table impossible. In his thorough study of the roll of 1305, Maitland shows that a week after the parliamentary session had begun thirty-two petitions had been expedited,[2] making it plain that they were not reserved until the end, but were treated concurrently with other business. Such a practice is not incompatible with the calendar in the *Modus*, which seems to be an order of importance rather than an order of time. In the narrative roll of the Lincoln Parliament (1316) it is stated explicitly that, during the delay caused by Lancaster's absence, the hearing of petitions was put in train.[3] When Lancaster came (February 12) a fortnight late, the cause of summons was declared and a request was brought forward for counsel and aid for the Scottish war.[4] Discussion of supply lasted for nearly a week and it was finally granted on February 19.[5] The order laid down in the *Modus*—royal business including supply, legislation and petitions—is a natural order and, no doubt, it was that preferred by the executive, but the evidence indicates that it was greatly modified in practice. To save time, petitions were expedited from the beginning of the session and, in the intervals caused by debates on taxation, legislative measures were brought forward.

The other formal rules laid down in the *Modus* may be briefly summarised. All members of Parliament shall sit ; no one shall stand, unless he is speaking ; all speaking must be audible (XXII and XI). No one shall come in or go out except

[1] We may compare this definition of parliamentary business with that in the Ordinances of 1311 : Parliament should meet once or twice a year to deal with petitions and with the delays and doubts of other courts (Ordinance 29). In the *Mirror of Justices* (Selden Society, 1895, p. 155), which is almost contemporary, we have a complaint that the king held Parliament rarely and then only " for the purpose of obtaining aids and for the collection of treasure." The *Modus* combines these two descriptions and adds law-making and the discussion of policy, as essential functions of Parliament.

[2] *Memoranda de Parliamento*, 1305, p. lxi.

[3] *Rot. Parl.* I, 350b.

[4] *Ibid.*, pp. 350b-1.   [5] *Ibid.*, p. 351.

by one door and it is the duty of the usher to know every one who has the right to enter, so that entrance be denied to none [1] (XX and XXII). No one may withdraw without leave given in full Parliament ; should anyone fall ill, he shall send excusers and his essoin shall be tested by two of his peers ; if it be found that he is malingering, he shall be amerced and if his essoin be accepted, he shall name a sufficient person to act as his attorney (XXIV). The king shall dissolve Parliament with the words : *Parliamentum nostrum licentiabimus.* It is impossible to compare these details with early fourteenth century practice ; they seem more like an attempt to reform irregular or casual behaviour than a statement of existing conditions, and, for that reason, they probably belong to an early stage of parliamentary history.

An examination of those sections of the *Modus* which deal with the formal side of parliamentary procedure brings out in a striking way the limits of the author's outlook. He was evidently anxious to suggest changes which would increase both the prestige and efficiency of Parliament, but when his proposals are analysed and set beside existing conditions, so far as we know them, it is evident that he was asking for nothing radical. What he demanded was mainly the hardening of custom into stereotyped rules, rigidly enforced. Early rising, punctual attendance exacted by heavy penalties, no concessions for delay or laziness, even to the king himself—these are to him matters of weight. Even the duties and position of the usher and the crier are defined with a detail that we could wish he had extended to more important affairs. He was certainly anxious to devise an orderly system of record, but showed as much concern for the breadth of the membranes and the fees charged for copies as for the subjects entered on the rolls themselves. His only new idea seems to be an increase in the number of clerks employed and a demand that they should answer directly to Parliament itself. It is the point of view of the over-anxious bureaucrat, irritated by interference or undue delay and determined that the machine should run smoothly in its appointed groove. Even this general attitude recalls the reign of Edward II. It was, as Tout said, a time when lesser men, engaged upon the business of ad-

---

[1] Archbishop Stratford may have cited this rule when he was turned away from Parliament in 1341.

ministration, gave their attention to " those simple inventions which enable the machine to do its work better and more economically." [1] The same zeal for efficiency which underlay reforms devised for the household, the chancery and the exchequer inspired the meticulous rules and inflation of clerical service which characterise these chapters of the *Modus*.

[1] *Place of Edward II*, p. 24.

CHAPTER XI

PARLIAMENT AND THE CROWN

THOUGH we have found in the author of the *Modus* a satisfaction in the petty detail of procedure deep enough to characterise him as a zealous and perhaps even a fussy bureaucrat, it must be emphasised that his main concern remained for the place and power of Parliament as a whole. His grasp of the fundamental importance of its composition appears plainly in the opening chapters and in his treatment of function we find the same firmness and the same coherent idea of an institution exercising permanent authority on behalf of the whole realm. It is true that the main points are blunted or obscured by bad arrangement, even in the A version of the manuscripts, and it is tempting to suppose that in the original draft the constitutional chapters were grouped together at the end of the document. Yet a close examination strengthens the opinion that the order of the A text is substantially as the author wrote it. The second part of the tract was clearly intended to describe the procedure of Parliament from the opening to the dissolution, treating all matters, great and small, in the order of their appearance : the whole account was then rounded off and summed up in the last chapter on the six estates. The only obvious divergence from this is the chapter on the rolls (XXV), which comes second from the end ; it seems to have slipped out of its place after the two sections on the clerks (XV-XVI). Instead, its natural position is occupied by the important chapter, *de casibus et iudiciis difficilibus* (XVII) which we would expect to find after *de auxiliis regis* (XXIII). The explanation is probably that chapter XVII begins by a reference to the duties of the clerks ; difficult cases should be put in writing for the consideration of Parliament and the secondary clerks should assist in laying business before each *gradus*. However, though the reasons for the jumble of great matters and small can be understood, the order remains confused. For purposes of discussion it will be convenient to discount it altogether and to consider first the constitutional chapters of the *Modus*, in so far as they deal with the Crown in Parliament and, in the succeeding chapters, to face the larger issues of representation and consent.

The king of the *Modus* is neither an autocrat nor a puppet, but a constitutional monarch, charged with the government of his realm in co-operation with the estates in Parliament. The business of Parliament is royal business and it is the king's duty to ensure that it is handled with efficiency and justice. In the calendar of matters to be handled in Parliament (XVIII) emphasis rests upon functions which are not primarily judicial, but royal, political and national. War, the affairs of the king and his family and the creation and modification of public law take precedence over strictly judicial business. At the same time the petitions of subjects have a particular claim on the attention of the king in Parliament, since he was bound by his coronation oath to cause his judgements to be executed with justice and discretion and in mercy and truth. He is perjured (*periurus est*) if Parliament should be dissolved before all petitions have been discussed (XXIV).[1]

Though petitions are put last in the calendar of the *Modus*, probably last in order of importance, we are left in no doubt that to answer them was one of the chief functions of Parliament. The treatment of the subject is, in fact, in harmony with the idea that Parliament met *pro iusticia omnibus exhibenda*, as bishop Orleton defined it in 1330.[2] There is no need to discuss more fully the proclamation that petitions will be received during the first six days of the session (IX), the duties of clerks with regard to them (XV) and the rule that they shall be heard in the order of filing. The matters which demand examination are the composition of the body by which petitions were heard and terminated (XV) and the instruction that Parliament should not be dissolved until every petition had been answered (XXIV). The second instruction is obviously a proposal of reform, not a

---

[1] A late MS., Harley 305, f. 282ᵛ, has at this point the marginal note : " Hoc loco manifestus patet error et merito abstergendus."

[2] *Grandisson's Register*, III, p. 1544, quoted in *Bulletin*, IX, p. 1.

statement of practice, but by its phrasing it raises the question whether the author had in mind only the petitions of private persons and groups, or also petitions from the estates themselves. There is nothing in the terminology of the *Modus* to suggest that the estates would or should present petitions in Parliament. The proclamation that petitions should be filed within the first six days of the session almost precludes the idea of common discussion and in the calendar petitions are explicitly classed as *negotia singularia* (XVIII). We are told (XXIV) that before dissolution inquiry should be made " if there be anyone who shall have delivered a petition to Parliament to which no answer has yet been given " ; the use of the singular number again seems to exclude the idea of common petitions of the estates. The instruction was intended to safeguard the interests of private suitors, even at the expense of long-drawn-out sessions and against established custom,[1] so far as we know it. The emphatic statement that the king will be perjured, that is, he will have broken his coronation oath, if Parliament should be dissolved before all petitions have been discussed, is evidently brought forward to bolster up a claim recognised to be hardly reasonable.[2] The line of argument was familiar in Edward II's reign, when references to the coronation oath were frequent,[3] and it helps to mark the date of composition.

The absence of all explicit reference to common petitions has special significance in a tract which exalts, not only Parliament as a whole, but the lesser estates within it. The practice of drafting general petitions certainly goes back to the thirteenth century, as the Articles of 1215, the Petitions of the Barons (1258) and the Provisions of Westminster (1259) remind us. Under Edward I there are a few examples of petitions presented in Parliament which cannot be classed as private. In 1290 a petition from *plures de populo*, put before the king and council, was entered on the Parliament roll ;[4] a *billa prelatorum et procerum regni* was presented in the Hilary Parliament of 1301 by

---

[1] E.g. in 1305, 1332 and 1336.

[2] Cf. the failure to deal with petitions in the Parliaments of 1332, *Rot. Parl.* II, 65, 67, 68, cited in *Bulletin*, Vol. VIII, where there are interesting remarks about petitions, pp. 72-4. See also *ibid.*, Vol. VI, pp. 75-6.

[3] See the references collected in *The Coronation Oath of Edward II*, B. Wilkinson, *Essays in Honour of James Tait*, pp. 413 *seq.*

[4] *Rot. Parl.* I, 47.

Henry of Keighley, addressed to the king in the name of " les gentz de la communaute de sa terre." [1] Other petitions of the same general type are recorded on the rolls in 1304, 1305 and 1307.[2] There is, however, no sign that they were given any separate treatment and, as Maitland says, " by no sharp line can the petitions of the assembled lords and commoners be marked off from the general mass of those petitions which are to be ' expedited ' in the Parliament by the king and his council." [3] The evidence for Edward II's reign is harder to interpret. Mr. Richardson and Mr. Sayles regard the few petitions of this period, which might be the work of the Commons in Parliament, as emanating from " the general body of suitors attending Parliament in contradistinction to the king and council by whom the petitions were considered." They understand by *communitas* or *commune* the " nation at large," including the magnates.[4] Professor Gray, on the other hand, arguing back from the form of petitions, undeniably put forward in 1333 and 1337 by the Commons in Parliament, maintains that the eleven articles presented in 1309 and the six of 1325 were " Commons bills " in the later meaning of the term.[5] Both sides agree in admitting that the " indented bill " presented in Edward III's first Parliament was a true Commons petition, but Professor Gray points out [6] that its form, expressing definitely the idea of a bargain between the king and commons,[7] was not that followed in later Parliaments.[8] The petitions of 1327 were not, therefore, the model followed in 1333, and 1337 and it seems more likely that the form of " Commons bills " was derived from those of 1309 and 1325. It is, however, certain that demands of the kind were rare under Edward II and we may conclude that the treatment of the subject in the *Modus* corresponds to normal parliamentary practice in that reign.

[1] Madox, *Exchequer*, II, 108 ; and *Parl. Writs*, I, 104, cited in *Bulletin*, Vol. IX, p. 7.

[2] *Rot. Parl.* I, 166-7, 219-20 ; *Memoranda de Parliamento*, 1305, nos. 87, 198, 203, 472 and 486.

[3] *Ibid.*, p. lxxiv.

[4] *Bulletin*, Vol. VI, p. 77, n. 2 ; Vol. IX, p. 8. Cf. *supra*, pp. 170-2, for a discussion of the meanings of the word *communitas*.

[5] H. L. Gray, *Influence of the Commons*, Chapter VIII, especially pp. 207-16. Cf. Statute of Westminster IV (1320), *ibid.*, p. 214.

[6] *Ibid.*, pp. 215-18.

[7] The Commons undertook to maintain the *querele* of the young king.

[8] The subsidy bill of the fifteenth century adopted the indenture form.

Chapter XV contains some important remarks on the way in which petitions should be heard. Judges may be assigned by the king and the peers of Parliament to act *cum aliis sectatoribus Parliamenti* in hearing and transmitting petitions and complaints. When peers of Parliament are appointed specially by themselves to hear and to examine petitions, their proceedings and unanimous judgement shall be recited in full Parliament. It is clear that the hearing of petitions was not intended to be the professional monopoly of the judges. If they take part in it, it must be by appointment of the king and Parliament ; even then other suitors or members of Parliament ought to be associated with them. It is also indicated that petitions may be heard without the judges' assistance. We find, in short, the same strict limit imposed on the power of the judges as we found in the treatment of the councillors. It has recently been shown that the petitions to the Parliaments of Edward I were heard mainly by trained lawyers and permanent officials in the royal service ; [1] only three barons, for example, served on the four panels set up in 1305. During the reign of Edward II a marked change in the personnel of the panels took place. The name of auditors appointed in four Parliaments (Hilary 1316, Mich. 1318, Mich. 1320 and Midsummer 1321) are on record and they show that the magnates outnumbered the technical experts.[2] Mr. Richardson and Mr. Sayles suppose that " in the earliest Parliaments of Edward II the precedents of his father's reign were followed . . . thereafter it is outweighed by the baronial element." [3] The new position of the magnates was probably the outcome of the Ordinances, which, though ignoring the Commons, had stressed the baronial as against the professional element in Parliament.[4] The change thus begun persisted under Edward III, though the duties of auditors declined in importance and we should not expect them to be emphasised except during the period of transition. The beginning of the independent action of estates, ultimately to take the form of common petitions, may be seen in the order (XVI) that the secondary clerks shall record the

---

[1] *Eng. Hist. Review*, Vol. XLVI, pp. 534-6, 542-6.
[2] *Ibid.*, Vol. XLVII, pp. 197-8. The appointment of prelates and earls as auditors of petitions in 1320 was commended by bishop Cobham in his letters to the Pope and one of the Cardinals (Cobham's Register (Worcester), pp. 97-8).
[3] *Ibid.*, Vol. XLVII, p. 199.
[4] Cf. Conway Davies, *Baronial Opposition*, pp. 511 *seq.*

dubitationes et responsiones of each *gradus*. These doubts and answers represent an early discussion of business which led in the end to the common demand, the common bargain and legislation by bill.

The most sensational chapters in the *Modus* are those entitled *de casibus et iudiciis difficilibus* and *de auxiliis regis* (XVII and XXIII). They are of primary importance for the interpretation of the document and it would not be helpful to discuss them fully at this stage. The committee of estates (XVII) has already been dealt with in relation to the deposition of Edward II [1] and the emphatic declaration of the doctrine of consent (XXIII) must be reserved for separate treatment.[2] We may, however, consider now the other constitutional questions raised in these chapters, as they fall into line with our discussion of specific restrictions on the royal power.

In Chapter XVII the difficult cases are defined in the first place as disputes or controversies relating to peace or war ; these ought to be decided by judgement of the majority, after full enquiry by each *gradus* sitting apart. More serious cases are : discord between the king and magnates, discord among the magnates themselves sufficient to disturb the public peace, perils of war and difficult cases arising before the chancellor or the judges. If a unanimous decision or even a decision of the majority cannot be reached, then the extraordinary committee of twenty-five must be set up. The remedy that the author anticipated was the drafting of ordinances, which the king and council had power to examine and amend, provided that they acted in and with the consent of full Parliament.

The difficulties which are described might be glossed as the Scottish war, the strife between Lancaster and Warenne and the discord over Gaveston and the Despensers, and they are as typical of Edward II's reign as the Ordinances themselves. The separate jurisdiction of the chancellor, indicated in the phrase " si casus difficilis coram cancellario Anglie emergat," was already growing up before the end of the thirteenth century and steadily increased under Edward II.[3] It is easy to find

---

[1] *Supra*, Chapter IX. [2] *Infra*, Chapter XII.

[3] Holdsworth, I, 401 *seq*. The development came partly by means of reference to the chancellor of petitions presented to the council or to Parliament. Cf. Conway Davies, *Baronial Opposition*, pp. 238 *seq*.

contemporary parallels for judicial doubts arising before the chancellor and judges ; for example, where the dispute over the Clare estates in 1316 was referred by the king to the chancellor, two judges and other councillors, they reported that they would not presume to give judgement or even to advise the king without the assent of the magnates.[1] In fact, the special mixture of technical, military and political problems described in the chapter is also a succinct statement of the problems confronting Edward II.

In the procedure laid down for these difficult cases a certain ambiguity is evident in the references to the Crown. On the one hand, it is supposed that the king may be at loggerheads with his Parliament and that ordinances may be drafted which he and his council are reluctant to accept ; on the other, the leave of the king and council is deemed necessary for the setting up of the committee of twenty-five and his personal leave must be given for the reduction of its numbers below three. An attempt to strike a balance between royal and parliamentary authority is plain in the reservation to king and council of the power to examine and to amend the ordinances of the committee, though only if they wish to exercise it, know how, and act in full Parliament and with parliamentary consent. What would happen if the king rejected the ordinances altogether, or if Parliament rejected the emendations is not considered. The author evidently had no fear of a permanent deadlock. The situation in his mind was not that of the Deposition Parliament of 1327, but rather that of 1322, when the king and council requested the Parliament of York to repeal the Ordinances and to put the good points in a statute.[2]

At the same time it cannot be denied that the general attitude to the king is severe. This comes out strongly in the chapter *de absentia regis* (XIII). The king is bound to attend Parliament in person. Should he fall ill he may keep his chamber, but he must not be outside the place where Parliament is sitting. His condition should be examined by a committee of the estates [3] and in their presence he should commission the archbishop of the province, the steward and the chief justice to act for him in

---

[1] *Rot. Parl.* I, 354.

[2] Conway Davies, *Baronial Opposition*, p. 583, Appendix 93.

[3] The committee should be composed of two bishops, two earls, two barons, two knights of the shire, two citizens and two burgesses.

Parliament. The committee and the commissioners should satisfy the magnates that the illness is genuine. The reason given for this remarkable royal essoin is that formerly clamour and murmurs have arisen because of royal absence, which is a hurtful and perilous thing for the whole commonalty of Parliament and for the realm.[1] There can be no doubt that the author was thinking of a king who feigned illness to avoid a parliamentary session. Edward II was charged with malingering for this purpose in 1313, according to the Chronicler of Malmesbury, he stayed away from Parliament *morbo ut putabatur ficto detentus*.[2] From the same source we learn that later in 1313 he delayed his coming to Parliament for almost a fortnight, so that the magnates departed in anger before he finally arrived.[3] He seems also to have withdrawn for a time from the Parliament of Lincoln, when he appointed two bishops and two earls to act for him until the coming of Lancaster.[4] It can hardly be questioned that the peculiar emphasis on the dangers of royal absence, which is characteristic of the *Modus*, points definitely to the behaviour of Edward II.[5]

The choice of commissioners to represent the king in Parliament also points to an early period. It is unlikely that the archbishop of the province in which Parliament met would be named after sessions had ceased to be held in the north,[6] or that the chancellor should be omitted, at least after 1327. As early as 1325, Edward II requested the chancellor and treasurer to open Parliament for him.[7] Under Edward III, when the king was often absent, a formal commission was granted to one of his sons, sometimes with the assistance of other persons.[8] The chief

---

[1] Cf. Chapters XVII and XIX for a similar attitude.
[2] *Vita Edwardi II*, p. 190.   [3] *Ibid.*, pp. 193-4.
[4] *Rot. Parl.* I, 350b. Cf. the postponement of the Lent Parliament of 1312 because of the king's absence (Reynolds' Register (Worcester), p. 34).
[5] When Richard II withdrew from the Michaelmas Parliament of 1386 this chapter may have been cited. See *supra*, p. 177, n. 1 ; *infra*, Chapter XV, pp. 353-5.   [6] *Supra*, p. 143.
[7] Chancery warrant 130/7247, cited in *Eng. Hist. Review*, Vol. XLVII, p. 389, n. 5.
[8] E.g. in 1339 and in 1351, *Rot. Parl.* II, 107, 225. In 1339 the archbishop of Canterbury, the dean of York (treasurer), John Stonor (chief justice of the Bench) and John de St. Paul (master of the rolls) were associated with Richard de Willoughby, C.J., to open and continue Parliament in the name of the king and the duke of Cornwall, then *custos regni* (*ibid.* II, 107).

justice was evidently closely associated with parliamentary business until the last years of Edward III's reign ;[1] between 1347 and 1362 it was he who regularly made the formal declaration of the causes of summons. After that time his office definitely lost its direct political importance to that of the chancellor.[2] It would be surprising to find him as a commissioner after the reign of Edward III.

The selection of the steward as one of the commissioners is more significant and will require fuller investigation. Elsewhere in the *Modus* the obligation is laid on him to see that the estates sit in Parliament in their appointed places, unless the king shall assign the duty to another (XIV). Of much greater importance is the special function allotted to the earl steward, the earl constable and the earl marshal in the chapter *de casibus et iudiciis difficilibus* (XVII) ; it shall be the duty of these three, or two of them, to choose the committee of estates who shall ordain for the whole Parliament. The high claims made here on behalf of the great hereditary officials are characteristic of the conflict between the crown and the baronage from the days of Simon de Montfort to the deposition of Edward II.

By the reign of Henry III the growth of royal power and the organisation of the household had reduced the great baronial offices to little more than ceremonial importance. The office-holders had precedence and special functions at coronations and other high festivals, but the domestic duties implied by their titles were performed by the king's servants.[3] The marshal and constable, however, retained their military importance in time of war and the prestige of the hereditary titles gave to all of them a certain superiority over the rest of the baronage. They were the natural leaders of their order and it was inevitable that at times of crisis they should arrogate to themselves special duties and privileges. That a certain residuum of power was acknowledged by the crown to lie with them, even in time of peace, is shown by an incident during the Hilary Parliament of 1290.[4]

[1] *Rot. Parl.* II, *passim.*
[2] The great, though indirect political importance of Tressilian under Richard II and the consultation of Thirnyng in 1399 must not be forgotten, though formal duties in Parliament were no longer assigned to the chief justice.
[3] J. H. Round, *King's Serjeants and Officers of State,* 1911, pp. 52 *seq.* ; Tout, *Chapters,* I, 201 *seq.*
[4] *Rot. Parl.* I, 17.

The earl of Cornwall was served with a summons to appear before the archbishop of Canterbury when he was crossing Westminster Hall ; those who procured the summons were prosecuted jointly by the king, the steward, the marshal, the earl of Cornwall and the abbot of Westminster.[1]

Mr. Richardson and Mr. Sayles comment on the prosecution as follows : " The steward and the marshal take part perhaps because they are in some special sense the guardians of the law, especially in Parliament ; since they do not try the case, their intervention can hardly be founded on the fact that the offence was committed within the verge." [2] The case is important because it shows that Edward I was prepared to allow that the great lay officers of state had a certain special responsibility in relation to Parliament.

It seems probable, as M. Bémont has suggested,[3] that neither king nor barons were sure what constitutional rights were united to the hereditary dignities. In 1265, after the battle of Lewes, Henry III (or Simon de Montfort in his name) wrote to Loretta, widow of Robert Fitz Parnel, earl of Leicester, and then a recluse of Hackington, to ask her to state what she knew of the rights and liberties appertaining to the stewardship of England.[4] The appeal for information to an elderly lady, who had retired from the world nearly fifty years before, is a sign that little can have been known on the subject. Similar ignorance was manifest in 1282 when the precedents of the constable's emoluments were investigated [5] and again in 1308, when a search was made in the rolls of the exchequer before the stewardship was granted to Thomas of Lancaster, as appertaining to his earldom of Leicester.[6]

The obscurity which surrounded the rights of hereditary officers proved an advantage to the holders when they wished to take the lead in public affairs. Simon de Montfort assumed the style of *senescallus Anglie* in 1255 ; [7] during the struggle with Henry III he made the stewardship the first great office of state

---

[1] The abbot appears because Westminster Hall was in his peculiar.

[2] *Bulletin*, Vol. V, p. 132.

[3] *Simon de Montfort*, translated by E. F. Jacob, Oxford, 1930, p. 14.

[4] Vernon Harcourt, *His Grace the Steward and Trial of Peers*, 1907, pp. 125-6 ; F. M. Powicke, " Loretta Countess of Leicester " in *Historical Essays in Honour of James Tait*, p. 267.

[5] J. E. Morris, *Welsh Wars of Edward I*, Oxford, 1901, p. 155.

[6] Madox, *Exchequer*, I, 52, n., cited by Vernon Harcourt, *op. cit.*, p. 142.

[7] M. Bateson, *Records of the Borough of Leicester*, Cambridge, 1899, I, nos. XXII, XXIII, etc., cited, as above, p. 47.

and the basis of his claim to be the new Mattathias, *zelans zelum legis*.[1] Under Edward I the office was virtually in abeyance [2] and when opposition to the crown revived in a dangerous form, the lead passed to Bigod of Norfolk and Bohun of Hereford, as marshal and constable. The father of each of them had been included in the council set up at Oxford in 1258 [3] and their own military service in the Welsh and Scottish wars had drawn attention to their peculiar status. Beginning, as Mr. Morris has shown,[4] with private grievances and a technical case against service abroad without the personal presence of the king, their refusal to go to Gascony developed into a constitutional struggle against the Crown. Arming themselves and their supporters, they marched on London and civil war was probably averted only by the alarm caused by William Wallace's victory at Stirling. The confirmation of the Charters (October 10, 1297) as " the rallying-point of the oppressed and offended " [5] was thus achieved under the leadership of the constable and marshal. The triumph was underlined in the following year at an assembly of estates at York (May 25, 1298) when Bohun and Bigod insisted on a second confirmation as a condition of military service in Scotland.[6] Edward I's good faith was rightly suspect and in 1299 and 1300 the same issues were revived, with special emphasis on the fulfilment of repeated promises to disafforest. Under the lead of the marshal and the archbishop, the *Articuli super Cartas* were exacted from the king in the Parliament of 1300.[7] The struggle over the charters was the centre of political agitation in the last decade of Edward I's reign and it served to mark out the constable and marshal as pre-eminent among the baronage. The contrariants under Edward II thus inherited a double tradition of leadership. That of the constable and marshal was strong by reason of the constitutional conflicts of the previous reign, but it was overshadowed by the memory of earl Simon's great stand against Henry III and by the enormous wealth and

---

[1] *Song of Lewes*, ed. C. L. Kingsford, Oxford, 1890, ll. 76-7.
[2] It was held by Edmund Crouchback, the king's brother, for the term of his life, and lapsed on his death in 1296 (Vernon Harcourt, *His Grace the Steward and Trial of Peers*, pp. 139-40, 163).
[3] *Select Charters*, pp. 380-1.   [4] *Welsh Wars*, pp. 274 *seq.*
[5] Stubbs, *Select Charters*, p. 489.
[6] Rishanger, *Chronica et Annales* (*Rolls Series*), p. 186.
[7] *Ibid.*, p. 404 ; Hemingburgh, II, 186.

prestige of Thomas of Lancaster, who had entered into his stewardship. The question had also its personal side. Bigod of Norfolk died in 1306 and the marshalship was in Edward's hands at his accession. After an unsuccessful attempt to separate the office from the estates,[1] the king conferred first the Norfolk lands and then the office of marshal on his young half-brother, Thomas of Brotherton.[2] Until the end of the reign, when he supported Isabella and Mortimer,[3] little is known of Thomas, though the formal importance of his office was shown by his appointment as *custos Anglie* in 1319.[4] The constableship of Bohun of Hereford, taken away from him for a time, was restored as his right in 1311 and he retained it until his death at Boroughbridge.[5] For the rest of the reign the office was in abeyance. It was inevitable, therefore, that official leadership should be exercised by Lancaster as steward, with Hereford as his first lieutenant.

It is unnecessary to recall in detail the history of baronial opposition to Edward II, in order to illustrate the dominating part played by the steward and the constable, as their leadership throughout the conflict is well known.[6] At what stage Lancaster began to claim for himself peculiar status as guardian of the public interest is obscure ; perhaps the occasion was the murder of Gaveston, carefully designed to take place on Lancastrian land.[7] Memory of earl Simon's exploits was probably revived at the same time ; the *Brut* chronicler, for example, describing the confirmation of the Ordinances in 1312, writes " the Kyng . . . helde a parlement and ordeynede the lawes of Sir Symond Mountford. . . ."[8] The first explicit reference to Lancaster's interpretation of his official duties belongs to the year 1317. When the king ordered his army to assemble at York, Lancaster caused bridges to be broken down and did all that he could to prevent the passage of men and arms. His defence was that he was acting as steward of England, " cujus interest utilitatibus regni prospicere, et, si rex contra aliquem arma vellet assumere, senescallo praecipue deberet innotescere." [9] A year later, in the

---

[1] Conway Davies, *Baronial Opposition*, p. 208.   [2] *Ibid.*
[3] *Supra*, Chapter IX, p. 189.   [4] *Annales Paulini*, p. 285.
[5] *Cal. Pat. Rolls*, 1307-13, p. 387.
[6] Cf. *Annales London*, pp. 160, 225 *seq.*
[7] *In feodo comitis, ibid.*, p. 207.   Blacklow is one mile from Warwick.
[8] I, 207.   [9] *Vita Edwardi II*, p. 230.

Parliament of York (October 1318), he claimed that his office entitled him to appoint the steward of the royal household and he renewed this demand in the succeeding Parliament at York in 1319.[1]   At the irregular assembly summoned by him to Sherburn in Elmet (1321),[2] the statement of grievances and the attack on *malos conciliarios* was expounded at Lancaster's command, probably in his official capacity.[3]   The constable, Hereford, was present as leader of the Welsh Marchers.[4]   They had already taken arms against the Despensers and now bound themselves by indentures to rid the realm of evil councillors.   Perhaps on the constable's advice, they attempted to justify their violence and threats of deposition by a statement of constitutional right, described in terms which are tantalisingly vague.   In the *Annales Paulini*, a trustworthy authority, it is stated that during the advance on London the Marchers drafted a certain tract, ordained and approved according to ancient custom.[5]   This tract was almost certainly the famous treatise on the office of steward, which embodied and expanded the Lancastrian claim.[6]

The special problems raised by the manuscript history of this document will be considered later ; at this stage we are concerned only with its content.   The function of the steward is " to supervise and to regulate, under and immediately after the king, the whole realm of England and all the officers of the law within the realm in times of peace and of war."   He must see to it that all complaints of subjects are heard in Parliament and that the failures of the chancellor, the judges and other officials are corrected.   If the law prove on examination to be doubtful, then the steward and the constable shall nominate a committee of estates who shall ordain a permanent remedy, which shall be approved in full Parliament and proclaimed throughout the realm.   Officials who fail in their duty shall be admonished or punished, according to the degree of negligence. It is the steward's special business to take action against evil

---

[1] Cole, *Documents*, pp. 3, 8, 48.   [2] Cf. *supra*, p. 163.

[3] Bridlington, pp. 61-4 ; for the indenture drafted at Sherburn see MSS. Tanner 12, f. 50, and Ashmole, 860, ff. 375-6 (Bodleian Library).

[4] *Ibid.*, p. 62.

[5] P. 293, " . . . fecerunt in scriptis quendam tractatum ex antiqua consuetudine ordinatum et approbatum."

[6] The text is printed in Vernon Harcourt, *His Grace the Steward*, pp. 164-7. Cf. *infra*, Chapter XV, pp. 358-60, for a discussion of the MSS.

councillors. Associating himself with the constable, magnates and others of the commonalty, he shall appeal to the king to dismiss those who dishonour the Crown and injure the realm. Should the king reject all advice, then the steward and constable of England, with the magnates and commons, shall go with banners displayed against the evil councillors, as public enemies ; they shall seize them and all that they have and keep them in custody to be judged by the realm in Parliament. In this way Godwin was banished before the Norman Conquest,[1] Hubert de Burgh was overthrown by the steward and other magnates under Henry III, and Gaveston was banished and on his return taken by the steward, the constable and other magnates and beheaded as a public enemy.

Here this most tendentious document abruptly ends. It is difficult to say exactly at what stage it was drafted, though it was obviously devised *ad hoc* to justify the attack on the Despensers, before their exile in the summer of 1321. It can hardly be earlier than the end of 1320, when the Middle Party broke up on the question of the lordship of Gower.[2] It may have been concocted during the negotiations between Edward II and the Marchers in April 1321,[3] when Hereford urged the king to remove the younger Despenser and to refer the complaints against him to Parliament. However, the open justification of civil war, which concludes the document, suggests that it was written when the Marchers were already in arms (May 1321) and it may have been prepared for the meeting at Sherburn (June 28) where the steward and the constable certainly played the leading parts. It will be remembered that the condemnation of the Despensers in the Parliament of 1321 was stated in the statute to be at the suit of Thomas of Lancaster, steward of England.[4] The whole tenor of the tract, especially the frank allocation of responsibility for the death of Gaveston to the steward and the constable, leaves us in no doubt as to the importance of the great hereditary officers in the crises of the reign.

Emphasis on the functions of the steward and the constable

---

[1] Cf. *Brut*, I, 128.
[2] Conway Davies, *Baronial Opposition*, pp. 473-4.
[3] *Ibid.*, p. 475 ; *Cal. Cl. Rolls, 1318-23*, pp. 296, 367-8.
[4] Preamble, stat. 1 Ed. III, *Statutes of the Realm*, I, 251.

is not the only point of connection between the tract on the steward and the *Modus*. Their association in manuscripts is highly significant, but discussion of this must be reserved for a later chapter. When the two documents are set side by side, the likeness between them is unmistakable. In each, Parliament occupies the centre of the stage and attention is to some extent concentrated upon its legislative business. Each has the same conception of law-making, as necessary to provide a remedy for the failure of the courts to do right to all men ; each even considers the same problem of a difficult case arising before the chancellor. More remarkable is the agreement in the provision of an extraordinary committee of estates to draft ordinances or statutes when the law is ambiguous or doubtful. In the steward's tract it is provided that to ordain a permanent remedy the steward and constable in Parliament shall chose a committee of twenty-five persons, or about that number, drawn from the earls, barons, knights of the shire, citizens and burgesses of Parliament. The analogy with the committee of estates in the *Modus* (XVII) is so plain that we cannot doubt that the one was known to the drafter of the other. There can also hardly be a doubt as to which has priority. The steward's tract was written *ad hoc*, from the point of view of the contrariants, and in its whole attitude it takes the offensive and threatens penalties for wrongdoing. In the *Modus* each point made in the other document is taken up and modified with considerable skill. Though not in any way reactionary, a working compromise is continually sought between punitive methods and licensed anarchy on the one hand, and the free exercise of the royal prerogative on the other. For example, the marshal is associated with the steward and constable in the exercise of power and the exclusively lay composition of the committee of estates is enlarged by the inclusion of the prelates and the proctors of the clergy.

If the date of 1321 be accepted for the steward's tract, that of the *Modus* must follow quickly after it. It must be after the ruin of the contrariants, the death of the constable at Boroughbridge and the execution of the steward at Pontefract (March 1321). Yet it must also have been written soon enough for Lancaster's claims to be fresh in men's minds and before the full force of the reaction under the Despensers had developed—say before the death of Pembroke (June 23, 1324), and the end of Stapeldon's treasurership (July 3, 1325). Within this brief period the Parliament of York (May 1322) was held. About that time, when the famous statute was passed and the good points of the Ordinances were incorporated into the law of the land, seems the most fitting occasion for the composition of the *Modus*.

The occasion cannot be separated from the whole question of the meaning of the document. We have found in the *Modus* a theory of monarchy, or of the Crown in Parliament, which is neither royal nor baronial. It contains no vestige of the idea of the ruler as *solutus legibus*, free from the limits of positive law. This was the position which Edward I seems to have tried to take up at the end of his reign, claiming for the kings of England " the free pre-eminence of the state of their royal dignity " [1] and securing absolution from the Pope for promises made *de nostra bona voluntate minime*.[2] The *Modus* leaves no room for *voluntas*, or royal pleasure ; what prerogatives the king enjoys must be employed in the service of Parliament. On the other hand, the attitude of the *Modus* cannot fairly be described as baronial or Lancastrian. The Commons are exalted at the expense of the magnates, both spiritual and temporal ; it is even laid down that the king can hold his Parliament without the latter (XXIII). As we have just seen, the marked way in which the claims put forward in the tract on the steward are reduced in the *Modus*, by linking him up with the constable and marshal, is a decisive argument against a particular Lancastrian bias.[3] The general attitude is one of confidence, not in men, but in institutions. Power is vested in the communities of the realm, represented by the *gradus* in Parliament ; it is exercised in accordance with the principle which necessity had constrained Edward I to assert in vague and high-sounding words. " It is the custom of the realm of England that in all things touching the state of the same realm there should be asked the counsel of all whom

---

[1] *Parl. Writs*, I, 102-3, in the letter sent from the Parliament of Lincoln (1301) to the pope, certainly inspired by Edward I ; cited by Stubbs, *Constitutional History*, II, 159.
[2] *Statutes of the Realm*, I, 147-9 (1306), cited by Stubbs, *op. cit.*, p. 162, n. 2.
[3] For the Lancastrian view, see Tout, *Chapters*, III, 138-9, n. 2, and the recent article by Professor Morris, *Eng. Hist. Review*, Vol. XLIX, pp. 407 *seq.*

the matter concerns." [1]   In the *Modus*, this principle was given shape and substance in the doctrine that the Parliament of estates rested on the pillars of representation and consent.

We reach here a definite challenge to the general medieval rule that if there were no absolute king, there was also no absolute community.[2]   It was a rule that stood firm only as long as kings and councils were under the supremacy of the law and custom of the community.   The author of the *Modus* admitted that public law might be corrected by legislation in Parliament and that taxation ought to be imposed on the realm only by the consent of its chosen representatives.   Though he certainly cannot have realised the full implications of these admissions, he was, in effect, maintaining a new supremacy, the supremacy of the Parliament of Estates.   This brings us to the final, intrinsic [3] difficulty with regard to the date of the document, since scholars are reluctant to allow that ideas of representation and consent had developed so far in the first quarter of the fourteenth century. It will, therefore, be necessary to submit their history to a fairly detailed investigation, before discussing the special treatment they receive in the *Modus*.

[1] Letter of Edward I, 1301, cited by Stubbs, *Constitutional History*, II, 159, from Matt. Westminster, p. 439.

[2] A. J. Carlyle, *Medieval Political Theory in the West*, Vol. V, 1928, p. 467. On this subject cf. Vol. V, Part III, Chapter II, *passim*.

[3] A difficulty of another kind, which still requires examination, is the manuscript history of the document.   Treatment of this is reserved until Chapter XV.

CHAPTER XII

THE DOCTRINE OF CONSENT

THE doctrine of consent to changes in the law has its origin in the inveterate conservatism of primitive people. Hostility to change and the belief that custom was the ultimate sanction of law led them to insist that all alterations of law and custom required the explicit consent of the community. The reluctance with which that consent was given was a formidable barrier to progress and nearly everywhere the effort to break it down destroyed at the same time the idea itself. In England, where continuity of law and tradition has been unbroken for over fourteen centuries, the primitive idea of consent has survived the successive shocks of foreign invasions and the more subtle infection of continental practice. It has become the keystone of the constitution, the principle upon which the rights of subjects and the powers of Parliaments ultimately depend. The process by which an idea, in origin archaic and obstructive, was translated into the motive force of modern democracy is complicated and obscure, especially in the early stages. It is, however, possible to suggest under what conditions and in what ways it came to be employed as a constructive principle in the architecture of Parliament.

In so far as the doctrine of consent in medieval society had roots in the secular politics of the ancient world, all that is important for our purposes is to be found in the Roman Empire.[1] For the *Politics* of Aristotle, which gave medieval thought direct contact with Greek political ideas, was unknown in Western Europe before the second half of the thirteenth century. Long

---

[1] For this, as in other passages in which the Roman Empire is discussed (*infra*, pp. 280-2, 293), I am deeply indebted to valuable notes given to me by Mr. C. G. Stone. I have drawn upon them freely, often verbally, but he is in no way responsible for errors into which I may have fallen.

before that time the political structure of the Christian West had been profoundly, though obscurely, influenced by Roman literature and Roman law.

The Roman Empire, as medieval jurists saw it mirrored in the Roman law, was governed by an absolute monarchy, but it was a monarchically governed commonwealth—a *respublica*—which had grown out of what we call the Roman Republic and what Romans of the imperial age called the Old Republic (*vetus respublica*). In the *vetus respublica* the sovereign legislative power had belonged to the Roman people in its assemblies, while the Senate had "authority" (*auctoritas*) as a permanent council for the chief annual magistrates to consult, as a body which contained the leading men of the community, and as exercising a regulative influence which had to be generally accepted if the Republican constitution was to be workable. That constitution broke down when, in a series of vehement disputes within the Italian people over the spoils and opportunities of Empire, the Senate could no longer effectively control the action of magistrates who had the right to initiate legislation in the popular assemblies.[1] There was, however, no clean break with the past and the means by which stability was restored to the Roman State may be described as the grafting of monarchy on to the Republican Constitution. Though in the early imperial age the legislative sovereignty of the Roman people fell into atrophy, yet it seems that a formal *lex populi* was still for a time needed to confirm the decree by which the Senate invested a new Emperor with his powers. Thus a later imperial jurist could say that what was in his time the absolute power of the emperor was the power of the Roman people, which the people had transferred to its prince. And so at least the theory of ultimate popular consent was maintained, and, through Roman law, it was transmitted to medieval Europe. The famous tag *quod principi placuit, legis vigorem habuit* was often cited in defence of absolutism, but in its context it was also a reminder of the popular basis of authority. The full sentence runs : " What has pleased the prince has the force of law, since by a royal law, enacted concerning his authority (*imperium*), the people have conceded to and have conferred upon him the whole of their *imperium* and

---

[1] Hence, among other things, the creation of great military commands by laws of the people for Pompey and for Caesar.

potestas." [1] Though the opening phrase was used in the middle ages and later to justify the most arrogant claims of princes, the whole passage contained within it the idea of popular sovereignty. With it must be associated a still more famous maxim which appears in the private law of Rome—" what touches all must be approved by all " (*quod omnes tangit ab omnibus approbetur*).[2] These two maxims sum up the main political contribution of Rome to Western Europe.

In the barbarian societies that succeeded the Roman Empire the idea of consent arose naturally out of the supremacy of law or popular custom. In a well-known passage Tacitus describes the public assemblies of the Germans at the end of the second century A.D. The chiefs discuss lesser matters apart, but all join in the discussion of important business, though the chiefs debate beforehand those things for which the decision (*arbitrium*) rests with the people. They meet on fixed days and are addressed by their king or chief, who adopts a tone of persuasion, never of command. If they are displeased they shout aloud and if they are satisfied they clash their spears.[3] Tacitus may have written this passage with the lost powers of the Roman people in his mind, yet its general sense is confirmed by other evidence, especially that of the Anglo-Saxon laws. The preambles of Anglo-Saxon codes repeatedly express the idea of consent, the consent of the council of the wise or the Witan, which, like the Roman Senate, had probably replaced the clamour of a popular assembly.[4] The same formula of consent appears in the laws of Canute, showing that the Danish conquest brought no change in this respect.[5] William the Conqueror claimed to be the true heir of Edward the Confessor and promised his English subjects to respect and to maintain their laws.[6] Under him the traditional Anglo-Saxon practice merged with feudal ideas of counsel and consent, so that it becomes hardly possible to distinguish the one from the other. But, whatever its origin, the practice continued and is expressed in all important enactments of the twelfth century. English law continued to rest on a basis of custom

---

[1] Justinian, *Institutes*, I, 2 ; § 6.   [2] Cf. *infra*, pp. 264-5.
[3] *Select Charters*, pp. 61-2.
[4] For examples, see *ibid.*, pp. 67, 70, 77, 82, 84.
[5] *The Laws of the Kings of England from Edmund to Henry I*, Cambridge, 1925, edited and translated by A. J. Robertson, pp. 154-5, 174-5.
[6] His *statuta* had the consent of *principibus*, *Select Charters*, p. 98.

and consent. This basis is finally expressed by Bracton in the opening paragraph of his treatise : " Though almost all countries use statutes and written law (*legibus et iure scripto*), England alone uses unwritten law and custom (*iure non scripto et consuetudine*). Unwritten law is established or defined by precedent. It will not be ridiculous to accept the unwritten law of England as law, since that has the force of law which has been defined and approved by royal authority and by the advice and assent of magnates and the common consent of the realm."[1] Thus in England the idea of consent was from earliest times closely bound up with law and the strength of the bond was due, at least in part, to Anglo-Saxon practice for nearly four hundred years.

It would be easy to make too much of the consent of the Anglo-Saxons and to distort perspective by seeing at work in the Witan the principles of modern democracy. Under the great kings of the house of Alfred it was probably purely formal, and it was kept alive more as a matter of habit than as the conscious expression of a political idea. We have no evidence that it was in any way associated with royal revenue. Alfred declared that a monarch required, as means of support, lands, gifts, weapons, meat, ale and clothing ; with these he maintained his subjects and administered the authority committed to him.[2] The monarch, thus endowed, made no demand for taxes and, therefore, no safeguards against his extravagance or greed were needful. We may suppose that, if a republic had been established in England soon after the death of Alfred, the taxation levied in the common interest as Danegeld might have escaped all connection with the private resources of a single person and thus have evaded permanently the pressure of consent. Roman society seems to have been at this stage when the Republic was established, and here we may recognise the first of many reasons why the Romans

---

[1] *Select Charters*, p. 412, from *De Legibus et Consuetudinibus Angliae*, ed. Woodbine, II, 19, I, c. 1. Cf. Glanvil, *Prologus*, p. 24 ; " Leges namque Anglicanas licet non scriptas leges appellari non videatur absurdum, cum hoc ipsum lex sit, quod principi placet legis habet vigorem, eas scilicet quas super dubiis in concilio definiendis, procerum quidem consilio et principis accedente auctoritate constat esse promulgatas. . . ." Professor Woodbine comments : " The most cursory reading of the opening lines of Bracton will reveal that he had read, and was more or less using, the prologue to Glanvil " (*Select Charters*, p. 184).

[2] *King Alfred's Version of the Consolations of Boethius*, translated by W. J. Sedgefield, Oxford, 1900, Book II, cap. XVII, p. 41.

never developed a specific doctrine of consent to taxation. In England the absence of a capital and the strength of provincial organisations not only made monarchy essential, even when the native dynasty failed, but also led naturally to the growth of safeguards against the abuse of royal power. It was, however, by no means inevitable that the doctrine of consent should be formulated as the greatest defence of public and private rights. The word consent (*consensus*) carried with it the idea of *concordia* [1] or unanimity and for that reason the act of consent tended to be automatic. Nothing more than general consent was required. Without either the duty to undertake the detailed scrutiny of particular issues or the stimulus of divided opinion, the right of consent might easily have atrophied, as it had done in ancient Rome. Its survival was, in fact, due less to the vigour of the primitive idea, than to its practical application within two systems of organisation unknown to the ancient world, feudal society and the Catholic Church.

Feudalism and the Catholic Church represent the two principles of order evolved in western Europe when, under pressure of the barbarian invasions, the order and civilisation of the ancient world disappeared in chaos. That chaos was a disaster that has, as yet, no parallel, but it was not irreparable, since continuity was never entirely lost. Both the destroyers and the destroyed refused to submit to the routine of anarchy. It was only in pockets and corners of western Europe, among the Lapps and the Celtic clans, that society stood still or turned stagnant, held fast by the chains of kindred and local custom.

From the ruins of Mediterranean civilisation the Church slowly built up the theocratic solution of the problem of anarchy : the order of the Christian life, maintained by a hierarchy of deacons, priests, bishops and cardinals and controlled in the last resort by the Pope, as the living medium through whom the divine purpose was continuously revealed. If the Catholic Church were indeed but the ghost of the Roman Empire, she was a ghost with an authority and an intelligence informed by all that could be salvaged and appropriated from the wreckage of ancient civilisation. Parallel in time but utterly different in origin, was the feudal concept of the northern barbarians : society organised

[1] Cf. *infra*, Chapter XIV.

round the personal bond between hero and war-band, lord and vassal. In their struggles against Rome and against each other the barbarians had been forced to prefer the contract between leader and follower above the rival bond of kindred. Their primitive economy, without cities and without mobile wealth other than cups and weapons, led naturally to the recognition of land, the fief or *feudum*, as the outward and visible sign of the personal bond. The fief in turn became the nexus of a whole series of relationships, covering or claiming to cover every public activity. The *milites* who formed the army were pledged to fight for their lord in return for their fiefs ; the law courts were the judicial sessions of landlords and tenants ; taxes were the obligatory dues rendered by vassals, supplemented by special offerings or " gracious aids " in time of need. The contractual idea spread steadily up and down throughout society. On the one hand, need of service and, on the other, need of land pushed on the process of stratification, until we can set against the hierarchy of the Church the feudal hierarchy of peasant, sub-tenant, tenant-in-chief, and suzerain or king.

Theocracy and Feudalism, formed in this way, were the solutions evolved for the problem of anarchy in the Dark Ages, each from a different angle illustrating the toughness and resil-ience both of the new barbarians and of " the obedient provinces of Trajan and the Antonines." The solutions were not com-plementary but mutually exclusive ; logically extended, neither had room within it for the other. As each moved forward and increased its claims, friction between the two grew more and more violent and gradually, by means of that friction—compli-cated at every turn by the friction of both with the monarchy— the new civilisation of the modern world was brought into life. With this triple friction we are not directly concerned, though it was, in fact, the forcing-house of all medieval political theory. For our purposes, it is sufficient to examine only the particular contributions to the doctrine of consent made in England by Feudalism and by the Church.

It is easy to understand how naturally the doctrine of consent would find a place in feudal law, which took shape at a time and in countries when no other idea of change was comprehensible. In addition to military service, the vassal was bound to perform other duties less clearly defined. On the negative side, he was under obligation neither to injure nor to assail his lord in any way ; on the positive, he owed advice and aid (*consilium et auxilium*), given in the lord's court, which he was bound to attend. Though his duties as suitor were mainly judicial, he was also called upon for counsel and consent. The legislation of English kings in the twelfth century was carried out on the advice of the tenants-in-chief, the idea of counsel being closely associated with that of assent. As in the earlier period, this consent was no more than general agreement or *concordia*, and we must look for the political contribution of feudal law not so much in *consilium*, as in the companion obligation of *auxilium* or aid.

Under the terms of his contracts, the lord was entitled to claim military service and other supplementary dues, known as the feudal incidents ; behind these lay a more general obligation, arising out of the personal bond between lord and man, the right to call upon tenants for help in time of need. This help or *auxilium* took the form of a money payment or gift. The obligation to pay it is difficult to define ; only a false or disloyal vassal would refuse necessary aid, but the right to determine both the necessity and the amount rendered lay, not with the lord, but with the suitors of his court. In this way the right of consent was attached to a definite object, something which directly and personally concerned every vassal. Unfortunately we know very little about aids in the twelfth century.[1] A few examples have been collected by Professor Stenton, but they throw only a dim light upon the way in which they were granted. A charter granted by Waleran of Sulgrave to Northampton Priory in 1183-84 records that the monks were bound to render " the . . . services which my free men do to me, that is, if need shall arise they shall help to redeem my body and to make my eldest son a knight, and to give in marriage my eldest daughter. And if my free men shall give me a common aid (*commune auxilium*), the monks shall give me what is appropriate to their holding." [2] Here two types of aid are mentioned, the aids for ransom, knighting and marriage, later known as aids of course, and the common aid given by the

---

[1] Closely allied to the aid was the *donum*, which was imposed from time to time by the king, either in connection with scutage or, as a polite term for tallage, on the towns (cf. *infra*, pp. 270-3). Here it is sufficient to note that the name *donum* or gift was a standing reminder of the idea of consent.

[2] F. M. Stenton, *English Feudalism*, Oxford, 1932, pp. 172, 276.

tenants.[1] By the second half of the twelfth century the lord had
established a prescriptive right to the three aids of course, but
for others the consent of vassals was necessary. Glanvil, writing
at the close of the century, stated the law of his time : An heir
might take reasonable aids from his men to help him to pay relief,
provided that the amount taken corresponded to the size of the
fiefs and the condition of the tenants and that it did not burden
them so much that they could not maintain their estate. " Nothing
is definitely fixed concerning the gift or exaction of such aids, except
that these rules should be maintained inviolate. Lords can also
exact aids on other occasions, as when the eldest son is knighted
or the eldest daughter is married, but it is doubtful if they can
demand aids to wage war ; the custom is that they have no right
to distrain tenants for this purpose, unless the tenants themselves
have granted it to them. They may distrain tenants for reasonable aids . . . provided that the tenants are being taxed justly,
on the advice of the court, and in accordance with custom. . . ." [2]
Here Glanvil makes the distinction, already noted, between aids
of course and gracious or voluntary aids given to the lord by his
men.

The gracious or voluntary aid was thus the one way open to
the feudal lord, as such, to increase his revenue, and it was natural
that the king should do all in his power to exploit it. Under
Richard I and John royal demands for aids began to multiply.
The huge sums raised for Richard's ransom, collected as an aid
of course in 1194, were followed by the carucages of 1198 and
1200, which were gracious aids ; taxes on personal property
were levied as gracious aids in 1202, in 1203 (a seventh as a fine
for deserting the king), and in 1207 (a thirteenth for the war with
France).[3] The writ for the collection of the thirteenth states
that it was granted to the king by the common advice and consent (*per commune consilium et assensum*) of the king's council
at Oxford [4] and a contemporary chronicler informs us that it
was the work of an enormous number of prelates and magnates

---

[1] For other examples of the common aid in the twelfth century see J. H.
Round, *Commune of London*, p. 126, and S. K. Mitchell, *Studies in Taxation
under John and Henry III*, Yale U.P. 1914, pp. 246-7.

[2] *De Legibus Anglie*, IX, c. 8, ed. Woodbine, pp. 130-1 ; *Select Charters*,
p. 193, where a slightly different reading is given.

[3] Mitchell, *op. cit.*, Chapters II and III.

[4] *Select Charters*, p. 278.

assembled at Oxford.[1] It is clear that the gracious aid was becoming an important source of revenue, and it is not surprising that the barons attempted to define their rights with regard to it in 1215. In Magna Carta we find a definite statement of the feudal theory of taxation. No scutage or aid shall be imposed unless by the common counsel of the realm, save for the three aids of course.[2] What was meant by " common counsel " was explained in Chapter XIV. " To have the common counsel of the realm in order to assess an aid or a scutage . . . we will cause to be summoned the archbishops, bishops, abbots, earls, and greater barons by our letters under seal ; and we will also cause to be summoned generally, by our sheriffs and bailiffs, all those who hold of us in chief . . . the business shall proceed on the appointed day, according to the counsel of such that are present, though not all who were summoned shall come."

The central idea underlying these arrangements is perfectly clear. The contract between lord and man covered certain obligatory duties and payments ; all others were outside the bargain and, therefore, were matters of grace, not of right. The original basis of the feudal contract, the personal bond between the hero and his war band, had been completely overlaid by a structure of legal obligations. By 1215 it was admitted that on three specific and exceptional occasions the king was entitled to reasonable aids ; all other additional levies were gracious aids for which the consent[3] of his vassals was necessary. On the other hand, scutage obviously fell within the contract and it was merely because John had been collecting it so often that the barons wished to bring it under their control. The attempt had no legal warrant and, probably for that reason, the clauses dealing with both scutage and aid were left out of the later redactions of the Charter. In practice, Henry III levied scutage as before, but he never attempted to raise a gracious aid without consent.

" The source of modern taxation was the feudal aid, the voluntary contribution which the vassal made to relieve the

---

[1] *Annals of Waverley (Rolls Series)*, p. 258 ; *Select Charters*, p. 268-9. This is the earliest description of the granting of a tax.

[2] Cap. 12.

[3] " Nullum scutagium . . . ponatur . . . nisi per commune consilium regni nostri."

wants of his lord." [1]   This is the conclusion reached by Professor Mitchell, the historian of English taxation in the thirteenth century. To explain the transition some comment is necessary. The general obligation of vassals to help their lord was freely admitted throughout the middle ages and, as feudalism declined, it became more and more a stringent obligation to render aid to the king. We find it, for example, clearly expressed by archbishop Fitzralph in the fourteenth century. He countered the argument that a tenant's revenues could not be used without his consent (*nisi velit*) by the argument of *raison d'état*. The king or overlord, he maintained, in virtue of his *dominium*, may impose burdens for the conduct of a common war; " iuste id ageret, nec baro sine iniuria eius posset obsistere ; sic in aliis casibus satis multis." [2]   These burdens, in terms of money, were aids of grace. In 1215 their future was by no means certain. It is true that the doctrine of consent had been established as a working principle, not only in the general sense of agreement to legislation, but with reference to taxation itself. There were, however, still obstacles in the way of a just and efficient exercise of the right. It was doubtful how far the king might be allowed to press the argument of *raison d'état*. Here no final settlement, short of an admission of autocracy, was possible and in England this solution was never seriously considered. Our attention must be given to obstacles of a more definite kind, which were inherent either in the composition and customs of the consenting body, or else in the relations between members of that body and the estates or orders below them in the feudal hierarchy.

In the first quarter of the thirteenth century, at least, consent to an aid was deemed to be, not corporate, but personal ; a member of the *concilium* could and did consent only for himself. Ideas either of an agreement by the majority or of power to bind the absent were still undeveloped, so far as the laity were concerned.[3] The thirteenth of 1207 seems to have been granted by the consent of individuals, rather than by the council as a body. An innovation is cautiously implied in clause fourteen of Magna Carta, where it is stated that " when all have been duly

---

[1] S. K. Mitchell, *Studies in Taxation under John and Henry III*, p. 346.

[2] *De Pauperie Salvatoris*, ed. R. L. Poole, 1890, p. 279. My attention was drawn to this passage by its citation by Professor C. H. McIlwain, *Growth of Political Thought in the West*, 1932, p. 357.

[3] *Infra*, pp. 340 *seq.*

summoned, the business shall proceed on the appointed day, according to the counsel of such as are present, though not all who are summoned shall come." This would hardly be worth saying if the bargain between the king and his tenants-in-chief were purely personal ; the implication is that those present shall act for and bind the absent. This idea was established very slowly, at least for the magnates themselves. In 1217 the bishop of Winchester refused to pay his share of a carucage on the grounds that he had not personally consented to it and his excuse was accepted by the barons of the Exchequer.[1] Similar examples may be found throughout the reign of Henry III ; as late as 1270 the bishops granted a twentieth to the king with a definite declaration that only those present were bound to pay.[2] The privilege of the absent magnate illustrates the stark individualism behind all feudal doctrine ; what gave reality to the principle of consent was nothing more than the self-regarding zeal of each baron for his own possessions. There was danger that the same individualism would bar the growth of the council as a corporate body, and that taxation, at least of the tenants-in-chief, would not advance beyond an innumerable series of private bargains. However, it so fell out that the danger was met in a way that led to the greater danger of over-riding the rights of sub-tenants.

It will be seen at once that, in accordance with strict feudal notions, there were difficulties in the way of taxing sub-tenants. The aids granted to the king were far too large to be paid by his tenants-in-chief out of their own resources and it was assumed that their vassals should help them. The king had no direct contractual relations with sub-tenants and, granted the feudal premise, he could not ask them for aids. There is, in fact, no evidence that the king attempted to gain their consent until the eve of the Barons' War, and there is no proof of the attendance of knights at the council before 1248. The magnates were thus compelled to apply to their own tenants for aid on the king's behalf, but means were devised to make refusal almost impossible. A theory was slowly and, perhaps not deliberately, formulated that the tenants-in-chief represented the rear-vassals and were able to give consent in their name. The growth of this idea can be traced in the changes in the phrasing of writs for collecting

[1] Mitchell, op. cit., p. 127, from Madox, I, 675, n. q.
[2] Mitchell, op. cit., p. 388, from Wilkins, II, 21.

the aids. In 1207 the thirteenth was granted merely by the council ; in 1220 the carucage was granted jointly (communiter) by the magnates and all the loyal men of the whole realm ; the fifteenth of 1225 was granted by the archbishops, bishops, abbots, priors, earls, barons, knights, free tenants and all men of the realm.[1] The formula used in the writ for the collection of the fortieth of 1232 even included villeins.[2] Thus a theory of the corporate existence of the council was developed in order to meet the difficulty of taxing sub-tenants. The danger of a system of private bargains instead of a common grant virtually disappeared, and the absentee or dissenting magnate gave up his right of personal veto in return for the right of coercing his sub-tenants. There are signs that absentee taxpayers did not surrender their rights without a struggle. In 1220 the barons of Yorkshire refused to pay their contribution to a tax which had been granted by the council, on the ground that they had not been summoned to the assembly and had not given their consent.[3] They took their stand strictly on the point of law, since they said that, if their consent had been sought by the king when he was in York, they would have given it willingly. Unfortunately it is not certain if these " barons " were great tenants-in-chief, who had received no summons to the council, or lesser men, poor tenants-in-chief or sub-tenants, who were seldom or never present. We do not know whether they were making a protest against binding absentee magnates or against the new assumption that the council represented all taxpayers.

If it were a protest of sub-tenants, it was undoubtedly a failure. Any attempt at resistance by them was made virtually impossible by a clever administrative device, probably adopted merely for reasons of convenience. Logically, aids should have been collected first by the king's officers from the tenants-in-chief, then by the tenants-in-chief from their sub-tenants, and so on to the bottom of the feudal ladder. Instead, the king relieved his own tenants of the burden of collecting aids from their men.[4] The taxes were assessed by royal officials, or by juries acting under them, and payment was enforced by all the weight of royal

---

[1] Mitchell, op. cit., pp. 384-5 ; Select Charters, pp. 351-2.
[2] Ibid., p. 356.
[3] Mitchell, op. cit., pp. 130 seq.   [4] Ibid., p. 383.

authority.[1] Thus the theory that the council was representative
of the whole realm and the practice of royal collection combined
to push taxation down through all the feudal strata to the villein
at the bottom. The dangers of such a system are self-evident ;
in countries where it was maintained it led inevitably to all the
worst abuses of aristocratic privilege.

. We may conclude, then, that the main contribution of feudal
theory was to make concrete the doctrine of consent, by relating
it to taxation. At the same time the practice was developing
by which the king and magnates acted together to compel or to
render nugatory the consent of sub-tenants. This was a grave
danger to the proprietary rights of all outside the circle of the
magnates and the doctrine of consent, thus expressed, was a
menace rather than a safeguard to the ordinary free-holder. No
doubt aristocratic insistence on the right of consent helped to
spread knowledge of the doctrine throughout society, and an
understanding of it was, perhaps, increased by the fact that the
lesser tenants-in-chief ceased to attend the Magnum Concilium
and threw in their lot with the sub-tenants. This nebulous
advantage was far outweighed by the oligarchic composition of
the consenting body. The natural line of development was that
the magnates would use their right to secure for themselves
permanent exemption from taxation. They would then be
able to shift the whole burden to the commons, whom it would
no longer be to their interest to defend. This is what happened
on the Continent ; it might have happened in England, if another
and more popular way of expressing the same principle had not
been devised.

The feudal doctrine of consent was drawn out of the contracts of individuals ; the ecclesiastical doctrine arose out of
the professional privilege of an international body, claiming
superiority over the whole of secular society. The ideas can

[1] The plan was probably not devised for the special purpose of coercing the
sub-tenants, though that advantage must have been realised quickly. The
first levy of a tax on property, assessed by local juries and collected by special
officials, was the Saladin Tithe 1188 (*Select Charters*, p. 189), in the later
carucages and fractional taxes on property, though the jury was not always
used, all men paid directly to the royal collectors, whatever their tenurial
qualifications might be. Stubbs and other historians have put emphasis mainly
on the use of the jury, and have ignored the danger of the exploitation of all
beneath the dignity of great tenants-in-chief.

be distinguished without difficulty, though in practice they were continually overlapping. In theory, the Church claimed to stand outside the feudal hierarchy ; in practice, all ecclesiastics who held by military service were within it. In England a rough compromise between conflicting claims was reached early in the twelfth century. It was admitted that the prelate had two capacities ; he was invested with the ring and staff by ecclesiastical authority, while, as baron, he swore fealty to the king for his lands.[1] As a consequence, bishops and abbots were taxed with lay tenants ; like them, they were members of the Magnum Concilium, and there they assented to or rejected royal demands for gracious aids. On the other hand, it was maintained that the income of the clergy, drawn for a spiritual purpose and derived mainly from tithes and alms—known as their spiritualities—was altogether exempt from taxation. It was deemed to be reserved for a sacred purpose and, therefore, outside secular control.[2] In the face of the king's growing needs it was plainly impossible for the exemption of spiritualities to pass unchallenged.

It is possible that the idea of bringing all the resources of the Church under contribution was suggested to English kings by the taxes levied for the Crusades. In 1166 a tax of sixpence in the pound, to which probably all the clergy contributed, was levied on personal property for the relief of the Holy Land.[3] In 1188 the fall of Jerusalem moved Henry II, with the consent of the Magnum Concilium, to impose a tax of a tenth on the personal property of all his subjects.[4] The Saladin Tithe fell on all clerks as well as on the laity, on spiritualities as on temporalities, and it is remarkable as the first tax on personal property for which local juries were used as assessors. Though the taxes of 1166 and 1188 were levied for a sacred purpose, the object lesson was not lost on the English Exchequer. When it

---

[1] *Select Charters*, p. 113, *sub anno* 1107.

[2] The term " spiritualities " was a varying one, but the distinction seems to have " rested on the use rather than the source of revenue " (T. S. R. Boase, *Boniface VIII*, 1934, p. 132)—like the modern exemption from income tax of money used for a charitable purpose—and it was difficult to apply it in practice. Land held in frankalmoign, for example, had been given for a spiritual purpose, yet it was land held in fee and the Crown never abandoned the claim to tax it (*Eng. Hist. Review*, Vol. XLVII, p. 7).

[3] Mitchell, *op. cit.*, p. 6.

[4] *Select Charters*, p. 189 ; Kate Norgate, *England under the Angevin Kings*, 1887, II, 249.

was necessary to raise Richard I's ransom in 1193 the same plan of a tax on moveables was employed ;[1] after his release Richard exacted another tax (the carucage of 1198), and again employed the juries of assessment, as for the Saladin Tithe.[2] He also insisted that the tax should be paid by the religious orders ; when they refused, he denied to them the protection of his courts and thus forced them into submission.[3] This action and the idea underlying it are significant. The king was no longer prepared to allow the clergy to benefit by his protection without exacting a full return.

It was inevitable that John, who was both unscrupulous and desperate for money, should carry his brother's policy further. In the first year of his reign he revived a device that had been used by Henry II in 1159, and exacted *dona* or free gifts from religious houses.[4] This exaction, which is sometimes called *commune auxilium*, in spite of its name appears to have been levied arbitrarily. The *donum* of 1199 was followed by others in 1203, 1204, 1205 and 1209 ; on the last occasion a chronicler states that £100,000 was collected, a figure that is certainly an exaggeration.[5] In 1207 John went a stage further and at a council held in London demanded that the bishops and abbots should make him a grant from spiritualities, that is, a grant from the income of the beneficed clergy.[6] The prelates refused, but at a second council held in Oxford he was granted a thirteenth, to be levied on the clergy as well as on laymen.[7] It is not clear whether in the end the beneficed clergy were included and, on the whole, it seems more probable that they escaped. It is, however, certain that John's demands must have seriously alarmed them as a class and prepared them to resist any similar proposals. The spoliation of ecclesiastical property during the Interdict no doubt led to a further hardening of hearts against royal needs.

The menace to ecclesiastical immunity was not confined to England ; in other countries, notably in France, the income of the clergy was also threatened. It is, therefore, not surprising that the whole matter came up for discussion and legislation at

---

[1] *Select Charters*, pp. 245-6.
[2] *Ibid.*, pp. 249-50.
[3] *Ibid.*, p. 251 (Rog. Hoveden, IV, 66).
[4] Mitchell, *op. cit.*, p. 32.
[5] *Select Charters*, p. 269 (Matt. Paris, II, 530).
[6] *Ibid.*, p. 268 (*Annals of Waverley*, p. 258).
[7] Mitchell, *op. cit.*, p. 87.

the Lateran Council in 1215,[1] where the decree entitled *de talliis a clericis non exigendis* was issued. If bishops and clergy, without coercion, recognised the need of lay rulers, they might grant subsidies from their churches and the laity should accept this help humbly, as an act of grace ; to avoid imprudent gifts, they should first of all consult the Pope, since it was his duty to provide for the welfare of all the churches.[2] Canonists were agreed that the words *consult* and *counsel*, when used of the Pope, carried the force of authority ; papal permission was, therefore, necessary for the taxation of churches. The decree did not, of course, apply to the feudal aid, as it concerned only the income from spiritualities. Thus, the protection of privilege belonged to the lower clergy rather than to the prelates—a reverse relation to that between the magnates and their sub-tenants. When the immunity was challenged, it followed naturally that resistance was organised from below.

To understand the peculiarly English consequences of the Lateran decree, the general relations between England and the Papacy in the thirteenth century must be recalled. The situation was suddenly altered by John's full submission to Innocent III in 1213. Henry III's minority gave the Papacy a great opportunity to exploit the surrender and an ever-increasing load of taxation and provision for foreign clerks was laid upon the Church in England. At the same time the interests of the young king were safeguarded by papal legates and, as he grew up, he showed a deference for and an obedience to papal authority which had been unknown at the English court since the Norman Conquest. With pope and king as allies, the clergy were unable to withstand new attacks on their immunity, though they showed remarkable vigour and ingenuity in the attempt. Not only were taxes imposed upon them for the benefit of the Papacy, but the support of the Crown was secured either by allotting a share of the papal tax to the king, or by granting to him licences to tax ecclesiastical revenues for a secular purpose. Throughout the reign of Henry III the Church in England was forced to submit

---

[1] In 1179 Alexander III had decreed that the exactions of secular rulers should be resisted, unless the clergy freely recognised urgent necessity. Professor Powicke (*Stephen Langton*, p. 91) has shown that Langton, when teaching at Paris at the end of the twelfth century, maintained this view.

[2] Mansi, *Collectio Conciliorum*, XXII, cap. XLVI, cols. 1030-31.

to a long series of financial exactions and nearly every time the spiritualities were included. In this way a formidable body of precedents was built up to justify the taxation of the total ecclesiastical revenue by the Crown.

Fortified by these precedents, Edward I demanded subsidies from the clergy, without papal licence, not as a grace, but as a right. In the first twenty years of his reign the clergy granted aids to him on seven separate occasions ; these grants were additional to the tenths granted by the Pope. So matters stood in 1296 when Boniface VIII made a last effort to recover the immunity. By the bull *Clericis laicos*, he altogether prohibited, under pain of excommunication, payment to secular rulers of taxes levied on the revenue of churches.[1] He was doing little more than reiterate the decree of 1215, but an express reference to *imperatores et reges* made evasion impossible. In England, after long delay and much debate,[2] the clergy refused a tax urgently demanded by the king. Edward was greatly enraged, as he was in need of money for his wars with Scotland and France.[3] Following the precedent set by Richard I in 1198, he declared the whole body of the clergy to be outlawed, that is, outside the protection of the common law and at the mercy of whoever might choose to invade their rights. Submission was thus constrained by what might be called a legal lock-out, a harsh, though logical, answer to a refusal to give aid in time of national need. Individuals hastened to buy themselves back into royal favour by heavy ransoms[4] and, in 1297, with papal consent, the clergy evaded the technical point at issue by making a voluntary grant or gift. In 1304 Benedict XI amended *Clericis laicos* to allow free gifts and in 1306 it was annulled altogether. The decree of the Lateran Council still survived, but it was disregarded by tacit consent. Victory plainly lay with the Crown, as " free " or

---

[1] See Boase, *Boniface VIII*, Chapter V, for the most recent account of *Clericis laicos*.

[2] Cf. *infra*, pp. 321-3.

[3] An Evesham chronicle (Bodley MS. Laud 529, f. 77) states that Edward said to Winchelsey : " quod si Papa haberet in Anglia temporalia, sicuti archiepiscopus, licenter de eisdem caperet, et capere posset pro defensione regni sui et ecclesie Anglicane."

[4] *Ibid.*, f. 76, states that the following made fine with the king almost at once—the bishops of Ely, Coventry and Bath, the keeper of the spiritualities of York, the proctors of Winchester, abbots, priors, secular canons, hospitallers, templars and many other religious, especially nuns and simple rectors.

" voluntary " gift was no more than a phrase ; the main body
of the clergy had failed to maintain their immunity from the
burden of contributing to royal revenue.

Though the clergy were defeated, they were not altogether
at the king's mercy, as they were able to fall back on a position
already prepared for defence. They had not submitted to the
heavy taxation of Henry III's reign without a hard struggle.
In the heat of conflict they not only expounded and popularised
the doctrine of consent, but they contrived màchinery to enforce
it. As their watch-word they took a maxim embedded in the
private law of Rome : *quod omnes tangit, ab omnibus approbetur*.[1]
The maxim, as Vinogradoff has shown,[2] was widely known in
the thirteenth century, but it is significant that in England it
almost invariably occurs in an ecclesiastical context.[3] The vogue
may be traced to its citation in a decretal of Innocent III, which
regulated the discipline of the lower clergy and was, therefore,
widely known. It was issued in reply to an enquiry as to whether
rural deans should be appointed and dismissed by the bishop
alone, or by the archdeacon, or by both together. The answer
ran : " According to the authority of imperial law, what touches
all ought to be approved by all ; therefore, since the (rural)
dean exercises his functions generally (*commune*) he ought to be
elected and dismissed by common assent (*communiter*)." [4] That
the decretal was taken literally in some English dioceses may be
proved from an entry made a century later in the register of
Bath and Wells : " Owing to laudable and immemorial custom
of Bath Archdeaconry, the incumbents of each Deanery yearly
elect their Dean." [5] Probably the more usual practice is
shown by an ordinance of the Salisbury chapter, issued in
1222 : " Rural deans shall be appointed and removed by the
common consent of the lord bishop and the archdeacons." [6]
The Salisbury ordinance has a particular interest as a proof that

---

[1] Justinian, Code V, Tit. 59, 5, cap. 3.

[2] *Collected Papers*, Oxford, 1928, II, 245.

[3] Bracton's use of it is the only important exception (ed. Woodbine, II, 21),
and he was referring merely to general consent to legislation.

[4] *Decretales Gregorii IX*, Liber I, Tit. 23, cap. vii, 6 ; Innocent III,
Collatio IV.

[5] Written in 1328 of an election of November 10, 1319, Register of
Drokensford, p. 286 (*Somerset Record Society*).

[6] *Register of St. Osmund* (*Rolls Series*), II, 20. No doubt the archdeacons
were deemed to express the consent of the clergy.

the decree of Innocent III, in which *quod omnes tangit* . . . is cited, was soon known and acted upon in England. As we shall see, it is also significant that it was known to the chapter of Salisbury.

To understand how the maxim came to be applied to the defence of the English clergy it is necessary to turn back to the years of Henry III's minority.[1] In 1225 the king asked the council for a grant of a fifteenth for the war in Gascony. It was granted in return for confirmation of Magna Carta and the charter of the Forest.[2] The Pope gave permission for the taxation of spiritualities and, in May 1226, the king informed the clergy that he had licence for an effective and competent subsidy to be levied on their benefices. He sent his demand to the bishop of each diocese, together with a supporting letter from the archbishop of the province.[3] We have record of what followed only in the diocese of Salisbury, where the register of the chapter has preserved the correspondence and also an account of the debates of the canons. It is worth noting that the diocese was at that time burdened with building the new cathedral, towards the expense of which the canons had voted a quarter of their income for seven years [4] and that the chapter then included certain men of outstanding ability and experience in public affairs.[5] The proposal to tax spiritualities, hitherto regarded as exempt from secular burdens, must have caused consternation among the clergy ; the canons of Salisbury had not only strong motives for resistance, but were fully qualified to set about it in the most effective way.

The royal demand, supported by the papal licence and the archbishop's letter, was laid before the chapter. In a second letter the archbishop asked that the clergy should grant either a

[1] The taxation of the clergy at this time and its important consequences has been fully discussed by Professor Barker, *Dominican Order and Convocation*, pp. 42 *seq.*, and by Professor Powicke, *Stephen Langton*, pp. 157 *seq.*
[2] *Select Charters*, pp. 322-3, 350.
[3] *Regist. of St. Osmund*, II, 55-8.   [4] 1218, *ibid.* II, 8.
[5] The bishop was Richard Poore, who had served Henry III as itinerant justice in 1217 ; the treasurer was Edmund Rich, afterwards archbishop of Canterbury ; another canon was Martin Pateshull, one of the great judges of the reign. At that time thirteen of the thirty-seven canons were masters of arts (*ibid.* II, 60-1. Cf. M. Gibbs and J. Lang, *Bishops and Reform, 1215-72*, Oxford, 1934, pp. 25 *seq.*).

twelfth or a fifteenth.[1]   It was decided to summon a full chapter, since, in the words of the record, " seeing that this business touches all the brethren (*omnes fratres suos tangere*) the chapter is unwilling to make answer without them." We may recognise here the maxim *quod omnes tangit* . . ., thinly disguised and applied to the question at issue. When all the canons were cited and twenty-seven of them had come on the appointed day, it was agreed that they dare not make answer alone on a matter so great, general and prejudicial to the Church in England. They requested that proctors from the churches might be assembled before the archbishop, in order that a conclusion might be reached which would protect the clergy in future. We do not know what action was taken in other dioceses, but the fact that the Salisbury suggestion was adopted indicates considerable support elsewhere. The archbishop summoned to a Convocation at St. Paul's the bishops, abbots, priors and archdeacons of the province, and also proctors representing collegiate and cathedral chapters. At this assembly the king was voted, not the twelfth or fifteenth that had been asked for, but a sixteenth, to be levied on the benefices of the clergy. Though it was expressly promised that the grant should not be drawn into a precedent, the occasion was of momentous importance. On the one hand, the first breach had been made in the immunity of the lower clergy ; on the other, the doctrine of consent was formulated and put into action, not only as regards taxation, but by use of the principle of representation.

Thus by the year 1226 the doctrine of consent was a living principle both in secular and in ecclesiastical society, yet so many difficulties stood in the way of its practical application that the chances of survival seemed small. There was danger that the idea of popular consent to legislation should disappear altogether, as it lingered only in the general approval of the king's council : there was danger that taxation arising out of the gracious aid should be pushed down to the lower strata of society ; and there was danger that the attempt of the lower clergy to develop their practical solution of the problem would be crushed by the double authority of Pope and Crown. The practical solution put forward

---

[1] For what follows see *Regist. of St. Osmund*, II, 58-9, 62-3, and the documents in *Registrum Antiquissimum*, I, 162-3 (ed. C. W. Foster, *Lincs. Rec. Soc.*, 1931).

by the canons of Salisbury was, in fact, the key to the situation, since the main obstacles in the way of free development were also practical. The theory of consent was generally admitted, but, on the one hand, it was impossible to secure unanimity and, on the other, it was impossible to consult all persons whose interests were involved. Where solutions were not found for these two problems, the doctrine of consent became a dead letter. However, in England, by 1226, we can see the possibility of success in both directions. The king's council was beginning to act in a corporate capacity and to claim power to bind the absent, whether they were summoned or not ; the lower clergy had found a way to express the consent or denial of large numbers through delegates or proctors. To understand how these two ideas came together, how the magnates of the king's council were afforced by the attendance of proctors of the Commons, it is necessary to trace the history of the representative principle. As a preliminary we must now consider why the English monarchy was forced, not only to accept the doctrine of consent, but also to develop it by means of representation in Parliament.

It will be recognised that for all national purposes the representative principle could not be applied without the king's consent, since the right of summons was his exclusive prerogative. We must ask why this prerogative was exercised more and more often as the thirteenth century advanced and how the king came to accept the doctrine of consent, with all its implications of control from below. At first sight the answer seems to be that no other alternative was open. The magnates had established the right of consent for the gracious aid and the lower clergy had done as much for the taxation of spiritualities, therefore, the king must summon them to grant him supply. Very little further enquiry shows that the problem cannot be solved so easily. We have already seen how the consent of the magnates was no bar to the exploitation of the lay commons and that the resistance of the clergy could always be overcome, in the last resort, either by calling in the *plenitudo potestatis* of the Papacy, or by a withdrawal of the protection of the courts. The barriers raised against arbitrary taxation in 1226 were not nearly as strong as they now appear, in the light of later events. It is partly for this reason that some historians—notably Pasquet[1]—have denied

---

[1] *Origin of the House of Commons*, translated by R. G. D. Laffan, pp. 178 *seq.*

that the origin of the House of Commons was in any special way connected with the doctrine of consent.

At the outset it will be useful to consider the full stretch of royal claims. The strongest and clearest statement of the king's financial position comes fittingly from the *Dialogus de Scaccario* [1] in a passage so significant that it deserves to be quoted in full :

> " It is necessary to serve and to submit in all fear to the powers ordained by God, since all power is from God. . . . It is right that princes should be served, not only by maintaining their dignity . . . but also by providing them with abundance of all things requisite to their estate. Now the power of princes stands or falls by the plenty or dearth of their possessions. . . . Though abundant riches may often come to kings, not by some well-attested right, but perhaps by ancestral custom, or by the secret counsels of their own hearts, or even by arbitrary decisions made at their pleasure, yet their deeds must not be discussed or condemned by inferiors. For the hearts and workings of the hearts of princes are in the hand of God and their cause—as those to whom God Himself has entrusted the care of subjects—stands or falls, not by human, but by divine judgement."

This may fairly be taken as the official or civil service view of the monarchical position at the end of the twelfth century. The king's necessity is paramount ; even his arbitrary decisions must not be challenged by his subjects, who are bound to submit themselves altogether to the powers ordained by God.

Turning from the theory to the facts, we find that English kings in the twelfth and thirteenth centuries were invested for a time with three fiscal privileges, each fully sanctioned by law and custom, any one of which might have defeated the doctrine of consent, if it had survived. These were Danegeld, or the right to impose a direct tax on the land ; tallage, or the right to levy an arbitrary tax on the royal demesne ; and the right to regulate exports and imports by means of custom duties. Each of these rights, it is now easy to see, was almost enough in itself to secure the financial independence of the monarchy. How they were, for all practical purposes, lost between the reigns of Henry II and Edward I, can be briefly stated ; why they were surrendered without much protest is a question to

---

[1] Ed. A. Hughes, C. G. Crump and C. Johnson, *Prefatio*, p. 1. Unfortunately this significant passage is omitted in the later editions of the *Select Charters*.

which no complete answer can be given. The situation will be clearer if the loss of each privilege is considered in turn.

Of Danegeld Vinogradoff wrote [1] : " The ravages of Norsemen had been felt all over Europe, and yet in no other place did they call forth such a systematic activity in the matter of building up a financial organisation, and nowhere else did the prosperity of the Royal Exchequer outlive the cessation of hostilities." What was originally a war tax was continued by Canute and, though Edward the Confessor is said to have given it up, the tradition of the levy was strong enough for William the Conqueror to revive it. Danegeld continued to be collected by William's successors, but it became less and less profitable and finally disappeared early in the reign of Henry II. The last general levy is recorded on the Pipe Rolls of 1162. Though the use of the old assessment and the number of exemptions (granted and prescriptive) had certainly reduced its value, the amount brought in was still, by contemporary standards, substantial.[2] It is extraordinary that Henry II neither developed nor retained it, but instead drew on other sources of revenue, such as scutage, the profits of justice and tallage. The explanation may lie in the brief and inaccurate statement in the *Dialogus* that it was a war tax, rarely imposed after the time of William I and then only when wars and rumours of wars threatened from without.[3] It may be that the original purpose of the tax was never forgotten, and that its disappearance should be regarded as a triumph of custom over the claim of the Crown to levy an arbitrary tax.[4] In other words, Danegeld as a tax in time of peace, was so alien to ideas of customary right and to the feudal doctrine of consent that the king was forced to give it up, hardly realising the extent of his loss. The suggestion is no more than an hypothesis, but whether it be correct or not, does not alter the facts. Danegeld was abandoned by Henry II and when the land tax reappeared as carucage, it almost at once came under the operation of the doctrine of consent.

Danegeld has only a negative bearing on the doctrine, showing how the king was forced to yield before the irresistible pressure

---

[1] *English Society in the Eleventh Century* (Oxford, 1908), pp. 140-1.
[2] See the Pipe Rolls for 1162-3, pp. 67-70.
[3] *Dialogus*, I, xi ; *Select Charters*, pp. 220-1.
[4] Cf. Ship Money in the seventeenth century.

of custom. With tallage and the custom duties we come to the direct consequences of the doctrine. Tallage, or the arbitrary taxation of royal boroughs, arose out of the anomalous position of towns in feudal society.[1] As it was impossible to bring them under the general system of contract, it was assumed that they were on royal demesne ; the king, as lord of tenants, was able to tax them at will, just as any lord could tax the villeins on his manors. Tallage was, in fact, primarily the right to tax serfs and the tallage of cities and boroughs seems merely an extension of this idea, combined with a less definite notion that the lord had some right to a return from the land on which the borough was built. Though the legality of the tax was not denied, it was naturally unpopular. As the boroughs grew stronger and began to enjoy a measure of self-government, they strove to evade the burden or to reduce the amount imposed. The history of these attempts is technical and obscure and here it is impossible to do more than to indicate main outlines, in so far as they seem to bear upon the doctrine of consent.

In the Pipe Rolls of Henry I and Henry II we find at intervals entries of heavy taxes paid by cities and boroughs ; they are sometimes called tallages and sometimes *auxilia* or *dona*.[2] It is also significant that certain taxes which Henry II negotiated for as *dona*, are entered on the rolls as tallages, suggesting that it was already easier for the king to ask as a favour what he could take as a right. Though the word *dona* was probably no more than a polite concealment of an arbitrary levy, it has interest as the first association of the boroughs with the idea of consent. The author of the *Dialogus* carefully distinguished between the free gift made to the king by the burgesses and the capitation tax imposed on them by judges in the king's name.[3] Liability for the gift lay upon the community as a whole, with power of adjusting the burden in accordance with the resources of each member, while the capitation tax fell on individuals, who could be compelled to contribute by distraint. Though both kinds of payment were, in fact, tallages, we can see in the distinction between them

[1] See Carl Stephenson, " Taxation and Representation in the Middle Ages " (*Haskins Anniversary Essays*, pp. 291 *seq.*).

[2] Ramsay, *Revenues of the Kings of England in the Middle Ages*, Oxford, 1925, I, 51. These *dona* were exacted from counties and towns by Henry II when he was taking scutage from his military tenants ; they are recorded mainly in the first decade of the reign.

[3] *Dialogus*, II, xiii ; *Select Charters*, pp. 237-8.

the first consequence of the new legal unity which the borough was acquiring. The common liability of the borough was the result of its own act, not that of the king ; that act was the result of the consent given by the burgesses to bear the tallage in common instead of *per capita*. We are obviously drawing near to a time when the borough will be anxious to consent to a gift in order to escape from tallage altogether.[1]

How this worked in practice may be gathered from the tallages levied by John and Henry III. Mitchell has calculated that John levied a tallage on an average once in every three years and that Henry III, taking fifteen tallages in all, raised them about as often as his father.[2] Through these exactions, both kings were involved in trouble with London [3] and there is no doubt that discontent regarding them was general. In the Provisions of Oxford it was stated that " London and all other royal cities have gone to shame and destruction by reason of tallages and other oppressions." [4] However, the hardships of the tax were mitigated by the growing bargaining powers of the boroughs, since they could avoid a head tax by offering a lump sum to the king. Thus in 1205 Exeter compounded for £100 and three palfreys and all towns seem to have compounded in 1223 and 1234.[5] The logical outcome of this practice was the free gift offered to Henry III in 1253.[6] He had levied a tallage so recently that he was afraid to ask for another. Instead he sent round officials to all tenants on his demesne, asking for a free gift, called *competens auxilium de gratia*. London, for example, gave him 500 marks and received a charter in return, making it plain that consent was bought by royal favour. The free gift, bargained for locally, was a natural preliminary to a grant made by burgesses in a central assembly ; it is even possible that the tallage of 1268 was granted or, at least, discussed by the representatives of twenty-seven cities and boroughs summoned to London in that year.[7]

---

[1] A further incentive towards this kind of bargain was the fact that the Crown almost invariably lost by commuting a tax *per capita* for a lump sum.

[2] *Studies in Taxation, op. cit.*, p. 340.

[3] *Select Charters*, pp. 288, c. 32, 294, c. 12 ; Madox, *Exchequer*, I, 712.

[4] *Select Charters*, p. 383.

[5] Mitchell, *op. cit.*, pp. 77, 148, 207.   [6] *Ibid.*, p. 256.

[7] *Eng. Hist. Review*, Vol. XL, pp. 580-5. Mr. Sayles, who discovered the draft of the writ of summons, comments : " A financial motive is usually, and perhaps in this case also, to be found " (p. 583). The representatives were summoned for April 22, 1268, and the first reference to the levy of tallage is dated May 10, 1268 (*Cal. Pat. Rolls, 1266-72*, p. 226).

Such was the position when Edward I came to the throne. The boroughs were certainly liable to tallage according to law, but it is equally certain that it was much easier to tax them if they had given their consent. It is clear that we must distinguish between what the monarch could legally do and what he found it expedient to do. The long series of concessions, which the boroughs had already bought from the Crown, made it natural for their representatives to sell taxes to the king, in return for even a beginning of a recognition of their right of consent. When Edward I began to summon burgesses to Parliament he probably hoped to secure a grant quickly and to collect it easily. He was also able, by the same means, to tax boroughs in private hands, which otherwise could be tallaged only by their lords. That he had no intention of letting go his right, though public opinion was moving strongly against it, may be seen by examining the two versions of the bargain made during the crisis of 1297. Certain of the demands made by the magnates were set out in the document known as *de tallagio non concedendo*, of which the first clause runs : " From henceforth no tallage nor aid (*tallagium vel auxilium*) shall be imposed or levied in our realm, by us or by our heirs, save by the will and common assent of the archbishops, bishops and other prelates, earls, barons, knights, burgesses and other freemen of the realm." [1] Here tallage is put beside the gracious aid and brought under the same conditions of consent.[2] However, if Edward I were ever asked to make so great a surrender, he certainly refused it. The form actually accepted by the Crown is preserved in the *Confirmatio Cartarum*. The significant clause for our purpose is the sixth : " We have granted for ourselves and for our heirs

---

[1] *Select Charters*, p. 493. It is doubtful at what stage of the negotiations this version was drafted, or indeed if it were anything more than " a mere imperfect and unauthoritative abstract of the formal document, in which the terms of pacification have been confused with the details of permanent legislation " (Stubbs, *Constitutional History*, II, 149). Cf. Bodley MS. Laud, 529, f. 79, for a popular version of the demand made to Edward I—" quod nullum auxilium vel vexacionem exigit a clero vel populo in postremum "—which suggests that tallage was included.

[2] A general protest against tallage had been made at an earlier stage of the dispute. See the *documenta* objected to in the document preserved by Rishanger (p. 175) and other chroniclers (*Select Charters*, pp. 434-5 ; Nicholas Trevet, ed. T. Hog (*Eng. Hist. Soc.*), 1845, pp. 360-61 ; Hemingburgh, II, 124-5 ; Cotton, p. 325).

. . . to all the community of the land, that from henceforth, for no business, shall we take such manner of aids, mises and prises from our realm, but by the common assent of all the realm and for the common profit thereof, saving the ancient aids and prises due and accustomed." [1] Tallage was omitted altogether ; mises and prises referred to the ancient customs.

The right of tallage thus retained was exercised by Edward I in 1304, but this was the last occasion upon which it was levied effectively.[2] Edward II collected it only once, at the height of the Gaveston crisis in 1312.[3] Then the Londoners, not challenging the king's general right, claimed a special privilege and Edward was forced to sell them a respite until the next Parliament, when the tallage was absorbed into the twentieth then granted.[4] Edward never again attempted to use his right of tallage and it lay dormant for twenty years. Edward III sought to revive it in 1332, but the interval had been too long and a storm of protest was raised.[5] When Parliament met over two months later (September 1332) the king withdrew the commission for collection, accepting instead a grant of a fifteenth and a tenth.[6] He also promised that in future he would levy tallage only " as it had been done in the time of his ancestors and as he had a right to do." The words seem meaningless, as his legal right was still clear, but it serves to illustrate the strength of the resentment it aroused. The end came soon afterwards and, when the French war made him desperate for money, Edward was forced to conciliate Parliament by agreeing to the abolition of tallage by statute.[7] The loss of tallage, which might have been used to keep the boroughs in permanent subjection, is a striking example of the way in which the doctrine of consent eroded or wore down an established royal right.

The same erosion may be seen at work on the prerogative right to regulate exports and imports by the imposition of duties.[8] The origin of the control of customs exercised by the Crown is

---

[1] Select Charters, p. 491.
[2] Cf. Edward I's letter of 1303 to the Treasurer and Barons of the Exchequer setting forth his reasons for levying tallage, Calendar of Chancery Warrants, 1927, Vol. I, p. 197. [3] Stubbs, Constitutional History, II, 546.
[4] Parl. Writs, II, ii, 59, 60, 61, 83-5 ; Liber Albus (Rolls Series), I, 428-9 ; Madox, Firma Burgi, pp. 6 seq., 248 ; Stubbs, Constitutional History, II, 547.
[5] Stubbs, op. cit. II, 547. [6] Rot. Parl. II, 66b.
[7] Statutes of the Realm, I, 290 (1340).
[8] On the history of the customs see N. C. B. Gras, Early English Customs System (Harvard U.P. 1918), Chapters I and II.

very obscure, but it probably grew up slowly when commerce was at a very early stage. Customs were at first levied arbitrarily, though, like all other early payments, they tended to become stereotyped. They were collected without question by the Angevin kings ; in Magna Carta " lawful and reasonable customs " were approved, though an attempt was made to limit the taxes imposed upon foreign merchants.[1] John certainly tried to develop a regular custom system and his experiments were continued under Henry III. In the Petition of the Barons (1258), complaint was made that the prises imposed on alien merchants were damaging trade,[2] and we may suppose that the discontent was widespread before the end of the reign. Probably passive resistance to the duties made them difficult to collect, and it may have been for that reason that Edward I brought the whole matter before the Parliament of 1275. It is significant that six or four burgesses from all cities, boroughs and merchant towns were summoned.[3] The king was granted by statute [4] certain fixed customs on wool and leather at a rate which came to be known as the Ancient or Great Custom. Anything raised in excess of this rate was called a maletolt or evil custom. In 1297, by the *Confirmatio Cartarum*, Edward I was forced to surrender his right to levy maletolts at will, that is, his right to raise the customs rate.[5] By this means English merchants were protected from arbitrary exactions on the staple articles of export. Six years later (1303) the alien merchants came to an agreement with Edward I, known as the New or Little Custom ; it was additional to the Ancient Custom paid by all alien or denizen merchants. The Ordainers first suspended (1309) and then abolished (1312) the New Custom, but in 1323 Edward II was strong enough to restore it and it was confirmed by statute in 1353. Thus both the *Antiqua Custuma* and the *Nova Custuma* were consolidated in the reign of Edward I and for centuries remained the basis of the customs revenue.[6]

The *Confirmatio Cartarum* bound the king not to raise the rate of the *Antiqua Custuma* without the common consent of the realm, but for some time after 1297 it was uncertain how and by whom that consent should be given.[7] The *Nova Custuma* was

---

[1] *Select Charters*, pp. 297-8, c. 41. [2] *Ibid.*, p. 376, c. 23.
[3] *Ibid.*, pp. 441-2. [4] *Ibid.*, pp. 443-4.
[5] *Supra*, pp. 272-3. [6] Gras, *op. cit.*, Chapter II.
[7] See *Finance and Trade under Edward III*, ed. G. Unwin, M.U.P., 1918, pp. 137 *seq.*

a private agreement between the king and alien merchants and, therefore, could be revised without " common consent." Edward III tried to use to the full the advantage left to him by the ambiguity of the terms of the agreements. He sought to read into the phrase " common consent " the meaning of " consent of the parties concerned " and to buy this special consent by concessions of monopoly rights to merchants. Resistance to his efforts to keep the customs outside the jurisdiction of Parliament was undertaken mainly by the Commons and it lasted throughout almost the whole of his reign. The details of the contest do not now concern us. It is sufficient to note the result. In 1340 Edward III was compelled to consent to two statutes, by which he renounced in perpetuity the right of the Crown to take more than the *Antiqua Custuma* without parliamentary consent ; no charge or aid whatsoever should in future be levied " without the common assent of the prelates, earls, barons and other magnates and Commons and that in Parliament." [1] The vague phrase " common assent " was replaced by a precise statutory definition and, though Edward made many efforts to evade it, Parliament insisted on its observance, reasserting the same principle again and again.[2] By the end of the reign it was firmly established that any levy of customs beyond the *Antiqua Custuma* was a subsidy which must have parliamentary sanction.[3]

Later history thus makes it clear that Edward I blundered fatally when he agreed to the fixed tariff of 1275. Why he allowed Parliament to control and to limit his undoubted prerogative is unknown. In the Latin version of the statute it is said to have been passed at the request of the merchants ; [4] we can merely conjecture that in consenting Edward secured some immediate practical advantage. He can hardly have understood the danger of admitting that control of the customs could in any way be shared with subjects. Gras, the historian of the English customs, writes : " Two ideas are the key to the tax, compromise and co-operation." [5] It was imposed on only a few articles, no

---

[1] *Statutes of the Realm*, I, 289-90
[2] For example, in 1348, 1362 and 1371.
[3] See Gras, *op. cit.*, Chapter II, for the consolidation of other lesser customs at this time.
[4] " ad instantiam et rogatum mercatorum . . ." *Select Charters*, p. 443. Cf. French version (Gras, *op. cit.*, pp. 223-4).
[5] Gras, *op. cit.*, p. 63.

exemptions were granted and king and subjects acted together in enforcing it. Through co-operation, thus invited, Parliament gradually gained control and, after nearly a century of contention, the prerogative of indirect taxation was virtually lost to the monarchy.

The way in which English kings surrendered in Danegeld, tallage and the custom duties their three great chances to build up a revenue independent of their subjects, demonstrates the immoveable resistance that the doctrine of consent could offer to royal power. Henry II and Edward I, the kings who made the surrender, were the strongest and most enlightened rulers of medieval England. Both were autocratic in temper and impatient of interference from below, yet each in his own way was forced to abandon key positions in the battle for royal revenue. They typify, as no Roman emperor ever did, the truth of Seneca's maxim : " Power pertains to kings, property to individuals." [1] It was what Gierke called " the absolute and imperishable value of the individual " [2] that impelled the English monarchy to exchange rights, fully recognised at law, for the practical advantages of free co-operation and consent. The stages by which this exchange was carried out remind us that expediency may exert as great an influence as custom in the shaping of laws and institutions. In the thirteenth century we can trace the beginnings of free co-operation, and by the reign of Edward III the balance is already slowly shifting to the side of popular control. Once the Crown had lost the legal right to levy taxes without consent, the gracious aid, extended throughout society, became the main source of revenue and the ultimate ascendancy of the body which gave consent was secured. That ascendancy is justly regarded as the triumph of the representative principle, but it must not be forgotten that representation in itself could have achieved little, unless it had gained direction and reality as the vehicle for the doctrine of consent.

---

[1] " Ad reges enim potestas omnium pertinet, ad singulos proprietas," *De Beneficiis*, VII, cap. 4, quoted by McIlwain, *Growth of Political Thought*, p. 394.

[2] " Moreover, a fugitive glance at Medieval Doctrine suffices to perceive how throughout it all . . . runs the thought of the absolute and imperishable value of the Individual. . . ." Gierke, *Medieval Political Theory*, translated by Maitland, pp. 81-2. Cf. the valuable remarks and citations by McIlwain, *op. cit.*, pp. 368 *seq.*

Though we have traced out the early history of the doctrine in relation to the practical needs of rulers and subjects, it must not for that reason be considered merely as a means to an end, a device by which certain definite advantages may be readily secured. In England, it is true, it was incorporated in a remarkable way into the visible structure of political society, but this concrete achievement must not be allowed to conceal its general importance as the governing principle of social order. In all communities which are more than prisons of the human will, where men have maintained any vestige of personal independence and dignity, law and the power to enforce it must rest on their consent, either explicit or implied. This broad principle of government was finely expressed by Hooker and we may take his words as the conclusion of this part of our enquiry. " . . . sith men naturally have no full and perfect power to command whole politic multitudes of men, therefore utterly without our consent we could in such sort be at no man's commandment living. And to be commanded we do consent, when that society whereof we are part hath at any time before consented . . . we were then alive in our predecessors, and they in their successors do live still. Laws therefore human, of what kind soever, are available by consent." [1]

---

[1] Hooker, *Ecclesiastical Polity*, I, c. X, 9 (Oxford ed. 1890, p. 191). Hooker, was, of course, thinking primarily of the social contract, an explanation of political origin, which would never have been generally adopted if it had not been founded upon the doctrine of consent.

CHAPTER XIII

THE PRINCIPLE OF REPRESENTATION

It is often said that the principle of representation was unknown to the ancient world, and that its discovery and application are the only significant contributions to political theory and practice made since the Stoics. This is true only in a limited sense ; the limits apply mainly to the political use of the idea and even here there are important anticipations. The principle itself, put in general terms, means that one or more persons stand or act on behalf of others and, at least for the purpose in hand, an identity of interests between them is assumed.[1] The idea of representation in the widest sense is probably as old as the first primitive community which was aware of itself as a whole. In its earliest application it appears in close association with religion, as part of the ritual of primitive worship. In more sophisticated societies its value for legal purposes was slowly recognised. Out of uses so different, the religious and the legal, its political importance was at last developed. To understand how this came about we may begin by a summary discussion of its rudimentary forms in primitive society and also its use by the Greeks and Romans. Fuller consideration must be given to its medieval development, both in secular affairs and within the Catholic Church.

The earliest sign of the representative principle may be found when, for a religious purpose, some creature or object is deemed to be the symbol or agent of hidden or unearthly power. In primitive society, as Frazer has shown in *The Golden Bough*, the king or chief stood half-way between his people and the unseen world, typifying or representing both humanity and divinity. His office carried with it responsibility for the weather and the fertility of the soil and in times of drought or other

[1] Cf. *infra*, pp. 289-92.

278

calamity he might even be offered up as a vicarious sacrifice for his subjects. Sometimes he was able to transfer his personal responsibility and to sacrifice in his place another person or creature, who, for purposes of ritual, represented his peculiar virtue.[1] Closely associated with these ceremonies were the magical practices by which it was believed that good or evil might be transferred to particular persons or objects. In this way arose the idea of the scape-goat upon whom the sins of a community were laid and thereby expiated. There are many parallels to the Jewish custom by which the iniquities of the people were borne away into the desert by a goat.[2] Plutarch, for example, describes how in his native town of Chaeronea a slave was periodically beaten and turned out of doors ; the ceremony was known as " the expulsion of hunger." Similar practices were used in Athens at times of public danger and in the Roman army before the festivities of the Saturnalia.[3] No doubt as civilisation advanced, the personification became less concrete and more symbolic, but from the first the general idea of representation, or substitution of the part for the whole, was constantly present. As the idea itself was familiar, its extension from religious to secular life was bound to occur.

The Greek city state was too compact for the idea of political representation to grow up easily ; every citizen was able to attend in person political discussions in the public assembly. In Greek law, however, the representative idea found expression. Vinogradoff has collected a number of examples showing how the city could be represented by a group of prominent citizens.[4] This was done in making treaties and in raising loans for public purposes, but there were no permanent officials or groups who were empowered to act regularly for the city as a whole. Representation was not so much a principle as a temporary administrative convenience. The nearest that the Greeks came to its

[1] Cf. H. M. Chadwick, *Origin of the English Nation* (Cambridge, 1907), Chapter X, *Cult of Nerthus* ; Frazer, *Golden Bough* (ed. 1924), Chapter XXVI, *Sacrifice of the King's Son.*
[2] Leviticus xvi, 21-2. For a more developed form of the same idea, cf. II Maccabees vi, 37-8, for the speech of the seventh son, tortured to death by Antiochus : " But I, as my brethren, offer up my body and life for the laws of our fathers . . . that in me and my brethren the wrath of the Almighty which is justly brought upon all our nation, may cease."
[3] Frazer, *op. cit.*, pp. 578, 583 *seq.*
[4] *Historical Jurisprudence*, II, 107 *seq.*

true political use was probably the Council of Five Hundred in Athens.[1] Its members were chosen by lot out of the whole body of citizens and certain administrative functions were delegated to them. Sometimes political trials, in form resembling the English bill of attainder, were conducted before the Five Hundred, which for a time was vested with full powers of punishment. These powers, however, were afterwards resumed by the people and it was enacted that no Athenian citizen could be sentenced to death, imprisonment, or confiscation without a direct, popular decision. The resumption of power is significant of a failure to recognise or understand the principle of representation.

The great territorial expansion of Rome did not make representation (in the ordinary political sense of the term) an element of the Roman Constitution. There was no such pressure on the Roman governing class as to induce it to replace the popular assemblies and the Senate of the old Roman city-state by a body or bodies of elected representatives from different parts of Roman territory.[2] There were disadvantages for that class in the city-state form of constitution, but there would have been other disadvantages for it in a representative system, besides the initial trouble and difficulty of making such a radical change in the political structure of the community. An Italian state with representative institutions might indeed have been formed if the country had been united, not by the Roman city-state, but by one of the old leagues or " names " of ancient Italy (Latin, Etruscan, Samnite and so on), or if Rome had been defeated by the Italic Confederacy which was formed against her in 90 B.C., and in the government of which there was a Council of delegates from the different states of the Confederation. But in fact none of the old leagues nor yet the Confederacy of the Italic war seems to have had any good chance of uniting Italy ; they had not enough coherence.

There were representative councils in the provinces of the Roman Empire from the time of Augustus onwards ; but they had been formed, not to take part in the regular provincial

---

[1] *Historical Jurisprudence*, II, 62-3, 142.

[2] Before the war by which Rome finally broke the Latin League (c. 340 B.C.), the Latins, it is said, offered the terms that they should be incorporated in the Roman state, but that in future one Roman consul and half the Roman Senate should belong to the admitted Latin element. Rome rejected this proposal, which did not at all suit her great houses.

administration, but to foster loyalty to Rome and the emperor, to give provincial feeling an outlet towards the central government, to promote provincial welfare, and to enable the local magnate to cut a figure in his province. Augustus (c. 29 B.C.) had first organised them for the ceremonies of a cult of himself and of Rome—a concrete way of venerating imperial authority and the majesty of Rome.[1] In the Asiatic provinces he made use of the *koina* or assemblies in which groups of cities were united, usually in connection with public worship. Temples were provided for Caesar-worship and the cult was maintained by games and ceremonies directed by the provincial assembly. The provincial organisation of this cult was introduced into one after another of the western provinces,[2] showing the same general characteristics wherever it appeared. We are concerned only with the composition and powers of the council. Its members were delegates sent by the cities or districts of the province ; they were usually chosen by local councillors, but in certain Asiatic provinces they appear to have been elected by the whole body of citizens. Cities sent one or more delegates in accordance with their standing in the province. The councils met annually and proceedings were regulated by a president whom the assembly chose. He was known in the West as the *sacerdos* or *flamen* of the province and, although the office involved a heavy outlay on the games, it seems to have been " the goal of provincial ambition." Apart from its main object of fostering the state cult, the council acquired few functions of political interest. A connection with Rome was established through the *laudationes* sent to the emperor by the assemblies and these compliments were soon followed by other messages of a less general kind. The privilege was gradually acquired of sending to Rome accusations directed against provincial governors, which were followed by trials before the Senate. A number of prosecutions, begun in this way, are recorded by Tacitus and Pliny ; the manner in which they began on the initiative of a representative assembly, recalls the English procedure of impeachment. The councils

---

[1] E. G. Hardy, " The Provincial Council " (*Studies in Roman History*' pp. 236 *seq.*).

[2] For example, from 12 B.C. the sixty-four *civitates* of Gallia Comata (which included the three provinces of Aquitania, Lugdunensis and Belgica) sent delegates to a council which had the care of a temple at Lyons, where an altar was consecrated to Augustus and to Rome.

also acquired certain fiscal powers ; by their authority taxes were levied on the *civitates*, in order to maintain the temples and to pay the expenses of the delegates and messages sent to Rome. Thus we find in the Roman provincial council three attributes characteristic of later representative assemblies. It was composed of delegates from the *civitates* and, therefore, was representative of the province as a whole ; it enjoyed a limited power of taxation for public purposes ; and it had the right to initiate proceedings against the head of the local administration. On the other hand, it had no general legislative authority and no direct control over the executive, but the example of these provincial assemblies may have helped in the development of the councils of the early Church.

Consideration of the secular development of representation in the middle ages must begin with the primitive concept of law. We have already seen how the idea of law as custom underlay the medieval doctrine of consent. The same concept played an even more direct part in the use of the principle of representation, at least for legal and administrative purposes. Customary law could not be administered without local knowledge. At first this was easily provided by the suitors or members of the local court, but as centralisation increased, or as men moved away from their native districts, it became more difficult to give judgement based upon particular customs and obligations. The barbarian invasions brought about both a mixture and a shifting of population and thus raised the problem on a large scale. For a time it was solved on the theory that a man's law was personal to himself and that he could be judged only in accordance with it. Agobard of Lyons, early in the ninth century, said that " often five men would be walking or sitting together and each of them would own a different law." [1] A conquered people retained their old law, but it naturally tended to become a mark of inferiority.[2] During times of transition law was associated with persons rather than with places. As an example of this we may take a famous passage in Frankish law : " This we also determine, that a Frank, a Burgundian, an Alaman or any of another nation, when accused in court in the country of the Ripuarian Franks, shall answer according to the law of the place

[1] Cited by Pollock and Maitland, I, 13.
[2] Cf. Celtic law after the English conquest of Ireland.

where he was born. And if he be condemned he shall bear the loss, not according to Ripuarian law, but according to his own law."[1] It is clear that "conflict of law" must have been frequent and that no arrangement of the kind could be permanent. For us it is important chiefly because it brings out the original close connection between law and knowledge of it by the parties concerned.

With the rise of feudalism local connections were again emphasised, this time with stress on the court of peers or co-vassals, who alone knew the law of the fief. Men ought to be tried only by their peers, since they alone had the knowledge necessary for judgement. In this way the association of local knowledge with law was re-enforced and permanently established. When the central courts and a common law began to take shape, it followed naturally that local knowledge should be expressed by sworn local representatives or juries. The jury of representatives was apparently first used for administrative rather than for judicial purposes, though no clear line of division can be drawn between the two. The Frankish kings employed it to establish royal rights and to check the abuses of provincial officials. An earlier stage of the same institution can be traced in the Danelagh at the end of the tenth century, when the twelve senior thegns of the wapentake, and the reeve with them, were ordered to swear that they would accuse no innocent man, nor conceal any guilty one.[2] Here the thegns and the reeve represent the public opinion of the district ; though the law is promulgated by the Witan, the purpose is strictly local. The findings of the Frankish jury, on the other hand, were made at the direct command of the king and in order to aid the central government.

The Norman sworn inquest followed the Frankish pattern. The methods of the Domesday survey provide the best known example of its use to represent the knowledge of particular

---

[1] *Lex Ripuaria*, Tit. XXXI, 3, cited by Ed. Jenks, *Law and Politics in the Middle Ages*, 1913, p. 16. Cf. the juries of Ostmen, used for the Scandinavian population of certain Irish towns after the English conquest.

[2] Laws of Ethelred, c. 997, *Select Charters*, p. 85. Cf. the judges of the three districts of the Gula-Thing, Norway : " . . . inside the ring sat the judges, twelve from the Firthfolk, and twelve from the Sognfolk, twelve from the Hordafolk : those three twelves of men must there judge the suits of men." The judges were nominated by the chief man of each district (Egil's Saga, translated by E. R. Eddison, Cambridge, 1930, p. 118).

districts.[1] The procedure of 1086 may be compared with two statements of custom, compiled early in the twelfth century, but containing much of an older period. In the *Leges Henrici Primi* it is stated that the lord or his steward may perform suit in the hundred court for all the lord's demesne lands in the hundred ; if both are absent, then " the reeve, the priest and four of the better men of the vill shall attend for all (*pro omnibus*) who have not been summoned by name to the court." [2] The words *pro omnibus* plainly express the representative idea. The companion passage occurs as the prologue to the *Leges Edwardi Confessoris* and claims to be a record of the way in which Anglo-Saxon law was preserved after the Conquest. " After the fourth year of the Conquest, William, king of this land, on the advice of his barons, caused to be summoned throughout all the counties of England, Englishmen who were noble, wise and learned in their law, in order that he might hear from them their custom. Twelve men, therefore, were chosen from each county and these in the king's presence swore to make known the provisions of their laws and custom, so far as they were able, omitting nothing and changing nothing by deception." [3] It is unlikely that a meeting of this kind was ever held ; the interest of the passage lies in the author's idea of the natural and just way in which law ought to be ascertained.

It is unnecessary to rehearse in detail the development of the jury under Henry II. The main point of interest is that it continued to maintain the principle of representation. The jury of recognition reported local information about particular matters of fact ; the indicting jury expressed local public opinion about the evil-doers of the district. The care with which the jury for the Grand Assize was chosen shows a definite recognition of the need to secure the best type of representatives. Four knights elected or nominated the twelve who gave the verdict ; " if some have knowledge and some have not, the ignorant shall be turned away and others shall be summoned until at last twelve agree ; if some take one side and some the other, more shall be added until twelve are unanimous." [4] What was

---

[1] *Select Charters*, p. 101.   [2] *Ibid.*, p. 124, c. 7.
[3] *Die Gesetze der Angelsachsen*, ed. Liebermann, 1898, I, 627.
[4] Glanvill, II, c. 17, ed. Woodbine, pp. 67-8 ; *Select Charters*, p. 192. Cf. *infra*, pp. 335-44, for a discussion of the question of unanimity.

required was the knowledge of representative men. The arrangements for the appointment of the Grand Jury in 1194 show a further development : " Four knights shall be elected from the whole shire, who shall elect on oath two lawful knights from each hundred or wapentake, and those two lawful knights shall elect on oath ten knights from every hundred or wapentake, or, if knights be lacking, lawful and free men, so that those twelve together shall answer for all the pleas of the whole hundred or wapentake."

This steady application of the representative principle through the jury would have been impossible without that framework of local boundaries and institutions which was the richest part of the Anglo-Saxon inheritance. The whole of England was honeycombed with small and seemingly insignificant districts to which tradition and geography had given a natural unity. By the thirteenth century even the youngest of the shires had been a centre of public life for three hundred years ; the hundreds, whatever their origin, were also ancient, and in their courts quarrels and common business had been heard and examined by generations of neighbours. Though many boroughs were relatively upstart, the narrow circle of their walls had compressed their inhabitants into a unity more obvious, if no deeper, than the slowly growing cohesion of rural communities. Perhaps this sense of place, this membership of a geographical hierarchy, is the part of the outlook of the medieval Englishman which is now most difficult for us to imagine, though all the evidence of the records goes to prove its existence. Either by the king at the centre or by the ordinary man in his village, political geography was deemed to determine something essential. John Green was not only a freeman of the parish and vill of Cow Honeybourne, he was also a member of the hundred of Kiftsgate, and, through that membership, had his part in the county of Gloucester. Each form of membership had its corresponding form of activity in the courts of the vill, the hundred and the shire.

These units of local government, with their courts, obviously played an important part in the history of representation. Professor McIlwain has pointed out that the use of the words *comitatus* and *hundredum*, both for the territorial area and for

<hr>

[1] *Select Charters*, p. 252.

the courts, proves the presence of a theory of representation.[1]
By a convenient fiction, the suitors of the courts were identified
with the whole area, though only a relatively small part of the
population was actually present. In this representative capacity
two or more persons were able to act for the rest. In the Assize
of Clarendon, for example, the sheriff was ordered to bring before
the king's justices " two lawful men to bear the record of the
county and the hundred," [2] the record being, not a written document, but oral testimony. In the first quarter of the thirteenth
century there are two instances of the summons of knights of
the shire to the king's court, to bear the record in this way. In
1213 John summoned four discreet knights from each shire to
speak (ad loquendum) with him at Oxford concerning business
of the realm.[3] This writ marks the faint beginning of a new
idea. No doubt the knights were expected to report on local
opinion, to pool their information for the king's benefit, but they
are to come less in a legal than in a consultative capacity. In
the same way in 1226 the sheriffs were ordered to cause the election of four law-worthy and discreet knights to come to the king
at Lincoln to explain (ad ostendendum) their complaints about
the execution of certain clauses of Magna Carta.[4] Again the
knights are summoned for a purpose which is as much consultative as judicial. It must, however, be noted that they are
not yet asked to do anything which could not be covered by the
older phrase " bearing the record." They are not summoned
ad faciendum or even ad tractandum ; their functions are still
limited to reporting on past or present conditions and have no
direct bearing on decisions for the future. The king does not
ask for and they are not given any mandate to act for their communities ; they come to find the facts, to declare their knowledge,
rather than to bind those whom they represent. In other words,
the function of giving counsel and consent was still the monopoly
of the magnates in the council.[5]

Thus between 1066 and 1226 the principle of representation
was, by means of the inquest and the jury, elaborated to such a

---

[1] Cambridge Medieval History, VII, 668, but cf. infra, p. 342, for the
failure to regard suitors at the shire court as true representatives.
[2] Select Charters, p. 170, c. 4.
[3] Ibid., p. 282.   [4] Ibid., p. 353.
[5] Cf. ibid., p. 277, for nobiscum tractaturi in the writ of summons to the
bishop of Salisbury in 1205.

point that the knights of the shire were brought to the frontiers of political responsibility. In local affairs they had already crossed the line between information and action, as they were being used with increasing frequency as assessors and as collectors of taxes. For example, in 1198 the carucage was assessed with the help of knights of the shire, acting in co-operation with two knights from each hundred and the reeve and four men from each vill.[1] The carucage of 1220 was collected by two knights elected in the full county court, by the will and consent of all in the county.[2] These fiscal duties show that the knights were extending their functions beyond the juror's obligation to "find the facts," but before 1226, at least, the extension was strictly limited to local tasks undertaken at the king's command. The importance of this limitation has been questioned by Professor McIlwain.[3] He thinks that it "implies a distinction between central and local institutions which is too sharp and too modern" and he maintains that there is little contemporary evidence for a cleavage "between the idea of representation for information and representation for action." However, the distinction seems to be expressed in the words of the writs themselves ; the knights were summoned to the king *ad loquendum* or *ad ostendendum*, while the magnates came *ad tractandum*, or to give their counsel and consent. It is true that in local government the knights represent their communities both for information and for action, by bearing the record and by acting as assessors and tax-collectors, but these tasks had no direct political significance. They were undertaken at the king's command and without any mandate from the communities, who had merely chosen the persons best suited to perform them. The authority upon which the knights acted came, not from below, but from above. The magnates, on the other hand, had full powers of counsel and consent, but each was present only for himself ; until the same powers were exercised by communities, through their delegates, the essence of political representation was still absent.

Though the subject bristles with difficulties, one other English application of the representative principle to secular administration

[1] *Select Charters*, p. 249.
[2] *Ibid.*, p. 349 ; the fifteenth of 1225 was collected by the reeve and four men of the vill and handed over to four knights elected by each hundred (*ibid.*, p. 352).
[3] *Cambridge Medieval History*, VII, p. 671.

must be briefly discussed. The internal organisation of the borough runs parallel to the development of the jury, and it began to take a new and more popular form soon after the death of Henry II. The growing prosperity of towns in the twelfth century, and the grants to them of royal charters, helped to draw the inhabitants more closely together, and to encourage the demand for control over their own affairs. Their new claims form a part of the general communal movement on the Continent, though in England complete autonomy was never demanded.[1]   Though not yet corporations in the technical sense, by the year 1200 English boroughs were beginning to be " persons who are not men " ; [2] by Bracton's time the term *universitas* was borrowed from Roman law to describe them and *universitas* stood for something more compact and united than the older *communitas*.   This new unity led naturally to the idea that one or more members might act for the rest ; the outward signs of change may be traced in the new office of provost or mayor, and in the elective governing body of the town.   The first reference to a mayor occurs in the oath of the London commune (1193) ; [3] the first mention of an official elected by the citizens appears in Richard I's charter to Lincoln : " the citizens of Lincoln may make one of themselves their provost every year, provided that he is a person suitable to us and to them " [4] (1194).   We have it on the high authority of Professor Tait that " an elected chief magistrate, whether new mayor or old bailiff, must be assumed to have had for his necessary complement an elected body of twelve or twenty-four " ; [5] these persons represented the community as a whole, and acted in co-operation with the chief magistrate.   The first clear reference to an elected council comes from London at the beginning of John's reign : " in this year there were elected twenty-five of the more discreet citizens, sworn to counsel the city, together with the mayor." [6] Other examples soon follow,[7] and it may be concluded that election of the common council by the whole body of citizens, or at least with their assent, was a common characteristic of the English

[1] The tendency of recent scholarship seems to run against the older idea of imitation of Norman models.
[2] Pollock and Maitland, I, 486.   [3] Round, *Commune of London*, p. 235.
[4] *Ibid.*, p. 262.   Cf. *ibid.*, p. 307 (1200), for John's charter to Northampton.
[5] *Eng. Hist. Review*, Vol. XLIV, p. 192.
[6] *Liber de Antiquis Legibus*, p. 2.
[7] Ipswich, 1200 ; Northampton, 1215 ; Leicester, a mediatised borough, 1225 ; Dublin, 1229.

borough in the thirteenth century. Thus, within their own limited sphere, English towns had carried the representative principle one stage further than that reached by the shires. By 1226 certain of them were already electing their own mayor and common council to govern the borough on their behalf. On the other hand, their activities, though genuinely political, were confined behind their own walls ; they had still no direct share in the central government, except in so far as they might be summoned to the courts as witnesses or jurors. The knights, elected in the shire courts, had been summoned at least twice (1213 and 1225) to meet the king in a central assembly, but they were asked only *ad loquendum* or *ad ostendendum* and were never, so far as we know, called to act with the magnates in council. None the less, the parallel lines of development are significant, as the scattered elements of popular government were clearly present. To achieve a national representative assembly, endowed with political power, knights and burgesses seemed to have little more to do than to pool the duties and privileges already assigned or granted to them by the king.

However, the lines of development were still far apart, and it is unlikely that they would ever have come together without the intervention of forces external to them both. It is not enough to say that their union was achieved through the royal summons, as we have still to explain how the monarchy came to apply the representative principle to forms capable of political growth. To understand the problem, it is necessary to submit to further analysis the loose description with which our enquiry began, and to attempt to isolate the characteristic signs of political action. At the outset we recognised the representative principle as at work when one or more persons stand or act for others, in such a way that, at least for the matter in hand, an identity of interests between them is assumed. We have used this general definition to cover things as foreign to each other as the scape-goat of the Old Testament and the mayor and common council of the medieval borough. It is now necessary to set apart in separate categories the various types of acts or appearances through which the general principle manifests itself. They may be classified broadly as personifications, specific acts undertaken for reasons of administrative convenience and political action bearing directly upon public law.

The most ancient examples of the first type are the personifications indissolubly bound up with primitive cults.   The priest-
king personified the unseen world, the order of nature and the
transient humanity of his subjects ;   the scape-goat, whether
beast or human, was the living embodiment of the sins or evils of
the community which cast him out.   Representation of this kind
is almost too closely joined to a bewildered failure to distinguish
between the powers of man and of God and to irrational ideas of
contagious magic to yield a definite result to close analysis.   None
the less, we cannot set it entirely on one side, since it made a
contribution of permanent value in the idea that a body of persons
are, for certain purposes at least, deemed to be one and, therefore,
may be represented by a single agent.   The history of despotism,
from the Renaissance to the present day, naturally inclines us to
consider the personification of a people or a country by a monarch
or dictator as deadly to political growth, but we must not on that
account ignore the great part that has been played by kingship as
a symbol of national unity.   It is, in fact, hard to see how men,
who dwelt in any but the smallest geographical areas, could have
acquired the coherence necessary for political development, if they
had not, for a long period of time, personified their common
habits and business under the figure of a king.

With representation for a legal or administrative end we pass
to another phase of development.   The half-irrational, half-
mystical elements disappear and are replaced by a precise application of the principle to specific problems of law and government.
The jury in all its forms, the lawful men who bore the record, and
the knights summoned in 1213 and in 1225 were alike called upon
to voice local public opinion for particular purposes.   Though
the need for the witness of men who knew the facts had its roots
deep in customary law, the growth of this type of representation
in England was a consequence not of popular, but of royal
authority.   The movements of representatives were evoked and
controlled by royal-writs, and it was assumed that they should act,
almost passively, as a living testimony to the truth, as it was
known to their communities.   Their right to speak for these
communities was at first also assumed.   Though by the end of the
twelfth century an elective form was sometimes employed, the
fact of election carried with it no general power or responsibility.
Representation along these lines was no more than an adminis-

trative convenience, ingeniously developed out of strong local custom, and there was no obvious reason why its growth should take a political form.

The first condition requisite for political representation, in the full sense of the term, is a coherent society, organised within its own frontiers and of considerable geographical extent. Such coherence is essential to its growth and in the middle ages it was seldom achieved except in the shape of a realm or kingdom. The condition of size is, as we shall see, necessary in order that the strain of responsibility may be distributed over a considerable area of territory. Within this area the ruler must be powerful, though not absolute ; he must be strong enough to secure the service of his subjects and yet not so strong that they render to him servile obedience. It seems hardly possible for political representation to be unilateral. Evocation of representatives by an authority of some kind is certainly essential, but mere evocation, as with the jury, simply calls together the agents of administration. Some mandate from below is a further necessary condition and this mandate must be of a particular kind. On the one hand, it cannot be a final transfer of responsibility from the electors to the representative ; the formal act by which power was shifted permanently from the *popolo* of an Italian city to a tyrant was political suicide, even though he were beyond all doubt their chosen representative. On the other hand, political representatives must be more than members of a deputation or delegates, primed with precise orders as to their words and deeds. If the main business of the Commons in early Parliaments had been no more than to push local petitions, their work could have no claim to be called political. No activity can properly be styled political which does not help directly to create or to modify public law. When this task is undertaken by a group of persons, a state of friction, due to the chafing of mind against mind, ought to be set up. This friction alone can throw off the spark that makes co-operation dynamic and, if representatives are to contribute to it, they must be charged under certain conditions. They must have a mandate to act for their constituencies, which is both temporary and general ; it must be acknowledged that they owe to their electors not obedience, but judgement ; that judgement must be exercised in co-operation with other representatives, in a like manner empowered.

In some of the examples already brought under review we can recognise certain of these essential characteristics. The Council of Five Hundred in Athens was not a deliberative or legislative body, but was concerned only with the duties of administration and executive. The delegates sent to Roman provincial councils were entrusted with duties which called for both co-operation and decision, but they were unable to develop the general powers necessary for effective political action. The mayor and councillors elected to govern a medieval borough fulfil our conditions of a temporary mandate from below, freedom (at least in name) to reach independent decisions, and the duty of co-operation with other representatives. However, their development was blocked either by interference from above or by the intolerable pressure of personal interests. For similar reasons the rich variety of urban experiments throughout medieval Europe had singularly little influence on the main stream of constitutional change. Like a machine over-driven by an engine too powerful for it, political life in small communities tends to break down under the moral strain of public responsibility. It appears that a certain mingling of diverse interests, the check of other standards, and the friction due to contact with unfamiliar minds are essential to the healthy growth of a society, representative in type. It is significant that the Swiss cantons, where these advantages were partially secured by the adoption of federal union, were the only small political communities to resist the rise of modern absolutism.

If this analysis of representation be accepted, it becomes plain that, though the general principle was almost universal, it was commonly expressed in forms that had no political value. In English secular society at the beginning of the thirteenth century the germ of political representation can be traced only in the boroughs and they were too weak and self-regarding to exert a decisive influence on society as a whole. The knights of the shire had indeed been summoned to central assemblies, but we have no evidence that they were required to exercise their judgement or to act in co-operation. We find, in short, that representative knights were beginning to share in public life through their employment in administrative business, both locally and in central assemblies ; representative burgesses were beginning to control the government of the tiny area within the circuit of their walls. To understand how these lines of development, which appear to promise so little, slowly drew together in the new direction of political representation, it is necessary to turn back again and to trace the history of the representative principle within the Catholic Church.

The Catholic Church has inherited so much from the Roman Empire that it is tempting to suppose that her legislative assemblies were an adaptation of the provincial councils established by Augustus.[1] There can be no doubt as to the general influence of Roman culture on the Church. As Maitland puts it—". . . into the debates of the spiritual Parliaments of the Empire go whatever juristic ability and whatever power of organisation are left among mankind."[2] Through the Church, the political traditions and the administrative practice of Rome were transmitted to the new world, but the details of the process cannot easily be followed. The provincial council certainly gave the Church some general guidance for its early organisation. A German historian of Caesar-worship writes : " It is a significant testimony to the continuity of human development . . . that the Christian Church has borrowed for her priests and for her councils the outward forms, names and marks of distinction which were used for three centuries in provincial Caesar-worship."[3] Apart from the name, continuity can be traced only in two things. The territorial area of the Roman civil diocese or group of provinces frequently corresponds to the ecclesiastical or metropolitan province, presided over by the archbishop ; the special privilege known as the *cursus publicus* —the right to use the imperial post or to travel free of cost—was enjoyed by members both of civil and of ecclesiastical councils.[4] However, what was transmitted seems to have been a general idea, not the transformation of a civil into an ecclesiastical assembly. The representative principle was applied by the Church in an entirely different way ; instead of nominated or elected representatives of the *civitas*, the bishop attended in virtue of his office, representing his diocese as the leader of the community and without any express mandate from his people.

[1] *Supra*, p. 281.   [2] Pollock and Maitland, I, 4.
[3] Hirschfeld, article *Concilium*, in Pauly-Wissova, *Real-Encyklopädie*, Stuttgart, 1901, IV, 824.
[4] E. Carette, *Les Assemblées Provinciales de la Gaule Romaine* (1895), p. 425.

The first Christian assembly, convoked for purposes of debate and decision, is described in the Acts of the Apostles,[1] when disputes over the Mosaic law led to a meeting of the Apostles, elders and brethren in Jerusalem. After " much questioning," an unanimous decision was reached and despatched to the churches in Antioch, Syria and Cilicia. This decision may be described as the earliest legislation of the Church. In the first three centuries of the Christian era diocesan and provincial assemblies met fairly often ; they seem to have been attended mainly by bishops, who represented their dioceses by reason of their sacred office. They were first described as *concilia* by Tertullian (*fl.* 200) ; he may have had heathen provincial councils in mind when he wrote " at councils of all the churches high matters are treated in common (in *commune*) and this representation of the whole Christian world is solemnised with great veneration." [2]   It can hardly be accidental that the word *concilia* first appears in close association with *representatio*.[3]   No elaborate organisation was possible during the centuries of persecution, but the conversion of the Emperor Constantine was soon followed by the summons of the first General Council at Nicea (325).   It is unknown whether the idea came from the Emperor or from the Church ; the question is of minor importance, as general councils were the logical consequence of the conception of the Church as one and indivisible.   The representative character of this first oecumenical Council has never been questioned ; over 200 bishops were present, drawn from the whole Christian world.   Its chief work was the condemnation of Arius, the insertion of *Homoousios* (" of one substance with the Father ") into the creed since called Nicene and the issue of a series of laws, which are the beginning of the canon law of the Church.   Thus the Council of Nicea was a representative assembly which exercised both judicial and legislative functions ; these powers were maintained in succeeding assemblies.

[1] Acts xv, 1-29.
[2] Cited in *Cambridge Medieval History*, I, 164.
[3] The idea of representation was specially familiar to Christians through the doctrine of Redemption, and was evidently much discussed. St. Paul wrote to the Corinthians (1 Cor. xv, 29) of baptism for the dead, and St. Chrysostom attacked the heresiarch Marcion on the subject of vicarious baptism, moving his audience to laughter by the very idea of salvation by the agency or proxy of another human being (Homily XI).   St. Augustine's declaration that St. Peter represented the Church (*figuram gestabat Ecclesie*) is an example of personification of this type (*Sermo* cxlix, cap. 7, cited E. Denny, *Papalism*, 1912, p. 60).

The first great age of Councils came to an end with the development of the schism between the Eastern and Western Churches. Long before that time, the practice of holding ecclesiastical assemblies was well established in the West. In fact, the Council of Arles (314), held before Constantine gained control of the Eastern Empire, was the link between the older provincial synods and the Council of Nicea. It was a representative assembly, attended by bishops from the whole of the Western Church (including three from Britain), which exercised both judicial and legislative authority in the condemnation of the Donatist heresy and by the issue of a series of canons. Provincial councils and synods continued to be held frequently until the general dislocation caused by the Viking invasions of the ninth century. In England, for example, though the records are scanty, we have evidence of forty-three distinctly ecclesiastical assemblies held between the Synod of Whitby in 664 and the Synod of Canterbury in 844 ; of these, fourteen were councils of the whole English Church, and the remaining twenty-nine were provincial or diocesan synods.[1] Towards the middle of the ninth century, the assemblies ceased to meet, and do not seem to have revived again until the Norman Conquest. In the interval, ecclesiastical business was dealt with in the Witan, a method typical of the close union of Church and Crown in Anglo-Saxon England.

Lanfranc's revival of ecclesiastical assemblies brought England into line with the general revival of synods and councils on the Continent. Under Pope Leo IX (1049-54) important decrees of reform were promulgated in councils held in Rome and elsewhere, and they were made known by means of metropolitan synods in the provinces. These and later reforms in the eleventh century were the prelude to the revival of the General Council. The first Lateran Council of 1123 was the ninth General Council, and the first to meet since the Council of Constantinople (869). Its sessions mark the beginning of the second great age of councils, falling between 1123 and 1274. Within that period six General Councils were held : the four Lateran Councils of 1123, 1139, 1179 and 1215, and the two Councils of Lyons, 1245 and 1274 ; they amount to almost a third of the total number (19) held between Nicea (325) and Trent (1548). It is significant that

---

[1] Haddan and Stubbs, *Ecclesiastical Councils and Documents*, Vol. III, *passim*.

this revival of the General Council should coincide in time with the rise of national legislative assemblies. The three General Councils of the twelfth century were chiefly concerned with particular issues ; [1] though important decrees were issued by each, the main attention of members was directed to policy and administration. At the fourth Lateran Council (1215) the emphasis was reversed. It was summoned by Innocent III, when the Papacy was at the height of its power, for the express purpose of reform. In Innocent's own words, it was called " to extirpate vices and implant virtues, to correct excesses and reform manners, to eliminate heresies and strengthen faith, to allay discords and establish peace, to end oppressions and to increase liberty." [2] To fulfil this vast design, the council was summoned in 1213, two and a half years before the time of session, and attendance was enjoined as a solemn obligation. Not only archbishops and bishops, but abbots and priors and all the monarchs of western Christendom were cited to appear. No such gathering had met in Europe since the great councils of the age of the Fathers ; 412 archbishops and bishops and over 800 abbots and priors were present, and many others were represented by proctors. The proctor representing an individual was not an innovation, but there were also proctors representing the chapters of cathedral churches. Innocent had commanded each bishop to see that every chapter in his diocese sent the provost, dean or other suitable men to act for the whole body ; he gave as a reason for this new departure that business relating to chapters would be brought before the council.[3] It was part of his scheme of reform to compel the chapters to allot one prebend for the support of a schoolmaster and, in commanding the attendance of their representatives, he was acting on the principle already expressed in his canons—*quod omnes tangit, ab omnibus approbetur*.

The Fourth Lateran Council put the representative principle into action on a scale and with a prestige which made it known throughout the whole of western Europe. Two decrees passed

---

[1] The first ratified the Concordat of Worms, the second ended a schism, and the third was concerned partly with schism and partly with the claims of Barbarossa.

[2] Mansi, *op. cit.*, Vol. XXII, col. 961.

[3] Barker, Dominican Order, p. 32, citing Labbe and Cossart, *Concilia*, XI, I, 124.

by the council expressed the same idea under other forms. The sixth canon decreed that metropolitans with their suffragans should not omit each year to hold provincial synods, for the correction of excesses and the reformation of manners, especially of the clergy ; that persons should be appointed to investigate what needed correction and reformation and to report to the metropolitan and his suffragans at the next council. Thus they should be able to proceed with prudent deliberation and to cause what they had enacted to be observed, publishing their decrees in annual diocesan synods.[1] The decree was enforcing an old canonical custom, which was often neglected ; it enjoined the annual meeting of provincial and diocesan synods for purposes of legislation ; further, by the addition *et alios* to the metropolitan and suffragans, it is clear that the assemblies should be attended by some at least of the lower clergy. The twelfth canon is also relevant to our enquiry. Triennial chapters were ordered to be held in each national province by those religious orders by whom the practice had not already been adopted.[2] The effect of this canon was, as Professor Jacob has said, " to generalise representation throughout the religious orders." [3]

Before turning away from the Lateran Council, it is necessary to note the immediate consequences of the new representation of chapters, as it will explain why the canons of Salisbury were so quick to put forward the plan of a representative assembly in 1226.[4] In 1225 a legatine council was held at Bourges to which a papal demand for two prebends from each chapter was presented.[5] The council was attended by proctors of the French chapters and an account of their debate is preserved in the Salisbury Register and in two English chronicles.[6] After some preliminary business, the legate attempted to dismiss the proctors and thus provoked a formal protest. " My lord," they said, " we have heard that you have special letters from the Curia to exact prebends from conventual churches and we wonder that you have proposed nothing of it in this council, while we, whom the matter specially touches, are present." [7] The demand was then

---

[1] Mansi, *op. cit.*, Vol. XXII, col. 991-2.　　[2] *Ibid.*, cols. 999-1002.
[3] *Cambridge Medieval History*, VI, 40.　　[4] *Supra*, pp. 265-6.
[5] See Barker, *op. cit.*, pp. 34 *seq.*, for a discussion of this council.
[6] *Regist. of St. Osmund*, II, 51-4 ; Roger of Wendover, II, 295-7 ; Walter of Coventry (*Rolls Series*), II, 276-9.
[7] *Regist. of St. Osmund*, II, 52.

brought before the assembly and the proctors stated their arguments against it at some length. In the following year the Pope demanded a subsidy from the English Church. Archbishop Langton held a provincial council on the model of Bourges, summoning to it, not only bishops, abbots and priors, but the deans of cathedral and collegiate churches, all archdeacons and proctors from all chapters of churches, colleges and religious houses.[1] All summoned were ordered to come fully instructed (*plene instructi*) to give answer to the pope. This was the first English ecclesiastical assembly to which proctors came with a mandate or instruction from their electors. The reply given to the Pope was copied from that given at Bourges the year before, so there can hardly be any doubt that archbishop Langton was copying the summons of proctors to the Lateran Council and to the legatine council of 1225.[2] His representative assembly met in London on May 3, 1226, that is, in the same summer as that in which the canons of Salisbury refused to agree to a subsidy until the proctors of chapters had been convoked.

Thus Innocent III's magnification of the representative principle had an effect upon the English church in little more than ten years' time. To understand why the idea was already familiar, we must turn back and see how it had been slowly worked out, as it were in miniature, by the religious orders.

Though some form of legislative assembly seems to have been prescribed by the first monastic rules of the Christian East, the idea was not transmitted to the West, where it was evolved independently by slow stages.[3] According to the rule of St. Benedict, each abbey was self-contained ; it was governed by its abbot, who also exercised full authority over dependent priories. Informal meetings of abbots may have been held from time to time, like the great assembly at Aachen in 817, though this is the only general meeting of which we have record. Provincial gatherings of abbots met in Italy, Germany and probably in England in the ninth and tenth centuries, but almost nothing is known of their deliberations. The power of the abbot remained unimpaired ; the position was stated with some bitterness by a discontented German monk in 1159 ; each abbot, he said, adds

---

[1] *Select Charters*, p. 445. The correct date is 1226, not 1225, as is printed.
[2] Cf. Powicke, *Stephen Langton*, p. 159.
[3] *Cambridge Medieval History*, V, Chapter XX.

or rejects as he pleases, according to his own inclination, and without the counsel or consent of his brother abbots.[1]

The same separatism characterised the secular canons, founded by St. Chrodegang in the eighth century, and the regular or Austin canons, who were organised about the year 1063 ; they followed a common rule, without common meetings to enforce it or to ensure uniformity of interpretation. It was by them, however, that the idea of the chapter or council of full members of a particular religious house seems to have been evolved. The chapter made ordinances and exercised judicial and executive authority ; without it the constitutional development of the religious orders would have been impossible. It was the first organised constituency and its common discussions, carried on by persons equal in rank and responsibility, were the foundation of the representative system, as developed by the Church.[2] During the Investiture contests, when quarrels over appointments were frequent, the chapter naturally became more compact and self-conscious. It soon developed the habit of appointing one or more agents or proctors to act for the whole body, at the king's court, in Rome or elsewhere. In England this stage was reached early in the twelfth century, as a natural consequence of the agreement about elections reached in 1107. The unity and equality of members of a chapter made it possible to elect delegates who could act for the whole body.

Another line of development was followed by the Cluniac order in the tenth century. They recognised the need for closer association and all the daughter houses were controlled from Cluny. Each priory owed full obedience to the abbot of Cluny and contact was maintained by annual councils, called chapters, attended by the priors. The decrees of these chapters were binding upon the whole order. Thus in the dark period of the tenth century the conciliar plan of legislation, based upon advice, was revived by Cluny ; its annual chapter was the first modification of Benedictine self-sufficiency and the autocracy of the abbot.

The plan of holding general chapters was carried further by the new religious orders of the twelfth century ; like General Councils, the use of assemblies for purposes of legislation and

[1] Herbord, *Dialogus*, I, 19 (Jaffé, Monum. Bamberg, p. 719), cited by Dom Berlière, *Mélanges Bénédictines*, Series IV (1902), p. 57, n. 1.
[2] Cf. the fellows of a college.

administration was characteristic of a great period of reform. The change was mainly the work of the Cistercians. By their *Carta Caritatis* (1118), the government of the order was entrusted to a general chapter of abbots, presided over by the abbot of Cîteaux. The absolute ascendancy of the abbot of Cluny was not imitated. The abbot of Cîteaux did not control the detail of administration in other houses and he had no power to levy temporal exactions. Arrangements were made for regular, visitations by abbots, from which even the mother house was not exempt ; final decisions in matters of excommunication or deposition were reserved for the general chapter. The fame of the order and the great personal influence of St. Bernard led to the adoption of some variant of these arrangements by the other new orders founded in the twelfth century. The Premonstratensian canons, established in 1129, followed the Cistercian model fairly closely. The Carthusian order (1142) gave further powers to the general chapter. Though each house elected its own head, the priors were " little more than officials of the general chapter," [1] to which they took vows of obedience. ' The prior of the *Grande Chartreuse* presided *ex officio*, but even his decisions might be over-ridden by the assembly. As a safeguard against hasty legislation, it was provided that a statute must be passed by three successive general chapters. The other orders, notably the Hospitallers and the purely English order of St. Gilbert of Sempringham, resembled the Carthusians rather than the Cistercians in entrusting larger powers to the general chapter. The contrast with the Benedictine rule is clearly marked ; a member of a twelfth-century order belonged, at least in theory, to that order as a whole, while the Benedictine monk belonged to his own house. The new orders achieved, within particular groups, the size and coherence essential for political representation.

Thus the general chapter expressed and put into action all over western Europe the idea of an assembly with legislative and executive powers, composed of members drawn from the communities which together made up the whole order. As a rule, these members were priors or heads of houses ; like the bishop of a diocese, they represented their convents only in a general sense and without any specific mandate. There is, however, one

[1] E. M. Thompson, *The Carthusian Order*, 1930, pp. 87 *seq.* See *ibid.*, Part I, Chapter V, *passim.*

interesting exception to the general rule, which shows that by the middle of the twelfth century the idea of representation of a community rather than of an office was understood. The order of Grandmont was founded in the diocese of Limoges about 1076, but its rule was probably not drawn up until about 1150.[1] It was an austere rule, designed for contemplatives who were strictly bound to extreme poverty. A special characteristic was the absolute equality which was at first maintained between the clerks and the lay brothers or *conversi* ; they used the same church, cloister and chapter and wore the same dress and tonsure. By 1163 there were sixty houses of the order, all small and all in France, chiefly in the domains of Henry II (Limoges and Poitiers). These peculiarities of organisation and geography no doubt help to explain the new form of election devised for the choice of the prior of Grandmont, the president of the order. The ordinary general chapter, which met annually, was attended by the *corrector* or head of each cell and the *curiosus* or head of the lay brothers ; this is an extension of the idea of representation, though still on official lines. However, for the election of the prior of the order a special general chapter was held. It was attended by two brothers from each cell ; they are called *fratres*, without any reference to office, and it is expressly stated that those who do not attend the chapter shall grant to those who go the power to make an election. Here we have a clear example of a mandate given by the community to its representatives. The same principle governed the election itself. It was carried out by twelve men, six clerks and six lay brothers, chosen by the whole chapter, who gave a pledge to accept their decision. It was also laid down that the decision of the majority should be binding on the rest.[2] The order was poor and its members lived in complete retirement from the world. Even though it enjoyed the special patronage of Henry II, it can hardly be maintained that the influence of its constitutional arrangements spread very far. It serves rather to show that the idea of representation was changing to something less official, more practical and more popular.

In theory, as we have seen, a member of one of the new orders

---

[1] For a full account of the order of Grandmont, see Miss Rose Graham, *English Ecclesiastical Studies*, 1929, pp. 209 *seq.*

[2] Cf. *infra*, p. 338, for the limitations imposed on a majority decision.

belonged to that order as a whole, rather than to a particular house, but in practice the large powers entrusted to the abbot or head of a house tended to interpose his personal authority between his convent and the rest of the order. It remained for St. Dominic to find a means by which the theory underlying twelfth-century monasticism could be translated into action.[1] The fourth Lateran Council had decreed that no more new orders should be founded [2] and St. Dominic was therefore compelled to adapt for his followers the rule of an order already established. He chose (1216) that of the Premonstratensian canons, which followed the general lines of Cistercian organisation. At the first general chapter (1221) the vow of poverty was adopted after the Franciscan model and the detailed constitution was probably drafted at the same time. The constitution was confirmed by a chapter general in 1228 and by the Pope in 1232.

The government of the Dominicans was entrusted to a hierarchy of chapters ; the conventual chapter ruled the house, the provincial chapter ruled the province, and the general chapter ruled the whole order. The " most general " (generalissimus) chapter was an extra-ordinary body—summoned only twice in the history of the order—to which certain powers of emergency legislation were given. The functions of the three normal chapters are well summarised by Mrs. Galbraith : " The general chapter laid down certain rules ; the provincial chapter amplified them according to the particular needs of the province ; the conventual chapter applied them to individual cases." [3] In addition, " both general and provincial chapters, especially the latter, made and executed ordinances." Power was not, as the hierarchy at first suggests, delegated from above, rather it ultimately derived from the convents or communities. This was secured by the use of representatives. " The general chapter was composed of representatives of the provinces, elected in the provincial chapter . . . the provincial chapter in its turn included in its ranks representatives of the convent." [4] The conventual chapter elected from its total number of professed friars a representative or socius to attend the provincial chapter with the prior ; this socius was invested with full power to deliberate and to vote for

---

[1] G. R. Galbraith, Constitution of the Dominican Order, passim.
[2] Canon 15.   [3] G. R. Galbraith, op. cit., p. 37.
[4] Ibid., pp. 37-8.

the rest.[1]   He was " burdened with the business of his convent " ; in speaking he was bound to distinguish between his own opinion and that of his electors.[2]   The conventual chapter also chose two electors for the election of the provincial prior and it had the right of forwarding petitions through the *socius*.   The provincial chapter, in addition to official members, thus consisted of the prior and one *socius* from each house in the province.   It was usually a large body ; there were, for example, forty-six houses in the English province by 1303 and an average of about thirty-five in most of the others at a slightly earlier date.[3]   The provincial chapter appointed a sort of cabinet of four ministers, known as *diffinitores*, by whom almost all business was transacted, except elections.   A special electoral chapter was held to choose the prior of the province.   The general chapter was a small body, consisting of one elected representative from each province.   To it belonged the function of altering the constitution (with the consent of three successive assemblies), and the power to elect, to punish and to depose the master-general of the order.   It is unnecessary to discuss in detail the elaborate rules for the conduct of business in each type of chapter.   They serve only to deepen the impression of a highly complex constitution, at the same time both representative and efficient.

The religious orders supply the link between the first and second series of General Councils.   The Benedictines and, much more, the Cluniacs slowly evolved the idea of general chapters for purposes of legislation and discipline under the control of the abbots.   In the twelfth century the Cistercians and Carthusians exalted the general chapter as the supreme executive of their orders and the plan was widely imitated.   The order of Grandmont first developed the idea of representing the community by elected proctors rather than by officials, and they also entrusted those elected with a definite mandate.   In the third decade of the thirteenth century the Dominicans made the representative principle the keystone of their constitution. The order of Grandmont spread to England early in John's reign ; only three houses were founded, one in Yorkshire (*c.* 1204) and two in the Welsh Marches (*c.* 1225).   The Dominicans came to

[1] G. R. Galbraith, *op. cit.*, pp. 61 *seq.*
[2] *Ibid.*, p. 61.
[3] As late as 1301 there were only eighteen provinces (*ibid.*, pp. 98-9).

England in 1221 and at once founded houses at Oxford and in London ; by 1236 nearly a score of houses had been established. It is, however, unlikely that knowledge of their organisation spread beyond the ranks of the clergy, or that their influence went further than to strengthen belief in the value of representation, already made familiar by the work of the Lateran Council and of Innocent III.

In England the practical application of the principle of representation in relation to the doctrine of consent was the work of the secular clergy. To understand the process, it may be helpful to recall how the Church in England was organised. At first the main ecclesiastical divisions were the provinces of Canterbury and York and the dioceses within them. At the centre of each diocese was the bishop and his cathedral. Gradually the clergy of the bishop's household became the canons of the cathedral, with a dean at their head ; it was mainly by them that the system of government by chapter was developed and they were also connected with the parishes by holding prebends. At one time, they may have been thought to represent, in a general way, the ordinary parish clergy, but as dioceses gained a more orderly structure, that function passed to special officials who had a more direct connection with the routine of parochial work. These officials were the archdeacon and the rural dean, or dean of Christianity, and they played a leading part in the organisation of the lower clergy. The archdeacon was originally the chief deacon of the bishop's household ; in the early Church, from the fourth century onwards, he gradually replaced the country bishop or *chorepiscopus*, who belonged to the missionary stage of organisation. The archdeacon had both administrative and judicial duties, especially the duty of visitation, and he gradually took over those episcopal functions which need not be performed by the bishop in person. He enforced the sentences of the bishop's court and became responsible for the discipline of the clergy and the upkeep of their churches. In England archdeacons of Canterbury appear in the ninth century,[1] but hardly any later references to them occur before the reign of Edward the Confessor. They were certainly very little employed before the Norman Conquest.

[1] *Eng. Hist. Review*, Vol. XLII, pp. 1 *seq.*

The rural dean is a dignitary of obscure origin, the obscurity being largely due to the varying meanings of the word *decanus* or dean. The late classical use of the word to describe a man set in authority over ten soldiers developed into the medieval meaning of a man in authority in civilian society, as the dean of a cathedral, the dean of a gild or the dean of a tithing.[1] Perhaps not earlier than the eleventh century, bishops and archdeacons began to delegate part of the supervision of the lower clergy to officials called deans, who executed the bishop's orders, looked after vacant benefices and collected and made known information from above. There is no trace of them in England before the Norman Conquest.

It seems that the organisation of the lower clergy under archdeacons and deans is one of the main positive results on the constitutional side, which can be definitely connected with the Norman Conquest. The Anglo-Saxon church was clearly behind continental practice in this respect and one of Lanfranc's chief reforms was to begin to divide dioceses into archdeaconries. Rather more slowly, the archdeaconries were divided into rural deaneries. The process of subdivision must have taken some time, but by the thirteenth century almost all dioceses were divided into archdeaconries, which were in turn divided into rural deaneries. The boundaries of the archdeaconries corresponded, whenever it were possible, with the county boundary and, sometimes at least, those of the deanery corresponded with the boundaries of the hundred. For example, the diocese of Salisbury was divided (1078) into the four archdeaconries of Dorset, Berkshire, Wiltshire and Salisbury and Lincoln (*c.* 1075-85) into the eight archdeaconries of Leicester, Northampton, Oxford, Huntingdon, Bedford, Buckingham, Lincoln and Stow. Dioceses, like Canterbury or Ely, which were co-terminous with shires or less than shires, had no territorial archdeaconries. The boundaries of the deaneries have not yet been fully examined ; though sometimes, as in Lincolnshire, a connection can be traced with the hundred, in some other counties no principle of

---

[1] Cf. the dean of a college. Professor Hamilton-Thompson tells me that the earliest ecclesiastical use of the word seems to be in monasteries, where the *decani* were set over sections of the community. At Durham there were two *decani* as late as the fifteenth century.

division can be detected.[1] A certain connection with the old units of local government was maintained and it may help to account for the unusual vigour of the institutions, especially the rural deaneries. In the deanery the clergy were organised in chapters, which were attended by all the parochial clergy and sat every three weeks, like the hundred and manorial courts.[2] The chapter of the rural deanery was the lowest unit of government in the English Church and it naturally became the unit either for ecclesiastical or for secular taxation of the clergy.[3]

The representative system evolved by the English Church in the thirteenth century followed the lines of territorial division, though it was only by degrees that the lowest units were brought into play. For a time the plan of representation by dignitaries was adopted, as it had been by the religious orders in the twelfth century. The bishop at first sight seems the natural agent for his clergy, but his powers were curtailed by a canon of the third Lateran Council (1179) which forbade him to tax his clergy without their consent.[4] It was thus virtually impossible for bishops to maintain the right to bind their clergy, though they sometimes tried to do so, if a papal demand for taxes were made. The archdeacon at first stood out as the representative of the

---

[1] Professor Hamilton-Thompson says in a note which he has kindly given me, " Throughout the whole diocese of Lincoln, the correspondence between deaneries and hundreds or wapentakes was nearly exact. The same thing is true of the Yorkshire deaneries, though small wapentakes were included with larger ones in the large deaneries of the West Riding (e.g. Doncaster deanery consisted of the large wapentake of Strafforth and Tickhill and the small one of Staincross). It is south of the Thames that the differences between civil and ecclesiastical boundaries become noticeable, e.g. in Hampshire, Wiltshire and Dorset."

[2] William Dansey, Horae Decanicae Rurales, II, Part V, pp. 22-5. Cf. Synod. Exon. 1287, Wilkins, II, 148, cap. 31. Lyndwood (Provinciale, I, Tit. II, ed. 1679, p. 14) distinguished between rural chapters held every three weeks and those held quarterly. In 1342 archbishop Stratford ordered that chapters should be held in more important places, where food was plentiful (Wilkins, II, 699). These meetings might be compared to the sessions held later by J.P.s.

[3] The archipresbyter who helped to collect the Saladin Tithe was the rural dean (Select Charters, p. 189). Cf. the valuation of the seven deaneries of the archdeaconry of Leicester, 1217 (W. E. Lunt, Valuation of Norwich, Oxford, 1926, Appendix I, p. 526), and Extrav. Commun., Tit. X, c. un (Corpus Jur. Can., ed. Richter and Friedberg, II., col. 1299), " decanis ruralibus duntaxat exceptis, qui in aliquibus regionibus archipresbyteri nominantur." I owe this reference to Professor Hamilton-Thompson.

[4] Canon VII, Mansi, Vol. XXII, col. 221-2.

clergy of his archdeaconry, as he had personal knowledge of their opinions and their resources. At the council of St. Alban's, held to discuss Romescot in 1206, archdeacons were present, perhaps for the first time.[1] They attended all three assemblies held to consider papal and royal demands in 1226 and they probably established their right to be consulted in that year. We cannot trace the history of their summons in detail, as the writs for ecclesiastical assemblies are not always preserved. However, they seem to have come fairly regularly from 1226 onwards and on several occasions their position as representatives of the clergy was officially admitted by prelates. At the same time a growing hostility to the heavy burden of taxation aroused discontent with the whole plan of representation by dignitaries. The assumption of identity of interests between either the bishop or the archdeacon and the lower clergy slowly broke down under the financial strain and it became necessary to devise a new plan of representation. The model was ready to hand in the proctorial system, already worked out by the new religious orders and by the chapters of cathedrals.

It is impossible to assign an exact date to this important extension of the proctorial system.[2] If Roger of Wendover be correct in his statement that rectors attended a royal council in 1229,[3] they must have appeared by elected or nominated representatives. More probably the change did not begin until about ten years later. In 1239 Gregory IX demanded an aid of a fifth from the English lower clergy and sent the legate Otto to enforce it. The main evidence for his negotiations is a letter addressed to the bishop of Bath and Wells, which was probably sent to every diocese.[4] From it we learn that he assembled the deans, proctors of chapters and archdeacons on at least three occasions in 1240.[5] The letter is a summons to the final meeting, at which the tax was partially granted. He wrote in a querulous key, complaining that the bishops had already persuaded the clergy to agree

[1] Wilkins, I, 514.
[2] For what follows I have had the great advantage of checking my own enquiry by reference to Dr. Lunt's essay, " Consent of the English Lower Clergy to Taxation during the Reign of Henry III " (*Essays in Honour of George Lincoln Burr*). [3] II, 375.
[4] Dated, London, October 14, 1240. MSS. of Dean and Chapter of Wells, I, 403. (Hist. MSS. Com.). Cf. *Tewkesbury Annals*, p. 116.
[5] At Reading (date uncertain) and in London, September 29 and November 8.

and that at an earlier meeting (Michaelmas) only four archdeacons had attended. Further, in the same citation he asked the bishop " with the help of his archdeacons, to admonish and persuade the lesser deans, rectors and vicars of his diocese to give a liberal aid." This request was tantamount to an admission that the archdeacons could not bind the lower clergy. The admission is strengthened by the facts that the diocese of Worcester made a separate grant in the course of the year [1] and that Otto himself appealed to the rectors of Berkshire. They presented him with articles of protest, amounting to a flat refusal ; [2] almost every article ended with the refrain—" unde dicunt quod nec volunt nec debent contributioni consentire." We have it on the authority of Matthew Paris that the bishops had declared, at an early stage of the negotiations, that the archdeacons must be consulted, as they alone knew the resources of the beneficed clergy—" omnes tangit hoc negotium ; omnes igitur sunt conveniendi ; sine ipsis nec decet nec expedit respondere." [3] We know also, from Otto's letter, that nearly all the archdeacons failed to attend the Michaelmas assembly. It seems as if each order of the Church were trying to escape the odium of consent by repudiating responsibility. Otto was thus forced either to consult the lower clergy themselves or to require the bishops to do it for him. The delays and inconveniences of the plan were probably a decisive factor in the extension of representation.

The first clear documentary evidence of the presence of clerical proctors at a central assembly belongs to the year 1254.[4] They were summoned to agree to the deflection of the triennial tenth, granted for a crusade, to the war in Gascony.[5] The bishops had refused to agree without the assent of their clergy, and royal writs were issued ordering each bishop to summon all the clergy

---

[1] Lunt, *Valuation of Norwich*, p. 30.

[2] Matt. Paris, IV, 38 *seq*. The document seems to have been used again by " omnes et singuli rectores ecclesiarum Anglie " in 1244 (*Burton Annals* (*Rolls Series*), pp. 265-7).

[3] Matt. Paris, IV, 37. See Lunt, *Consent of Lower Clergy*, pp. 126 *seq*., on the chronological difficulties raised by Paris.

[4] Indecisive evidence from chronicles suggests that they may have attended councils in 1229, 1231, 1237, 1239, 1246 and 1247 (Wendover, II, 375 ; Wilkins, I, 629 ; Matt. Paris, III, 400 ; *Tewkesbury Annals*, p. 105 ; Wilkins, I, 663 ; Matt. Paris, IV, 580 *seq*., and Cole, *Documents*, 352 *seq*. ; Matt. Paris, *Addit.*, p. 145).

[5] Matt. Paris, V, 423 *seq*. ; VI, 283 ; *Dunstable Annals*, p. 195 ; *Royal Letters, Henry III* (*Rolls Series*), II, 101.

of his diocese to persuade them to grant a gracious aid to the king, and to send discreet men from each diocese to report the decision to the council.[1] This writ was issued on the same day as the writs to the sheriffs, ordering consultation of the shire courts and the election of knights of the shire for the same purpose.[2] A Durham manuscript has preserved an account of what the clergy did at Westminster.[3] The *nuncii* of the chapters, colleges and clergy of England consented to the deflection of the tenth on five conditions ; these conditions included, not only a general protection of ecclesiastical liberties, but also particular stipulations that the tax should not be paid unless the king invaded Gascony and that the collection should be in accordance with the old assessment. These terms were, in effect, a refusal and they were not accepted by the king. They show that the *nuncii* had full power to act for their dioceses, as it cannot be supposed that the five conditions were drafted independently in each local assembly. The proctors of the clergy thus conformed to certain conditions necessary for political action, in so far as they had temporary and general mandates from their constituencies and had used them to exercise independent judgement, in co-operation with others. On the other hand, their assemblies were not public, but sectional, and for that reason their deliberations are not yet entitled to be called political.

The action taken by the clergy in 1254 cannot have been altogether unexpected, as the tenth had been unpopular, even in its original form. It had been granted by the Pope in 1250 (April 11) and in order to make the task of collection easier, Henry III had asked the prelates for their consent.[4] A series of councils was held,[5] and it was not until May 1253 that the prelates finally consented. In the interval the lower clergy were apparently consulted locally ; we know, for example, that the York clergy met at Blyth in 1252 (September) and declared that the

---

[1] Lunt, *Consent of Lower Clergy*, pp. 140 *seq.* The writ is printed in Prynne, *Register*, I, 3-4 ; H. Hody, *English Councils and Convocations*, 1701, Part III, 339.

[2] *Select Charters*, pp. 365-6.

[3] British Museum, Stowe MS. 930, ff. 57ᵛ-58. This important document was discovered and printed by Lunt (*Consent of Lower Clergy*, pp. 142-3).

[4] See Lunt, *Consent of Lower Clergy*, *passim*, for the question of local consent and the *plenitudo potestatis* of the Pope.

[5] *Cal. Cl. Rolls, 1251-53*, p. 217 ; Matt. Paris, V, pp. 359 *seq.* ; Lunt, *Valuation of Norwich*, pp. 55-63.

matter concerned equally both provinces of the English Church and that a joint discussion was therefore necessary.[1] It is clear that the discontent of the clergy was so strongly expressed that the bishops did not dare to agree to the deflection of the tax to the Gascon war on their own authority. It may be that their demand that the lower clergy should be consulted suggested to the Regents the plan of consulting the county courts and calling up the knights of the shire in the same way. The use of the vague word *nuncii* in the writs to the bishops indicates that the procedure of representation by proctors was not then fully worked out, and it is probable that in 1254 the clergy were for the first time regularly represented in a central assembly by men of their own choice. Early in 1256 a Convocation held in London was attended by three or four proctors from each archdeaconry [2] and statements of grievances were presented in the name of the clergy of each diocese or archdeaconry.[3] From this date the right of the lower clergy to representation may be taken as established. That they fully understood the position may be seen by the declaration of the archdeaconry of Lincoln in 1255 : " when it is proposed to lay a burden on anyone, it is necessary to have his express consent." [4]

The exact form that representation should take was not fixed for nearly thirty years. In 1257 and in 1258, for example, the archdeacons were summoned to Convocations with special instructions that they should bring with them proctorial letters from their clergy.[5] The most significant event was the refusal of the clergy of Canterbury to grant an aid in 1269 for the lord Edward's crusade. The abbots, priors, rectors and vicars of the province drafted a reply to the prelates in which they stated their grievances, said *non possumus* to the proposed taxation, and cited the canon of 1215 in their defence.[6] The document was put forward in the name of the proctors of nineteen dioceses, including the three in the northern province.[7]

---

[1] *Gray's Register*, Surtees Society, p. 211.
[2] Matt. Paris, *Additamenta*, p. 314-15.   [3] Burton *Annals*, pp. 360-3.
[4] " . . . cum agitur de aliquo obligando, necessarius est eius expressus consensus " (Burton, p. 360). Cf. protest of proctors of Coventry and Lichfield, *ibid.*, p. 362.   [5] Burton, pp. 401-2, 411 ; *Select Charters*, p. 446.
[6] Wake, Appendix, pp. 5-7.
[7] " Procuratores Coventr. Linc. Norwyc. Helyens. Roffens. Cant. London. Cicestr. Winton. Sar. Bathon. Exon. Landav. Menev. Hereford. Wigorn. Ebor. Dunelm. Carl. abbatum, priorum, rectorum, et vicariorum, earund. diocesium " (*ibid.*, Appendix, p. 7).

In the early years of Edward I's reign the king's demands brought about the final organisation of the provincial convocations, since he began to claim the right to tax the clergy directly instead of contenting himself with grants made through the Pope. Before the grand struggle provoked by *Clericis laicos* (1296-97) he was granted aids by the clergy on seven different occasions,[1] each time after more or less open resistance. The habit of consulting the lower clergy was already established [2] when a dispute with the king in 1283 served to crystallise the constitution of the provincial assemblies of the Church. It is worth recalling the sequence of events, as they had a permanent effect on the relations between the clergy and the Crown.

Edward I summoned the knights and burgesses of North and South to meet at Northampton and York respectively on January 20, 1283.[3] For the same day he issued writs to the archbishops of Canterbury and York requiring them to secure the attendance of lesser dignitaries and clerical proctors at the same assemblies.[4] His intention was to extract an aid for the war in Wales. In the writs to the archbishops he used a new formula— *mandamus . . . venire faciatis*—which was, in effect, a peremptory royal order. He was probably anxious to avoid delay by insisting upon simultaneous sessions of the clergy in both provinces. Had his plan been well received, clergy and lay commons might have coalesced into provincial estates, summoned only for purposes of taxation. Any chance that he had of success was destroyed by the formula in the writs, which was deeply resented by the clergy of Canterbury province. The principle had already been admitted by the Crown that *convocacio laicorum* pertained to the king and magnates and *convocacio clericorum* to the prelates.[5] The southern clergy refused to go to Northampton on the grounds that they had not been properly summoned, and it was necessary for archbishop Peckham to summon a new assembly later in the same year.[6] This second summons was

---

[1] In 1273, 1279, 1280, 1283, 1290, 1294 and 1295.

[2] For example, the bishops were ordered by archbishop Kilwardby to bring to London on January 14, 1278, " personis maioribus de suis capitulis et locorum archidiaconis et procuratoribus tocius cleri," *Register*, Bronescombe of Exeter, pp. 53-4. Cf. summons of York clergy to Pontefract, February 9, 1280, *Register*, Wickwane of York (Surtees Soc., 1907), p. 53.

[3] *Select Charters*, pp. 457-8.   [4] *Ibid.*, p. 459.

[5] Cole, *Documents*, p. 356, no. XIII.

[6] *Peckham's Register of Letters* (*Rolls Series*), II, 508 *seq.* ; cf. *supra*, Chapter VII, p. 129.

issued to the bishops ; they were ordered to assemble their clergy, to explain to them the king's request and then to see to it that the archdeacons, two proctors from each diocese and one proctor from each chapter should attend convocation in London, with full and express power (*plenam et expressam potestatem*) to treat with the bishops and to consent to those things which the community of the clergy shall provide.[1] This assembly became known as Peckham's model convocation and, as Stubbs says, the writ " was then or soon afterwards accepted as authoritative, and has been treated as having the force of a canon." [2] The form of the Convocation of York was fixed at about the same time ; it was slightly different from Canterbury as, owing to the small number of dioceses, two proctors came from each archdeaconry instead of from the larger unit.[3] It may be concluded that by 1283 the English clergy had perfected the machinery by which the doctrine of consent was put into action through representatives. All that was lacking to give them true political representation was the inclusion of their proctors in an assembly empowered to create or to modify public law.

Evidence for the action taken by the laity during the same period is less abundant and more difficult to interpret. We have already seen how the doctrine of consent was accepted in theory, but, as far as the lay commons were concerned, it was evaded in practice by means of the general formula in the writs of collection. This was the position in the minority of Henry III and, if he had remained on good terms with the magnates, taxation of the laity through the Great Council might have become a custom of the constitution. The determining factor in the situation was the refusal by the magnates of every royal request for supply between 1237 and 1269.[4] It was natural that the king should try, by a sort of short circuit, to go behind the great tenants-in-chief to the commons, whose consent had been assumed in the earlier formula. We have definite evidence that attempts of this kind were made in 1254 and 1258. Possibly the provoking cause of the innovation was the summons to the lower clergy at the same time. In 1254 two knights were summoned from each

---

[1] *Select Charters*, pp. 459-60.   [2] *Constitutional History*, II, 207.
[3] Cf. *infra*, Chapter XIV, pp. 326-9.
[4] A thirtieth was granted in 1237, *Select Charters*, pp. 358-9 ; a twentieth was granted in 1269, Mitchell, p. 295.

shire to come before the council at Westminster ; the knights were to be elected in the shire courts " to provide, together with knights of other shires . . ., what aid they were prepared to grant in such necessity."[1] They were to come prepared to answer exactly (*precise respondere*) for their shires, and we can see here the old idea that the knights came to " bear the record " combined with something new. They represent the shires in a novel way ; they are to come with a mandate given them from below, not merely to report on local information or local opinion. The expedient was adopted at a time of great financial strain, when the king was out of the country, fighting in Gascony. It gave no promise of permanence, and the fact that the request for an aid was refused was discouraging to those who had advocated the plan. A similar experiment was probably tried in 1258, though it is uncertain if the purpose for which the knights were summoned in that year was definitely fiscal.[2] In 1254, at least, we have a clear association of the doctrine of consent with the principle of representation.

Between 1258 and 1265 an advance was made in another direction. The lesser landowners, as the community of bachelors, forced the magnates to publish the Provisions of Westminster,[3] and, partly on account of this incursion into politics, both king and magnates began to compete for their support. In 1261, 1264 and 1265 elected knights of the shire were summoned to treat with the king and in 1265 the citizens and burgesses were also summoned.[4] After Evesham there is no decisive evidence that either the fiscal precedent of the 'fifties or the political precedents of 1261-65 were followed. In 1268 twenty-seven cities and boroughs, chiefly county towns, were ordered to send six representatives to Westminster ; they were to come with letters patent under the borough seal, empowering them to act in the name of their communities. They were summoned, not merely to bear the record, but " to bring what was virtually a power of attorney " to act for the boroughs. We are not told what form this action was to take, but it is significant that in the first draft of the writ the representatives were to be not only

---

[1] *Select Charters*, pp. 365-6.
[2] Cf. Pasquet, pp. 35-7. We have writs *de expensis* for knights from five counties, who had come to the king on business of the shires at a time when the council refused the king's request for an aid (*Report on the Dignity of a Peer*, I, 461-2 ; *Tewkesbury Annals*, p. 163).
[3] *Select Charters*, pp. 390 seq.
[4] *Ibid.*, pp. 394-5, 399-400, 403-4.

the " more discreet," but the " more upright, richer and more powerful " members of the communities.[1] It seems probable that the underlying motive was fiscal, and it is possible that the tallage collected in this year was negotiated with these persons.[2] It is also possible that the *potentiores* brought from the cities and boroughs in the autumn of 1269 for the translation of the relics of Edward the Confessor were consulted about the grant of a twentieth made immediately afterwards by the Great Council.[3] However, on the evidence, we cannot say that taxation and consent had more than a casual connection at the end of Henry III's reign, so far as the laity were concerned.

It is unnecessary to discuss in detail the definitive association of consent and representation under Edward I. Mr. Edwards has recently shown how the phrase *plena potestas* in the writs of summons was slowly evolved during the central period of the reign ; [4] he has also pointed out that the significance of the demand that knights should have power to bind their counties did not altogether escape the notice of contemporaries.[5] The express demand that full powers should be granted by constituencies first appears in 1268 ; it was clearly expressed in 1283 (January), 1290, 1294 and finally in 1295.[6] The variations of wording before the complete phrase *plenam et expressam potestatem . . . ad faciendum quod tunc de communi consilio ordinabitur* was achieved show how the chancery clerks were searching for a formula to express both what the king required and what the communities were prepared to perform. On the evidence of the writs we must conclude that the conditions already laid down for political representation were fulfilled under Edward I. The Commons came to Parliament empowered to act by express mandates from their constituencies, and their action involved

---

[1] *Eng. Hist. Review*, Vol. XL, 580-5.

[2] Mitchell, *op. cit.*, p. 294 ; *supra*, p. 271.

[3] Wykes, *Annales* (*Rolls Series*), pp. 226-7 ; Mitchell, *op. cit.*, p. 295 ; McKisack, *op. cit.*, p. 4.

[4] " The *Plena Potestas* of English Parliamentary Representatives " (*Oxford Essays in Medieval History*, ed. F. M. Powicke, Oxford, 1934, pp. 141 *seq.*).

[5] Cotton, p. 254.

[6] The evolution of a like formula for the lower clergy was perhaps older, and at least simultaneous. The words *plenam et expressam potestatem* first appear in the writ of 1283 (*Select Charters*, p. 460), but it was implicit in the action of the *nuncii* in 1254 and in the proctorial letters given to the archdeacons in 1258 (*ibid.*, p. 446).

both the exercise of independent judgement and co-operation with others. They were thus qualified to contribute to that friction of minds which is the driving force of political discussion. The Parliament of estates was the public assembly of a coherent society, organised within its own frontiers and of considerable geographical extent ; in dependent partnership with the Crown, especially in connection with taxation, it had a direct share in the creation or modification of public law.

Though the influences underlying this great achievement are strangely different in their origin and history, the credit for the heavy task of co-ordination must be given to the Crown. Modern scholars are returning to the view that Edward I's governing purpose in summoning the Commons was to win their consent to taxation.[1] It is true that on certain occasions when the Commons attended no taxes were granted. Dr. Pasquet has enumerated six assemblies at which, he claims, no pecuniary demands were made, that is, in 1283 (Shrewsbury), 1298, 1300, 1302, 1305 and 1307.[2] At best, these occasions make up less than half of the total number of times (six out of sixteen) that the Commons were summoned in the reign. It seems probable that the number should be smaller still, as Dr. Pasquet does not consider whether taxes were asked for and refused. A promise of supply was certainly made in 1300, when Edward I gave a conditional assent to the *Articuli super Cartas* and in return was granted a twentieth.[3] In 1302, as Dr. Pasquet himself suggests, a request was probably refused [4] and something similar perhaps happened in 1305 when tallage was discussed.[5] We are thus left with only three occasions when there is no indication of a discussion of finance in which the Commons could have had a share. The evolution of the *premunientes* clause (*premunientes . . . plenam et sufficientem potestatem*) [6] to bring the proctors of the clergy to Parliament was frankly fiscal in intention, as there was no other reason why Edward I should require their

---

[1] See J. G. Edwards, *op. cit.* ; Carl Stephenson, *Haskins Anniversary Essays*, pp. 311-12 ; C. H. McIlwain, *Cambridge Medieval History*, VII, 678.

[2] *Origin of the House of Commons*, Eng. trans., p. 178.

[3] *Select Charters*, pp. 437-8 ; *Parl. Writs*, I, 104-5 ; Pasquet, *op. cit.*, pp. 114-16.

[4] Pasquet, *op. cit.*, p. 118.

[5] *Memoranda de Parliamento*, 1305, pp. 54-5.

[6] Cf. the clause *vocantes prius . . . plenam et sufficientem potestatem* of 1294, *Select Charters*, p. 476.

presence. Whatever his legal theories may have been, Edward's practice shows that he knew that he could not impose taxes on his subjects, outside the towns, without their consent. When he threatened and bullied the clergy, as in 1294 and 1297, he was seeking to force their consent and thereby tacitly admitting their right to withhold it, if they chose to risk the consequences. In the *Confirmatio Cartarum* he acknowledged that his subjects' goods were their own and that he could enjoy a share in them only " by the common assent of all the realm and for the common profit thereof." [1] When we distinguish between legal theory and actual practice, between what the king could do and what it was expedient or even possible for him to do, it is clear that the doctrine of consent was in fact recognised by Edward I. We may go still further and claim that his tacit acceptance of it was a main cause of the summons of the Commons, both clerk and lay, to Parliament. No phrase could express more succinctly the union of the doctrine of consent with the principle of representation than the formula of the writs of 1295 and we must set beside it that phrase, with so much history behind it, which found a place in the writs to the prelates in the same year—" quod omnes tangit, ab omnibus approbetur." [2]

[1] *Select Charters*, p. 491, c. VI.   [2] *Ibid.*, p. 480.

CHAPTER XIV

REPRESENTATION AND CONSENT IN THE MODUS

A SUMMARY examination of the history of representation and consent has shown that both were undoubtedly understood and put into practice in England before the end of the thirteenth century. It has also served to show that evidence for their widest and most various expression comes definitely from ecclesiastical sources. This is, perhaps, due only to more favourable conditions of record and it may be that, if we had evidence of debates in shire courts or in boroughs, we should find there the same lively perception of the need for corporate assent to corporate burdens. It is, on the whole, more likely that the shock of taxation of spiritualities, following hard on the teaching of the fourth Lateran Council and the new constitutional forms adopted by certain religious orders, roused the lower clergy to a peculiar condition of anxious activity. Urged by the spur of necessity, they translated their old claim to immunity into the doctrine of consent and enforced it by methods which could be used by all the king's subjects. Evidence is lacking to prove that their influence was decisive. It is impossible to be dogmatic about origins when dealing with ideas as pervasive and as useful as representation and consent. None the less, it must be admitted that the clergy seem to be the first to bring the two ideas together in a way that had general political utility. When we come to examine the details of the process, as it is recorded in the early fourteenth century, we find on the ecclesiastical side that same weight of evidence which is remarkable in the previous century. Such an examination must, for our special purpose, be conducted in close relation to the statements in the Modus. So far we have seen that its general doctrines certainly cannot be used as an argument against an early date. It will now be profitable to consider the text in more detail and to compare it with what we know independently of representation and consent in England in the first part of the fourteenth century. It will be convenient to discuss first the division of estates into orders or *gradus*, together with what evidence we have about the way in which representatives were chosen ; then particular applications of the doctrine of consent ; and, finally, the manner of consent, with special reference to unanimity and decisions of the majority.

The general doctrine of the *Modus*, with regard to representation, is clearly expressed in the famous chapter (XXVI) on the six orders (*gradus*) or estates, which concludes the document. These orders are the king, the prelates who hold by barony, the proctors of the clergy,[1] the lay magnates who hold lands to the value of an earldom or a barony, the knights of the shire and the citizens and burgesses. Stubbs long ago pointed out that the later idea of three estates does not properly describe the " subordinate distinctions " and " cross divisions " which are characteristic of the early history of Parliament,[2] but he rejected the six orders of the *Modus* as neither legal nor historical.[3] His main objection was probably grounded upon the inclusion of the king, about which he wrote in strong terms. " It is scarcely necessary to add that on no medieval theory of government could the king be regarded as an estate of the realm. He was supreme in idea if not in practice ; the head, not a limb, of the body politic ; the impersonation of the majesty of the kingdom, not one of several co-ordinate constituents."[4] Here Stubbs seems to be thinking of the estates more in relation to Parliament than as component parts of society and to make an arbitrary distinction between the head and the limbs of the body politic. In so doing he puts the monarch outside the social structure in a way that no medieval lawyer or theorist would allow. The position of the king in the *Modus* as the head, the first and last of Parliament, (*caput, principium et finis Parliamenti*), who has no peer in his order, shows him as the leader of the society of which he is also a part. This is only another expression of the common medieval

---

[1] Note the omission of proctors of chapters and lesser ecclesiastical dignitaries, as in Chapter II.
[2] *Constitutional History*, II, 202.   [3] *Ibid*. II, 174, n. 3.
[4] *Ibid*. II, 176.

idea of head and members, so elaborately worked out by John of Salisbury [1] and it was from this attitude to monarchy that the later idea of king in Parliament was derived.

The estate of the Crown alone is essential to Parliament ; " although any of the said five orders, below the king, be absent, if they have been summoned by reasonable summons of Parliament, the Parliament shall nevertheless be deemed complete " (XXVI). Provision for the absence of the king through illness was made by an elaborate arrangement for the appointment of a commission (XIII), but the author of the *Modus* did not contemplate, or venture to discuss, a state of affairs in which the king would stay away out of ill-will, as Richard II did in 1386, or would be forcibly detained by his subjects, as Edward II and Richard II were detained in 1327 and in 1399. In such circumstances no Parliament, in the strict sense of the word, could be held ; even if the king were compelled to appoint commissioners, the fact of constraint would invalidate the commission. In the last resort, however, the other estates could take action, which though not properly parliamentary, would be effective and justifiable, on the ground that they represented the community as a whole. This was clearly recognised by certain lawyers in the seventeenth century, who wrote, no doubt, with the obstinacy of Charles I in their minds. In the " Discourse of the Laws and Government of England," collected by Nathaniel Bacon from manuscript notes of Selden's, we find this passage on the deposition of Richard II :

"And albeit that by the Resignation of Richard the Second, the Parliament might seem in strict construction of Law, to be expired, together with the King's power who called them together ; yet did not that Parliament so apprehend the matter, but proceeded not onely to definitive Sentence of deposing him, but declared themselves by their Commissaries, to be the Three States, and Representative of the People of England : maintaining thereby their subsistency by the consistence of the Members together, although their Chief was for the present like a head in a Trance, till they had chosen Henry the Fourth to succeed in the Throne : by this means preventing the conceit of discontinuance in the very Bud of the Notion." [2]

[1] Cf. the reference to the *state of kyng, Rot. Parl.* III, 424, cited by Pollard, *Evolution of Parliament*, p. 69.

[2] Pt. II, p. 69, London, printed for John Starkey, 1689. The problem was obviously relevant to the authority of the Convention Parliament.

In spite of some inaccuracy in detail, we have here a substantially correct account of what happened in 1399, when the Parliament summoned in Richard II's name met *rege absente* and, therefore, was no more than an assembly of estates. As Mr. Lapsley has recently shown,[1] the distinction was clearly recognised by contemporaries ; for example, Thirnyng, the chief justice, who must have chosen his words with care, is reported to have told Richard that his abdication had been laid before " all the states and all the people " gathered at Westminster.[2] It seems certain, therefore, that the principle laid down in the *Modus* that the king was the essential element in Parliament, was a recognised part of constitutional practice.

Professor Pollard has shown in some detail that early Parliaments in England cannot properly be described as assemblies of three estates.[3] He suggests that the semi-official use of the term may have been borrowed from the French at the time of the Treaty of Troyes (1421).[4] Though he does not equate the *Gradus* of the *Modus* with estates, he points out that the classification corresponds to what we know of early parliamentary history.[5] Unlike Stubbs, who fully accepted the phrase three estates, Professor Pollard considers the growth of Parliament to be a gradual turning away from the original idea of a number of estates to the later form of two houses, representing " a meeting of council and community." [6] With this later development we are not here concerned. It is sufficient to note that the orders of the *Modus* are in full accord with what we know of the early history of Parliament. They are by no means the same as the ancient broad division of society into *oratores*, *laboratores* and *bellatores*, which Stubbs took to be the origin of the parliamentary estates [7] and we must look elsewhere for their beginning. They rested not upon literary generalisation, but on practical arrange-

---

[1] " The Parliamentary Title of Henry IV," *Eng. Hist. Review*, Vol. XLIX, pp. 423 *seq.* and 577 *seq.*

[2] " . . . per pares et proceres regni Anglie, spirituales et temporales, et ejusdem regni communitates, omnes status ejusdem regni representantes. . . ." *Rot. Parl.* III, 422*b*, from the sentence of deposition ; in his speech to Richard, Thirnyng spoke of " all the states of this londe " and of " all the states and all the poeple that was ther (Westminster) gadyrd " (*ibid.* III, 424).

[3] " The Myth of the Three Estates " (*Evolution of Parliament*, Chapter IV).

[4] *Ibid.*, p. 70.

[5] *Ibid.*, pp. 68 *seq.*   He finds in the *Modus*, not too many, but too few estates.

[6] *Ibid.*, p. 79.   [7] *Constitutional History*, II, 172, n. 1.

ments, undertaken when men met together to discuss common business, for different reasons and in different capacities. No simple lines of division will account for these practical distinctions, which arose naturally from the complexity of medieval society. Prelates were sharply divided from secular magnates by the privileges and responsibilities of their order, though they held their temporalities by the same tenure. We find them debating apart from the laity at an early date [1] and in one of the first committees of estates (1244), consisting solely of magnates, it was necessary to have the four categories of bishops, abbots, earls and barons.[2] In the same way knights were divided from citizens and burgesses and the religious orders ; the lesser ecclesiastical dignitaries and the diocesan clergy stood apart from the laity, from the prelates and from each other. Common business was not enough to break down barriers of status and of function.

Both the term *gradus* and its application to an assembly divided into orders for purposes of debate and decision are ecclesiastical and can be traced back to the reign of Edward I. The earliest reference to it in this connection occurs in a letter of the bishop of Worcester sent to archbishop Peckham in 1283 ; the bishop excused himself from attending a congregation of prelates and clergy at London and appointed two proctors to act, as the archbishop should propose and as *alii gradus* should determine.[3] There is here no indication of separate sessions. The first accounts of the way in which discussions were conducted in Convocation belong to the stormy years of 1296 and 1297. At the Parliament of Bury St. Edmunds, the royal demand for a subsidy was brought before the clergy in the chapter house of the abbey, of course with special reference to the situation created by *Clericis laicos*. For purposes of discussion the assembly divided into four *partes* or orders—the archbishop, the bishops and their proctors ; abbots, priors and other religious ; other ecclesiastical dignitaries ; and all proctors of the community of the clergy (*omnes procuratores communitatis cleri*).[4]

[1] E.g. in 1229, at a Great Council of tenants-in-chief, which may have included some of the lower clergy. The laity refused a papal demand, to which the clergy gave consent, after three days' debate (Wendover, II, 375 ; *Select Charters*, p. 323).
[2] Matt. Paris, IV, 362 ; *Select Charters*, pp. 326-7. Cf. *supra*, pp. 174-5.
[3] *Peckham's Register of Letters* (*Rolls Series*), II, Appendix, p. 753.
[4] Cotton, pp. 314-15.

The same procedure was followed in the Convocation held at St. Paul's in January 1297. The whole assembly was addressed by the archbishop and by messengers from the king ; then it divided into four *gradus*, as at Bury ; according to one chronicler, each *gradus* debated for many days and finally made answer (*quilibet gradus . . . finaliter respondebat*) that they could reach no decision.[1] Another writer styles the divisions *ordines sive turmae ;* his doubt about the correct word suggests that the practice was novel.[2] That the word *gradus* was not yet the official term is shown by the use of *partes* in a letter from archbishop Winchelsey to Edward I in which he described the proceedings in Convocation : " . . . totus clerus in IV partes dividebatur : in prima parte allocabantur episcopi presentes, et procuratores episcoporum absentium ; in secunda vero parte religiosi, tam exempti quam non exempti ; in tertia, omnes in dignitatibus constituti ; et in quarta, omnes procuratores cleri. . . ."[3] Later in the same letter, he states : " unde iidem gradus saepius intuitu et per plures dies, continuo et diligenti studio, super hoc meditantes, et per disputationes arduas cum magna angustia et labore negotiorum huiusmodi disserentes. . . ." Evidently the terminology was not yet fixed and, perhaps, the organisation of Convocation did not take definite shape before the critical debates of these years.[4] A note in Winchelsey's Register describing the Convocation of August 10, 1297 states that the royal demand for supply was debated " communement par touz les degrez du clerge,"—each order presenting their advice in writing to the archbishop.[5] *Degrez* is certainly a translation of *gradus* and the procedure prescribed is that in the *Modus*.[6] The same word was used in 1298 in a letter sent by Canterbury Convocation to the king, in which they stated that four requests would be considered " par chescoun degre du clerge, par eux, sicome costome est. . . ."[7] These words show that separation into *gradus* for purposes of debate and

[1] Cotton, pp. 317-18.
[2] *Annals of Dunstable*, pp. 404-5.   Here it is stated that the answer sent to the king under the archbishop's seal came from the *ordines seu turmas.*
[3] The letter is preserved in the chronicle of Evesham (Bodley MS. Laud 529, f. 78) ; part of the letter is printed by Wake, *op. cit.*, Appendix, pp. 23-4.
[4] But cf. a remark of Cotton's (p. 249) that royal messengers were sent in 1294 to the place where the clerical proctors meet.
[5] *Register*, pp. 189-90.   [6] XVII.   Cf. *supra*, p. 235.
[7] *Winchelsey's Register* (Canterbury), p. 260.

decision was by 1298 regarded as an established practice. We know from many sources that it continued during the first half of the fourteenth century. For example, the revocation of the judgement on the Despensers was sanctioned by the prelates and *omnes gradus ceteros cleri*[1] (December 1, 1321). The arrangement, according to the latest authority,[2] was fairly soon simplified in the Canterbury Convention by a division between the prelates and the rest, that is, into two houses only. However, we find religious and diocesan proctors debating apart from each other as late as 1370[3] and it is possible that the general language of the records may conceal a permanent subdivision of the lower house. We know also that the separation of estates survived, to some extent at least, in the northern province well into the fifteenth century.[4]

The parallel between Convocation and the Parliament of the *Modus* is unmistakable. The four orders of the clergy first met together to hear their archbishop and, sometimes, a charge delivered by royal messengers ; then they separated, *gradus* by *gradus*, to discuss and to reach a decision on the matter in hand ; finally, they delivered their answers in writing to the archbishop in the general assembly. In the *Modus* each *gradus* withdrew by itself (*quilibet gradus adeat per se*) and, after due consideration, reported in writing their answers and advice (XVII).[5] Probably this is as near as we can come to a description of procedure in the first Parliaments of estates.[6] It is evident that the several parts were stronger than the whole and that there was danger that the strength of each local or functional *communitas* would act as a centrifugal force, flying off from the common centre. To bring representatives together was not enough. As an acute observer of modern society has put it, " the theory of national harmony issuing from mere mechanical interplay of

[1] Mortival's Register (Salisbury MS.), II, f. 129.

[2] I. J. Churchill, *Canterbury Administration*, Vol. I, Part II, Chapter VIII, Section V.

[3] Cf. *supra*, Chapter III, p. 28.

[4] E.g. the separation of estates (*seorsim se diverterent*) in York Convocation, August 1426 (*Records of the Northern Convocation*, Surtees Soc., pp. 158-9).

[5] Cf. a description of the same procedure in XXIV.

[6] Separate discussion of taxation by burgesses is explicitly recorded at the Parliament of 1306 (Pasquet, *op. cit.*, pp. 234-6). This is not, as Pasquet (pp. 152-3) seems to argue, a mark of burgess inferiority, but the normal procedure of the period.

private activities is an impossible one. . . ." [1] However, in medieval society at least, no rigid division of private groups along lines of class or function could be maintained. Pressure driving men together was steadily exerted by the poverty and small size of the population, by conditions of ownership and by the inheritance of a common ideal of unity, derived alike from Christianity and from the tribalism of primitive peoples. The monarch represented his kingdom as a whole and at the coronation his vows were undertaken on behalf of all his subjects. Below him men were grouped according to the diversities of their function, but they were also united by common loyalty to him and by the general burden of social responsibility. That the prevailing idea of a highly complex society, simplified for purposes of action, was understood by all might be proved by many citations from literature, but perhaps a more convincing example may be found in the game of chess. At the end of the thirteenth century reading and writing were still mainly the business of clerks, but chess was the common pastime of the laity.[2] The pieces and their moves expressed concretely a struggle between two groups of men, each defending their king from the attacks of the other, by means of highly specialised and formalised action within the group.[3] The hierarchy of pawns, knights, castles, bishops, queen and king may be taken as symbolic of the living hierarchy of orders expressed in the *gradus* of the *Modus*. Without their help, at the same time specialised and co-ordinate, anarchy must reign.

> " Take but degree away, untune that string,
> And, hark ! what discord follows ; each thing meets
> In mere oppugnancy ; the bounded waters
> Should lift their bosoms higher than the shores,
> And make a sop of all this solid globe :
> Strength should be lord of imbecility,
> And the rude son should strike his father dead :
> Force should be right ; or rather, right and wrong—
> Between whose endless jar justice resides—
> Should lose their names, and so should justice too.

[1] W. McDougall, *The American Nation*, p. 39.
[2] See H. J. R. Murray, *History of Chess*, Oxford, 1913, Part II, Chapter II.
[3] Cf. the exclamation put into the mouth of David II at Neville's Cross— " even in chess a king cannot be taken."

Then every thing includes itself in power,
Power into will, will into appetite :
And appetite, a universal wolf,
So doubly seconded with will and power,
Must make perforce a universal prey,
And last eat up itself . . .
This chaos, when degree is suffocate,
Follows the choking.
And this neglection of degree it is
That by a pace goes backward, with a purpose
It hath to climb. . . ." [1]

The same idea was tersely expressed in a rebuke administered to the earl of Devon by bishop Grandisson in 1335 : " May it please God, sire, that each man maintains himself in his own estate and concerns himself with that which belongs to it. It ought to be enough for you to be a knight and an earl, and to leave to others to be kings and bishops." [2]

The degrees or orders of the *Modus* express a deeply rooted belief in unity through diversity, though not in the aristocratic form of a pyramid, with a declension of right and an increase of burdens from top to bottom. It seems deliberately assumed that the principle of representation is a counter-balance to the privilege of wealth and rank. The magnates come to Parliament for themselves (*per se*), unlike the Commons, both clerk and lay, who come for their communities. Special care is taken to be explicit about the mandate or *plena potestas* of elected lay representatives ; they shall come as *attornati* with sealed letters to authenticate their actions on behalf of their constituents (IV).[3] The representation of the diocesan clergy is as carefully defined ; their proctors shall come with sealed warrants, prepared to act as those who had elected them would do, if present in person (II). A peculiarity in the account of proctorial elections draws attention to a remarkable system of choice worked out by the clergy, which deserves scrutiny, as an example of their strong resolve to give full expression to local opinion.

---

[1] *Troilus and Cressida*, Act I, Sc. III.
[2] *Grandisson's Register* (Exeter), I, p. 290. It is worth noting that the bishop had no doubt that kings had their estate.
[3] The general conditions laid down for the barons of the Cinque Ports applied also to the knights, citizens and burgesses.

Chapter II of the *Modus* states that bishops and other persons in authority shall cause to be elected in each deanery and archdeaconry in England, by the deaneries and archdeaconries themselves, two proctors from their archdeaconries (*de proprio archidiaconatu*). In the chapter on the opening of Parliament (IX) it is stated that bishops shall be fined 100 marks for every archdeaconry that has not sent proctors punctually to Parliament. It seems plain that, in the author's opinion, proctors came or ought to come to Parliament, not from the diocese, but from the smaller unit of the archdeaconry. There is no warrant for direct representation of archdeaconries in royal or archiepiscopal writs. The obvious explanation is either that he was thinking of the practice in the northern province, or that he wished to increase the representation of the diocesan clergy to balance the exclusion of deans, archdeacons and proctors of chapters. However, as we have already seen,[1] the author was more concerned with the form of summons than with the numerical representation of the clergy. Writing with his head full of the controversy over the *venire faciatis* writ, he gave a muddled and careless summary of the procedure and of the constituencies by which proctors should be elected. His meaning, especially his emphasis on deaneries and archdeaconries, cannot be understood without an examination of the form of election actually followed.

The form of election adopted by the clergy was naturally based upon the territorial divisions of the diocese. We do not know what units chose the *nuncii* of the lower clergy in 1254,[2] but it is certain that the proctors of 1256 were the representatives not of dioceses, but of archdeaconries.[3] The lower unit of the rural deanery was probably brought into play from the outset, as it was in normal use for all business concerning the lower clergy, especially with regard to taxation.[4] The first clear indication of the method of election comes from the diocese of Coventry and Lichfield in 1257. Alexander IV had granted to Henry III certain heavy taxes to be levied on the clergy and it

---

[1] *Supra*, pp. 151-2.   [2] *Supra*, p. 309.

[3] Matt. Paris, *Additamenta*, pp. 314-15.

[4] We may take as an example of another kind of use the announcement of Grosseteste in 1238 that he proposed to preach to all his clergy, deanery by deanery, since he had not time to visit each parish. *Epistolae* (Rolls Series), p. 146.

was proposed at a council in London that they should compound by payment of 52,000 marks.[1] It was agreed that preiates, religious, deans and archdeacons should treat with their chapters and clergy and return to London to give a full answer, or to compound *per procuratores instructos*.[2] At this assembly (April 22, 1257) conditions were laid down by the clergy which were so displeasing to the king that a second Convocation was summoned for the following August. The Burton annalist has preserved a letter from the official of the archdeacon of Stafford to the rural dean of Tamworth and Tutbury, transmitting the archbishop's mandate ; in it, *inter alios*, the archdeacons of the diocese were summoned to Convocation, bearing letters of authorisation from the clergy subject to them (*ex parte clericorum qui subsunt eisdem*).[3] The dean was ordered to see that the mandate was executed in his district, that is, he was to exact from the clergy the authorisation for their archdeacon. The Burton letter makes it probable that the deans and chapters consulted earlier in the year were the rural deans and sessions or chapters of their clergy, which met at regular intervals.[4] Out of this plan, perhaps used for the first time in 1257, the system of proctorial elections seems to have developed.

The fullest illustrations of the system come from the diocese of Lincoln. Among the muniments of the Dean and Chapter of the cathedral are mandates relating to the Parliament of 1300 (March 6), issued by the official of the diocese, *sede vacante*, to the archdeacons of Bedford and Northampton.[5] Each archdeacon was commanded to cite the clergy subject to him to appear on Wednesday, February 23, at Northampton, by one suitable proctor, with sufficient power to elect two proctors to go to Parliament for the clergy of the diocese.[6] Details of the procedure

---

[1] W. E. Lunt, *Consent of the English Lower Clergy*, p. 148.
[2] Burton, p. 389.   [3] *Ibid.*, pp. 401-2.
[4] Cf. William Dansey, *Horae Decanicae Rurales*, Vol. II, Part V, *The Capitular Functions of Deans Rural.*
[5] Muniment Room of the Dean and Chapter of Lincoln, Dii. 59/1/3 & 5. My thanks are due to Canon C. W. Foster for drawing my attention to these documents and for providing me with transcripts.
[6] " . . . citent subditum sibi clerum, quod die mercurii in prima septimana quadragesime apud (Northampton' per) unum compareat procuratorem ydoneum qui potestatem habeat sufficientem eligendi et constituendi duos procuratores pro clero (dioces' Linc' ad) parliamentum predictum London' destinandos ad faciendum dicto die et consenciendum hiis que de communi

are made clearer by certain writs, issued for the Convocation held at Lincoln in January 1323, and preserved in a register of Peterborough. The official of the archdeacon of Northampton ordered the rural deans of his archdeaconry to summon the proctors of their deaneries to come to Northampton to elect a proctor to send to Stamford ; the bishop in turn enjoined his archdeacons to cause one proctor from each archdeaconry to come to Stamford to elect two proctors to represent the diocese in Convocation.[1]

In other dioceses evidence for primary election in the rural deaneries is lacking though the share of the archdeaconries is well established.[2] The Salisbury registers from 1305 onwards contain a series of episcopal letters to the four archdeacons, ordering each to cause one, or sometimes one or two, proctors to be elected to meet with the rest at Salisbury to choose two proctors for Parliament or Convocation.[3] Similar evidence appears in the registers of Winchester, Worcester, London,[4] and (later) Bath and Wells[5] and Durham.[6] Here variations occur of some significance. In the diocese of Winchester the two archdeaconries of Surrey and Winchester each elected one

consilio pro (utilitate regni) et ecclesie ordinabitur seu providebitur tunc ibidem." The words in brackets are supplied from the second mandate. The returns state that the archdeaconry of Bedford elected John de Clare and that of Northampton Henry de Stok', rector of Ravensthorp.

[1] Cotton MS. Vespasian E, XXI, ff. 50ᵛ-51ᵛ and 100ᵛ-101. Cf. like orders for the election of proctors for a Convocation at St. Paul's in 1334, *ibid.*, ff. 100-101ᵛ.

[2] The following letter, written by the bishop of Lichfield to the archbishop of Canterbury on April 4, 1685, may be compared as a statement of later procedure :—

" May it please yr. Grace,
    " In the Mandate I receeved for electing proctors for the ensuing Convocation, it is required, that two be returned out of the Archdeaconry of Coventry. Now I understand it is the custom to chuse two out of every Archdeaconry in the Diocese, and that the persons so chosen are to meet at the Bishops Consistory in the Cathedral, and to chuse two of themselves, who are to be returned for the whole Diocese. I humbly acquaint your Grace herewith, desiring to know if your Grace will please to have us to continue this practice and custom. . . ." (Bodley, MS. Tanner 31, f. 22.)

[3] See the registers of Simon de Gandavo and of Mortival, *passim.* Between 1300 and 1327 there are over twenty references to preliminary elections in the archdeaconries, either for Parliament or for Convocation.

[4] *Register of Baldock*, ed. R. C. Fowler (Canterbury and York Soc., 1911), p. 41, Carlisle Parl., January, 1307.

[5] *Register of Ralph of Shrewsbury*, ed. T. S. Holmes, *Somerset Rec. Soc.*, p. 649, Parl., February 1351 ; p. 746, Parl., 1354 ; pp. 656-7, Convoc., 1351.

[6] *Northern Convocations*, pp. 119 *seq.*, Convocation, York, 1396.

proctor to go to Parliament without any further choice.[1] This plan may have been followed in other dioceses where there were only two archdeaconries, as, for example, Worcester[2] and Chichester. The valuable list of proctors present at the Parliament of Carlisle (1307) shows that eleven archdeaconries were directly represented, some coming from dioceses with more than two archdeaconries ; three archdeaconries (Surrey, Winchester and Salop) sent two proctors each.[3] On the other hand, some archdeaconries were apparently not represented at all ; for example, two proctors from Salop were the only delegates from the diocese of Hereford.[4] The conclusion to be drawn from this evidence is that, at least at first, the order to return two proctors from each diocese was not taken literally, probably because small importance was attached to mere numbers.[5] Emphasis fell mainly on representation and the *plena potestas ;* the question of numbers was perhaps determined only by consideration of personal merit and the payment of expenses.[6] The description in the *Modus* suggests that the rural deaneries were regarded as the primary units of election and that great weight was attached to the choice of proctors locally. The direct representation of archdeaconries laid down in the text was probably intended to standardise a practice sometimes actually followed. It is, perhaps, a sign of an entirely distinct secular development that no trace of primary elections has been found in the shires, though the unit of the hundred might have been used for the purpose.

How closely the idea of representation in the *Modus* was bound up with that of orders or estates may be seen by the composition of parliamentary committees. The committee of

---

[1] Register of Woodlock (Winchester MS.), ff. 49-9ᵛ for Parl. of Carlisle, 1307 ; ff. 198-8ᵛ for Parl. Lincoln, 1316.

[2] Worcester *Sede vacante* Register, ed. J. W. W. Bund, p. 74, for Convocation of April, 1302. Cf. *ibid.*, p. 266, for citation to archdeaconry of Worcester only to elect proctors for *Parl.*, 1339 ; Gloucester may have been omitted in error.

[3] *Rot. Parl.* I, 188-91. The archdeaconries are—Chichester, Surrey (2), Winchester (2), Gloucester, Worcester, Lewin' [Lewes, Chichester dioc.], Salop (2) ; Suffolk and Sudbury and Norfolk and Norwich sent a proctor from each pair.

[4] Cf. the instruction of the bishop of Salisbury (*Register of Sim. de Gandavo*, p. 96) to the archdeacon of Wilts, and another unnamed to elect one proctor for two to save expense (Convocation of June 1302).

[5] Cf. *infra*, p. 343.

[6] Cf. the representation of the clergy of Carlisle diocese by four proctors at the Parliament of Carlisle, 1307 (*Rot. Parl.* I, 191).

twenty-five (XVII) consisted of two bishops and three proctors, two earls and three barons, five knights, five citizens and five burgesses ; the less important committee appointed to visit the king, if he stayed away from Parliament owing to illness (XIII), was made up of two bishops, two earls, two barons, two knights, two citizens, and two burgesses. The composition of these bodies shows plainly where the author thought the weight of authority ought to lie ; in the first the Commons have a majority of eleven and in the second they are equal with the magnates. This prejudice in favour of the Commons is carried still further in the chapter *de auxiliis regis* (XXIII), where it is laid down that the king may hold a Parliament with his Commons and without the magnates, provided that they have been duly summoned. Consideration of this remarkable statement brings us to scrutiny of the doctrine of consent, as it is set out in the *Modus*.

The main passage is that in Chapter XXIII where it is explicitly claimed that all things which ought to be affirmed or annulled, granted or denied, or done by Parliament ought to be done by the three estates of the commons. The chapter *de casibus et iudiciis difficilibus* (XVII) contains a reference to consent of a more general kind ; the decisions of the committee of twenty-five are subject to royal assent in a way which is quite alien to the treatment of taxation in the section *de auxiliis regis*. It seems that for general legislation or in the settlement of disputes, the king and council may exercise an authority which is denied in matters relating to supply. This is in harmony with the enacting power which the king, beyond question, enjoyed and may be compared with the doctrine laid down in the statute of York.[1] Aids are distinguished from legislation and they require the formal written consent of the estates, given in full Parliament. It is proper [2] that all members (*pares*) of Parliament should consent, but knights or proctors have greater weight in assent or denial than an earl or a bishop. Hence the author deduces that magnates are not essential to Parliament and for this he invents an historical explanation, that king and Parliament go back to a time when there were no distinctions of persons.

---

[1] Cf. *supra*, Chapter VIII, especially pp. 171-2.
[2] To translate *oportet* by *needful*, as Hardy does (*Modus*, p. 40), is to suggest confusion. The consent of all was *fitting* or *proper*, but only that of the Commons was essential.

The statement about primitive Parliaments has, of course, no historical foundation, nor is it even based upon current legends, such as appear in the Brut chronicle. It represents a deduction from the facts, as the author had observed them, and is obviously an attempt to explain the pre-eminence of the Commons in matters of supply. A later date than the first quarter of the fourteenth century is usually given to this pre-eminence. It was not until 1395 that grants of money were made expressly by the Commons, with the advice and assent of the Lords,[1] though it is generally admitted that the decisive share of the Commons was established under Edward III.[2]   However, if the history of consent, already outlined, be remembered, it becomes clear that the superiority of the Commons in matters relating to taxation was a logical inference from the long line of development in the thirteenth century. The magnates, both directly and indirectly, allowed the gracious aid, granted by tenants-in-chief, to be transformed into a tax on the whole community for which the consent of representatives was required. Into this general taxation the tallage paid by the boroughs was slowly merged. The prelates, for different reasons, though with a like result, had failed to establish a right to consent on behalf of the lower clergy. It followed, therefore, that those by whom consent was given had, in fact, superiority, though the full significance of this was for long concealed by the forms and traditions of an aristocratic society. The author of the *Modus* nowhere shows himself so acute and so far-seeing as in this chapter on taxation. He penetrates behind the pride and outward dignity of kings, barons and princes of the Church and half reveals the ultimate sovereignty of the Commons who, as the representatives controlling supply, are paramount in Parliament. The full force of the conclusion was not yet apparent, as parliamentary grants were still not deemed to be the main source of revenue : the prevailing belief in a hierarchy of orders or estates no doubt helped to cloud the issue. The author of the *Modus* was no theorist. He was plainly a man experienced in the business of government and less concerned with appearances than with the source and springs of power. It might, however, be argued

---

[1] *Rot. Parl.* III, 330*b*.   Cf. *ibid.* III, 611*b*, for a definite assertion of the principle under Henry IV.
[2] For example, Stubbs, *Constitutional History*, III, 270.

that he saw things, not as they were, but as they were becoming and that no such superiority of the Commons was claimed or understood in the early fourteenth century. It is, therefore, necessary to consider the position in the light of contemporary evidence.

Once more we find that the explicit evidence comes from ecclesiastical records. The lay commons under Edward II were not vocal, or, at least, we can seldom hear their voices. Grants of supply are recorded and from time to time petitions were presented, in the name of the commonalty or from the people of the realm, which sometimes may represent the work of the lay commons in Parliament.[1] A few references, like the petition of St. Albans against disfranchisement [2] (1315) and Matthew de Crouthorn's complaint that the sheriff of Devon had refused to return him, though he was duly elected by the shire (1318),[3] suggest that representation in Parliament was more highly valued than some scholars suppose. Yet, on the whole, it must be admitted that the opinions and even the acts of knights and burgesses remain in shadow throughout the reign. For the clergy, on the other hand, we have direct, though fragmentary, evidence in the episcopal registers, which, if eked out by the comments of chroniclers, amounts to something substantial. A summary examination of it will serve to illustrate the attitude of the ecclesiastical orders to the doctrine of consent.

Edward II demanded subsidies from the clergy on eight distinct occasions ; two were refused altogether [4] and six were granted, usually after long delay.[5] The first request (1307) seems the only one to which consent was promptly given. The pretext for delay was nearly always some defect in the form of summons or in the returns.[6] In addition to grants made in Parliament or in Convocation, eight tenths were imposed on the clergy by the Pope [7] and there were also requests (1310 and 1317) for the acceleration of these taxes. No consent was necessary for papal tenths, but the clergy were able to bargain on the

---

[1] On these petitions see G. Lapsley, " Knights of the Shire in the Parliaments of Edward II " (*Eng. Hist. Review*, Vol. XXXIV, pp. 168 *seq.*).

[2] *Rot. Parl.* I, 327*b*. The immediate object of the town was probably to assert its independence of the abbey. Cf. Pasquet, *op. cit.*, pp. 162-5.

[3] Cole, *Documents*, p. 16.   [4] In 1316 and in 1323.

[5] 1307, 1311, 1313, 1314, 1315, 1321-22.

[6] *Supra*, Chapter VII, pp. 128 *seq.*   [7] 1309, 1317 and 1319.

matter of acceleration. Archbishop Winchelsey made this clear in his writs summoning Convocation to discuss the acceleration proposed in 1310 ;[1] the request was granted on condition that the last term for collection was not advanced and that the collectors were men appointed by the Pope.[2] At the same time, the idea that the Pope alone could levy a tax on spiritualities had gone for ever and the Scottish war served as an unanswerable argument to coerce the clergy. The position, therefore, was that papal consent was no longer necessary for grants made *ad commune negotium*. This was explicitly stated by the prelates when the clergy refused to vote supply in 1316 ; apostolic sanction was not required, since the king, fighting within his own frontiers for the common advantage, ought to be helped by the community.[3] On the other hand, papal authority could be called in to enforce a grant which the clergy had already refused, as was done in 1319.[4] Thus the clergy were pierced by the two swords of ecclesiastical and secular dominion [5] and they had every incentive to maintain their right of consent.

All accounts of the clergy in Parliament and Convocation agree that for purposes of secular taxation the consent of proctors was essential. This is plainly stated in the writs of summons issued by the archbishops ; for example, in 1313 the archbishop of York summoned his Convocation to consider a grant of four pence in the mark for the Scottish war, because " without the convocation of prelates and clergy . . . business of this kind can by no means be despatched." [6] The same principle was asserted by the clergy in the Canterbury Convocation of January 1315.[7] At the Parliament of York (May 1322), though ten bishops were

---

[1] " . . . attendentes quod totum clerum nostre Provincie supplicacio dicta tangit, quodque id nequivimus concedere prout nec decuit per nos ipsos sine cleri nostre Provincie voluntate, propterea clerum nostre provincie, de consilio fratrum unanimi, decrevimus convocandum " (*Stapeldon's Register* (Exeter), p. 120).

[2] *Ibid.*, pp. 120-1. [3] *Vita Edwardi II*, p. 225.

[4] *Annales Paulini*, p. 286.

[5] Wilkins, II, p. 495. The metaphor was used by the prior of Christ Church, Canterbury, in a protest (1319) directed against the double collection of taxes from monks both on lay and on ecclesiastical subsidies.

[6] *Durham Register* (*Rolls Series*), I, 415.

[7] " Let it be ordained by the prelates and the clergy, *quorum approbacio est necessaria quod subsidium concedendum non in usus extraordinarios. . . .*" (*Swinfield's Register* (Hereford), ed. W. W. Capes (Canterbury and York Society, 1909), pp. 497-8).

present and others had sent sufficient excuse, the proctors refused to consent to a grant, since many of them were absent and could not be deemed contumacious because of the defect in the method of summons.[1] It was, therefore, necessary to summon the Canterbury Convocation in the following month.[2] On this occasion bishop Mortival of Salisbury seems to have secured the separate consent of his diocese ; he wrote to the archbishop that he had assembled each *gradus* of his clergy and that all except a few, whose names he forwarded, had agreed to the subsidy.[3] In 1323 the clergy of Canterbury gave a point-blank denial to the king's request for supply, refusing to yield to the threats and flattery of judges and magnates, sent as royal messengers.[4] The general attitude of the lower clergy throughout the reign was summed up in a letter from the bishop of Salisbury to Edward II, refusing a loan of grain for the Scottish war : " . . . we cannot and dare not make a loan of this kind without the assent of our sovereigns (*suvereins*) and without the assent of those under us (*nos subjetz*), who are blaming us greatly, as they have done in the past. They complain bitterly of prelates and, in reproof of them, array their grievances, because they have made grants, though they should not do, save for themselves alone, which may afterwards be a precedent for heavy demands on those under them." [5]

This letter, in which the bishop drew attention to the bitter discontent of the lower clergy, also serves to indicate another danger to which they were exposed. There is evidence that the bishops were often on the side of authority in the struggles against taxation. No doubt they were both more sensitive to pressure from the Crown and more willing to admit the need for aids to defray the expenses of war. Also, they had other ways of recouping themselves ; for example, in public service, and they must seldom have felt the pinch of taxation in the same personal way as their clergy. The evidence from the debates on supply points

---

[1] *Register of Rigaud de Asserio*, Winchester (*Hants Record Soc.*), pp. 489-90. Cf. *supra*, p. 144.

[2] June 9, 1322, Mortival's Register (Salisbury MS.), Liber II, f. 135ᵛ.

[3] *Ibid.*, f. 135ᵛ-136.ᵛ Cf. a similar return made by bishop Burghersh of Lincoln, *Register*, f. 310-311.

[4] Convocation at Lincoln, January 1323. Wilkins, II, 517 ; *Anglia Sacra, I*, 362 ; Peterborough Cartulary (Cotton MS. Vespasian E. 21, ff. 50-51).

[5] *Register of Sim. de Gandavo* (Salisbury), p. 394, c. July 1310.

in the same direction ; the bishops, following the lead of archbishop Reynolds, acquiesced in the king's demands and the protests, delays and conditions were nearly always *ex parte cleri*. Resistance by the bishops was connected with matters of summons rather than with questions of taxation. Though the need for the consent of the lower clergy was never denied, a tendency to take it for granted may be detected. Taxes which had been referred in Parliament to a later Convocation are sometimes described as granted in that Parliament. The Salisbury Register refers to the tenth of 1316 as granted by the Parliament of Lincoln, though it was actually made by Convocation in the following autumn ;[1] Cobham's Register (Worcester) has a similar reference to the tax of five pence in the mark, as authorised by the Parliament of York (May 1322),[2] though it was granted either in diocesan assemblies or by the convocation at St. Paul's. A chronicler, who is usually trustworthy, also states that the clergy granted five pence in the mark in the Parliament of York in 1322.[3] This evidence suggests that the bishops were inclined to assume that the consent of the clergy would be given, as indeed it generally was in the long run. It may be that the emphatic statements in the *Modus* were directed against this assumption as much as against the totally unauthorised opinion that the bishops could answer for their clergy altogether.

The author of the *Modus* did not merely express the doctrine of consent ; he also gave an indistinct indication of how it should be put into action. Twice he referred explicitly to the consent of the *maior pars*, but when his statements are looked at carefully a certain confusion of thought becomes evident, suggesting that he was not thinking of the decision of the majority as merely a matter of counting heads. Decisions in difficult cases (XVII) shall be taken in accordance with sound and wise counsel and with the agreement of the majority (*maior pars*) of Parliament ; if all, or at least the majority cannot agree (*concordare*), that is can reach no decision, then the committee of twenty-five shall be set up. Here the majority are associated with sound and wise counsel (*melius et sanius consilium*) ; if the greater number do not follow in the right way we may suppose that their decision

---

[1] Mortival's Register (Salisbury MS.), Liber I, f. 137ᵛ.

[2] *Cobham's Register* (Worcester), p. 125. Cf. *supra*, p. 144. Other more ambiguous references may refer to taxes granted at an earlier date and still uncollected. [3] *Annales Paulini*, p. 303.

is not binding. The only escape from the deadlock is the committee of twenty-five, which, by reducing itself to one, will in the end arrive at unanimity, since one man cannot disagree with himself.[1] To achieve unanimity is the whole purpose of this committee which diminishes itself, thus showing plainly that the decision of the majority was deemed unsatisfactory. Further light is thrown on the author's attitude by his remarks on the superiority of the Commons in Chapter XXIII. " Two knights who come to Parliament for their shire have a greater voice (*maiorem vocem*) in Parliament in agreeing or dissenting than an earl of England, who is greater than they are, and in like manner the proctors of the clergy of a single diocese have a greater voice in Parliament, if they all agree, than the bishop himself. . . ." *Maior vox* certainly seems to imply a majority, but it is not, in fact, a majority of heads, but a superiority of orders ; within the superior orders, unanimity is essential (*si omnes sint concordes*), if their will is to prevail. The underlying idea seems to be that elected agents, who represent *totam communitatem Anglie*, must reach a unanimous decision, unlike the magnates who come to Parliament each for himself and for no other. Such an idea obviously belongs to a particular stage in political development ; to set it in its place we must consider the process by which the majority verdict began to separate itself from the older notion of unanimity.

It is not hard to see why a high value has always been set on the idea of an unanimous judgement, as it not only carries with it the compulsion of authority, but is the outward sign of that permanent harmony which ought to be the basis of all united action. In a society made up of many orders, the best conditions are achieved when the members of each order are in full agreement with each other and when all orders together co-operate to reach a common end for the common good. This is the ideal of action in the *Modus*, a familiar medieval ideal, which at a later date was sometimes compared to the harmonious movement of the spheres.[2] We have already seen how it found

---

[1] " . . . que cum se ipsa discordare non potest . . ." *Numerus maior* in the preceding phrase refers, not to a majority, but to the committee before it was reduced to one.

[2] E.g. Hooker, *Ecclesiastical Polity*, I, iii, 3 (*Works*, Oxford, ed. 1868, I, p. 155), and Du Bartas, *Days and Weeks*, translated by J. Sylvester (ed. 1641), pp. 35-6. My thanks are due to Miss M. Lascelles for calling my attention to these references.

expression in the doctrine of consent or *concordia* in its general sense and how the same notion in other forms may be found in the ancient world.[1] In practice, full unanimity was impossible and it was necessary either to assume it or else to accept the judgement of the majority as a working compromise. The Greeks used the compromise for judicial decisions—Socrates was condemned by a verdict of a majority—and normally in politics, though in that sphere the sentiment, " ours is the city," often led to the expulsion of leading members of a minority.[2] Judgement by the majority appears in Roman public law[3] and thus influenced ecclesiastical development. How the Church tried to secure both the great moral advantage of ünanimity and the practical advantage of a majority decision is worth a brief examination, as the attempt stamped its mark deeply on medieval theory.

The majority decision appears in the version of the rule of St. Benedict set out in the code of Justinian[4] (530). There it is stated that the election of an abbot should be by all the monks or by a majority of them ; the senior monk ought not to succeed automatically. Commenting on this, Dom Chapman wrote— " the source of this ' addition ' to the imperial laws . . . might be common sense, or it might be the rule of St. Benedict. I cannot think of any third view." [5] The fact that later versions depart from the plan of a majority decision suggests that it had its origin in legal rather than Benedictine practice. Five years later (535), the plan of electing the senior monk was reverted to,[6] but this was quickly found unsatisfactory. In little more than a decade (546), it was definitively stated that the abbot should be elected by *omnes monachi (vel) melioris opinionis existentes*.[7] " The Code had wrongly understood the manner of election, as being by unanimity or the majority of votes : for the Rule says ' quem sive omnis concors

---

[1] *Supra*, Chapter XII, p. 251.

[2] Cf. the *fuorusciti* of the Italian city states.

[3] Both the Senate and the *Comitia* made use of the majority vote. Senators divided to vote, walking to opposite sides of the house ; the majority of the *Comitia* was not reckoned by heads, as the final vote was by groups (*curiae, centuriae or tribus*), not equal in size, though the vote of each order depended on a majority decision within it. See W. Ramsay and R. Lanciani, *Roman Antiquities*, 15th ed., 1894, pp. 137-8, 261.

[4] *Code*, Book I, III, 46 (47) ; cited by Dom John Chapman, *St. Benedict and the Sixth Century*, 1929, pp. 59-60.

[5] *Ibid.*, p. 60.　　　　　[6] *Novella*, V, cap. 9, cited *ibid.*, p. 62.

[7] *Ibid.* CXXIII, cap. 34, cited *ibid.*

congregatio . . . sive etiam pars, quamvis parva, congregationis saniore consilio elegerit ' . . ." [1] The Benedictine rejection of the decision of the majority for that of the *sanior pars* was in fact a reversion to the idea of unanimity, or as near to it as practical considerations would allow. It was probably assumed that the will of the *sanior pars* would in the end be adopted by all ; failing agreement, appeal to outside authority would be necessary, and the wish to avoid this must often have helped to bring about a unanimous decision. The precise form of the Benedictine election was not fixed until the Lateran Council of 1215. Before that date, the immense value of a majority decision, as a lever to action, had acquired both special sanction and wide publicity by its adoption for papal elections in 1178.

Benedictine practice was followed fairly closely in monastic and capitular elections, the variants merely emphasising the dominant demand for unanimity. The strength of the demand may be illustrated from the rule of Grandmont (*c.* 1150). The election of the Grand Prior was entrusted to twelve representatives, six clerks and six lay brothers, chosen in the general chapter.[2] " If indeed some among the twelve dissent about the election, the decision shall rest with the *maior pars*, which is understood to be the wiser and more faithful party, anxious for nothing but the common good. The dissentients shall be turned out of the council and even out of the convent, so that all shall be done without them. From the same convent and in the same proportion of clerks and lay brothers, as many shall be added to the council as were ejected, in order that twelve persons shall always make the election." [3] Here the practical use of the majority was combined in a striking way with the principle of unanimous consent.

We may compare with the rule of Grandmont examples of the same combination, practically applied, as we find it in two elections at York in the early fourteenth century.[4] In 1310 the chapter of York met to elect a new dean, and it was decided to proceed by way of scrutiny. Three canons were appointed to act as scrutineers, with power to examine secretly the votes of all and to publish the result. The votes were examined in the chapter

[1] Chapman, *op. cit.*, pp. 62-3.   [2] Cf. *supra*, p. 301.
[3] Migne, *Patrologia*, Vol. CCIV ; *Regula S. Stephani*, cap. 60, p. 1160.
[4] Greenfield's Register (Surtees Society), Vol. I, nos. 125, 165.

house ; the scrutineers voted first, probably in order that they should not have casting votes. It was announced that votes had been cast for three persons, thirteen for Robert of Pickering, seven for his brother William, and two for John of Markenfeld. William's supporters then agreed to transfer their votes to Robert, Markenfeld was tacitly dropped and Robert was unanimously elected. The electoral act was formally carried out by one person, who by the mandate of all announced that the canons had unanimously consented to the choice of Robert and, therefore, he solemnly elected him. The archbishop was asked to confirm the election and, as a sign of unanimity, the electoral decree was sealed by the chapter and by each member of it. The account of a second election in 1312 adds a few new details. All the votes but one were cast for the same person. His election was proposed on the grounds of the majority of votes and the candidate's zeal and merit ; the other candidate withdrew with the consent of his proposer ; the electoral act was then performed by one of the canons—" vice tocius capituli et mea ex potestate michi concessa." [1] The whole procedure shows that the majority decision was no more than a necessary preliminary to an unanimous election.

It was obviously very difficult for ecclesiastics to escape from the tradition that *melior et sanior pars* ought not to be automatically equated with *maior pars*. In all grave matters men were reluctant to reduce their decisions to a problem in arithmetic and the use of a system of representation served only to increase their uneasiness. In 1226 the canons of Salisbury instructed the proctors elected to attend Langton's council, to enquire what ought to be done if some canons opposed what a majority in the chapter had decided.[2] The Dominicans faced the issue with characteristic ingenuity and common sense. The general chapter (1259) ruled that the *socius* of a convent could not legally represent his house, unless half of the *fratres* had voted for him.[3] The intention was plainly to set a limit to split votes and party intrigue and to establish the principle that the representative must be the choice of more than a fraction of the community. In the effort to secure this they

---

[1] Greenfield's Register, I, p. 77.
[2] " . . . inquiratur ab aliis quid faciendum sit si aliqui canonicorum singulariter contradixerint his quae a majore parte capituli provisa fuerint " (*Register of St. Osmund*, II, 64).
[3] G. R. Galbraith, *Constitution of the Dominican Order*, p. 62.

discovered what was, in effect, the idea of an absolute majority. If they could not have unanimity, at least they would come as near to it as the facts would allow.

The same reluctance to give up the principle of unanimity left its mark on secular history. The procedure described by Glanvil for the Grand Assize offers a close parallel to the rule of Grandmont. " If some of them know the truth of the matter and some do not, the ignorant shall be sent away, and others shall be summoned to the Court until at least twelve are found in agreement on the matter. Again, if some of them declare for one, and some for the other litigant, others must be brought in until at least twelve are in agreement for one of the parties." [1]   A decision was deemed essential, but it was secured by afforcing the jury until twelve on one side or other were agreed. Britton, writing of the petty jury over a century later, pronounced definitely in favour of a decision of the majority, though only in particular circumstances. " If the greater part of them know the truth and the other part do not, judgment shall be according to the opinion of the greater part. And if they declare upon oaths that they know nothing of the fact, let others be called who do know it . . ." [2]   The earlier plan of afforcing the jury to secure the unanimous testimony of twelve witnesses gradually was changed and stereotyped into the later practice, by which the judgment rested on the unanimous verdict of the twelve empanelled to hear the evidence. The way in which the half-grown idea of the majority was squeezed out of English procedure at common law is the most striking example of the survival of the principle of unanimity.[3]

Such a survival was impossible in public affairs wherever it was understood that " the end of politics was not knowledge but action." The ill-famed *liberum veto* of the Polish Diet was the hall-mark of an irresponsible and helpless assembly. In England party conflict brought the idea of the majority into prominence long before it was recognised by theorists. It was plainly stated in the sanction clause of Magna Carta, though with an ambiguous reservation which shows that it was still distrusted ; " if perchance . . . the twenty-five disagree among themselves . . . let that be

[1] *Select Charters*, pp. 192.
[2] Britton, ed. F. M. Nichols, Oxford, 1865, cited by J. F. Stephen, *Criminal Law*, 1883, I, 258-9.
[3] Cf. the majority verdict of the Scottish jury.

held as firm and established which *maior pars eorum qui praesentes fuerint* shall provide or command, *ac si omnes viginti quinque in hoc consensissent.*" [1] The majority reach the decision, but it must be assumed that it is the work of all. In the Provisions of Oxford (1258) the majority principle was expressed without qualification. The chancellor shall seal no gifts of wardships or escheats without the consent of the council or the majority therein (*u de la greinure partie*) ; what is done by the fifteen shall be confirmed by the twenty-four, or by the majority of them, and if all cannot be present, that which the majority do shall be firm and established.[2] Magna Carta and the Provisions are documents of rebellion, drafted when the compelling need of decision outweighed tradition and when the fiction of unanimity had worn too thin for daily use. It was not until rebellion was translated into political strife and became a normal part of the activities of council and Parliament that the decision of the majority won permanent recognition.

A more complex situation arose when those who differed were not mere individuals, but the agents of others. Then the demand for unanimity was even stronger, because of the need to express the general will behind the representatives. Any clash of opinion between them was regarded as different in kind from a clash between individuals acting for themselves alone. The difference was, perhaps, partly due to the feudal idea of contracting in or out of a bargain, which applied to individuals only. It may also have been part of a tradition of joint action, formed in the thirteenth century when the first knights or proctors were summoned to central assemblies. We can hardly suppose that all the knights who came to Westminster in 1254 or 1258 were of the same mind in refusing the royal demand for an aid, or that all the archdeacons or proctors summoned in 1254 or in 1256 were agreed as to the exact terms of the bargain offered to the king, yet on each occasion the idea of unanimity or a united front was strong enough to coerce the minority into acquiescence. On the analogy of ecclesiastical elections we may guess at the procedure adopted ; for example, in the elections made at York at the beginning of the fourteenth century [3] a unanimous decision was reached by the surrender of the minority to the general will of the chapter. It seems strange that the *plena potestas*, granted on

---

[1] *Select Charters*, p. 302. [2] *Ibid.*, pp. 380, 383.
[3] Cf. *supra*, pp. 338 *seq.*

election, did not at once carry with it the power to dissent from the majority, as in practice dissent must have been expressed by word of mouth from the outset. But the idea of unanimity died hard, and there is no indication in the early records of a clash of opinion where we would most expect to find it, that is, among the proctors in Convocation or in Parliament. It is possible that the king's object in consulting local assemblies, as he occasionally did, was to secure the local consent of groups, which would have been swallowed up in the unanimous refusal of a Parliament or Convocation. An attempt of this kind was made in 1337, and some details have been preserved in episcopal records. Edward III's request for a local subsidy was refused by the shire court of Devon, and a letter from bishop Grandisson, the earl of Devon and John de Raleghe describes how they had first expounded the royal demand to the whole assembly and then had discussed it in turn with knights, stewards, bailiffs of hundreds and other liberties, and others present, using the procedure of scrutinising votes (*de modo singulorum vota scrutandi*).[1] It seems that a vote could be taken in this way because the shire court was not representative, but each member was there for himself alone. In the previous year a similar attempt had been made to secure an ecclesiastical grant, by ordering that the consent of all the clergy of each diocese should be sought separately. The clergy of Exeter replied, after long debate *per eos adinvicem*, that the notice given was too short for the royal demand to be discussed, or for a scrutiny to be taken of the votes either of those present, or of those absent for good reason.[2] If they had been willing, the correct procedure was plainly to act on the decision of the majority, presumably because, not proctors, but all had been summoned. It was, no doubt, either from these local assemblies or from ecclesiastical practice that the procedure by majority was derived. The process of adoption was certainly slow. In the interval a strong element of artificiality must have entered into many unanimous decisions, the minority agreeing *nolens volens*, constrained by the strong tradition which forbade any dissent but the dissent of all.

The doctrine of the majority, as we recognise it in the *Modus*, thus bears all the marks of the period of transition. Some special bond with ecclesiastical practice is probably indicated by the

---

[1] *Grandisson's Register* (Exeter), Vol. I, pp. 300-1.
[2] *Ibid.* 1336 (?), Vol. I, pp. 300-1. Cf. *ibid.*, p. 355 (1328).

juxtaposition of *melius et sanius consilium* with *maiorem vocem*. The indifference to the precise number of clerical proctors also reflects the prevailing idea that a unanimous decision must be reached. Unfortunately, it is impossible to say exactly at what time representatives acquired the right to differ, which was essential to the appearance of the political majority. On the Continent a change in attitude may be detected in the second quarter of the century. In the *Defensor Pacis* (1324) Marsilius of Padua stated that the dominant part (*valentior pars*) of the citizens represents the whole ; it is dominant by reason of its number and quality, and is, in fact, the *maior et sanior pars*, superior in virtue rather than by counting of heads.[1] If the idea of the binding force of the will of the majority had been current in his day, we may be sure that Marsilius would have used it, as it was necessary to complete his theory of the state. Only thirty years later Charles IV frankly adopted it in the Golden Bull (1356), as part of the procedure at imperial elections. The change had already been advocated by Leopold of Bebenburg (*c.* 1340) on the ground that " the electors vote, not as individuals, but as members of a body which represents the people as a corporate whole." [2] The swing-round of opinion seems complete ; the use of the majority is justified as the special privilege of representatives. The older idea of unanimity did not at once disappear,[3] but the form in which we find it in the *Modus* belongs to the first rather than to the second half of the fourteenth century.

The long survival of the idea was not an altogether empty tradition. It served to express the permanent need of ultimate social unity, to give formal acknowledgment to the truths that the whole is greater than its parts and that a house divided against itself cannot stand. It is not surprising that an immense value was set on the appearance of harmony as long as society was not robust enough to bear the shock of open dissent without the relief of armed conflict. That political sense which guides men

---

[1] *Defensor Pacis*, ed. C. W. Previté-Orton, Cambridge, 1928, *Dictio I*, cap. XII, 3, p. 49. Cited by McIlwain, *op. cit.*, p. 303.

[2] *Tractatus de iuribus regni et imperii Romani*, ed. Basel n.d., cap. XVII, pp. 200-1, cited by McIlwain, *op. cit.*, p. 291.

[3] McIlwain (*op. cit.*, p. 304, n. 1) notes that Cardinal Zabarella, *c.* 1400, uses *pars valentior* as *pars potior*—a body superior, but not necessarily by virtue of its numbers.

to admit a fundamental difference between opposition before and after the event, has from its nature grown very slowly, since the high demand that it makes on the good will of minority and majority imposes an almost intolerable strain both on party allegiance and on personal conviction. Its strength is still, perhaps, the final test of an honourable and intelligent political society. We need not look in the early stages of political development for that frank avowal of a permanent defeat, which marks, say, the Tamworth manifesto. It is enough that the principle of harmony was respected by the outward forms of unanimous consent.

We may suspect that for a long time political minorities were voiceless and that formal unanimity was often no more than *nemine contradicente*. In the angry Parliaments of Richard II, for example, the Commons cannot always have been of one accord, as we see them through the records.[1] The same men cannot all have given ungrudging support alike to the punishments of the appellants and to the revenge of Richard II.[2] When we examine this appearance of unanimity we find that it was secured mainly by the actions and words of the Speaker. He alone reported the decisions of the Commons and expressed for them that harmony in opinion which the theory of representation supposed. We must, therefore, consider in conclusion the origin of his office, as it cannot be separated from the whole question of unanimity, as we find it in the *Modus* and in contemporary practice.

For the Speaker's antecedents we must turn once again to ecclesiastical records. Though examples of the chief man of a group, who answered for them in a general representative sense, can be traced far back in legal procedure,[3] there is no definite evidence of an agent of this kind in early deliberative assemblies. The law-speaker of the Icelandic Thing was the embodiment of

---

[1] The three conflicting returns of election in the Dublin county court in 1375 suggest that even the idea of a majority decision was not then understood in Ireland (*Windsor Documents, op. cit.*, pp. 128-9).

[2] For the changes in the personnel of the Commons under Richard II, I have had the advantage of reading unpublished evidence collected by Miss McKisack. Cf. N. B. Lewis, "Re-election to Parliament in the Reign of Richard II," *Eng. Hist. Review*, Vol. XLVIII, pp. 364 *seq.*

[3] For example, the *decanus* of a tithing or the professional expert appointed to *find* and to declare customary law, the *asega* of Frisia, the Swedish *laghman* or the *logsogu-madr* of Iceland (Vinogradoff, *Historical Jurisprudence*, Oxford, 1920, I, 361-2).

legal tradition rather than the mouthpiece of the assembly.[1] We
cannot, on the evidence, describe Edwin's councillor, who made
the famous speech comparing man's life to a bird flying through
a lighted hall from darkness into darkness, as the speaker for the
laity of Northumbria. Later, the strong individualism of feudal
society worked against the choice of a representative spokesman
in the king's council, while the special position of the clergy
made some officer of the kind essential, as soon as they began
to meet regularly in Convocation. Their *prolocutor* grew naturally out of the proxy or attorney, whom corporate bodies were
freely employing by the end of the twelfth century ; the men
sent by Bury St. Edmunds to Henry II or by Canterbury to
Innocent III were *procuratores* for their chapters, the forerunners
of the speakers for a general assembly. It was also natural that
when a particular decision was reached, or when the terms of
a bargain were drafted, that only one man should be entrusted
with the task of making a formal report. This was not merely
convenient, but it also expressed the idea of unanimity in a concrete form. The same plan was followed at capitular elections
when a single person was appointed to perform the formal
electoral act and to report it to the archbishop.[2] As *instructor
electionis*, he represented the unanimous decision of the chapter ;
the speaker of an assembly had for long no other function ; he
was simply an improvised agent, appointed *ad hoc* and without
any permanent status.

Early examples of the representation of assemblies in this
way are not numerous, but they are sufficient to illustrate a
practice which chroniclers probably took for granted. At the
council of Westminster in January, 1226, held to hear a
papal message, the bishops and prelates consulted together and
made answer by John, archdeacon of Bedford.[3] At another
council summoned in 1244 to meet a papal collector, Master
Martin, the dean of St. Paul's, as *prolocutor* for *universitas prelatorum Anglie*, refused to give an answer in the absence of the

---

[1] *Origines Islandicae*, ed. Gudbrand Vigfusson and F. York Powell, Oxford,
1905, Vol. I, pp. 346-9.

[2] For example, the elections already described at York, *supra*, p. 339.

[3] Wilkins, I, 621, from Matt. Paris. A remark in the *Vita Magna S.
Hugonis Linc.*, describing the council at Oxford in 1198 (*Select Charters*, p. 248)
suggests that the bishop of London was for a time regarded as the official
spokesman of the bishops.

king, the archbishops and other bishops.[1] Something of the
difficulties of the position is shown by Cotton's account of the
council of bishops and archdeacons which met in 1256 (January
13).[2] The nuncio, Rostand, had convened an assembly of bishops,
archdeacons and proctors of the clergy to demand a stricter
collection of the papal tenth ; he was resisted by Master Leonard,
as speaker *pro universitate*. When Rostand asked if he were
speaking for himself alone, or as *synodicus procurator universitatis*,
all were silent ; his name and those of all who had supported him
were taken down at Rostand's command.[3] A similar desertion
of the speaker by the men on whose behalf he was acting occurred
in 1268. At a council held at St. Paul's certain statutes were
promulgated by the legate Otto ; a clerk appealed against them
nomine totius cleri, but afterwards all the clergy renounced the
appeal.[4] All these examples, it will be noted, relate to protests
and complaints and we may suppose that they were recorded
because the men who undertook to outface the papal nuncios
were deemed to be exceptionally bold. By the end of the century,
when for purposes of debate the division of Convocation into
orders was fixed,[5] the practice of appointing one man to answer
for each *gradus* was probably established. We have a clear
example from the northern Convocation in 1311, in the answer
of the clergy to a royal demand for a subsidy. The archbishop
and other bishops informed Edward II that the clerical proctors
of their province had debated his request for three days and had
finally decided to refuse it ; their formal reply would be brought
to the king by Sir William de Melton.[6]

Thus the *prolocutor* became the proctor of proctors. He
was, in fact, none other than the *sola persona* of the *Modus*, who
cannot disagree with himself. In that form he marks an early
stage of political development, not only before majorities and
minorities have a recognised part in parliamentary debates, but
even before a formal and permanent embodiment of unanimity

---

[1] Matt. Paris, IV, 374 *seq*.   [2] *Historia Anglicana*, pp. 135-6.
[3] *Ibid*. At this time the clergy appointed the dean of St. Paul's and others
to go to Rome *pro universitate ecclesiae Anglicanae* (Matt. Paris, V, 539-40).
[4] Cotton, *op. cit.*, p. 143.
[5] *Supra*, pp. 321-3. Cf. I. J. Churchill, *op. cit.*, pp. 368-9, 378-9, for valuable
notes on the later *prolocutor* or *referendarius* of Canterbury Convocation.
[6] Greenfield's Register (York), II, p. 96 ; *Northern Registers*, p. 211. Later
the speaker of the clergy of York Convocation bore the title of *referendarius*
(*Northern Convocations*, pp. 155, 158-60, *s.a.* 1426).

in the person of the Speaker was deemed essential. The *sola persona* of the *Modus* was devised for rare occasions of exceptional difficulty, when something more than a mere mouthpiece of the estates was required. Probably he was used for the first time at the deposition of Edward II, when Trussel as *procurator totius Anglie*, renounced allegiance to the king.[1] Only by slow degrees in the reign of Edward III was he shaped into the permanent Speaker of the Commons. It was not before the sensational leadership of Peter de la Mare in the Good Parliament (1376) that the political significance of the office was understood by king and Parliament.[2] From that time onwards the Speaker ceased to be an improvisation and his actions became a normal part of parliamentary procedure.

We may conclude, therefore, that the *Modus* is in accord with what we know of consent and representation under Edward II. The general theory there set out is the theory of the time and it is confirmed in detail by certain significant peculiarities. The curious reference to rural deaneries and archdeaconries corresponds to the form of proctorial elections in some dioceses and it served as a reminder of how carefully the clergy elaborated their system of representation. The statement that a Parliament of king and commons existed before there were prelates or magnates is, in fact, a deduction from the superiority of elected members in matters of supply, which has the full support of ecclesiastical records. The *gradus* of the *Modus* are in agreement with our knowledge of early parliamentary history and with the familiar and hierarchic conception of society expressed concretely in the game of chess. Finally, in its treatment of unanimity and majority and in the *sola persona* as the forerunner of the Speaker, the *Modus* embodies ideas of representation and consent which are of ancient origin and can hardly be later in date than the first half of the fourteenth century.

[1] *Supra*, p. 191.

[2] For the Speakers under Richard II see N. B. Lewis, *Eng. Hist. Review*, Vol. XLVIII, pp. 392-4. Mr. Lewis omits Robert Plessynton, the Speaker of the Merciless Parliament (*Historia Mirabilis*, p. 14, Camden Miscellany, XIV), who was posthumously condemned in 1398 (*Rot. Parl.* III, 384*b*). Another Speaker, Sir James Pickering, about whom Mr. Lewis is doubtful, had been a supporter of William of Windsor in Ireland between 1368 and 1376 (*Windsor Documents, op. cit., passim*) and his choice as Speaker in the Parliaments of 1378 and 1383, probably indicates the persistent influence of the " gang " impeached in the Good Parliament.

CHAPTER XV

THE MANUSCRIPTS OF THE *MODUS*

M. Bémont was the first scholar to attempt a systematic survey of the manuscripts of the *Modus ;*[1] few of importance escaped his notice, and his work must be the beginning of all later enquiry. He compiled a descriptive list of forty-seven manuscripts ; of these thirty-two are in the British Museum, four in Oxford, three in Cambridge, and seven in private hands. Only one, the Gruthuyse manuscript in the Bibliothéque Nationale, is outside England. M. Bémont included in his list many late transcripts of little interest ; he did not attempt to arrive at any classification based on textual detail, and it is not clear when he was merely working from catalogues and when he had actually handled the manuscripts. He was the first to note that the *Modus* was generally associated with particular documents, more particularly the coronation order of Richard II and certain tracts on the functions of the constable, marshal and steward. The fact that in two out of the three oldest manuscripts [2] the *Modus* immediately follows the coronation order of Richard II was his chief reason for proposing a date soon after 1377. He did not distinguish a second group of manuscripts, descended from or connected with the third exemplar of the fourteenth century.[3]

Over twenty years later, M. Bémont's work was carried further by Miss Hodnett and Miss White, who undertook a thorough

---

[1] *Mélanges Julien Havet*, Paris, 1895, *La Date de la Composition du Modus Tenendi Parliamentum in Anglia*, pp. 465-80.

[2] Cotton, Nero D, VI, and MS. Lat. 6049, Bibl. Nat. (the Gruthuyse MS.). These MSS. are almost identical, and both appear to belong to the last decade of the fourteenth century. My thanks are due to Miss L. S. Sutherland for examining the MS. in Paris on my behalf.

[3] Cotton, Vespasian B, VII, also of the late fourteenth century.

examination of the manuscripts in the British Museum.[1] They gave special attention to the text, and the order of the chapters, and they found no signs of revision or drastic change, either by omission or by interpolation. On the other hand, study of the order of the chapters brought to light a discovery of great positive value. They were able to establish that the manuscripts fall into two main groups, according to the order in which the chapters are arranged. In both groups, which they call A and B, the arrangement of the introduction and first seven chapters is the same, while the order of the remaining nineteen varies in a complicated way. Chapters VIII to XIV of the A type become Chapters XIV to XX of the B type, and their place is taken in B by Chapters XIII to XIX and XXVI of A. From this change it follows that Chapters XX to XXV in A are Chapters XXI to XXVI in B.[2] When the text is examined, it is obvious that the original order is that of A. Not only is it the logical order, treating of Parliament from its opening to the dissolution, but it is the order plainly indicated in the chapter *De Modo Parliamenti* (VIII). This is an interim chapter, joining the first section on parliamentary summons to an account of the procedure and powers of the assembly. It begins : " Having first shown how, to whom, and at what time the summons of Parliament ought to be issued, and who ought to come by summons, and who not, it is, secondly, to be related, who they are who, by virtue of office, ought to come . . . without summons. . . ." The officials and servants who are bound to attend without summons are then enumerated, and it is explicitly stated that the duties of clerks will be treated *specialius post*. As the chapters on the clerks are IX and X in the B group, that order cannot be correct.

It is not easy to see why the change in the order was made. Chapters VIII to XIV and XIV to XX are almost exactly the same length, and they may have been transposed in the first place by a scribe's error. The change of the chapter *De Gradibus* (XXVI) from its place at the end to the middle looks as if it were deliberate. In four fifteenth-century manuscripts of the B type, this chapter

[1] " Manuscripts of the *Modus Tenendi Parliamentum*," *Eng. Hist. Review*, Vol. XXXIV, pp. 209-15. The article also contains useful references to MSS. of the *Modus* in other English Collections.

[2] In Miss Hodnett and Miss White's table (*Eng. Hist. Review, loc. cit.*, pp. 210-11) the introduction is counted as Chapter I. The chapter numbers must, therefore, be altered accordingly.

reverts to its correct place at the end ; [1] several later manuscripts in the same group, including the copy prefixed to the Lords' Journals,[2] show the chapter at the beginning.[3] It seems that some scribes of the B text, perhaps having seen a copy of the A version, realised that the section *De Gradibus* expressed the central idea of the whole document and altered its position in order to bring out its importance. The discovery of the true order, found in the A group, was the first and most important contribution to the interpretation of the *Modus ;* study of other manuscripts has served only to confirm the classification put forward by Miss Hodnett and Miss White.

These scholars published, as an appendix to their article, a fifteenth-century English *Modus* of the A type,[4] the first appearance in print of the true order of chapters. D'Achery [5] and Duffus Hardy [6] both printed from the Gruthuyse manuscript in Paris, and Stubbs [7] merely reproduced Hardy's text. For this reason, the full meaning of the *Modus* has hitherto been obscured, as it was not possible to read it in its original language and sequence. The change in order at once gave new significance to the whole document, and a new emphasis to its several parts.

It is now necessary to enquire what conclusions as to the date and authority of the *Modus* may be based upon a study and classification of the manuscripts. At the outset it must be admitted that, if the A order be accepted as the original form, it is most unlikely that departure from it would begin soon after the first appearance of the document. Two manuscripts of the B type

---

[1] Two Latin MSS., Petyt 511, VI (Inner Temple), and MS. EL. 35, B. 61, Huntingdon Library, California ; two French translations, Finch-Hatton Roll (Northamptonshire Record Society, Northampton) and a copy in the Courtenay Chartulary (in private hands, but transcribed in MS. Harley 305).

[2] MS. Vol. I ; described by A. F. Pollard, *Transactions of Royal Historical Society*, 3rd Series, Vol. VIII, pp. 36-7. Cf. Miss Hodnett and Miss White, *loc. cit.*, p. 214.

[3] For example, MS. Bodley Additional A. 85a, of the eighteenth century.

[4] MS. Harley 930, *c.* 1450.   [5] *Spicilegium, 1653-77*, XII, pp. 557 *seq.*

[6] *Modus Tenendi Parliamentum* (1846). Hardy consulted a number of other MSS., but did not attempt any classification or description of them, though he sometimes cited alternative readings. He refers to (pp. xxx-i) " several manuscript copies of the English translation extant in the British Museum and College of Arms, the library of Sir Thomas Phillipps, Bart., and elsewhere." In another passage (p. VII) he refers to a Cotton MS. which must be Nero B. VI.

[7] *Select Charters*, first eight editions, pp. 502 *seq.*

belong to the end of the fourteenth century;[1] both, as we shall see, are handsome volumes, carefully prepared for important people, and we must suppose that some pains were taken to secure accuracy in transcription. If the original order were already so much disturbed by this date, the date of composition must be pushed back at least a generation, that is, to the first half of the century. By 1400 the condition of the text of the *Modus* was such as to create a strong presumption in favour of an early date.

In order to test this presumption, it is necessary to examine the manuscripts themselves in some detail. The simplest line of approach will be to adopt the test of association, suggested by M. Bémont, but applied by him to only a few manuscripts. For this purpose there will be no need to consider the numerous transcripts of the sixteenth and seventeenth centuries, as they were either copied in a block from older exemplars, or else were included in that heterogeneous mass of material which is found in an antiquary's rag-bag. It will be convenient to confine our enquiry to medieval manuscripts, choosing the year 1500 as a limiting date. As the manuscripts can seldom be dated exactly, border-line cases will be given the benefit of the doubt and treated as medieval.

The *Modus* is extant in twenty-five manuscripts,[2] which belong to the period between the end of the fourteenth and the beginning of the sixteenth century. Of these six are translations, four into English and two into French. Obviously, only the Latin versions are in the main tradition, though the translations are also important as definite evidence of interest outside professional circles. It is, however, an indication of the more formal and, probably, more authoritative character of the A version that only one medieval translation belongs to that group.[3] The nineteen Latin manuscripts divide almost exactly into the categories of A (10) and B (9), but here again the A group seems superior. In two of the manuscripts of the B type the order is disturbed by shifting the chapter *De Gradibus* from the middle to the end of the document,[4] thus showing that in this group the form was not

---

[1] Cotton, Nero D. VI and MS. Lat. 6049, Bibl. Nat.
[2] See the descriptive list at the end of this chapter.
[3] MS. Harley 930.
[4] MSS. Petyt 511, VI, and Huntingdon EL. 35, B. 61. The two French versions have the same change.

definitely fixed. Within each group the manuscripts are closely associated with each other ; in fact, from a glance at the contents of a volume, one can usually be fairly certain which order the text of the *Modus* will follow. At the same time, the two groups differ sharply, and it is impossible to suppose that they were descended from a common archetype.

It will be convenient to consider first the manuscripts in group B, as they are more numerous, less regular and better known than those of the A type. Also, it will certainly be an advantage to begin by finding out what we can about the date and authority of the text which had obviously degenerated from the original version. There are fourteen medieval manuscripts in this class, nine in Latin, two in French and three in English ; in four, two Latin and two French, the normal B order is disturbed by shifting the chapter *De Gradibus* from its place in the middle to the end of the document. When the volumes in which these examples occur are examined in detail, it at once becomes clear that most of them, ten out of fourteen, appear to be connected with each other. In fact, the evidence points directly to Nero D, VI as the common ancestor from which the other nine are more or less directly descended.

Nero D, VI is a handsome folio, which both from its contents and on palæographical grounds may be said to belong to the last two decades of the fourteenth century.[1] The latest entries to which dates can be assigned are the ordinance for the Scottish campaign of 1385 and the royal charter granted in January 1386, by which Mowbray, earl of Nottingham, was created earl marshal. The contents of the manuscript fall into two unequal parts, though not without some connection between them. The first part,[2] consisting of some sixty folios, is a transcript of forty-five military and diplomatic documents relating to the wars with France and Scotland in the reign of Edward III. The second part [3] begins with the coronation claims and order of Richard II. It is followed by the *Modus*,[4] a well-known little tract on royal

---

[1] When the MS. was in Cotton's possession, he caused it to be blazoned with shields representing variants of the royal arms together with those that he claimed for himself, through his alleged descent from Robert Bruce. The work was well executed, and might easily deceive the student, anxious to use heraldic evidence for dating.

[2] Ff. 4-64ᵛ.   Nearly all the documents belong to the years 1357-62.

[3] Ff. 65-71ᵛ.   [4] Ff. 72-5.

obsequies, and a short chronicle on the kings of England from the time of Noah to the accession of Richard II.[1] The remaining folios [2] contain a group of documents about the rights and duties pertaining to the marshalship of England ; in this group are *Modus faciendi duellum coram Rege*, the Nottingham charter, January 1386, the Usages of Thomas of Brotherton and the ordinances for the campaign in Scotland, July 1385. Except the chronicle, which was probably inserted as a chronological guide, all the items in the second part are connected with the marshal's office ; he was closely concerned with the crowning and burial of kings and, according to the *Modus*, with the procedure of Parliament. The treaties, truces and diplomatic agreements in the first part may have been collected because of the military and chivalrous duties of the marshal, but of this we cannot be certain. It is as probable that the second group was appended as an after-thought, to complete a volume begun as a record of the diplomatic history of the Treaty of Brétigny.

As a result of his study of this manuscript, Round came to the conclusion that " we have at least a fair presumption that the *Modus*—at any rate in the form that has reached us—dates from the constitutional crisis of 1386." [3] He had approached the problem by the side-track of the marshalship and was, therefore, inclined to overstate the importance of the duties assigned to the great hereditary officials in the chapter *De Casibus et Iudicibus Difficilibus* (XVII). He pointed out that " the three chiefs of the opposition at the time were Gloucester, Derby and Nottingham, who respectively represented the Constable, the Steward and the Marshal." He also drew attention to the chapter *De Absentia Regis* (XIII) and argued that it accorded well with Richard's angry withdrawal from the Parliament of 1386.[4] As a clinching proof, he cited the Nottingham charter from the Nero manuscript, by which the style *comes marescallus* of the

---

[1] Ff. 76-81. The chronicle is of little interest, though the account of Edward II's death is, perhaps, worth noting, as it represents the view maintained by Richard II, f. 81 " . . . in castro de Berkeley occisus, quasi per martirum, expiravit et Glovernie sepelitur, ubi providente divina clemencia per eum plura et diversa fiunt miracula."

[2] Ff. 82-94.

[3] *The Marshalship of England*, in *The Commune of London*, 1899, pp. 302 *seq.*

[4] Knighton, II, 215.

Modus was first formally granted, with the express words *una cum nomine et honore comitis Marescalli*. Though plausible at first sight, Round's arguments do not bear close examination. The three great officials, assuming—and it is a big assumption [1] —that Derby could act as steward, were not united in opposition until a full year after the Parliament of 1386 ; [2] in fact, as the impeached chancellor, de la Pole, was a Lancastrian retainer, it was very unlikely that Derby and Nottingham would unite under Gloucester against him in 1386. As for the king's withdrawal from Parliament, Round was on the right track when he connected the *Modus* with the efforts of the magnates to persuade Richard to return, but he overlooked a specific statement in a contemporary chronicle describing the argument then put forward. When Gloucester and bishop Arundel interviewed Richard at Eltham, they warned him that *ex antiquo statuto* he might not depart from Parliament unless from illness or other necessary cause.[3] It seems almost certain that the *Modus* was the " statute " to which they referred and, though *antiquo* need not cover a long period of time, it could not be used to describe a document concocted during the crisis.

Finally, as Round himself admits, the style of earl marshal was used loosely before 1386. *Comes marescallus* occurs three times on the Parliament roll of 1318 [4] and in 1330 Thomas of Brotherton petitioned the king for the rights enjoyed by his predecessors, *countes mareschauls*.[5] Though his conclusion cannot be accepted, Round was probably right in recognising in the Nottingham charter the *raison d'être* of the Nero manuscript. Nottingham acted as marshal in the Scottish campaign of 1385 and it was no doubt at that time that attention was drawn to the

---

[1] His father, John of Gaunt, was then in Spain, and there is no evidence that he was willing or able to vest his rights as steward in his son.

[2] Derby and Nottingham did not join in the original appeal issued by Gloucester, Arundel and Warwick on November 14, 1387 (*Rot. Parl.* III, pp. 229) ; they did not throw in their lot with the other appellants until de Vere's army was on the march in December.

[3] Knighton, II, 217. Cf. *ibid.* II, 219, for a second reference *ex antiquo statuto*, this time cited in connection with the deposition of Edward II. See also *Rot. Parl.* III, 376*b*.

[4] Cole, *Documents*, pp. 8, 11, 14.

[5] Thomas Hearne, *Curious Discourses*, 1771, II, 135-7 ; in the official return of fees due to Thomas he is styled *counte mareschaul* (Round, *op. cit.*, p. 311, n. 1).

rights and dignities of the office.[1] When the royal army returned from Scotland there was a lavish distribution of honours ; the king's uncles, Cambridge and Buckingham, were created dukes of York and Gloucester, de Vere was made marquis of Dublin, and de la Pole earl of Suffolk. Nottingham's reward was plainly the charter of January 1386, and it is probable that Nero D, VI, or at least the second part of it, was compiled under his direction. The date of compilation cannot be later than early in 1397, as the manuscript does not include either Nottingham's elevation to the rank of duke in September 1397 or the grant to him of additional privileges as marshal in February of the same year.[2] It is hardly conceivable that these new honours would have been omitted from a collection on the marshalship gathered after 1396. It must, therefore, have been undertaken within the previous decade, perhaps during the conflict of 1387 and 1388. As we have just seen, the *Modus* was almost certainly cited in the Parliament of 1386 and it may be that in this way Nottingham became aware of the parliamentary duties which it assigned to him. Certainly the association of the *Modus* with the documents on which he based his claims to the rights and perquisites of his office suggests that it was deemed to bear the stamp of authority.

Whether prepared for Nottingham or not, we cannot suppose that the matter contained in Nero D, VI was regarded as in any way disloyal or dangerous. This may be deduced from the other fourteenth-century manuscript which contains the B version of the *Modus*, that is, the Gruthuyse manuscript now in the Bibliothèque Nationale. It was apparently copied from Nero, very soon after the original compilation was made. It seems to contain almost exactly the same subject matter, except the Nottingham charter ;[3] the only difference of any note is that the

[1] The question had been raised in 1377. The order of coronation includes the *Servicia dominorum*, defined in the Court of Claims held before Lancaster, as steward ; here Nottingham's grandmother, Margaret, countess of Norfolk, put forward her claim to the marshalship, based on the rights of her father, Thomas of Brotherton. Settlement was postponed owing to Richard's minority.

[2] *Rot. Parl.* III 343*b*-4*b*. Nottingham was then granted, *inter alia*, the right to substitute for the customary wooden baton of office a golden baton with black rings, bearing the royal arms on the upper end and the Mowbray arms at the other.

[3] F. 97ᵛ has a list of the names of those who came with William the Conqueror from Normandy in 1066, which does not appear in the Nero D, VI.

treaties and truces of Edward III come at the end instead of the beginning. On the first folio the royal arms of France are illuminated, a shield bearing three gold fleur-de-lys on a blue ground. If this shield be contemporary [1] with the rest of the manuscript, it is possible that the book was prepared as a gift for · Charles VI on the occasion of the marriage of Richard II to his daughter in 1396. The fine penmanship and coloured capitals, ornamented with formal patterns, show that it was executed with great care ; if not for the French king, perhaps it was a gift to some other member of the royal family, or even to Richard himself.

We are left in no doubt as to the popularity of the Nero collection, as it continued to be copied frequently throughout the fifteenth century. Of the dozen other manuscripts in the B group, eight show some connection with the Nero archetype. Five follow the original fairly closely, with some omissions or additions.[2] Two of these contain additions of heraldic interest. Additional 29,901 has transcripts on the creation of heralds by Julius Caesar, the founding of the order of the Garter, how an esquire should be knighted, and tracts on arms by Johannes de Badeo Aureo [3] and Bartolus of Sassoferrato.[4] Domitian XVIII contains certain of the Nero documents on the marshal, and much of the heraldic matter in Additional 29,901.[5] The strong interest which heralds and antiquaries showed in the collection thus began in the fifteenth century ; more than anything else, it helps to explain the number of transcripts made in the sixteenth and seventeenth centuries. In the other three manuscripts [6] dependent on the Nero original, the documents on the marshal are usually selected for transcrip-

---

[1] As the book came into the Royal Library, the arms may well be a later addition.

[2] MSS. Vitellius C, IV ; Additional 32,097 ; Additional 29,901 ; Domitian XVIII ; Cambridge University, IV, 207 (English).

[3] He wrote a tract on arms at the instance of Anne of Bohemia (edited by Ed. Bysshe, 1654). Mr. E. Lobel has suggested to me that his real name was John Guildford.

[4] F. 86ᵛ " . . . Hunc tractatum de insigniis et armis a domino Bartholo de Saxeferrato, excellentissimo legum professor . . . publicavit post mortem dicti domini Bartholi Alex. suus gener solempnissimus legum doctor, qui disputavit primam questionem sub annis domini MCCCLVIII . . . ."

[5] Dom. XVIII also contains material, including maps, for Irish history, the *Encomium* on Henry VII by Bernard Andreas and, as a later addition, the famous record of the runes on the Bewcastle cross.

[6] MSS. Antiquaries 58 ; Leconfield 17 ; Huntingdon EL. 35, B. 61.

tion, but the handsome folio now in the Huntingdon Library contains nothing but the *Modus* and a coronation order for kings and queens, an English translation of the fifteenth century.[1] The preservation of the *Modus* in all these manuscripts shows that it was regarded as a work of importance and authority.

The last four manuscripts in the B group might be called *Extravagantes*, as they have strayed away from all connection with the archetype, in that they contain no other documents relating to the marshal or to the coronation. Two are in French, and belong to the early years of the fifteenth century. Their existence must be taken as definite evidence of an interest in the document extending beyond the circle of those who could read Latin. The parchment roll from which the Irish *Modus* was probably translated back into Latin has already been described.[2] Differing from it only on one minor point [3] is the copy preserved in the Courtenay cartulary.[4] Why it was entered there it is impossible to say until the manuscript has been thoroughly examined ; it is tempting to suppose that it was taken from a copy used by archbishop Courtenay during the political excitement of 1386-88. The third manuscript has a special interest, as it once belonged to Fortescue.[5] Its contents are a strange jumble. Beginning with a shortened form of the *Brut* to 1437,[6] there follow various theological treatises or extracts from them ; then an English tract on the four occupations ; and finally the *Modus* and the Treaty of Troyes. One of the theological works was cited by Fortescue in *De Laudibus* [7] and we may assume that the collection was made

---

[1] Ff. 1-11ᵛ. " Modus sive forma regum et reginarum coronacionis in regno Anglie sequitur in hunc modum." It is printed in *English Coronation Records*, ed. L. Wickham Legg, 1901, pp. 172 *seq.*

[2] MS. Finch-Hatton 2995, printed *Archæological Journal*, Vol. XI͞X, pp. 266 *seq.*, and discussed *supra*, pp. 87-9.

[3] The omission of one of the three aids in the chapter *De Auxiliis Regis* (*supra*, p. 88).

[4] Now in the possession of Sir A. P. Vivian. My knowledge of it is derived from the transcript made by D'Ewes, Harley 305, ff. 274 *seq.*

[5] Bodley, Rawlinson C, 398. It bears Fortescue's arms, a bend engrailed and on the fly-leaf a note in a later hand " . . . liber quondam Johannis Fortescue militis sub Hen. 6ᵗᵒ Angliae Rege Cancellarii." The date must be soon after 1437.

[6] The end of this chronicle is printed in Kingsford's *English Historical Literature in the Fifteenth Century*, Oxford, 1913, pp. 310 *seq.*

[7] Cap. 4, from Parisiensis (William of Auvergne, bishop of Paris, 1228-48). Cf. *Governance of England*, ed. C. Plummer, Oxford, 1885, pp. 180-1.

under his direction.   The Petyt manuscript,[1] the last in the group,
is unique in that it alone has the B version as the preface to the
book of statutes.   As we shall see, this is characteristic of the A
group.   It differs from the regular B order in having the chapter
De Gradibus at the end.   Perhaps the scribe inadvertently began
to copy the wrong version and, realising his error, transposed the
chapter in the hope of making it look like the text normally used
for the purpose.   But it is curious that the two French *Extravagantes*, both of which are early, also shift the chapter to the end.
It may be that we should postulate for these four irregular
texts a fourteenth-century original no longer extant.[2]

We may conclude that the manuscripts of the B type are
nearly all associated with documents of definite historical value,
which were plainly not collected at haphazard.   It is true that
there was as yet no critical attitude to documents and that all
kinds of nonsense were accepted at their face value.   The re-
spectable companions of the *Modus* are, therefore, no proof of its
intrinsic worth, but they show that a tradition of confidence in it
had been established.   This could hardly have happened in less
than a full generation.   We may be sure that the *Modus*, well
known and respected in the reign of Richard II, cannot be later
in date than the first half of the century.

Turning to the A group, we find that eight out of eleven
manuscripts are collections of statutes or other legal documents,
more or less official ; in the ninth, the *Modus* appears among a
miscellaneous jumble of documents, ranging from Latin stories
to receipts for the diseases of horses ;[3] in the two others no other
documents are bound up with it.[4]   In seven cases the *Modus* is
followed by the tract on the seneschal.[5]   It may, therefore, be
said that nearly all the A manuscripts have a certain official
character.   The close attachment of the seneschal tract is significant.   As we have already seen, it cannot be as late as the exile
of the Despensers in July 1321, and it was probably drafted not
long before that date.[6]   The internal evidence connecting the

---

[1] MS. Petyt 511 VI.

[2] The Huntingdon MS., which has the same peculiarity, may have been
derived from the same source.

[3] MS. Leconfield no. 8.

[4] MSS. Harley, 930 (English) and Winnington 2.

[5] MSS. Nero C, I ; Lansdowne 522 ; St. Audries, No. 15 ; Vespasian B,
VII ; British Mus. Addit. 24,079 ; Leconfield no. 8 ; Holkham 232.

[6] *Supra*, pp. 243-4.

two documents is strong enough to make it almost certain that they were associated, not only because of their subject-matter, but because they were extant together from an early date. How closely they were united is illustrated by the Leconfield manuscript, where the tract is placed between the last chapter of the *Modus* and a postscript on the speaker. It is also worth noting that the office of steward lost all permanent importance with the death of Thomas, duke of Clarence in 1421 [1] and from that time onwards the tract was of little but antiquarian interest. Its inclusion in collections of the late fifteenth century can hardly be explained, except on the ground that it was regarded as a dependent part of the *Modus*. Two manuscripts which omit it are special collections. Julius B, IV deals exclusively with the Cinque Ports, and there a statement of certain liberties enjoyed by the Ports is substituted as an alternative appendix.[2] Some postscript was evidently thought to be necessary ; that on the seneschal was rejected as irrelevant, and in its place a document of local interest was transcribed, although it appears in two other places in the same volume.[3] The other example, Oriel 46, is, as we shall see, a London collection. The evidence thus indicates that the tract was the normal appendage of the A version.

Though there is a general similarity between nearly all the manuscripts of the A group, it is impossible to distinguish one as the common original from which the rest are descended. The oldest manuscript is Vespasian B, VII, which on palæographical grounds cannot be earlier than the end of the fourteenth century. It contains the statutes of the realm before 1327, known later to lawyers as *vetera statuta*, and that " apocrypha " of *statuta incerti temporis* which hangs in a sort of limbo between the reigns of Edward II and Edward III. These contents, as Miss Hodnett and Miss White pointed out in 1919,[4] indicate that the scribe was copying from a volume which belonged to a considerably earlier period. The manuscript begins with a list of the kings of England to the reign of Edward I ; a much later hand has carried it on to Henry VII. Then follows a list of statutes and kindred documents, with a summary of those relating to the

---

[1] Vernon Harcourt, *His Grace the Steward*, pp. 190-1.
[2] *Supra*, pp. 202-3.
[3] It appears on ff. 13ᵛ-14ᵛ and 88ᵛ-89, with slight variations.
[4] *Eng. Hist. Review*, Vol. XXXIV, pp. 214-15.

crisis of 1297. The statutes themselves do not include any later than the statutes made at York in 1318, but among the miscellaneous documents appears the oath of the Justices of the Peace, in the form in which it is recorded on the Parliament Roll of 1380.[1] A second list of kings, headed *Data Regum*, entering the month and day of accession from Henry III to Richard II, was evidently intended as an aid to fixing the regnal year. The *Modus*, the tract on the steward and the tract on the marshal [2] are the last items in the volume. Though nearly everything belongs to the reign of Edward II or earlier, the presence of *Data Regum* to Richard II and the oath of the justices makes it impossible to argue that the scribe copied, without making additions, from a much older manuscript. Vespasian B, VII, seems to be an early statute book, of the type to which we often find reference in the fourteenth century.[3] The absence of any statutes later than 1318 shows that no attempt had been made to bring the book up to date and we may suppose that the scribe or his employer regarded the *Modus* and the tracts which follow it as a part of the ancient " apocrypha " of *statuta incerti temporis*.

Nearest to the Vespasian manuscript in point of time is the collection of laws, legal documents and tracts preserved in Oriel College, Oxford.[4] It is a composite work, made up out of two mutilated volumes ; folios 1 to 108 are the second part of a book from which the first 96 leaves are missing.[5] A table of

---

[1] *Rot. Parl.* III, 85 ; B. Putnam, *Enforcement of the Statutes of Labourers*, New York, 1908, p. 42.

[2] The tract on the marshal is a portion of the well-known document entitled " Les Usages de Thomas de Brotherton." He was earl of Norfolk, and was granted the marshalship to hold as an hereditary office by his half-brother, Edward II, in February 1316. The tract was probably drawn up before his death in 1338, perhaps at the time of the petition on his office addressed to the Parliament of Winchester in 1330 (Hearne, *Curious Discourses*, II, 135-7).

[3] Cf. the " liver des estatutes " used by Peter de la Mare in the Good Parliament (*Anon. Chronicle*, p. 86) and " un petit livre veil' des estatuz dengleterre " in Gloucester's library at Pleshy in 1397 (*Archæological Journal*, Vol. LIV, p. 302).

[4] MS. Oriel 46. My thanks are due to the Provost and Fellows of the College for leave to consult this manuscript. I understand that it is one of a group of MSS. formerly in the London Guildhall.

[5] This is clear from the numbering of the gatherings, f. 1 being numbered IX, f. 13 X, and so on to f. 91, which is numbered XVII. F. 108 is the last sheet in the last gathering in this series ; the signatures of the gatherings after this point follow an entirely different arrangement. My attention was drawn to this feature by Mr. Denholm Young, to whom my thanks are due.

contents at the end shows that folios 109 to 208 were once in a huge manuscript of which 271 leaves are now missing.[1] The *Modus* occurs on folios 102 to 104^v of the first section. It is preceded by a transcript of laws from the Anglo-Saxon period to the time of Richard I, with short notes between the collections of each king.[2] The handwriting belongs to the first half of the fourteenth century. The *Modus* is written in a rather later hand, falling within the years 1380 to 1420.[3] After the *Modus*, still another scribe has copied an account of the meeting of Richard II and Charles VI at Guines on October 28, 1396.[4] The next folio (107) is blank and on the dorse of the one after (108^v), in another and probably contemporary hand, is a list of the names of those who came to England with William the Conqueror. It is unfortunate that the exact date of the *Modus* transcript remains uncertain. It might, perhaps, be argued that the interview at Guines was of slight interest after Richard's deposition (1399) and the return of his child wife to France (1401) and that the *Modus*, which precedes it, was copied in the reign of Richard II. Against this it could be urged that the document was of interest at the time of the marriage of Henry V to Katherine of France in 1420. However, the precise date would not be of great use for our enquiry, as it certainly cannot be put back earlier than 1380.

The book to which this *Modus* once belonged was evidently, in part, a *Liber de Veteribus Legibus Angliae*. Liebermann has shown how closely it is connected with a group of manuscripts which were altogether at the London Guildhall in the early fourteenth century.[5] He argues that the first part of the Oriel manuscript (*c.* 1330), Corpus Christi College, Cambridge, 70

[1] F. 210. This table of contents shows that the first 213 folios have been lost ; also ff. 304-62, another 58 folios. Evidently the lost ff. 1-99 closely resembled the leaves extant in Part I, but the three last items—the *Modus*, the Guines Interview and the list of followers of William I—are not referred to. The matter lost altogether from Part II appears to be charters, writs, royal letters and ordinances.

[2] Ff. 1-101^v.

[3] Marginal notes, indicating the subject-matter, occur in a later hand.

[4] Ff. 104^v-106^v. Printed by P. Meyer, *Annuaire Bulletin de la Société de l'Histoire de France*, Vol. XVIII, pp. 210-24. Another and slightly different version, entitled *Nuptie Regis Richardi*, appears in the Merton Register (Bodley MS. Laud, 723, ff. 68^v-70).

[5] F. Liebermann, *Über die Leges Anglorum saeculo XIII ineunte Londoniis collectae*, Halle, 1894, pp. 101 *seq.*

(c. 1320) and Claudius D, II (c. 1310) were all derived from a
common exemplar, now lost, which was a collection of royal
dooms and laws from Ine to Glanvil, with some additional
matter relating either to Anglo-Saxon custom or to the history
of London.[1] He also observed a close connection between the
second part of the Oriel manuscript and two others still at the
Guildhall ; *statuta*, Magna Carta to *Visus franci plegii*, correspond
to entries in the first part of the *Liber Custumarum* and certain
early law tracts and a register of writs are in the *Liber Horn*.[2]
Though the evidence for a close connection between all five
manuscripts is undeniable, Liebermann's grouping of them is
not altogether convincing. He supposed that Oriel 46 was a
copy conflated from the other volumes at the Guildhall and did
not consider the possibility that at least a portion of it was once
actually part of one of them. He seems to have failed to note that
two defective volumes had been bound up as one.[3] Fortunately,
what seem to be the full tables of contents of both original manuscripts were retained and with their help it is possible to establish
a closer link between part one and the *Liber Custumarum*.

The *Liber Custumarum*, now at the Guildhall, has a table of
its contents, drawn up in the early fifteenth century, which shows
that it then contained 284 folios.[4] Not half the items described
appear in the volume now extant. Its editor, H. T. Riley,
argued that its missing folios are now in Claudius D, 11, but his
proof was not altogether convincing.[5] The first folio of the table
corresponds to folio 103 of the *Liber* manuscript, as it is to-day,
and between folios 78 and 187 there is another break in the
original contents. This second gap is almost exactly filled by the
Oriel documents, the table of contents roughly corresponding to

[1] For C.C.C.C. 70 see the description in the Catalogue by M. R. James, and
also that by Maitland in the *Mirror of Justices* (Selden Society), pp. xv-xviii.
In the early fourteenth century it belonged to Andrew Horn (1328).
[2] Liebermann, *op. cit.*, p. 90.
[3] He noted that the two tables of contents did not appear to belong to the
MS., *op. cit.*, p. 102.
[4] F. 284, printed in *Liber Custumarum* (*Rolls Series*), Pt. II, pp. 488-90.
[5] *Ibid.* Pt. I, pp. xi *seq.* Owing to illness, I have been unable to examine
the Guildhall MS. However, Mr. V. H. Galbraith has very kindly examined
it for me, and, with Mr. W. A. Pantin, has compared its make-up with that of
Oriel 46. He has also reached the conclusion that Oriel 46 was once part of
the *Liber Custumarum*. It seems that a detailed investigation of the whole
problem ought to be undertaken.

the items in the manuscript. The *Modus* appears in the table just before *Chronicon de Calys*, which must be the Guines interview, and it is followed by the names of those who came with William in 1066.[1] The numbers of folios are almost exactly the same—108 in Oriel and 107 in the table of the *Liber Custumarum*. On the other hand, 96 folios are missing from the Oriel manuscript, while the table allows only for 80. We must suppose that some long item, perhaps a chronicle, once stood in the first place in the volume, and either was not included in the table, or else was removed before it was made. That the original book was certainly mutilated is proved by an entry in the *Repertory* of the Court of Alderman, dated January 1608.[2] It follows a series of entries recording the efforts which were then being made to recover certain books missing from its custody. "Item, one booke newly bound, conteyning a part of an olde boke heretofore belonging to this Cittye, called *Liber Legum Antiquorum Regum*, and a part also of another of the Cittyes boke, called *Liber Custumarum*, which bokes have been long missing out of the boke-howses of the Guildhall, and now lately restored by Francys Tate of the Middle Temple, Esquire, in whose custodye the same have long remayned, was then delivered into this Court to be safely kept in the boke-howses among other the bokes belonging to this Cittye." The name of Francis Tate is written many times on Oriel 46, and we cannot doubt that he was the owner.[3] We may conclude that the first part of the Oriel manuscript probably belonged to the original *Liber Custumarum*, which differed more in title than in name from the *Liber Legum Antiquorum Regum*. Judging by the original table, the Oriel folios once stood after a selection, beginning with Magna Carta, from the *Vetera Statuta* and its apocrypha ; following them came a large collection of documents mainly relating to London, but ending with the coronation order of Richard II and the charter of the duchy of Lancaster. It seems that the manuscript was either made up or

---

[1] *Liber Custumarum*, Pt. II, p. 490. Liebermann, *op. cit.*, p. 90, mistook the Guines interview for the Calais expedition of 1346.

[2] Quoted by Riley, *Liber Custumarum*, Pt. I, pp. xviii-xix.

[3] The details of the process by which Tate retained portions of two MSS. are still obscure, but it is certain that Sir Robert Cotton was his accomplice. Probably part of Claudius D, II represents another share of the spoils. C.C.C.C. 70 may have wandered from the Guildhall at the same time. The four volumes have obviously a close connection between them.

completed in the reign of Richard II, though far the larger part of it belongs to a much earlier period. Oriel 46 thus links up the old *Leges Regum* with the later *Vetera Statuta*, representing a type of legal collection still older than the Vespasian manuscript.[1] To find the *Modus* in such company is significant of its established place in legislative tradition.

It is not necessary to delay long over the remaining medieval manuscripts in the A group. The most important for purposes of classification are the four volumes of statutes. Three are *Nova Statuta*, each containing the *Modus* as a preface.[2] The fourth, Holkham 232, consists both of *Vetera* and of *Nova Statuta*, with the *Modus* sandwiched between them. The only English example in the A class, Harley 930, had also an official connection, already pointed out by Miss Hodnett and Miss White.[3] They show that it is the original of a sixteenth-century transcript, which ends with the note : " Taken out of a little old parchment book remaining with the clerk of the Parliament." [4] It may be concluded from this entry that the *Modus* was in use as a handbook on parliamentary procedure about the middle of the fifteenth century, the time to which Harley 930 belongs.[5] Its appearance as an introduction to the first volume of the Lords' Journals (1509), noticed many years ago by Professor Pollard,[6] is thus entirely natural, as it carried on a tradition already well established. The other four manuscripts are not of the same definitely public or official character. Julius B, IV is exclusively concerned with the Cinque Ports. Additional 24,079 (British Museum) and the Winnington manuscript each contain only the *Modus ;* they were probably either once part of larger volumes or else were little handbooks of the same type as Harley 930. The Leconfield manuscript (no. 8) is obviously a compilation made up to the taste of the original owner.

---

[1] Mr. Richardson and Mr. Sayles (" Early Statutes," *Law Quarterly Review*, Vol. L, p. 47, additional note) describe Oriel 46 as the " best representative " of a small group of MSS. which combine the older laws with the statutes.

[2] MSS. Nero C, I. ; Lansdowne 522 ; St. Audries ; Holkham 232. All four belong to the late fifteenth century.

[3] *Eng. Hist. Review, loc. cit.*, pp. 213-14. The MS. also contains an English translation of the Treaty of Troyes.

[4] Additional 25,457, British Museum, f. 9.

[5] The omission of the Seneschal tract, as no longer of practical value, is thus easy to understand.

[6] *Transactions of the Royal Historical Society*, 3rd Series, Vol. VIII, pp. 36-7.

Thus an examination of the manuscripts of the A type brings out much that is valuable, even though it does not help us to fix dates with exactitude. No common archetype has been traced, but the evidence points definitely to the kind of collection to which this version of the *Modus* belonged. We find it in two important volumes of *Vetera Statuta*, each containing hardly any matter later than the reign of Edward II ; we find it as the preface to three medieval copies of the *Nova Statuta* and, in one copy, as the bridge between *Vetera* and *Nova ;* we find it also in the " little old parchment book," which was in the custody of the clerk of Parliament. It appears seven times with the Seneschal tract, probably written in 1321, as an appendage ; it is also found in two great collections, made for the Cinque Ports and London respectively, each time with associations which point to the reign of Edward II or earlier. On this evidence it seems justifiable to argue first, that the *Modus* was accepted as an orthodox and official description of Parliament from the end of the fourteenth century onwards ; and, secondly, that by its position in manuscripts, it seems to form part of that apocrypha of *Statuta incerti temporis*, generally accepted as belonging to a time not later than 1327. Sir Mathew Hale long ago declared that the *Vetera Statuta* and other like documents ascribed to the reigns of Henry III, Edward I and Edward II, were regarded as " incorporated into the very common law, and become a part of it." [1] Into this great body of law, miscellaneous in date and content, and authoritative by reason of antiquity and use, the *Modus* was certainly received by the end of the fourteenth century.

It will hardly be profitable to follow the manuscript history of the *Modus* far beyond the end of the medieval period, as it does no more than confirm the conclusions which have already been reached. It is, however, worth noting that with the renaissance of historical and legal study in the Elizabethan age, interest in the *Modus* increased also. About the year 1575 John Hooker, *alias* Vowell, incorporated the *Modus* in his " Order and Usage of the Keeping of a Parliament in England " ; [2] John Hales or another [3]

---

[1] *Hist. Comm. Law,* 9, cited by Holdsworth, II, 223.

[2] Somers Tracts, I, 175. It was also published separately in the sixteenth century, probably in London, 1575. The British Museum and Bodley have each a copy, the only examples known.

[3] Hales was also author of the *Discourse of the Commonweal* (ed. E. Lamond, Cambridge, 1893) and M.P. in 1548.

used it in the " Treatise of the Parliament," written, perhaps, in the reign of Edward VI. The quarrels over parliamentary privilege, which became more frequent as the century drew to an end, naturally increased the popularity of the *Modus*, with its exaltation of the Commons. Lambarde's " Orders, Proceedings, Punishment and Previledges of the Lower Howse of Parliament " was based, in the first place, on the " old Treatise, *Modus tenendi Parliamenti* " and also on the works of Hooker and Hales.[1] In the stormy Parliament of 1593, when lord-keeper Puckering gave his famous definition of freedom of speech,[2] the speaker, the learned Coke,[3] drew on the *Modus* for argument and eked it out with some invention of his own. The passage deserves full quotation :—

" . . . At the first we were all one House and sat together, by a precedent which I have of a Parliament holden before the Conquest by Edward the Son of Etheldred. For there were Parliaments before the Conquest. This appeareth in a book which a grave Member of this House delivered unto me, which is intituled ' Modus tenendi Parliamentum ' ; out of that book I learn this, and if any man desire to see it, I will show it to him. And this book declareth how we all sat together, but the Commons sitting in the presence of the King and amongst the Nobles disliked it, and found fault that they had not free liberty to speak. And upon this reason that they might speak more freely, being out of the Royal sight of the King, and not amongst the great Lords so far their betters, the House was divided and came to sit asunder.

" A bold and worthy Knight at the time when this was sought (the King desiring a reason of this their request, and why they would remove themselves from their betters), answered shortly, that his Majesty and the Nobles being every one a great person, represented but themselves ; but his Commons, though they were but inferiour men, yet every one of them represented a thousand of men. And this answer was well allowed of. . . ." [4]

Coke's clever and highly disingenuous citation of the *Modus* has an interest beyond the history he concocted out of it, to support

---

[1] Bodley MS. Rawlinson A. 78, f. 136ᵛ. Another MS. is in the British Museum, Addit. 5123. It was published separately in 1641, and in the *Harleian Miscellany*, but Professor Neale has issued warning that both these texts are " incomplete and corrupt " (*Eng. Hist. Review*, Vol. XXXIX, p. 50, n. 3).

[2] *Ibid.*, Vol. XXXI, pp. 136-7.

[3] The MS. now at Holkham may have belonged to Coke.

[4] D'Ewes, *Journals of all the Parliaments during the Reign of Queen Elizabeth*, p. 515.

the demand for freedom of speech. Though, by his tale of a " bold and worthy knight," he embellished the plain words of his text, which contrast magnates attending *per se* with the Commons *qui representant totam communitatem Anglie* (XXIV), his assertion of the representative principle was an assertion of the principle underlying the *Modus* itself.

Thus the evidence of the manuscripts is decisive in favour of the high reputation enjoyed by the *Modus* from the end of the fourteenth century onwards. With the value of this reputation we are not, at the moment, concerned ; as Maitland said, " in the middle ages the clumsiest forgers deceived the gravest critics." [1] For purposes of dating it is enough to prove that a tradition of respect was established in Richard II's reign, as it must have taken at least a generation to grow up.[2] The manuscripts also show the *Modus* fairly steadily associated with documents which belong to the first quarter of the century ; here the use of the Seneschal tract as an appendage is specially significant. The evidence of association is confirmed by the condition of the text, which by the late fourteenth century had already become disordered, for no reason that can now be discerned. We cannot prove an exact date from the manuscripts, but we find in them general confirmation for the conclusions already reached. Examination of them has brought forward nothing which might be urged against the conclusion that the *Modus* was written in the year 1322, in order to expound and define the parliamentary theory and practice upheld by moderate men of that time.

NOTE A

MEDIEVAL MANUSCRIPTS OF THE A TYPE

British Museum.

Vespasian B, VII. *Vetera Statuta.* Late fourteenth century.
Nero C, I. *Nova Statuta*, Edward III to Richard III.
Lansdowne 522. *Nova Statuta*, Edward III to Richard III.
Julius B, IV. Collection on the Cinque Ports. Second half of the fifteenth century.

---

[1] *Mirror of Justices* (Selden Society), p. l.
[2] Cf. the scepticism shown by the first generation to Geoffrey of Monmouth's work.

Additional 24,079. Contains only the *Modus* and the Seneschal tract. Fifteenth century.

Harley 930. Contains only English translations of the *Modus* and the Treaty of Troyes, *c.* 1450.

Oxford.

Oriel College, MS. 46. Statutes of early kings ; formerly contained *Vetera Statuta.* Transcribed *c.* 1396-1420.

Private Collections.

MSS. of the earl of Leicester, Holkham Hall, Norfolk. No. 232. (*Not examined.*) *Vetera* and *Nova Statuta*, with the *Modus* between them, Edward I to 11 Henry VII. Contains also the Abridgement of Statutes.

MSS. of Lord Leconfield, Petworth House, Sussex. No. 8. (*Not examined.*) A miscellaneous collection, *c.* 1450.

MSS. of Lord St. Audries, St. Audries, Somerset. No. 15. (*Not examined.*) Contains *Nova Statuta*, Edward III to 7 & 8 Edward IV ; a roll of ordinances, 5 Edward III ; English translations of Trivet and *Brut* to 1420.

MSS. of Sir Francis Winnington, Stanford Court, Worcester. No. 2. (*Not examined.*) Contains only the *Modus*. Fifteenth century.

NOTE B

MEDIEVAL MANUSCRIPTS OF THE B TYPE

British Museum.

Nero D. VI. Late fourteenth century.
Additional 32,097. Fifteenth century.
Additional 29,901. Fifteenth century.
Domitian, XVIII. Fifteenth century.
Vitellius C, IV. Damaged by fire. Probably before 1450.

Oxford.

Bodleian Library, Rawlinson C, 398. Soon after 1437. Fortescue's copy. A Miscellany.

Cambridge.

University Library, IV, 207. English translation. Fifteenth century. (*Not examined.*)

Paris.

Bibliothèque Nationale, MS. Lat. 6049. Late fourteenth century. (Examined and reported on to me by Miss L. S. Sutherland.)

The Inner Temple.

Petyt MS. 511, Vol. VI. Fifteenth century. The *Modus* is a preface to *Nova Statuta*, Edward III to 3 Henry VII.

Society of Antiquaries.

MS. 58. English, *c.* 1450. Contains also table of contents of the Marshal tract.

Northamptonshire Record Society, Northampton.

MS. Finch Hatton 2995. A roll of two membranes of the early fifteenth century. On the dorse a petition to the Irish Council and a prophecy of St. Hildegard. *Modus* in French.

Huntingdon Library, California.

MS. EL. 35 B. 61. Late fifteenth century. Contains also the coronation order for kings and queens, in English.

Private Collections.

MSS. of Lord Leconfield, Petworth House Sussex. No. 17. (*Not examined.*) An English translation of the fifteenth century.

MSS. of Sir A. P. Vivian. (*Not examined.*) The *Modus*, in French, is the preface to the Courtenay Cartulary. Early fifteenth century.

Unless other contents are indicated, all these MSS. of the B type appear to be derived directly or indirectly from Nero D, VI.

CONCLUSION

By the investigation of the whole problem of the *Modus*, we have been drawn gradually into a study of the larger problems of constitutional development and, in particular, we have been led to examine both the doctrine of consent and the principle of representation. We have found that the conflict between the proprietary rights of persons and the royal right to demand competent subsidies was resolved, not on personal, but on corporate lines. For this reason, Parliament took shape as *communitas communitatum ;* not an Assembly of Notables, brittle in substance and dependent on personal caprice, but an institution slowly shaped and informed by the traditional habits of the communities from which its roots had sprung. In the study of this process in its early stages, we have turned to certain units of medieval society which have been little regarded hitherto. The reason for this is perhaps partly psychological. It is natural to value institutions by our knowledge of the individuals who compose them ; not only are standards of value difficult to separate from personal experience, but also it is through individual behaviour that communal activities are best understood. We tend to overlook those institutions where we lack knowledge of the persons by whom they were made up, though the mere absence of this type of evidence is no argument for their insignificance. As the human element is a constant factor, it is necessary to work by analogy from the known to the unknown. Analogy, however, cannot be legitimately used unless it is strictly controlled at both ends ; the only legitimate control is evidence, definite in itself, but not necessarily of the same order.

For example, no one can deny, though it is easy to forget, how the strong life of a monastic community, a borough or a college has often been enlarged and as often endangered by the action of individuals. Here there is ample evidence, even from the middle ages, in chronicles, letters and legal records. There are, however, no corresponding documents to throw light on the rivalries or parties of certain other medieval communities, ecclesiastical or lay. In tracing the early history of representation and consent, we have seen in action the diocese, the archdeaconry and the rural deanery ; without the help of a Jocelyn of Brakelond or a medieval Trollope, we cannot trace the designs and projects of the individual clergy who composed them. But we may press into service whatever knowledge we can gather from other communities of the same date, or from the same communities at a later stage, and test it by comparison with the impersonal evidence which has survived. We then find these communities of secular clergy were in vigorous motion, displayed in strong corporate activities, guided or thwarted, we may suppose, by men as ambitious or as inert as the Slopes, Grantlys and Proudies of nineteenth-century Barchester. Quickened by the spur of taxation, the lower clergy showed both ingenuity and resolution in protecting their rights. Their local and professional attachments were at once an advantage and an hindrance ; on the one hand, they were taught to apply the representative principle, and, on the other, they were blind to the permanent significance of that Parliament which they themselves had helped to bring into being. It is by the further study of these and other local communities—chapter, hundred, borough and shire—that we may hope to penetrate the mystery of medieval political structure.

APPENDIX

THE TEXT OF THE ENGLISH AND THE IRISH VERSIONS OF THE *MODUS TENENDI PARLIAMENTUM*

I. THE TEXT OF THE ENGLISH VERSION

THE text is based upon the collation [1] of sixteen manuscripts, with that already printed by Hardy from the manuscript in the Bibliothèque Nationale (MS. Lat. 6049). Though the manuscripts vary in date from the end of the fourteenth to the beginning of the sixteenth century, it seemed necessary to consider all of them closely, since not one is free from careless errors and omissions. The readings preferred are those of Vespasian B, VII, as the oldest manuscript with the chapters in the A order; obvious mistakes have been corrected from other manuscripts, usually from Oriel 46, which has some interesting readings, though often very careless, and from Nero D, VI, the oldest manuscript of the B type. It is remarkable that þe good text of the *Modus* has survived, an indication that the original version belonged to a date considerably earlier than any manuscripts now extant.

The following manuscripts have been collated :—

A. order.

> Vespasian B, VII (abbrev. Vesp.).
> Oriel 46 (O.).
> Nero C, I (N.).
> Julius B, IV (J.).
> Lansdowne 522 (L.).
> Additional 24,079 (A.).
> Harley 930 (English) (H.)

B. order.

> Nero D, VI.
> Additional 32,097.
> Additional 29,901.

[1] My thanks are due to Miss K. M. E. Murray who has collated fourteen of the manuscripts with Hardy's text and to Miss Dominica Legge for a collation of Oriel 46.

MEDIEVAL REPRESENTATION AND CONSENT

Domitian A, 18.
Tiberius E, VIII.
Vitellius C, IV.
Society of Antiquaries, 58 (English).
Huntingdon E. L. 35, B. 61 (Hunt.).
Petyt 511, VI (P.).

MODUS TENENDI PARLIAMENTUM

Hic describitur modus, quomodo Parliamentum regis Anglie et Anglorum suorum tenebatur temporibus regis Edwardi filii Etheldredi regis ; qui modus recitatus fuit per discretiores regni coram Willielmo duce Normannie conquestore et rege Anglie, ipso conquestore hoc precipiente, et per ipsum approbatus, et suis temporibus ac etiam temporibus successorum suorum regum Anglie usitatus.

I. *Summonitio Parliamenti.*

Summonitio Parliamenti precedere debet primum diem Parliamenti per quadraginta dies.

II. *De Clero.*

Ad Parliamentum summoneri et venire debent archiepiscopi, episcopi, abbates, priores et alii maiores cleri, qui tenent per comitatum vel baroniam, ratione huiusmodi tenure, et nulli minores nisi eorum presentia et eventus aliunde quam pro tenuris suis requiratur, ut si sint de consilio regis, vel eorum presentia necessaria vel utilis reputetur ad Parliamentum ; et illis tenetur rex ministrare sumptus et expensas suas in veniendo et morando ad Parliamentum ; nec debent huiusmodi clerici minores summoneri ad Parliamentum, sed rex solebat talibus pariter mandare brevia sua rogando quod ad Parliamentum suum interessent.

Item, rex solebat facere summonitiones suas archiepiscopis, episcopis, et aliis exemptis personis, ut abbatibus, prioribus, decanis, et aliis ecclesiasticis personis, qui habent iurisdictiones per huiusmodi exemptiones et privilegia separatas, quod ipsi pro quolibet decanatu et archidiaconatu Anglie per ipsos decanatus et archidiaconatus eligi facerent duos peritos et idoneos procuratores de ipso archidiaconatu ad veniendum et interessendum ad Parliamentum, ad respondendum, subeundum, allegandum et faciendum idem quod facerent omnes et singule persone ipsorum decanatuum et archidiaconatuum, si ipsi et eorum omnes et singuli personaliter interessent.

Et quod huiusmodi procuratores veniant cum warantis suis duplicatis, sigillis superiorum suorum signatis, quod ipsi ad huiusmodi procurationem electi et missi sunt, quarum litterarum una liberabitur clericis de Parliamento ad irrotulandum et alia residebit penes ipsos procuratores. Et sic sub istis duobus generibus summonicionum debet totus clerus summoneri ad Parliamentum regis.

III. *De Laicis.*

Item, summoneri et venire debent omnes et singuli comites et barones, et eorum pares, scilicet illi qui habent terras et redditus ad valentiam comitatus integri, videlicet viginti feoda unius militis, quolibet feodo computato ad viginti libratas, que faciunt quadringentas libratas in toto, vel ad valentiam unius baronie integre, scilicet tresdecim feoda et tertiam partem unius feodi militis, quolibet feodo computato ad viginti libratas, que faciunt in toto quadringentas marcas ; et nulli minores laici summoneri nec venire debent ad Parliamentum, ratione tenure sue, nisi eorum presentia aliis de causis fuerit utilis vel necessaria ad Parliamentum, et tunc de illis fieri debet sicut dictum est de minoribus clericis, qui ratione tenure sue ad Parliamentum venire minime tenentur.

IV. *De Baronibus Portuum.*

Item, rex solebat mittere brevia sua custodi Quinque Portuum quod ipse eligi faciat de quolibet portu per ipsum portum duos idoneos et peritos barones ad veniendum et interessendum ad Parliamentum suum ad respondendum, subeundum, allegandum, et faciendum idem quod facerent baronie sue, ac si ipsi de baroniis illis omnes et singuli personaliter interessent ibidem ; et quod huiusmodi barones veniant cum warantis suis duplicatis, sigillis communibus Portuum suorum signatis, quod ipsi rite ad hoc electi attornati sunt et missi pro baroniis illis, quarum una liberabitur clericis de Parliamento, et alia residebit penes ipsos barones. Et cum huiusmodi barones Portuum, licentia optenta, de Parliamento recessuri fuerant, tunc solebant habere breve de magno sigillo custodi Quinque Portuum, quod ipse rationabiles sumptus et expensas suas huiusmodi baronibus habere faceret de communitate Portus illius, a primo die quo versus Parliamentum venerint usque ad diem quo ad propria redierint, facta et expressa mentione in brevi illo de mora quam fecerint ad Parliamentum, de die quo venerint, quo licentiati fuerint redeundi ; et solebat mentio aliquando fieri in brevi quantum huiusmodi barones capere deberent de communitatibus illis per diem, scilicet aliqui plus et aliqui minus, secundum personarum habilitates et honestates, nec solebat poni pro duobus baronibus per diem ultra viginti solidos, habito respectu ad eorum moras, labores et expensas, nec solent huiusmodi expense in certo reponi per curiam pro quibuscumque personis sic electis et missis pro communitatibus, nisi persone ipse fuerint honeste et bene se habentes in Parliamento.

V. De Militibus Commitatuum.

Item, rex solebat mittere brevia sua omnibus vicecomitibus Anglie, quod eligi facerent quilibet de suo comitatu per ipsum comitatum duos milites idoneos, honestos et peritos, ad veniendum ad Parliamentum suum, eodem modo quo dictum est de baronibus Portuum, et de warantis suis eodem modo, sed pro expensis duorum militum de uno comitatu non solet poni ultra unam marcam per diem.[1]

VI. De Civibus.

Eodem modo solebat mandari maiori et vicecomitibus Londoniarum, maiori et ballivis vel maiori et civibus Eboraci et aliarum civitatum, quod ipsi pro communitate civitatis sue eligerent duos idoneos, honestos et peritos cives ad veniendum et interessendum ad Parliamentum eodem modo quo dictum est de baronibus Quinque Portuum et militibus comitatuum ; et solebant cives esse pares et equales cum militibus comitatuum in expensis veniendo, morando et redeundo.

VII. De Burgensibus.

Item, eodem modo solebat et debet mandari ballivis et probis hominibus burgorum, quod ipsi ex se et pro se eligant duos idoneos, honestos et peritos burgenses ad veniendum et interessendum ad Parliamentum regis eodem modo quo dictum est de civibus ; sed duo burgenses non solebant percipere per diem pro expensis suis ultra decem solidos et aliquando non ultra dimidiam marcam, et hoc solebat taxari per curiam, secundum magnitudinem et potestatem burgi et secundum honestatem personarum missarum.

VIII. De Modo Parliamenti.

Ostensa primo forma qualiter, cuilibet et a quanto tempore summonitio Parliamenti fieri debet, et qui venire debent per summonitionem, et qui non ; secundo est dicendum qui sunt qui ratione officiorum suorum venire debent, et interesse tenentur per totum Parliamentum, sine summonitione ; unde advertendum est quod duo clerici principales Parliamenti electi per regem et concilium suum, et alii clerici secundarii de quibus et quorum officiis dicetur specialius post, et principalis clamator Anglie cum subclamatoribus suis, et principalis hostiarius Anglie, que duo officia, scilicet officium clamatorie et hostiarie, solebant ad unum et idem pertinere, isti duo officiarii tenentur interesse primo die ; cancellarius Anglie, thesaurarius, camerarii et barones de scaccario, iusticiarii et omnes clerici et milites regis, una cum servientibus ad placita regis, qui sunt de concilio regis,

[1] MSS. L., A. and N. add " et nunc per diem viii s., videlicet pro quolibet eorum quatuor solidos."

tenentur interesse secundo die, nisi rationabiles excusationes habeant
ita quod interesse non possunt, et tunc mittere debent bonas excusationes.

IX. De Inchoatione Parliamenti.

Dominus Rex sedebit in medio maioris banci, et tenetur interesse
primo, sexto die Parliamenti : et solebant cancellarius, thesaurarius,
barones de scaccario et iusticiarii recordare defaltas factas in Parliamento sub ordine qui sequitur. Primo die vocabuntur burgenses et
cives totius Anglie, quo die si non veniant, amerciabitur burgus ad
centum marcas et civitas ad centum libras : secundo die vocabuntur
milites comitatuum totius Anglie, quo die si non veniant, amerciabitur
comitatus unde sunt ad centum libras : tertio die Parliamenti vocabuntur barones Quinque Portuum, et postea barones, et postmodum
comites : unde si barones Quinque Portuum non veniant, amerciabitur
baronia illa unde sunt ad centum marcas ; eodem modo amerciabitur
baro per se ad centum marcas et comes ad centum libras ; et eodem
modo fiet de illis qui sunt pares comitibus et baronibus, scilicet, qui
habent terras et redditus ad valenciam unius comitatus vel unius
baronie, ut predictum est in titulo de summonitione : quarto die vocabuntur procuratores cleri ; qui si non veniant, amerciabuntur episcopi
sui pro quolibet archidiaconatu qui defaltam fecerit ad centum marcas :
quinto die vocabuntur decani, priores, abbates, episcopi et demum
archiepiscopi, qui si non veniant, amerciabitur quilibet archiepiscopus
ad centum libras, episcopus tenens integram baroniam ad centum
marcas, et eodem modo de abbatibus, prioribus et aliis. Primo die
debet fieri proclamatio, primo in aula vel in monasterio, seu alio loco
publico ubi Parliamentum tenetur, et postmodum publice in civitate
vel villa quod omnes illi qui petitiones et querelas liberare voluerint ad
Parliamentum, illas deliberent a primo die Parliamenti in quinque dies
proximo sequentes.

X. De Predicatione ad Parliamentum.

Unus archiepiscopus, vel episcopus vel unus magnus clericus
discretus et facundus, electus per archiepiscopum in cuius provincia
Parliamentum tenetur, predicare debet uno istorum primorum quinque
dierum Parliamenti in pleno Parliamento [1] et in presentia regis, et hoc
quando Parliamentum fuerit pro maiori parte adiunctum et congregatum, et in sermone suo consequenter subiungere toti Parliamento
quod ipsi cum eo humiliter Deo supplicent, et ipsum adorent, pro pace
et tranquillitate regis et regni, prout specialius dicetur in sequenti
titulo de pronuntiatione ad Parliamentum.

[1] MSS. J., L., A., Vesp., O., N. and H. omit *in pleno Parliamento*.

XI. *De Pronuntiatione pro Parliamento.*

Post predicationem debet cancellarius Anglie vel capitalis iusticiarius Anglie, ille scilicet qui tenet placita coram rege, vel alius idoneus, honestus et facundus iusticiarius, vel clericus, per ipsos cancellarium et capitalem iusticiarium electus, pronunciare causas Parliamenti, primo in genere, et postea in specie, stando : et inde sciendum est quod omnes de Parliamento, quicumque fuerit, dum loquitur stabunt, rege excepto, ita quod omnes de Parliamento audire valeant eum qui loquitur, et si obscure dicat vel ita basse loquatur dicat iterato, et loquatur altius vel loquatur alius pro eo.

XII. *De Loquela Regis post Pronuntiationem.*

Rex post pronunciationem pro Parliamento rogare debet clericos et laicos, nominando omnes eorum gradus, scilicet archiepiscopos, episcopos, abbates, priores, archidiaconos, procuratores et alios de clero, comites, barones, milites, cives, burgenses et alios laicos, quod ipsi diligenter, studiose et corditer laborent ad pertractandum et deliberandum negotia Parliamenti, prout maius et principalius hoc ad Dei voluntatem primo, et postea ad eius et eorum honores et commoda fore intelligerint et sentierint.

XIII. *De Absentia Regis in Parliamento.*

Rex tenetur omni modo personaliter interesse Parliamento, nisi per corporalem egritudinem detineatur et tunc potest tenere cameram suam, ita quod non iaceat extra manerium, vel saltim villam, ubi Parliamentum tenetur, et tunc mittere debet pro duodecim personis de maioribus et melioribus qui summoniti sunt ad Parliamentum, scilicet, duobus episcopis, duobus comitibus, duobus baronibus, duobus militibus comitatuum, duobus civibus et duobus burgensibus, ad videndam personam suam, et ad testificandum statum suum, et in eorum presentia committere debet archiepiscopo loci, senescallo, et capitali iusticiario suo, quod ipsi coniunctim et divisim inchoent et continuent Parliamentum nomine suo, facta in commissione illa expressa mentione adtunc de causa absentie sue, que sufficere debet, et monere ceteros nobiles et magnates de Parliamento una cum notorio testimonio dictorum duodecim parium suorum ; causa est quod solebat clamor et murmur esse in Parliamento pro absentia regis, quia res dampnosa et periculosa est toti communitati Parliamenti et regni, cum rex a Parliamento absens fuerit, nec se absentare debet nec potest, nisi dumtaxat in casu supradicto.

XIV. *De Locis et Sessionibus in Parliamento.*

Primo ut predictum est, rex sedebit in medio loco maioris banci et ex parte eius dextra sedebunt archiepiscopus Cantuariensis, episcopi Londoniensis et Wintoniensis et post illos seriatim alii episcopi, abbates et priores linealiter ; et in parte sinistra regis sedebunt archiepiscopus Eboracensis, episcopi Dunelmensis et Karlioliensis, et post illos seriatim comites, barones et domini ; habita semper tali divisione inter predictos gradus et eorum loca, quod nullus sedeat nisi inter suos pares, et ad hoc tenetur senescallus Anglie prospicere, nisi rex alium velit ad hoc assignare. Ad pedem regis dextrum sedebunt cancellarius Anglie et capitalis iusticiarius Anglie et socii sui, et eorum clerici qui sunt de Parliamento ; et ad pedem eius sinistrum sedebunt thesaurarius, camerarii [1] et barones de scaccario, iusticiarii de banco et eorum clerici qui sunt de Parliamento.

XV. *De Principalibus Clericis Parliamenti.*

Item, duo clerici principales Parliamenti sedebunt in medio iusticiariorum, qui irrotulabunt omnia placita et negotia Parliamenti.

Et sciendum est quod ille duo clerici non sunt subiecti quibuscumque iusticiariis, nec est aliquis iusticiarius Anglie iusticiarius in Parliamento, nec habent per se recordum in Parliamento, nisi quatenus assignata et data fuerit eis nova potestas in Parliamento per regem et pares Parliamenti, ut quando assignati sunt cum aliis sectatoribus Parliamenti ad audiendum et terminandum diversas petitiones et querelas in Parliamento porrectas ; sed sunt illi duo clerici immediate subiecti regi et Parliamento suo in communi nisi forte unus iusticiarius vel duo assignentur eis ad examinanda et emendanda eorum irrotulamenta. Et cum pares Parliamenti assignati sunt ad audiendum et examinandum aliquas petitiones specialiter per se, cum ipsi fuerint unanimes et concordes in iudiciis suis reddendis super huiusmodi petitionibus, tunc recitabunt huiusmodi petitiones et processum super eisdem habitum et reddent iudicium in pleno Parliamento, ita quod illi [2] duo clerici principaliter irrotulent omnia placita et omnia iudicia in principali rotulo Parliamenti, et eosdem rotulos liberent ad thesaurarium ante Parliamentum licentiatum, ita quod omni modo sint illi rotuli in Thesauraria ante recessum Parliamenti, salvo tamen eisdem clericis inde transcripto, seu contrarotulo si id habere velint. Isti duo clerici, nisi sint in aliis officiis cum rege, et feoda capiant de eo, ita quod inde honeste vivere poterint, capiant de rege per diem unam marcam pro expensis suis per equales portiones, nisi sint ad mensam domini regis ; et si sint ad

---

[1] MSS. J., L. and A. read *camerarii*, Vesp. and N., *camerariis*, the rest have the singular number. Cf. *supra*, pp. 204-5.

[2] MSS. Vesp., O., J., L., N. and A. read *alii.*

mensam domini regis, tunc capient preter mensam suam per diem dimidiam marcam per equales portiones per totum Parliamentum.

XVI. De Quinque Clericis Parliamenti.

Dominus rex assignabit quinque clericos peritos et approbatos quorum primus ministrabit et serviet episcopis, secundus procuratoribus cleri, tertius comitibus et baronibus, quartus militibus comitatuum, quintus civibus et burgensibus, et quilibet eorum, nisi sit cum rege et capiat de eo tale feodum seu talia vadia quod inde possit honeste vivere, capiet de rege per diem duos solidos, nisi sit ad mensam regis ; et si sit ad mensam, tunc capiet duodecim denarios per diem ; qui clerici scribent eorum dubitationes et responsiones quas facient regi et Parliamento, intererint ad sua consilia ubicumque eos habere voluerint ; et cum eis vacaverit, iuvabunt [1] clericos principales ad irrotulandum.

XVII. De Casibus et Iudiciis Difficilibus.

Cum briga, dubitatio seu casus difficilis pacis vel guerre emergat in regno vel extra, referatur et recitetur casus ille in scriptis in pleno Parliamento, et tractetur et disputetur ibidem inter pares Parliamenti, et si necesse sit, iniungatur per regem seu ex parte regis, si rex non intersit, cuilibet gradui parium quod quilibet gradus adeat per se, et liberetur casus ille clerico suo in scriptis, et in certo loco recitari faciant coram eis casum illum ; ita quod ipsi ordinent et considerent inter se qualiter melius et iustius procedi poterit in casu illo sicut ipsi pro persona regis et eorum propriis personis, ac etiam pro personis eorum quorum personas ipsi representant, velint coram Deo respondere, et suas responsiones et avisamenta reportent in scriptis, et omnibus eorum responsionibus, consiliis et avisamentis hinc inde auditis, secundum melius et sanius consilium procedatur et ubi saltim maior pars Parliamenti concordat. Et si per discordiam inter regem et aliquos magnates, vel forte inter ipsos magnates, pax regni infirmetur, vel populus vel patria tribuletur, ita quod videtur regi et eius consilio quod expediens sit quod negotium illud tractetur et emendetur per considerationem omnium parium regni sui vel si per guerram rex et regnum suum tribulentur, vel si casus difficilis coram cancellario Anglie emergat, seu iudicium difficile coram iusticiariis fuerit reddendum, et huiusmodi, et si forte in huiusmodi deliberationibus omnes vel saltim maior pars concordare non valeant, tunc comes senescallus, comes constabularius et comes marescallus, vel duo eorum, eligent viginti et quinque personas de omnibus paribus regni, scilicet duos episcopos, et tres procuratores, pro toto clero, duos comites et tres barones, quinque

---

[1] MSS. Vesp., L. and N. read *mutabunt* ; A. reads *mittabunt*.

milites comitatuum, quinque cives et quinque [1] burgenses, qui faciunt
viginti quinque ; et illi viginti quinque possunt eligere ex seipsis, si
velint, duodecim et condescendere in eis, et ipsi duodecim sex et condescendere in eis, et ipsi sex adhuc tres et condescendere in eis, et illi
tres se in paucioribus condescendere non possunt, nisi optenta licentia
a domino rege, et si rex consentiat illi tres possunt in duos, et de
illis duobus alter potest in alium descendere et ita demum stabit sua
ordinatio supra totum Parliamentum ; et ita condescendo a viginti
quinque personis usque in unam solam personam, nisi numerus maior
concordare valeat et ordinare, tandem sola persona, ut est dictum, pro
omnibus ordinabit, que cum se ipsa discordare non potest ; salvo
domino regi et eius concilio quod ipsi huiusmodi ordinationes postquam
scripte fuerint examinare et emendare valeant, si hoc facere sciant et
velint, ita quod hoc fiat ibidem tunc in pleno Parliamento, et de consensu Parliamenti, et non retro Parliamentum.

XVIII. *De Ordine Deliberandi Negotia Parliamenti.*

Negotia pro quibus Parliamentum summonitum est debent deliberari
secundum kalendarium Parliamenti, et secundum ordinem petitionum
liberatarum et affilatarum, nullo habito respectu ad quorumcumque
personas, sed qui prius proposuit prius agat. In kalendario Parliamenti
debent rememorari omnia negotia Parliamenti sub isto ordine ; primo
de guerra si guerra sit, et de aliis negotiis personas regis, regine et
suorum liberorum tangentibus ; secundo de negotiis communibus regni,
ut de legibus statuendis contra defectus legum originalium, iudicialium
et executoriarum, post iudicia reddita que sunt maxime communia [2]
negotia ; tercio debent rememorari negotia singularia, et hoc secundum
ordinem filatarum petitionum, ut predictum est.

XIX. *De Diebus et Horis ad Parliamentum.*

Parliamentum non debet teneri diebus dominicis, sed cunctis aliis
diebus, illo die semper excepto, et aliis tribus, scilicet Omnium Sanctorum, Animarum et Nativitatis Sancti Johannis Baptiste, potest
teneri ; et debet singulis diebus inchoari hora media prima, qua hora
rex Parliamentum tenetur interesse, et omnes pares regni. Parliamentum debet teneri in loco publico, et non in privato, nec in occulto
loco ; in diebus festivis Parliamentum debet inchoari hora prima
propter divinum servitium.

XX. *De Hostiariis Parliamenti.*

Hostiarius principalis Parliamenti stabit infra magnum hostium
monasterii, aulae, vel alterius loci ubi Parliamentum tenetur, et

---

[1] MSS. O., P. and H. alone have *quinque burgenses ;* J. has *V° burgenses.*
[2] MSS. Vesp., O., J., L., A., N. and H. omit *communia.*

custodiet hostium ita quod nullus intret Parliamentum, nisi qui sectam et eventum debeat ad Parliamentum, vel vocatus fuerit propter negotium quod prosequitur in Parliamento, et oportet quod hostiarius ille habeat cognitionem personarum quae ingredi debent ita quod nulli omnino negetur ingressus qui Parliamentum interesse tenetur ; et hostiarius ille potest et debet, si necesse sit, habere plures hostiarios sub se.

XXI. De Clamatore Parliamenti.

Clamator Parliamenti stabit extra hostium Parliamenti, et hostiarius sibi denunciabit clamationes suas ; rex solebat assignare servientes suos ad arma ad standum per magnum spatium extra hostium Parliamenti, ad custodiendum hostium, ita quod nulli impressiones nec tumultus facerent circa hostia, per quod Parliamentum impediatur, sub poena captionis corporum suorum, quia de iure hostium Parliamenti non debet claudi, sed per hostiarios et servientes regis ad arma custodiri.

XXII. De Stationibus Loquencium in Parliamento.

Omnes pares Parliamenti sedebunt, et nullus stabit nisi quando loquitur, et loquitur ita quod quilibet de Parliamento eum audire valeat ; nullus intrabit Parliamentum, nec exiet de Parliamento, nisi per unicum hostium ; et quicumque loquitur rem aliquam que deliberari debet per Parliamentum, stabunt omnes loquentes ; causa est ut audiantur a paribus, quia omnes pares sunt iudices et iusticiarii.

XXIII. De Auxiliis Regis.

Rex non solebat petere auxilium de regno suo nisi pro guerra instanti, vel filios suos milites faciendo, vel filias suas maritando, et tunc debent huiusmodi auxilia peti in pleno Parliamento, et in scriptis cuilibet gradui parium Parliamenti liberari, et in scriptis responderi ; et sciendum est quod ad huiusmodi auxilia concedenda oportet quod omnes pares Parliamenti consentiant, et intelligendum est quod duo milites, qui veniunt ad Parliamentum pro ipso comitatu, maiorem vocem habent in Parliamento in concedendo et contradicendo, quam maior comes Anglie, et eodem modo procuratores cleri unius episcopatus maiorem vocem habent in Parliamento, si omnes sint concordes, quam episcopus ipse, et hoc in omnibus que per Parliamentum concedi, negari vel fieri debent : et hoc patet quia rex potest tenere Parliamentum cum communitate regni sui, absque episcopis, comitibus et baronibus, dumtamen summoniti sunt ad Parliamentum, licet nullus episcopus, comes vel baro ad summonitiones suas veniant ; quia olim nec episcopus fuerat, nec comes, nec baro, adhuc tunc reges tenuerunt Parliamenta sua, sed aliter est econtra, licet communitates, cleri et laici, summonite essent ad Parliamentum, sicut de iure debent, et propter aliquas certas causas venire nollent, ut si pretenderent quod rex non regeret eos sicuti deberet, et assignarent specialiter in quibusdam articulis [1] quod ipse eos disrexerat,[2] tunc Parliamentum nullum esset omnino, licet omnes archiepiscopi, episcopi, comites, barones et omnes eorum pares, cum rege interessent ; et ideo oportet quod omnia que affirmari vel infirmari, concedi vel negari, vel fieri debent per Parliamentum, per communitatem Parliamenti concedi debent, que est ex tribus gradibus sive generibus Parliamenti, scilicet ex procuratoribus cleri, militibus comitatuum, civibus et burgensibus, qui representant totam communitatem Anglie, et non de magnatibus, quia quilibet eorum est pro sua propria persona ad Parliamentum et pro nulla alia.

XXIV. *De Departitione Parliamenti.*

Parliamentum departiri non debet dummodo aliqua petitio pendeat indiscussa, vel, ad minus, ad quam non sit determinatum responsum, et si rex contrarium permittat, periurus est ; nullus solus de omnibus paribus Parliamenti recedere potest nec debet de Parliamento, nisi optenta inde licentia de rege et omnibus suis paribus et hoc in pleno Parliamento, et quod de huiusmodi licentia fiat rememoratio in rotulo Parliamenti, et si aliquis de paribus, durante Parliamento, infirmaverit, ita quod ad Parliamentum venire non valeat, tunc per triduum mittat excusatores ad Parliamentum, quo die si non venerit, mittantur ei duo de paribus suis ad videndum et testificandum huiusmodi infirmitatem, et si sit suspicio, iurentur illi duo pares quod veritatem inde dicent, et si comperiatur quod finxerat se, amercietur tanquam pro defalta, et si non finxerat se, tunc attornet aliquem sufficientem coram eis ad interessendum ad Parliamentum pro se, nec sanus excusari potest si sit sane memorie.

Departitio Parliamenti ita usitari debet : primitus peti debet et publice proclamari in Parliamento, et infra palacium Parliamenti, si sit aliquis, qui petitionem liberaverit ad Parliamentum, cui nondum sit responsum ; quod si nullus reclamet, supponendum est quod cuilibet medetur, vel saltim quatenus potest de iure respondetur, et tunc primo, scilicet, cum nullus qui petitionem ea vice exhibuerit reclamet, Parliamentum nostrum licentiabimus.

XXV. *De Transcriptis Recordorum et Processuum in Parliamento.*

Clerici Parliamenti non negabunt cuiquam transcriptum processus sui, sed liberabunt illud cuilibet qui hoc petierit, et capient semper

---

[1] MSS. Vesp., J., L., A., N., H., Hunt and P. read *in quibus articulis ;* O. reads *in quibusdam articulis.*

[2] The reading of MSS. Vesp., L., A., and N. ; O. reads *direxerat.*

pro decem lineis unum denarium, nisi forte facta fide de impotentia, in quo casu nihil capient. Rotuli de Parliamento continebunt in latitudine decem pollices. Parliamentum tenebitur in quo loco regni, regi placuerit.

XXVI. *De Gradibus Parium Parliamenti.*

Rex est caput, principium et finis Parliamenti, et ita non habet parem in suo gradu, et ita ex rege solo est primus gradus. Secundus gradus est de archiepiscopis, episcopis, abbatibus, prioribus, per baroniam tenentibus. Tertius gradus est de procuratoribus cleri. Quartus gradus est de comitibus, baronibus et aliis magnatibus et proceribus, tenentibus ad valentiam comitatus et baronie, ut predictum est in titulo de laicis. Quintus gradus est de militibus comitatuum. Sextus gradus est de civibus et burgensibus : et ita est Parliamentum ex sex gradibus. Sed sciendum est quod licet aliquis dictorum quinque graduum post regem absens sit, dum tamen omnes premuniti sint per rationabiles summonitiones Parliamenti, nihilominus censetur esse plenum.

Explicit Modus Parliamenti.

II. THE TEXT OF THE IRISH VERSION

The text is that of the inspeximus of 1419. There are a few gaps as the right-hand edge has been mutilated ; and these show that Hakewill's copy (printed by Dr. Steele in *Tudor Proclamations*, Vol. I, pp. clxxxviii-cxcii) must have been transcribed from this document.[1] The words in square brackets are taken from Dr. Steele's text.

MODUS TENENDI PARLIAMENTA ET CONSILIA IN HIBERNIA

Henricus,[2] Dei gratia Rex Anglie et Francie et dominus Hibernie, omnibus ad quos presentes littere pervenerint salutem : INSPEXIMUS tenorem diversorum articulorum in quodam rotulo pergameneo scriptorum, cum Cristoforo de Preston' milite tempore arrestacionis sue apud villam de Clane per deputatum dilecti et fidelis nostri Iohannis Talbot de Halomshire, chivaler, locum nostrum tenentis terre nostre Hibernie, nuper facti invento, ac coram nobis et consilio nostro in

---

[1] Cf. *supra*, p. 80.

[2] " A Copie of an Exemplificacion under the Greate ⟨Seal of Ireland⟩ 6 H. 5, of which I have seene the original under seale, reciting a ⟨charter⟩ of H. 2 sent into Ireland, conteyning the form of holding Parliaments." Hakewill's transcript has this introduction.

eadem terra nostra apud villam de Trym, nono die Ianuarii ultimo preterito ostenso, in hec verba :

Modus tenendi Parliamenta.

Henricus rex Anglie, conquestor et dominus Hibernie, mittit hanc formam archiepiscopis, episcopis, abbatibus, prioribus, comitibus, baronibus, iusticiariis, vicecomitibus, maioribus, prepositis, ministris, et omnibus fidelibus suis terre Hibernie, tenendi Parliamentum.

1. In primis somonicio Parliamenti procedere debet per XL^a dies [I] ante Parliamentum.

2. Sommoniri et venire debent ad Parliamentum omnes archiepiscopi, episcopi, abbates, priores et alii clerici qui tenent per tenuram comitatus vel baronie integre, et nulli minores custubus propriis causa tenure sue. Item, somoniri debent archiepiscopi, episcopi, abbates et priores, decani et archidiaconi, exempti et alii previlegiati, qui habent iurisdiccionem, quod ipsi de assensu cleri pro quolibet decanatu et [II] archidiaconatu Hibernie et [de] se ipsis decanis et archidiaconis faciant eligere duos sapientes et competentes procuratores pro propriis archidiaconatibus, ad veniendum et essendum ad Parliamentum ad respondendum et supportandum, locandum et faciendum quod quilibet et omnes de deacanatibus et archidiaconatibus facerent vel faceret si personaliter interessent. Et quod procuratores veniant cum warantibus suis duplicatis, sigillatis sigillis superiorum suorum, unde unum deliberetur clerico Parliamenti irrotulandum, et aliud secum remaneat, etc.

3. Sumoniri et venire debet etiam omnis et quilibet comes et [III] baro et pares eorum, videlicet, qui habent terras et redditus ad valenciam unius comitatus integre, quod est viginti feoda militum, quodlibet feodum computatum ad XX libras, que facit CCCC li, vel valorem baronie integre, videlicet, tresdecim feoda militum et tercia pars feodi, que faciunt CCCC marcas, et nulli minores laici vel clerici custibus propriis, causa tenure sue, nisi rex sumoneat consiliarios suos vel alios sapientes necessaria causa : quibus mittere solet precando eos, custibus ipsius regis, venire et esse in Parliamento suo, etc.

4. Item, per breve Rex mittere debet cuilibet senescallo libertatis et cuilibet vicecomiti suo Hibernie, quod faciant eligere, quilibet de assensu communitatis libertatis et comitatus sui, duos milites competentes, honestos, et sapientes, ad veniendum ad Parliamentum ad respondendum, supportandum, allocandum, et faciendum quod omnis et quilibet communitatis vel libertatis comitatus facerent vel faceret si personaliter interessent. Et quod milites veniant cum warantis suis, [V] ut supradictum est de procuratoribus, et quod sine licencia parliamenti non discedant a Parliamento. Et post licenciam, habeant breve directum senescallo vel vicecomiti, quod faciat dictos milites suos

habere de communitate sua racionabiles custus et expensas suas a die remocionis eorum versus Parliamentum usque racionabilem diem quo ad propria revenire a Parliamento poterunt. Et quod expensa non excedat I marcam de duobus militibus per diem, etc.

[VI-VII]   5. Item, eodem modo mittendum est maioribus, ballivis, propositis civitatum et burgorum franches', quod de communi assensu communium suorum elegant II cives vel burgenses, etc., ut dictum est supra de militibus. Et quod expensa II civium vel burgensium non excedat dimidiam marcam per diem.

[XV]   6. Et memorandum quod rex inveniet, custibus suis, principalem clericum parliamenti ad irrotulandum communia placita et negotia Parliamenti, qui tantum modo subiectus erit sine medio regi et Parliamento suo in communi. Et quando pares Parliamenti sunt assignati ad examinandum peticiones per seipsos, et sunt concordes in iudicio suo, tunc clericus predictus repetet peticiones et processus super ipsos, et pares reddent iudicium in pleno Parliamento. Et iste clericus sedebit in medio loco iusticiariorum. Et memorandum, quod nullus iusticiarius est in Parliamento, nec habet per ipsum recordum in Parliamento, nisi nova potestas ei assignetur per regem et pares Parliamenti in parliamento. Et dictus clericus deliberabit rotulos suos in thesaurum ante finem Parliamenti.

[XVI]   7. Item rex assignare solet, custibus suis, unum bonum clericum probatum ad scribendum dubitaciones et responsiones quas archiepiscopi et episcopi facere velint regi et Parliamento ; et secundum clericum procuratorum, eodem modo ; tercium pro comitibus et baronibus et paribus eorum, eodem modo ; quartum militibus libertatum et comitatuum, et quintum civibus et burgensibus. Qui clerici semper predictis erunt in eorum consiliis intendentes, quod si vacaverint, vel aliquis eorum vacaverit, adiuvare debent principalem clericum ad irrotulandum. Et ad minus assignare debet unum dominis et communibus spiritualibus, et alium dominis et communibus temporalibus. Et etiam rex assignabit cum quolibet predictorum clericorum unum hostiarium et I clamatorem.

[XXVI]   8. De rege solo est primus gradus Parliamenti, quia est caput, comensor et finis Parliamenti. De archiepiscopis, episcopis, abbatibus, prioribns, et paribus [1] eorum, per comitatum vel baroniam tenentibus, est secundus gradus. Tercius gradus est de procuratoribus. Quartus gradus de comitibus, baronibus et eorum paribus. Quintus gradus est de militibus libertatum et communitatum. Sextus gradus est de civibus et burgensibus. Et si contingat quod aliquis predictorum graduum, excepto Rege, absens a Parliamento fuerit, et debite sumonitus fuerit, nihilominus Parliamentum iudicatum est esse plenum.

---

[1] *MS.* pares.

9. Rex tenetur semper esse in Parliamento, nisi infirmitate impedi- [XIII] atur, et tunc infra maneriam (*sic*) vel villam Parliamenti debet esse, et mittere debet pro duobus episcopis, II comitibus, II baronibus, II militibus comitatuum, II civibus, et II burgensibus ad videndum personam suam, et testificandum statum suum. In quorum etiam presencia committere debet archiepiscopo loci, comitibus [1] terre, et capitali iusticiario suo, quod incipient et continuant Parliamentum nomine suo. Et rex absentare non potest nisi modo et causa supradicta, nisi sit eorum assensu parium Parliamenti.

10. Rex sedebit in medio principalis scamni, et ad eius dexteram [IX & XIV] archiepiscopus loci,[2] et si extra Dublin' provinciam Parliamentum fuerit tentum, tunc ad sinistram archiepiscopus Dublin', et deinde Cassellen' et Tuamen' ex utraque parte, deinde episcopi, abbates, et alii, secundum ordinem suum. Cancellarius stabit iuxta regem. Thesaurarius sedebit inter barones ; iusticiarii de uno banco et de altero ad pedes regis, et omnes procuratores super terram.

11. Rex cum concilio suo tenetur esse primo die in parliamento, et [VIII & IX] quarto die omnes somoniti ad Parliamentum erunt vocati, et eorum defectus recordati, et per consideracionem regis et omnium parium parliamenti amerciamenta defectuum taxata.

12. Parliamentum non debet teneri diebus dominicis, nec die [XIX] Omnium Sanctorum, nec die Animarum, nec in Nativitate Sancti Johannis Baptiste. Omnibus aliis diebus Rex cum gradibus Parliamenti debet esse in Parliamento media hora ante primam, festivalibus diebus propter servicium divinum ad horam primam, et sit Parliamentum in aperto loco semper.

13. Peticiones sunt affilati (*sic*) sicut deliberantur, et sic per ordinem [XVIII] legantur et respondeantur. Set primo determinentur que ad guerram pertinent, postea de persona regis et regine et pueris suis ac gubernacione eorum, et postea de communibus negotiis terre, sicut est de legibus faciendis et emendandis, videlicet, orginalibus iudicialibus et executoriis post iudicium redditum, et postea singulares peticiones secundum quod sunt super filator'. Et primo die Parliamenti sit proclamacio facta in villa et loco Parliamenti, quod omnes qui querelas

---

[1] *MS.* pares.

[2] Rex sedebit in medio principalis Scamni et ad eius dextram Archiepiscopus loci Ardmachanus vel Dublin., et si extra eorum limites Parliamentum fit, tunc a dexteris Regis Archiepiscopi Armach. et Casselen., et a sinistris Regis Archiepiscopi Dublin. et Tuamen., deinde vero a dextris Episcopi, Abbates Priores in secunda formula secundum ordinem, a sinistris in formula Comites Barones et eorum Pares secundum ordinem ad pedem per terum Regis sedebit Cancellarius, Capitalis Iusticiarius, cum suis sociis et eorum clericis, et ad pedem sinistrum sedebunt Thesaurarius et Camerarii et Barones de scacario : Iusticiarii de Banco et eorum clerici, si sint de Parliamento, deinde procuratores terre sedebunt. Dopping, *op. cit.*, p. 16.

vel peticiones velint deliberare Parliamento id faciant infra quintum diem sequentem.

[X-XII]   14. Quarto die Parliamenti vel quinto, predicacio fiat de aliquo solempni clerico eiusdem provincie, et post predicacionem cancellarius, vel alius sapiens et eloquens ac honestus per cancellarium electus, monstrabit causas Parliamenti, primo generaliter, postea specialiter, stando (quia quilibet loquens in parliamento tenetur stare loquendo excepto rege), ut ab omnibus audiatur. Et post promocionem Parliamenti rex debet predicare clericos et laicos quod quilibet in suo gradu diligenter studiose et corditer laboret ad tractandum et deliberandum negotium Parliamenti, sicut principaliter intendunt hoc esse, primo ad voluntatem Dei, et postea ad honorem et proficuum regis et ipsorum presencium.

[XXIII]   15. Rex non solebat auxilium petere de populo suo, nisi pro guerra existente vel pro filiabus maritandis. Que peticiones in pleno Parliamento debent in scripto deliberari cuilibet gradui Parliamenti, et in scripto responderi. Unde sciendum est, quod in talibus concessionibus necessarium est ut maior pars cuiuslibet status sit ad hoc consensiens. Et sciendum, quod duo milites electi habent plus vocis in concedendo vel negando pro comitatu suo quam comes eiusdem comitatus : eodem modo, procuratores clericorum plus episcopis suis in concedendo et negando ; quod apparet, quia rex cum comunitate sua potest tenere parliamentum suum [sine] episcopis, comitibus et baronibus, si racionabiliter sumoniti non venirent, quia aliquando fuit quod non fuerunt episcopus, comes, nec^ebaro, et tunc reges tenuerunt Parliamenta. Et si [communes] clericorum et laicorum sint sumoniti modo debito ad Parliamentum, et pro racionabili causa venire nolunt, scilicet si assignaverint specialiter causas in quibus rex eos non recte gubernaverit, tunc Parliamentum tenebitur pro nullo, quamvis omnes alii status plenarie ibidem intersint. Et ideo, necessarium est quod in omnibus concedendis, faciendis, affirmandis et donandis per Parliamentum, quod sunt concesse per communes Parliamenti, que consta⟨n⟩t ex tribus gradibus, videlicet de procuratoribus clericorum, militibus libertatum et comitatuum, civibus et burgensibus. Et quilibet parium Parliamenti est pro seipso in Parliamento, et omnes pares [1] Parliamenti sunt iudices et iusticiarii in Parliamento, et sedebunt [omnes], nisi quando locuntur, communes vero querentes et auxilii concessores vel negatores.

16. Si dubius casus vel durus guerre vel pacis in terra advenerit,
[XVII]   vel extra terram, ista causa sit scripta in pleno Parliamento, et sint ibidem inter pares Parliamenti disputata et tractata, et tunc, si necesse sit, per regem m[andetur] cuilibet gradui, quod eat quilibet gradus per se habens clericum cum causa scripta, ubi recitabunt eandem, ita

[1] MS. parí.

quod ordinent et considerant inter eos in quo meliori modo et iusto
procedere possint in casu illo, sicut pro persona regis et seipsis, ac pro
quibus presentes sunt, velint coram Deo respondere. Et respon-
ciones eorundem [in scriptis reportarent] ut omnibus responsionibus
et consiliis auditis, secundum melius consilium procedatur, sicut
si sit discordia inter regem et alios magnates, vel inter magnates pax
terre fracta fuerit, vel inter populum, ita quod videtur Parliamento
quod talis causa sit per omnes gradus terre tractanda, et per eorum
consideracionem emendanda [vel per] guerram rex et terra turbe(n)tur,
vel si durus casus coram cancellario vel iusticiario, aut durum iudicium
advenerit, vel aliquis alius similis casus, et si in talibus deliberacionibus
omnes, vel saltem maior pars cuiuslibet gradus, non consenserint, tunc
de quolibet gradu Parliamenti, excepto rege, eligatur unus, qui omnes
vel eorum maior numerus eligant duos episcopos, tres procuratores pro
toto clero, duos comites, III barones, quinque milites comitatuum, V
cives et V burgenses, qui faciunt XXV personas ; et ipsi de seipsis
possunt eligere duodecim, et condiscendere in ipsis ; et ipsi XII in
sex, et condiscendere in ipsis ; et ipsi sex [in] tres, et condiscendere in
ipsis ; et tunc per licenciam regis illi III in duobus, et illi duo in
altero ipsorum potest condiscendere [qui cum se ipso discordare] non
possit, cuius ordinacio erit pro toto parliamento, nisi maior numerus
consentire possit, salvo rege et consilio, quod ipsi tales ordinaciones,
postquam scripte fuerint, examinare et corrigere, si convenerint,[1] in
pleno Parliamento et non alibi, ex Parliamenti assensu.

17. Clerici Parliamenti non denegabunt alicui [transcriptum, vel [XXV]
processus sui,] aut recordi [2] Parliamenti, si qui solvere voluerint pro
quolibet decem lineis continentibus X polices in longitudine, que est
mensura rotuli Parliamenti, unum denarium.

18. Parliamentum erit tentum in quo loco competenti terre regi [XXIV]
placuerit, et Parliamentum departire non debet quando aliqua peticio
est pendens non determinata ; quod si rex contrarium fecerit, periurus
est. Et de omnibus gradibus Parliamenti nullus solus potest nec
debet decedere a Parliamento sine licencia regis et omnium parium
Parliamenti ; et hoc in pleno Parliamento, ita quod inde fiat mencio
in rotulis Parliamenti. Et si aliquis Parlia[menti] durante Parliamento
infirmitate detineatur, ita quod Parliamento accedere non possit, tunc
infra quartum diem mittet excusatores Parliamento, quo die si non
venerit, mittantur ei duo de paribus suis ad videndum et testificandu
infirmitatem suam, et per recordum eorum sit excusatus, vel in misericordia cum [pro defectu amercietur] ; quod si non ficta infirmitas sit,
tunc attornabit aliquem sufficientem coram ipsis essendum pro ipso in
Parliamento, quia sanus et de sana memoria non potest excusari. Ad

---

[1] MS. *somerint*.   [2] *MS. recordum.*

departicionem Parliamenti, primo demandari et proclamari debet in aperto in Parliamento, si aliquis deliberavit peticionem Parliamento, cui [factum non] est responsum, et si nullum reclamatum est, supponendum quod cuilibet peticioni medicina racionabilis facta est. Et tunc cancellarius, vel alius assignatus per regem et Parliamentum, debet dicere alta voce : Nos damus licenciam Parliamento dissolvi. Et sic finitur Parliamentum.

19. Et eciam rex vult quod ea[dem forma] in consiliis per somonicionem factam observetur, excepto quod pro rege et legibus in ipsis consiliis erunt ordinaciones, in Parliamento vero statuta.

20. Et etiam rex vult ut absente rege a dicta terra, sine procuratore vel gubernatore eiusdem terre, quocunque alio nomine censeatur,[1] per ipsum regem constituto quod statim [cum] celeritate concilium regis ibidem mittat pro archiepiscopis, episcopis, abbatibus, prioribus, comitibus, baronibus, et eorum paribus, aliisque proceribus et discretis viris ad minus proximorum trium comitatuum proximi,[2] ut[3] festinius convenire possint ad certum brevem diem et locum coram ipsis essendum, ad tractandum consulendum et consensiendum cum iusticiis regis terre Hibernie, qui vices regis ut domini Hibernie in nomine ipsius regis in omnibus supplebit, super quo statim concilium regis predictum sub magno sigillo regis terre predicte, iusticiarium Hibernie constituant (sic) terram predictam in omnibus, nomine regis, iustificandum.

21. Hanc formam rex vult ut in terra sua Hibernie in omnibus . . . observetur. Et quod in custodia archiepiscopi Cassellen., tanquam in medio terre, hoc scriptum populo eiusdem terre remaneat custodiendum· Constitutus a rege custos suus terre Hibernie, quocunque nomine cenceatur,[4] tactis sacrosanctis evangeliis, hoc sacramentum prestet coram cancellario, consilio et [populo] : Custodiet Deo et populo terre Hibernie, leges libertates et custumas rectas, quas antiqui reges Anglie, predecessores regis nunc, et ipse rex, Deo et populo Anglie et terre Hibernie concesserunt ; et quod observet Deo et sancte ecclesie clero et populo pacem et concordiam in Deo integriter, secundum potestatem suam, et quod fie[ri faciat] in omnibus iudiciis[5] suis equam et rectam iusticiam, cum discrecione, misericordia, et veritate. Et quod tenebit et custodiet rectas leges et custumas quas populus terre elegerit sibi esse tenendum, et ipsas defendere et fortificare debet ad honorem Dei, pro posse suo.

22. Et memorandum quod hoc iuramentum est a iuramento regis Anglie.

---

[1] MS. senciatur. [2] ? delete. [3] MS. vel.
[4] M.S. scenciatur. [5] MS. iudicibus

23. Et accepto iuramento, investitur iuratus potestate sibi concessa, et non antea. Finitur.

24. INSPEXIMUS etiam tenorem cujusdam articuli in quadam cedula de papiro scripti, et cum predicto Christofero tempore predicto similiter inventa, ac coram predicto locum nostrum [tenente et consi]lio nostro predicto, apud dictam villam de Trym, eodem nono die Ianuarii similiter ostensa, in hec verba :

Electus a plebe in regem ut consecretur postquam ad idem iterum consenserint, metropolitanus electum mediocriter distinctaque interroget voce : si leges et consuetudines ab anti[quo a] regibus plebi Anglorum concessas cum [1] sacramenti confirmacione, eidem plebi concedere et servare voluerit, et presertim leges et consuetudines et libertates a gloriosissimo rege et sancto Edwardo clero populoque concessas. Si autem omnibus hiis assentire se velle promiserit, exponat ei metropolitanus, ita dicendo ;

" Servabis ecclesie Dei cleroque populo pacem ex integro et concordiam inde secundum vires tuas ? "

Respondebit : " Servabo."

" Facies fieri in omnibus iudiciis tuis equam et rectam iusticiam et discretionem in misericordia et veritate secundum vires tuas ? "

Respondebit : " Faciam."

" Concedis iustas leges ess . . . per te esse protegendas, et ad honorem Dei roborandas quas vulgus eligerit secundum vires tuas ? "

Respondebit : " Concedo et promitto."

Sequitur admonicio episcoporum ad regem, et legatur ab uno episcopo coram omnibus clara voce, sic dicendo :

" Domine rex, a vobis perdonari petimus, ut unicuique de vobis et ecclesiis vobis [commissis canonicum privi]legium ac debitam legem atque iustitiam conservetis, et defensionem exhibeatis, sicut rex in suo regno debet unicuique suo episcopo, abbatibus et ecclesiis sibi commissis."

Respondebit : " Animo libenti et devoto promitto vobis et perdonoque nicuique de vobis et ecclesiis vobis comissis canonicum privilegium, et debitam [legem atque iustitiam] servabo, et defencionem quantum potero, adiuvante Domino, exhibeo, sicut rex in suo regno unicuique episcopo abbatibus et ecclesiis sibi comissis per rectum exhibere debet." Adiciantur preteritis interrogacionibus que iusta fuerint.

Pronunciatis omnibus supradictis, dictus princeps conservet se omnia predicta observaturum, [sacramento super] altare coram cunctis protinus prestito, rege itaque in solio suo taliter collocato, pares

---

[1] MS. *causa.*

regni dictum regem undique circumstantes manibus palam extentis in signum fidelitatis, offerent se ad dicti regis et dicte corone sustentacionem.

Nos autem tenores articulorum predictorum de assensu prefati [locum tenentis] et consilii nostri predicti, tenore presentium duximus testificandum, in cuius rei testimonium has litteras nostras fieri fecimus patentes.   Teste prefato locum nostrum tenente apud Trym, xii die Ianuarii Anno regni nostri sexto (1418-19).

Per ipsum locum tenentem et consilium.

Examinatur per Iohannem Parsant et Willelmum Sutton, clericos.

INDEX